THE GRAND EMPORIUMS

"It's as thick as a Sears catalogue and as comprehensive. I'm glad to own it, and I will keep it on my reference shelf as a standard reference."
—Leonard Fleisher, editor of "Sales & Bargains"
for *New York Magazine*, in *The Washington Post*

"*The Grand Emporiums* gets this consumer's nod....Valuable social history and spicy biography."
—*Newsday*

"Here it all is: the enterprise, the honesty, the chicanery, the hokum, and yes, the hard work and ingenuity behind the rise of the American department store. Impressive research, total coverage of the subject, and a lively style make this book highly recommended."
—*Library Journal*

"Packed with information and colorful stories....Lively....Consistently holds the reader's interest."
—*Publishers Weekly*

"A book worth reading. The writing is lively, the photos have been carefully selected and the anecdotes tell some unusual things about the kind of people Americans are."
—*Wall Street Journal*

"Great fun."
—*Newark Star-Ledger*

"Astonishing....Fascinating." —*San Francisco Examiner & Chronicle*

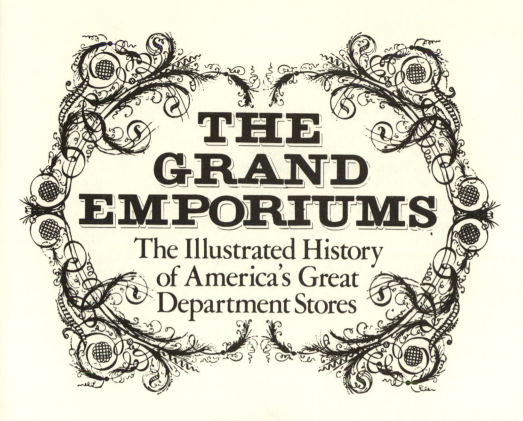

THE GRAND EMPORIUMS

The Illustrated History of America's Great Department Stores

ROBERT HENDRICKSON

A SCARBOROUGH BOOK
Stein and Day/*Publishers*/New York

For my brother, John Laurence Hendrickson

ACKNOWLEDGMENTS

Though essentially the story of the rise of the department store in America and the great merchants who made it a national institution, often in the face of tremendous odds, this book necessarily covers the whole spectrum of selling, from yesterday's pack peddlers to today's multi-million-dollar shopping malls and billion-dollar chains. General stores, dry goods stores, company stores, employee stores, specialty stores, *tiendas,* mail-order houses, variety stores, furniture stores, drugstores, supermarkets, surplus stores, shlock stores, even jewelers like Tiffany's and dealers in Orientalia like Gump's make their appearance in these pages, along with the people who made them great, the customers who patronized them, and the crooks who tried to bankrupt them. They are all here, some 700 of the most famous retailers of the past three centuries—from Crazy Eddie and the City Dump to A. T. Stewart's, Macy's, I. Magnin's, and Henri Bendel—all grand emporiums for one reason or another. I am greatly indebted to the many people who helped make *The Grand Emporiums* the most complete book on stores in America by generously opening company archives to me or supplying information or photographs unavailable anywhere else. I only wish that there was space enough here to thank each one individually for assistance that proved indispensable.

First Scarborough Books Edition 1980
The Grand Emporiums was originally published in hardcover by Stein and Day/*Publishers*.

Copyright © 1979 by Robert Hendrickson
All rights reserved.
Designed by Ed Kaplin
Printed in the United States of America
Stein and Day/*Publishers*/Scarborough House,
Briarcliff Manor, N.Y. 10510

Library of Congress Cataloging in Publication Data

Hendrickson, Robert, 1933-
    The grand emporiums.

Includes index.
    1. Department stores—United States—History.
I. Title.
HF5465.U5H46   1978   381'.06'573   78-7555
ISBN 0-8128-6092-6

THE GRAND EMPORIUMS

Want a teddy bear that wears a lorgnette and drinks Dom Perignon, or do you favor bargain basements? One famous Southern department store takes back everything, no questions asked—it's accepted altered shirts and suits, high button shoes thirty years old, a dead canary, and even goods from competitors down the street. And a haughty Gotham emporium used to accommodate its rich carriage trade customers with an electric numbering system installed above its marquee so that chauffeurs waiting across the street could be signaled right on time to pick up weary dowagers.

They've replaced the movies, baseball and football games, eating out, Sunday driving, and lovers lanes as our favorite haunts. We spend more time in department stores, shopping centers, and malls than anywhere except home and work. They're the places where we not only fill our needs, but indulge our fantasies and sustain our dreams.

The Grand Emporiums is the illustrated story of the rise of the great department stores, the merchants who made them, the customers who patronized them, and the crooks who preyed upon them. A monumental social history of the whole spectrum of selling in America, this fascinating romantic, nostalgic, and documentary epic covers everything from yesterday's pack peddler to the mail-order houses and discount marts, to the most elegant stores you can name. From peeping toms in dressing rooms to what it takes to make an Easter Parade, this is *the* complete store-by-store look at the real fabric of the American way of life.

ROBERT HENDRICKSON is the author of *The Great American Chewing Gum Book, The Great American Tomato Book, Human Words, Food for Love,* and *Rip-Offs,* and he has published more than 500 articles in *Time, Reader's Digest, The New York Times, Saturday Review, Sports Illustrated,* and many other prominent periodicals. He lives in Far Rockaway, New York.

Contents

vii

PART ONE

ROOTS: ANCESTORS OF THE GREAT DEPARTMENT STORES

From Peddlers
to Grand Emporiums

"Buy more, buy now, and be happy!" has been their slogan for well over a century; housed in what are often America's most beautiful buildings and characterized by elegant open vistas, they set their customers free in fantasy land, offering them EVERYTHING, while parades with elephants dyed pink pass by and Santas parachute from planes to dandle kids upon their knees ... while fireworks flare, rock bands blare, grand organs resound, and electronic cash registers are *blip-bleep-bleep-blipping* billions of dollars in sales.

Most anything under the sun can be bought in the great department stores, which are surely the most Barnumesque of American big businesses. It's said, in fact, that the man who recently walked into Macy's and ordered a complete kingdom wasn't considered a lunatic. He was simply told that while there was no kingdom for sale presently, Macy's might be able to get him a duchy or a principality or even a small republic tucked away in some corner of Europe. More than a few people have actually bought some of the following "truly unique" items offered by a certain high-toned specialty department store:

• A sterling silver "think tank," or privacy capsule, completely soundproof, with options ranging from film projection to music and dictation, which can be entered only by the insertion of a sterling silver punched card in the entry slot—merely $800,000.
• His and her robes made of shatoosh, an incomparably fine fabric woven from the hair of the Himalayan ibex goat. The fabric is the rarest and most costly in the world because the hair has to be collected from bushes on mountainsides where the goat catches its coat while foraging.
• Unset diamonds as a very real investment—a grab bag of loose

diamonds; some round, some pear, some marquise or emerald. The diamonds come in a special chamois bag with a 14K gold drawstring as an extra touch. The price of this precious cache of security: between $50,000 and $250,000, "depending on selection."

• His and her (male and female) *Bison* calves from the first certified 100 percent purebred buffalo herd in the United States. Starter calves, with a certificate from the American Buffalo Association attesting to the purity of the blood line. Delivered anywhere in the coterminous Unied States. The pair: $11,750.

• The ultimate omelette pan—made of pure gold. Stainless steel is sealed under the surface of gold—the most efficient heat conductor known, excepting silver. Finished with a rosewood handle, packed in a French oak box along with four pounds of truffles, four dozen double yolk eggs, and a documented assay on the 8-inch omelette pan. Only $30,000.

• A Noah's Ark for the person who believes Providence doesn't look too benevolently on all this blatant materialism. In addition to containing 92 mammals, 10 reptiles, 26 birds, 14 fish, and 38 insects, the ark is staffed by a French chef, an English valet, a Swedish masseur, a French maid, an Italian couturier, an English curator/librarian, a Park Avenue physician, and a Texas A & M veterinarian. Only well-to-do pessimists need order, for the price is $588,247, FOB Mount Ararat.

These are, of course, selections from various Neiman-Marcus Christmas catalogues (more about which later), in several cases taken word for word from the inspired world-famous fun books themselves. But they are memorable exaggerations of similar offerings from all of America's grand emporiums. Marshall Field, for example, offers as a service the reweaving and repair of oriental rugs and even restores the gesso ornamentation of picture frames, a job many major museums won't attempt. Macy's, Bloomingdale's, and other department stores outdo many gourmet shops by carrying foods like pâté de foie gras and caviar at $200 a pound, delicate raspberries in winter at $6 a half pint, and "frozen convenience foods" like shrimp de Jonghe, quiche Lorraine, and bouillabaisse. Roaming the aisles of I. Magnin's, Altman's or Bergdorf Goodman you might see a Saudi princess pick out $30,000 worth of dresses in a few hours, a Texas oilman purchase three mink coats—one for his wife, one for his daughter, and one for his mistress—or a shabbily dressed woman peel a hundred bills off a large roll of 100s to buy a Picasso etching. Customers can go to church or college, vote, bank, give blood, consult a doctor, dentist, or psychiatrist, attend plays and concerts, swim, skate, jog, dine well, even live and love luxuriously in the great department stores or the suburban and city malls they anchor. About the only services not provided are undertaker departments, although the stores once did carry a complete line of coffins and "black goods," the contemporary euphemism for the mourning clothes of black crêpe all members of a bereaved family wore.

But the bargain hunter in every shopper isn't overlooked, either; the grand emporiums have always been "all things to all people," and the Me Generation flocks to them from every possible place, every walk of life. Noted department store bargain basements like Filene's Automatic Bargain Basement have precipitated the most fatal charges since the Light Brigade, and some of their habitués are footnoted in psychology rather than retailing texts. Marvin Traub, Bloomingdale's president, recalls his first day on the job in the bargain basement of a large department store. "A customer came up to me and asked me where the fitting rooms were for the cheap cotton dresses," he says. "When I told her there were no fitting rooms, she proceeded to undress right in front of me. That problem had certainly never been covered in the curriculum at Harvard."

Amid all the glamour, while the enchanted are indulging, deluging, and indebting themselves (only the tooth fairy pays cash today), there are indeed problems in Paradise. Exhibitionists, peeping Toms, burglars, robbers, shoplifters, kidnappers, dognappers, and con men of every description have long plagued the grand emporiums. So have the unbalanced, the cases for the store shrinks, their extremes the pathetic bag lady who sneaks past security guards, looking as if she had hobbled out of hell . . . or the crazies who attacked Governor George Wallace and Senator Benjamin Jordan at shopping center rallies . . . or all the mad bombers political or apolitical . . . or David Berkowitz, the .44 caliber killer, who scrawled on a paper found in his room that he had once stalked the stores in Yonkers's Cross County Shopping Center: "I must have walked over every square foot of space there. I went there to look for a friendly face and I found none. . . . I only wish I had a machine gun. . . ."

Yet the great stores have survived and will survive, just as they survived the vilifications, window smashings, and firebombings of small merchants when they began to grow, just as the *grands magasins* of Europe literally rose from the ruins of World War II and America's grand emporiums survived the deterioration of the cities. Now an American institution, they have achieved mythical status and after a century are still working their magic. Department stores and the shopping malls they dominate, which might be termed huge department stores themselves, typify civilization in America today; in fact, some sociologists believe that the malls are no longer part of the community in many places, but *are* the community. Studies have shown that both men and women find more mates in them than they do in singles bars or discos, that they are the preferred haunt of teenagers, that strolling in them rivals sex as America's favorite pastime. In any case, their hold on the imagination of the millions who wander the wonderlands within their commodious walls shows no sign of weakening; they remain "places where almost all the operations of life can be conducted," as one observer put it, places where bodies and houses can be completely furnished and at least all material prayers can be answered for a price.

Strangely enough, the grand emporiums that fulfill millions of dreams and earn hundreds of billions of dollars (Sears alone has annual sales equaling one percent of the gross national product) have their roots in what seems at first glance rather prosaic country peddlers and country stores. Among the first of any stores were those erected on the hunched backs of the all-purpose itinerant peddlers, those who shouted their wares from house to house, heartily singing their "cries:"

> Scuttles and cans
> Buttons and bows
> I'll cure your ills
> And cheer your woes!

It was from these colorful hawkers, from their love of dealing and the sight, feel, and song of coin itself that the raw beginnings of retailing emerged in America. Their sturdy backs may even have been the first department stores, in the loosest sense of the word. From earliest times, in ancient Greece, Rome, and medieval Europe, following animals runs and trails Indians had worn in the American wilderness, these peddlers traveled the sparsely settled countryside crying their wares. At the very least, permanent stores everywhere developed from their backpacks when they settled down to sell. It could be said that their packs were the first "stores" to be divided into "departments," for weren't the goods inside carefully separated: the buttons n' bows, pins and needles, Bibles and gunpowder, patent medicines, whatever they came to hawk.

No one can say exactly how far back the peddlers go, but their antiquity is attested to by the grandiloquent word *emporium* that we use today for a large posh store carrying many goods. This derives from the Greek *emporion,* "a place where merchants come together," the Greek word for merchant being *emporos,* which was formed from the prefix *en,* "in," and *porous,* "travel"—the first merchants thus being peddlers or hawkers who traveled about the country.

The peddlers (their name comes from the Old English *ped,* "a pack in which articles were stored to be hawked about the streets") were considered "evill disposed persons" almost everywhere they went, and in America they were no better liked than elsewhere. One of the earliest records of peddlers here is of an itinerant hawker named Richard Graves, who in 1642 "kissed Goody Gent twice" and was sentenced to the whipping post and stocks. "The whole race of Yankee Peddlers," wrote an observer of American character in 1833, "are proverbial for dishonesty. They go forth annually in the thousands to lie, cog, cheat, swindle; in short to get possession of their neighbor's property in any manner it can be done with impunity."

Northerners probably got the name "damn Yankees," coined long before the Civil War, from Yankee peddlers who worked the rural South. Yankee peddlers were known as far away as Europe for their trickery, especially for their fabled wooden nutmegs. It is doubtful that anyone would take the trouble to carve wooden nutmegs (it took an expert wood carver a full day to make just *one* in a recent experiment) when these kernels of an evergreen tree cultivated in the Spice Islands sold for less than a penny a piece. But whether carved wooden nutmegs ever existed or not (no one has ever turned up an authentic one), many country people did believe that Yankee peddlers sold them, along with carved wooden hams painted pink ("Basswood Hams") carved cigars, and wooden pumpkin seeds! Connecticut is still called the Nutmeg State for this reason, and the warning, "don't take any wooden nutmegs," probably influenced the coining of the still current phrase, "don't take any wooden nickels."

"Know how to revive a Yankee peddler when he drowns?" an old joke went. "Just turn out his pockets!" But immigrant peddlers were as maligned as their Yankee predecessors. The Jews among them suffered most, prey to not only a general chauvinistic dislike of "foreigners" but to the anti-Semitism that followed them here. In fact, the vulgar offensive term *kike* for a Jew, among other op-probrious words, may have its origins in peddling. According to one story, Jewish peddlers refused to sign contracts with the customary English cross and instead made a *keikel*, the Yiddish word for a circle, a peddler who signed with a *keikel* being called a *keikel* and finally a *kike*.

Everybody with an ax to grind, from disgruntled customers to local merchants, maligned the American peddler, who suffered a distinct disadvantage—being on the road and not around to defend himself. Derogatory poems were circulated about the peddlers:

> There is, in famous Yankee-land
> A class of men yclepted [called] tin-peddlers,
> A shrewd, sarcastic band
> Of busy meddlers.

Many humorous stories were invented about peddlers. In one a German peddler sells a farmer a liquid for exterminating insects. "How do you use it?" the farmer asks, after buying the product. "Ketch the insect und drop von little drop into his mouth," the peddler replies. "The duce with that!" the customer cries. "I could kill it in half the time by stomping on it." Says the peddler: "Vell, dot is a good way, too."

But, no matter what their background, hawkers weren't usually the cheap, chousing vagrants folklore makes them. If they were crooked, the itinerant hawkers were generally "penny-snatchers not pirates"; they practiced and perfected an oblique kind of dishonesty, the old Yankee ability to give people "a steer in the wrong direction," as Barnum put it, and to bring novelty, fun, and excitement into their lives while doing so. The peddler actually had less opportunity than most merchants to cheat his customers, whom he dealt with on a firsthand basis, often over a long period of time and in unfamiliar territories where *he* was the outsider and had no crooked politicians, police, or judges to protect him. Young, tough, courageous, resourceful, shrewd, ambitious, and lucky he did have to be in order to survive, but if he had been basically dishonest there wouldn't have been many peddlers on the road—and a conservative estimate puts their number at about twenty thousand in 1860, peddlers that manufacturers entrusted with wagonloads of consigned goods valued at up to $2,000.

Hawking his wares throughout America, the adventurous, often reckless peddler was almost ubiquitous. Wherever a man swung an ax in the woods, it was said, a peddler would show up in the clearing the next day. In the course of making his living or fortune, the American peddler practically settled the South and Middle West, carrying the materials of civilization to those sparsely settled regions. Although some peddlers had circular routes near home that they serviced each year, most were wanderers and trips of 1,500 miles weren't uncommon—often with loads of 50 pounds strapped to their backs. Many started out on long journeys and were never heard of again.

Peddlers sold everything from specialized goods to specialized services. Indians in New York State, for example, hung carved "souvenir" plates from their horses and hawked them from settlement to settlement. Other peripatetic merchants were tinkers, carpenters, preachers, dentists, and even "breeders" who offered farmers the services of stallions and bulls for their mares and cows. Itinerant portrait painters carried stock paintings, filling in their customer's faces on assembly line canvases; women who sat for portraits could choose from various backgrounds and different-sized breasts.

But the true peddler tended to pack his back or wagon with many items, it being more profitable and safer to carry large assortments of goods, to anticipate what people needed and wanted. A red box wagon might have tinware hanging and banging on the sides, a Franklin stove or a large farm implement inside, even an organ or a piano. Somewhere among these items, however, would be the famous "Yankee notions"—pins and needles, buttons, razors, brooms, books, the window glass that in the nineteenth century began to replace windows covered with paper made translucent with bear grease. Often, too, there were novelties, like the brass combs that many southerners believed would straighten kinky hair and restore gray hair to its natural color. Most housewives put aside their "pin money" from the sale of eggs and other produce to buy these notions, but the peddler would often offer credit or barter for furs and other valuable goods with those who didn't.

Peddling was a "way out" for America's poor from colonial days; the process didn't begin with the immigrant peddlers of the nineteenth century. It is surprising how many notable Americans began their careers as peddlers. Laboring mightily as they did, these hawkers were the most resourceful of men. Typical of them was old Parson Weems, so renowned for his charming fabrication of George Washington chopping down the cherry tree, not to mention his bold, Homeric yarns about Ben Franklin and General Francis "The Swamp Fox" Marion. History often forgets that Weems, whose stories have become folklore, worked all his life as a book peddler; in fact, this vagabond preacher died in harness on the southern roads where he began hawking books in 1794. Fiddle at his side, the lively colporteur drove his Jersey wagon over bumpy rural roads for some 30 years, often playing gay tunes to stimulate his horses, dreaming up schemes for selling the books behind him and implementing his plans with soaring spirits. When a Tory clergyman complained that Weems was selling Tom Paine's radical *The Age of Reason,* he pulled out the Bishop of Llandaff's refutation of Paine, advising that he sold the antidote as well as the poison.

Parson Weems certainly wasn't the first or last of the famous or infamous peddlers. Benedict Arnold started out as an itinerant merchant, peddling stockings and other woolen goods up and down the Hudson Valley more successfully than he peddled the plans to West Point. On the other hand, peddler Enoch Crosby, prototype for Cooper's hero in *The Spy,* was a secret agent who worked for

General Washington. Stephen Girard, the great Philadelphia banker who helped finance America in the War of 1812, began his career as a peddler, as did Donald Alexander Smith, the Canadian fur trader who eventually headed Canada's giant Hudson Bay Company. John D. Rockefeller's father called himself "Dr. William A. Rockefeller, the Celebrated Cancer Specialist"; this shrewd, lusty, quack peddler claimed he could cure all cases of cancer ("unless too far gone") with patent medicines and once bragged, "I cheat my sons every chance I get" in order "to make 'em sharp."

Like many frontier Americans in the nineteenth century, Abe Lincoln's father was a part-time peddler. When he moved his family from Kentucky to Illinois, he took along a trunk full of notions to hawk from his wagon and help offset the expense of the trip. Bronson Alcott, that Socrates of Concord who fathered both a school of philosophy and Louisa May Alcott, author of *Little Women,* took to the road as a full-time peddler of tinware and almanacs instead of going to college. Inventors John Fitch and Thomas Edison both peddled for a time. Railroad magnate Collis B. Huntington started his financial career as a hawker, journeying far west, and from his backpack grew a vast railroad empire, the Southern Pacific. Big Jim Fisk was another railroad man and manipulator who began as a peddler, as was Daniel Drew. It is from the latter's activities peddling cattle from country to city that we get the financial term "watered stock." Drew routinely fed his cattle salt before they reached city stockyards; this, of course, caused them to drink until they were bloated, a herd of a thousand cattle commonly putting on over ten thousand pounds in water just before it reached the weighing scales.

Countless American fortunes were amassed by men who honed their business wits on the road. Their lives all read like a mixture of Frank Norris and Horatio Alger stories, and, in fact, Alger did write a rags-to-riches story called *Paul The Peddler.* Stanley Tools was founded by a peddler; B. T. Babbitt, America's first soap millionaire, began by peddling his soap in upstate New York; and Cyrus McCormick first peddled door to door the reapers that revolutionized American agriculture. Not the least of peddler success stories are today's department store giants themselves. Peddling seems to have been one of the best possible ways to learn merchandising, for at least a score of the grand emporiums, from Gimbels and May's to Saks Fifth Avenue and Macy's were founded or headed by reformed peddlers.

Ironically, former peddlers themselves helped hasten the end of the peddling era in American retailing history. In their wanderings peddlers were usually the first outsiders to realize that an area had become thickly populated, and they often opened general or country stores when they happened upon a good location or found the right girl and decided to settle down. Naturally, these former peddlers quickly altered their footloose philosophy and contended that the whole territory was rightfully theirs, that itinerant traders were intruding on their business rights. As early as 1700, permanent Connecticut merchants petitioned the House of Magistrates to outlaw "the multitude of foreign or peregrine peddlers," who were "stealing our business." These "foreigners" (most peddlers were actually native-born Americans at the time) paid no taxes, said the local merchants; neither did they contribute to local charities and they were financially irresponsible, as no merchandise could be returned to them. The merchants also used a scare tactic that was to be a feature of numerous campaigns against the peddlers; these dirty foreigners, they said, would surely introduce "many raging and contagious diseases" into the colony.

Through the years widespread taxation, among other restrictions, contributed heavily to the American peddler's demise and by the end of the nineteenth century, itinerant hawkers were already an anachronism. License fees, cheaper, more efficient transportation for the country folk, enabling them to journey to town for supplies, and the ability of country store owners to offer a wider variety of goods at lower prices, had eliminated all but an obstinate handful of the breed. All that remains of them today are the peddlers still thriving on city streets (there are twelve thousand in New York City alone, much to the dismay of local department stores, who complain about them in letters to the *New York Times*) and the three thousand or so firms like Fuller Brush and Avon Cosmetics engaged in house-to-house selling. In fact, several communities have ordinances against a peddler calling at a house unless he has previously been invited to do so, laws that have been upheld by the Supreme Court and which were inspired by con artists such as the

infamous Williamson clan, who are still peddling wooden light-
ning rods and other "bargains" door-to-door.

Peddlers probably founded the first real American country stores,
which are often described as primitive department stores, in remote
backwoods areas during the late 1600s. Specialization was impossible in such places; there just weren't enough people to support a
great many stores in a small village, and merchants had to carry a
mixed line of goods to survive. Therefore, a store operation evolved
that was influenced very little by English methods and was adapted
to American conditions.

Stores of course go back ages before the American country store,
to a time when some enterprising Ug H. Macy or Og Bloomingdale
set up a stall outside his or her cave. The word "store," in fact,
takes its name from the roofed colonnades called *stoas* that housed
the small shops of merchants in the ancient Athenian Agora, that
same market place where Socrates and his followers gathered to
argue philosophical questions, where Solon the great law giver
made his fortune as a merchant, and St. Paul addressed the Athe-
nians. In this marketplace the philosopher Zeno taught that "what
will be will be," man must accept his fate calmly in this world. He
and his pupils came to be called *stoics* because they met in a *stoa.*
Thus the Greek word *stoa* for a shop yielded both the English word
"store" and the word "stoic," this last something many a store-
owner has been forced to be by war, weather, fire, flood, plague,
recession, and other calamities over the centuries.

"Shop" is another old word, deriving from a Saxon term meaning
the porch or lean-to of a house—such "open rooms or stalls"
eventually developed into enclosed stores. As for "retailing" itself,
one old story speculates that French peasants used the word *taill*, a
corruption of the Latin *talea* (twig), to describe the process of
cutting up into large sections trees that they were barely able to
drag to market. Dealers who bought this bulky firewood from them
had to *re-taill* the wood into small sections before selling it to their
customers, so they became known as *retaillers*, as did all merchants
who broke large lots down into smaller ones customers could better
afford. Not long after, the term "wholesale" came into use; it was at
first two words meaning the sale of whole cloth: that is, cloth in
large lengths.

American country stores enjoyed their heyday between 1820 and 1860, at a time in our history when personal income was rising and population was growing rapidly. In 1800 there were only 5.3 million people in America, but by 1860 she claimed over 31 million. Into the vacuum caused by the lack of rural trading facilities, a vacuum far greater than the peddler could fill, poured the ubiquitous country stores. They spread out across America, became both trading and gathering places for the communities they served. Usually located in the center of town, the unimposing country store was the hub of community activity; "town," in fact, was often no more than a "four corner store" at the crossroads. The old country or general store was characterized by its informality—its bare wood shelves and hodgepodge of goods, the cat cuddled up in the cracker barrel; by its distinctive aroma—an indescribable compound of the smells of apples, cheese, tobacco, and a hundred other essences; and, in summertime, by the swarms of flies that always managed to evade the streamers of sticky flypaper suspended from the ceiling. (The flies and flypaper, incidentally, inspired the old country saying, "You can kill a fly, but ten flies come to fly's funeral.") Trading was informal, too, the storekeeper often dickering with his customers over prices, which were not fixed in many cases.

Might as well not try to peddle in the vicinity of a country store, one nineteenth-century peddler lamented, for all the customers want to go to the store for free gossip. Farmers and "loungers" sat in a few rickety chairs around the potbellied or box stove. Horses and livestock were traded, wagers made. Amusements ranged from spitting contests, with saliva, tobacco juice, or seeds aimed at the stove or a sawdust spit box, the ancestor of the spittoon, to the swapping of gossip, earthy jokes, and tall tales of tomcatting, farming, fishing, and hunting. A reporter for an Illinois paper wrote, "There are more ducks killed around the stoves [in an afternoon] than are slain in twenty-four hours along the Illinois River. . . ." On the other hand, a noted historian has observed: "It may not be too much to say that here the tariff question, government bank, internal improvements, foreign policies and other important national matters were ultimately settled. American statesmen for many years had to reckon with the force of public opinion generated and cultivated around the stove of the country stores."

From the Neiman-Marcus Christmas catalogue: A "gravy train" with four control switches that delivers salt, pepper, and condiments to diners. The engine is silver plate, the four cars sterling silver.

From the Neiman-Marcus Christmas catalogue: Unset diamonds as a very real investment—a bag of loose diamonds, some round, some pear, some marquise, some emerald. The diamonds held in a special chamois bag with 14K gold drawstring as an exotic touch. The price of this special cache of security: between $50,000 and $250,000.

Neiman-Marcus has also offered matched sets of buffalo.

HIS AND HER GIFTS, 1976

GIVE US A HOME FOR OUR BUFFALO TO ROAM!

Here's an unusual addition to your existing stock — or a way to get started with a herd of shaggies. A male and female calf from the first certified 100% pure bred buffalo herd in the United States. This remarkable beast is known as the American Bison (Bison Bison), but he's been buffalo to almost everybody else since long before Bill Cody's day. The ubiquitous buffalo has symbolically adorned many things in our history from the real nickel content nickel (see opposite page), to the heads of Amerindian braves. No longer a mere symbol, or on the way to extinction, the buffalo emerges as a greatly rekindled interest. With recognition of their financial and ecological potential, the numbers of buffalo are dramatically on the increase, and while it may be precipitate to guarantee anything like the herds of 60 million or so which once grazed our continent, this year's His and Her Gift gives each of us a chance to do his part. 25A. MALE AND FEMALE STARTER CALVES, six months old, from the herd of Bison Enterprises Ltd: Hartsel, Colorado. The calves, with a certificate from the American Buffalo Association attesting to the purity of their bloodline, will be delivered anywhere in the conterminous United States. They must be ordered no later than Monday, November 29th to insure delivery by Christmas. The pair, 11,750.00. For information, call AC 214/741-6911, ext. 1225.

23.

Old print from *Leslie's Magazine* shows a persistent peddler trying to sell his wares.

In South Dakota, Deadwood's main street shows what many frontier stores of the late 19th century looked like.

A country store in the rural south.

Peddlers often graduated to permanent sites such as these in this market on Chicago's Wentworth Street, and then worked their way up to an enclosed store.

At these oases in deserts of rural isolation the storekeeper was a link with the outside world. Frequently serving as postmaster, he passed on news in the form of long-awaited letters. As a further indispensable service, he often read and wrote letters for the many illiterates in the community. Religious life sometimes centered in his store, too, as the local church was frequently located in the attic above it, sometimes sharing its quarters with a fraternal order or a political club, and containing the shopkeeper's home as well.

It has been said that the country storekeeper was "all things to all men—things good and things less good." But he was usually respected, a man of consequence as often as not self-educated from his periodic buying trips to big cities and from the magazines and books that he carried in his store. One small-town Missouri storekeeper in 1829 sold a line of books that included Homer, Herodotus, Josephus, Shakespeare, Cervantes, Milton, Defoe, Bunyan, Smollett, Hume, Fielding, and Scott, in addition to the Bibles and popular works he carried. A town's most educated man aside from the schoolteacher or preacher, and generally the most knowledgeable, the country storekeeper was usually the local "crackerbarrel philosopher" who made flowery patriotic Fourth of July speeches for a political candidate and was the man chosen to make erudite toasts at weddings and other occasions. He frequently served as the local notary and justice of the peace as well.

His store, with the inevitable flour, cracker, and cookie barrels near the counter, carried what was a wonderland of goods to the civilization-starved settlers, and usually extended credit liberally. Shopping was a holiday here for men and women who came into town "storeing" late on a Saturday afternoon after a hard week on the farm. There were packaged foodstuffs, huge barrels of pickles, and great blocks of cheese waiting to be cut into five-cent slices. Pickled or dried fish was available from the seaboard. Salt was stored in barrels outside under a shed attached to the building. Soap was sliced off loaves until Benjamin Babbitt, the first soap millionaire, got the idea of wrapping it and selling it as a bar, giving premiums for the used wrappers. For the kids, penny candy ranging from licorice whips to all-day suckers were prominently displayed in jars atop the counter.

An interesting department was the "white work," "white sew-ing," or "under wardrobe" section—the lingerie department, as it was later called. Modesty wasn't confined to these euphemisms used for underwear, either; in at least one country store the merchant would put his wife in charge and leave the store entirely as soon as a lady hinted that she was shopping for an "unmentionable" like a corset.

In the country store shoe section, shoes were piled in wooden bins arranged according to size, but there was no separation by style. Until the nineteenth century all shoes were sold as "straights"; that is, they were made alike for each foot and only assumed the shape of right or left shoes after a buyer broke them in. People were so used to this that they initially ridiculed the "lefts" and "rights" some anonymous genius invented, calling them "crooked shoes."

Off to one side of the stores were the dry goods: shelves there held bolts of cloth, laces, ribbon, hooks and eyes, buttons, thread, and skeins of cotton, wool, and silk yarns. Our expression "getting down to brass tacks" (getting down to business) may have been born on the dry goods counters. Merchants in country stores, it's said, hammered brass-headed tacks at intervals into fabric department counters to indicate lengths of a yard, a half yard and a quarter yard. After a customer selected the cloth she wanted, the store-keeper might say, "All right, now we'll get down to brass tacks—I'll measure it up for you."

The plethora of pills and patent medicines available in the country stores led one historian to remark that it is a tribute to the robustness of pioneer Americans that they weren't exterminated by the medicines they took. There were "cures" on the counter for everything from "female sickness" and the "French disease" to drug addiction (addiction became a problem because of the mor-phine indiscriminately used during the Civil War). Many of these medicines were nothing but alcohol disguised so that "respectable" folk could buy it. One Colonel Hobstetter of Hobstetter's Bitters satisfied the national craving for booze in medicine bottles so well that he accumulated an $18 million fortune. To disguise the telltale breath of patent medicine drinkers, the stores often carried a product called Hunkidori. This "breath refresher," introduced in

1868, may have given us the saying "everything is hunky-dory" (okay).

In the backrooms of the general stores, where spirits like hard cider, beer, and whiskey often flowed and many a customer got fired up, fractious, and fried, another expression may have been added to the language. The backroom bars were sometimes no more than a large barrel serving as both booze container and counter. Before a customer got a smack of white mule, tarantula juice, fortyrod ("warranted to kill at forty rods"), or any rotgut likely to make him brave enough not to pay, he was required to put down "cash on the barrelhead" or counter. Naturally no credit was extended, as the coffin varnish might embalm him.

The country merchant's storekeeping methods could be unsophisticated. An early store owner, for example, might hang up two boots, one on each side of the chimney, and put all the money he received in one, all the receipts for money he paid out in the other. At the end of the year he would empty both boots and make an accounting. But, as a rule, bookkeeping methods were quite complicated, as were weighing and measuring techniques. There was even a complicated code system for marking goods so that the merchant could tell what every piece of merchandise cost him without the customer knowing, which gave the storekeeper an advantage when bargaining. A merchant for instance, might make the phrase NOW BE SHARP represent 12345678910 (an *N* would equal the numeral 1, an *O* the numeral 2, a *W* the numeral 3, and so on). Every trusted clerk would be given this equation, and if a piece of merchandise was marked, say, NWW on the back, anyone with the formula would know its cost was $1.33.

Country stores were far from being fashionable, "fancy," or "citified." For more than twenty years after paper bags were invented in 1850, clerks were still wrapping most packages in "pokes," brown wrapping paper adeptly shaped into cornucopias, folded over and tied with string. Trading in the stores was often conducted by barter, "country pay" as it was called, customers exchanging corn, wheat, rye, and flax, or articles of household manufacture like blankets and baskets for goods on the merchant's shelves. Homemade Indian brooms, maple syrup, barrel staves, skeins of wool, dried apples, blackberries and blueberries, churned butter, potash and charcoal left when forests were burned down to clear land—all these and a hundred other things were used as "cash crops" for barter at the country store. Aphrodisiac ginseng was gathered wild in the woods and sold to country stores, from where it was resold for export to China. Even wampum was accepted by the storekeeper, for wampum was often used by white men for trade with the Indians: In 1775 one enterprising storekeeper actually set up a wampum factory in what is now Park Ridge, New Jersey.

Storekeepers often had to deal with the many suave con men passing through their bailiwicks. The English encouraged counterfeiting during the Revolution, in fact, sending confidence men with cartloads of bogus money, "Not worth a Continental," into the provinces and even manufacturing fake ha'pennies for export to America at a Birmingham factory. Later, merchants protected themselves against the many types of bogus money in circulation by keeping a copy of *Day's New York Bank Note List and Counterfeit Detector* (1826) on the shelf by the cashbox. Another method was to nail all counterfeit coins one had been cheated with to the counter as an aid against clerks being deceived in the future and a warning to would-be sharpies trying to pass money in the store. Some say that this practice was the inspiration for the phrase, "To nail a lie to the counter," to expose anything false.

In any event, only resourceful shrewd men could hope to cope with the varied types of customers, ranging from Indians and trappers to settlers and confidence men, who wheeled and dealed in the country stores. Connecticut merchant Charley Thompson, who made a fortune in mail order before opening a country store, once sold five boxcar loads of kerosene lanterns by stringing them up all over town and lighting them. Farmers came from miles around that night to see if Bridgewater was burning down—only to find Charley pitching his lanterns from atop a soapbox. Another country store merchant arranged a reunion of all the Smiths in the state at his store every year, selling thousands of dollars of merchandise to his "relatives" during the festivities. Not surprisingly, these American institutions nurtured a good number of men who gained national prominence in other fields. John James Audubon ran a country store in Henderson, Kentucky, before beginning the wanderings that made him a world-famous painter of wildlife. Ulysses S. Grant clerked in his father's store in Galena, Illinois, and Grover Cleveland worked at a village store in New York where he made $50 a year. Everyone knows that Abraham Lincoln clerked in a country store as a youth, and the story of young Abe walking several miles to return a penny to a customer is of course part of American folklore. As for P.T. Barnum, he ran a general store in Bethel, Connecticut, where he claimed he learned many a trick from country people who cheated him as adeptly as any city slicker could.

Among the founders of great modern-day American department stores who operated or clerked in country stores Adam Gimbel, J. L. Hudson, Charles A. Stevens, Aaron Montgomery Ward, and Herbert Marcus should be mentioned. Gimbel, a former peddler, set a standard for country store honesty in his time. Not only did he distribute handbills announcing that his Vincennes, Indiana, store sold to everyone at the same fixed price, a revolutionary concept in 1842, but a sign hung prominently over the counter in his store read: "If anything done or said in this store looks wrong or is wrong, we would have our customers take it for granted that we shall set it right as soon as it comes to our knowledge. We are not satisfied unless our customers are."

Unfortunately, Gimbel's honesty wasn't emulated by all country storekeepers. Unconscionably high prices were in fact one of the major reasons for the decline of the general store. It is true that farmers were often dissatisfied with the quantity and quality of goods stocked in country stores. Despite his crowded shelves, the country merchant couldn't keep up with the manufacturers of his day. He was, quite simply, inefficient. And settlers in outlying areas had to travel great distances to reach the stores, frequently entrusting the shopping to a hired hand, with predictably unhappy results. But prices were the farmer's major complaint. "Meat was five to seven cents a pound in 1894," one historian notes, "flour $3 to $5 a barrel and sugar from four to six cents a pound. But before any of these commodities were loaded onto a customer's wagon the price was practically doubled."

To the charges of price gouging the merchants replied that they were squeezed on all sides. Their dishonesty wasn't like Barnum's.

Many farmers were poor credit risks, the merchants claimed justly, and when these credit risks turned out poorly, the good risks had to absorb the losses store owners took on the poor ones. Furthermore, sources of supply were uncertain, turnover slow, and wholesalers and jobbers took their profits before the country merchant could take his. All of these factors did conspire to raise prices, but there is no doubt that the merchants themselves, relatively few in number, found it easy to eliminate competition among themselves and fix prices *high*. To what extent this occurred isn't known, but farmers believed that such practices were widespread. This belief and their bitter resentment of middlemen who fixed prices *low* for the commodities the *farmer* sold, resulted in the farmers' cooperatives within the Grange organization that both sold farmers' produce and purchased clothing, household goods, and farm machinery at wholesale prices.

Most of these cooperative ventures failed, but they do show the resentment rural people had for the country store merchant. With the rapid, widespread improvement of roads and transportation beginning in the early 1870s, rural free delivery of mail, and the introduction of the Model "T" Ford, the stage was set for mail-order department stores like "Monkey Wards" to fill the needs of country folk, and by the turn of the century country stores were already marked as relics of the past.

Some of the old country stores became grocery stores; a few evolved into department stores. Many held out for another thirty years—there were said to be fifty thousand country stores doing over $2.5 billion worth of business in 1910. Some still serve out-of-the-way communities, for the concept of general stores is too simple and practical ever to die; but as a major force in American retailing, country stores had gone the way of the peddlers before them by the end of the nineteenth century. They are mostly relegated to museums like Sturbridge Village or Old Bethpage today, or are tourist attractions like the "Worst General Store" (run by a fellow named Worst). The modern department store is far from a "glorified general store." But it is too often forgotten that these simple beginnings provided an inspiration for the first grand emporiums, as well as for the mail-order stores and chain stores to follow—a purely native inspiration every bit as important to the development of the grand emporiums here as the department stores in Europe that preceded those in America. Mainly this was because the democratic country store, with its wide variety of goods, tried to be all things to all people, just as the department stores would try to do after the country store's demise.

PART TWO

DEPARTMENT STORES
FROM PAST
TO PRESENT

❧ II ❧

The Founding Fathers

Hercules Poirot would have to enlist C. Auguste Dupin, Inspector Maigret, and the whole Paris police force to establish with absolute certainty the identity of the world's first department store—even if it was a French store, as it almost surely must have been. There are many suspects in this retailing detective story, but few solid clues. England's Equitable Pioneer's Society Ltd., which opened in Rochdale, England, in 1844, has been nominated by a few writers, but Equitable probably didn't evolve into a true department store until much later. The same applies to New York's A. T. Stewart's founded in 1826, New York's Lord & Taylor, which opened in the same year, and at least fifty other early stores.

The department store does not derive directly from the medieval fair or the bazaar, despite the fact that it is composed of a number of "stores" gathered in one place. As Ralph Hower puts it in his groundbreaking study of Macy's:

> In contrast with those amorphous antecedents, the department store is not a haphazard agglomeration of independent enterprises. It is a formally created and managed organization, with a hierarchy of control culminating in one man or, at most, a mere handful of executives. It has an intricate and responsive nervous system and an alert brain, so that it can adjust quickly to new situations and ideas. It anticipates public demand and tries to direct it into certain channels. The fair and the bazaar . . . were essentially passive retailing institutions, depending on the active participation of the consumer to determine what goods should be offered and the prices at which they should be sold. The modern department store is far from passive. By means of skillful advertising, special exhibitions, and tempting bargains, it actively attempts to influence our behavior.

There may have been true department stores in the shadows of the pyramids, in ancient Corinth, or perhaps around the corner from the Forum on the banks of the Tiber. Cleopatra may have bought her aphrodisiacs for Antony at a bargain sale in an Alexandria department store. But that is all guesswork. As far as anyone knows, the first true department store arose in France in the mid-nineteenth century. The best evidence ascribes its beginnings to Bon Marché of Paris. Founded as a small shop in 1838, Bon Marché began to assume the proportions of a department store by the early 1850s. Paris even at that time had a long history as a retail and fashion center, its Mercer's Bazaar, called the *Pardis des Femmes* and very similar to a modern shopping center, dating back to 1300. According to Thomas Costain in his novel *The Moneyman*, a department store existed in France as early as 1450, but the store he describes was probably just a large specialty shop. Even at the time Bon Marché was founded, Paris was noted for these large retail stores employing up to 100 people and going by such colorful names as The Lame Devil, The Poor Devil, The Little Sailor, The Two Maggots, The Iron Mask, and the Beautiful Farmer's Wife.

Bon Marché, whose name means "cheap" or a bargain in French, was started by Aristide Bouçicaut as a small retail shop selling piece goods. Little is known about Bouçicaut, but journals of the day say that he founded the store with hardly any capital. The son of a fairly prosperous hatmaker, Bouçicaut was employed by a manufacturer of novelties and worked as a clerk in a large dry goods store on the Rue du Bac before he and his friend Paul Videau pooled their limited resources to open a small shop on the same street. This little man, no bigger than Napoleon and ultimately much more successful, was destined to lay the foundation for the world's enormous department store industry. He was nearly forty-three when he went into business for himself—an old man for the day— but from the very beginning he proved a source of fresh, innovative ideas. Since the neighborhood was a poor one, Bouçicaut gave away needles and thread to lure customers into the store. Little by little, saving, purchasing wisely, and organizing with rare intelligence, he built his shop into a great emporium that did an annual volume of over $1,400,000 by 1862. All the while he had added to the scope of his operation, branching out from piece goods to women's coats and dresses, underwear, millinery, and shoes until, sometime in the early 1850s, the store assumed the characteristics of a department store.

Bouçicaut stuck to his principles at a time when the respected *Journal des Economistes* denounced the selling of "diverse goods" such as stockings and handkerchiefs in the same store as "horrible." But his timid partner Videau grew frightened of the expansion, agreeing with other retailers that Bouçicaut's new ideas were too radical and romantic. "I prefer to leave you to continue your experiments alone," he told his partner. Bouçicaut was forced to buy him out in 1863 with money borrowed from another farsighted French merchant named Maillard—not with the help of Jesuits as some petty shopkeepers whispered.

Aristide Bouçicaut's innovations were revolutionary for retail stores of the era; he was far ahead of his time, and when people finally realized he was right, they said, as they usually do, that it was obvious all the while. To begin with, he let customers come in and browse about without any moral obligation to buy. This was a radical idea in an age when merchants commonly instructed their clerks never to let a customer leave without purchasing something; if a customer resisted all blandishments, a clerk was often expected to block his way until the proprietor came to the rescue with more propositions. A vestige of this custom remains today in the superstition some small merchants have that the first customer who enters a store when it opens must be sold something, even if the merchant only breaks even on the deal.

Bouçicaut wisely allowed his customers to exchange merchandise they bought or get their money back. His "money-back guarantee" was a new concept that built up his trade substantially, and he reversed the prevalent practice of taking a high profit on goods that turned over slowly. The presiding genius of Bon Marché sold his merchandise at a small markup, depending on a rapid turnover of goods to make his profit. Furthermore, he clearly marked all his goods with fixed prices and permitted no haggling between customers and clerk. This was heresy to some shopkeepers; indeed, as late as the eighteenth century, the distribution of handbills by a few daring retailers advertising sales at fixed prices had actually been prohibited by French law, just as merchants had earlier been forbidden by the state to sell more than one kind of merchandise in their shops.

John Wanamaker, who followed in Bouçicaut's footsteps, once commented on the uncertainty of trading that prevailed in America before the democratic fixed price. "The law of trading was then the law of the jungle" he said, *"take care of number one.* The rules of the game were: don't pay the first price asked; look out for yourself in bargaining; haggle and beat the seller as hard as you can. Naturally the purchaser felt that the concessions he secured from the shopkeeper were so much money made for himself. But how little he knew! Most assuredly the store-keeper, butcher or grocer, always added to the price enough to cover what he had learned was what the customer would beat him down to. And when a thing was once sold, it was sold—no returns. Exchanges of goods were rare and discouraging; the return of money was never admissible unless for goods damaged when purchased."

It would be misleading to say that Bouçicaut originated fixed prices and all the other new retail techniques he used. The incubation period between the conception of an idea and its realization can be centuries and was almost always at least decades in those days, so no one can say with any assurance that Bouçicaut invented marked and fixed prices, low markup and rapid turnover, the money-back guarantee, freedom of entrance for customers, and the display of a wide variety of goods in distinctly separate departments. In the last of these innovations we know that he was certainly anticipated by trading posts, general stores, and cooperative trading societies, while several contemporary merchants fixed prices before him. The hazy origins of the fixed price show just how difficult it is to establish "firsts" for ideas. An undated business card of A. T. Stewart & Company, which could have been issued as early as 1827 or as late as 1841, advises that the firm's prices are "regular and uniform." Adam Gimbel guaranteed fixed prices at his Indiana trading post in 1840, and several New York merchants were advertising one-price as early as 1842. Finally, Quakers Potter Palmer (an early partner of Marshall Field), Rowland Macy, and the founders of Strawbridge & Clothier established one-price cash policies long before their stores became department stores, perhaps because Quaker leader George Fox had urged his followers to eschew sharp bargaining two centuries earlier. Daniel Defoe, in his retailing history *The Compleat English Tradesman* (1826), observes that

English Quakers "resolved to ask no more than they would take upon any occasion whatsoever and chose rather to lose the sale of their goods, though they could afford at some time to take what was offered, rather than abate a farthing from the price they had asked."

Massachusetts law had regulated the price of shoes as early as 1676, and during the Revolutionary War, Rhode Island passed a law fixing prices on many commodities to provide for "the better supply of our troops in the army." Nevertheless, by making fixed prices and other innovative ideas firm policies in his store, Bouçicaut created the first true department store, even though his lines of merchandise were at first limited to clothing apparel and textiles. It is interesting to note that Zola visited Bon Marché to research *Au Bonheur des Dames,* his novel about department stores. When Bouçicaut died in 1877, his childless widow Marguerite immediately sold the shares of the business to his employees, who continued its expansion under her guidance until her death a decade later. For many years Bon Marché remained the greatest department store in the world—it did a total business of over $30 million in 1897—and not a franc's worth of its stock was held outside of the people in the store; the leadership of the strictly cooperative venture vested in three persons elected from the heads of departments by the employees. With Bon Marché began a new thing under the sun, the age of *les grands magasins* in Paris, with great stores like the Printemps joining its ranks. At Les Grands Magasins du Louvre, founded in 1855, which was inspired by Bouçicaut's success but catered to a higher class clientele, home furnishings departments and others were added, and soon there were practically no restrictions on what the department store could sell.

Bon Marché inspired the creation of department stores all over the world, unaffiliated stores in Brooklyn, London, Seattle, and Liverpool actually adopting its name. Nowhere was the influence of the original *grand magasin* greater than in America, where A. T. Stewart's, Wanamaker's, Macy's, Strawbridge & Clothier, Marshall Field, and other great emporiums all credited Bouçicaut's advanced trading practices as the source of many of their ideas in their transitions from dry goods or specialty stores to department stores.

Many American merchants sent observers overseas to study the great original in Paris. R. H. Macy visited the store himself and, when he got back home, outfitted his doormen in uniforms like those worn by Bon Marché employees. Frank Woolworth made it a point to take in the great store when he stopped in Paris during his 1890 continental tour, even though he knew no more French than *oui* and *non.* "This afternoon I visited the world famous store 'The Bon Marché,' which is probably the largest store in the world," the dime store genius wrote in his diary. "They employ 4,000 people regular and feed them all in the same building. It is as near like Wanamaker's store in Philadelphia as any store I know of, but on a much larger scale. On the busy days the sales would run up to 1,500,000 francs ($300,000). They use no cash system whatsoever but each customer must go to the desk and pay for what they buy. They are not allowed to pay the clerks who wait on them, a system that would not work in America."

Although Bon Marché and native country stores provided American merchants with the inspiration for creating department stores, the great majority of the first grand emporiums, probably three-quarters of them by rough count, made the transition from dry goods stores to department stores. These stores were common in both English and American cities, but their appellation has no counterpart among English retailers. Dry goods stores take their name from shops run by New England merchants, many of whom were shipowners and direct importers in colonial times. Their two chief imports were rum and bolts of calico, which were traditionally carried on opposite sides of the store—a "wet goods" side containing the rum and a "dry goods" side holding the calico. "Wet goods" disappeared from the language, though the taste for same certainly didn't abate, but stores that sell piece goods, and even some small town department stores, are still occasionally called dry goods stores.

Neither Bon Marché nor any of the world's early department stores would have evolved if economic conditions hadn't been favorable at the time. The American department store is largely a product of the years from 1860 to 1910, with several factors particularly important in its development besides the example of Bon Marché. First, population became far more dense in many regions of the country in the nineteenth century, at the beginning of which only 12 cities had populations of over five thousand. By the time of the Civil War, the American Industrial Revolution had wrought a great increase in the size of our cities, not to mention the creation of numerous new cities that literally doubled in population within a few years. Large numbers of people lived within comparatively small areas and were easily able to reach almost any place in town with the development of improved mass-transportation systems. Horse-drawn trolleys, precursors of urban electric trolley systems, charged a reasonable fare to carry a city's many potential customers from every section of town to the point of sale, and more and better advertising, enabling merchants to lure customers to their stores, was made possible by the lowering of the price of paper in about 1830. Ads, in fact, came down so in price from 1820 to 1850 that the earlier typical one-column wide advertisement that simply announced the location of a store and the kind of goods sold evolved into a much larger, profusely illustrated ad.

There were problems of course. Several epizootics, epidemic diseases that ravaged livestock, immobilized cities that depended on horsepower and actually forced men in harness to pull trolley cars, delivery wagons, and fire engines on the streets of New York, Boston, and Chicago. There was little window display advertising to attract impulse buyers, for plate glass wasn't made in America until 1868, and not until the 1880s was it used extensively here. Merchants tended to be cautious, too, after the panic of 1837, but this proved a good thing, for it led to the development of the mercantile agencies. Lewis Tappan started the first of these in 1841, and eight years later the Bradstreet Company, today's Dun & Bradstreet, came into being. By giving merchants information about the financial reliability of their suppliers and customers, these agencies eliminated much of the risk for retailers, reduced losses, and increased profits.

More available capital during the Industrial Revolution, low taxes, and cheap labor to build and staff stores also contributed to the rise of the department store in America. These factors together with an improved standard of living and a demand for more and better goods, encouraged many small merchants to create more efficient distribution systems by expanding their operations. Between 1840 and 1860 all of these factors came into focus at the same time, giving birth to the American department store.

Other factors also contributed to the rise of the native grand emporiums, notably the cutthroat competition among many of the 57,565 retail stores counted by the 1840 census. Most of these were located in New York, Pennsylvania, Ohio, Massachusetts, and Virginia. The average investment in the stores was only $4,350, but most merchants began to compete fiercely against one another. Dry goods stores, furniture stores, and specialty stores cut prices to the bone. As a result, little profit remained to be made on standard goods and the most farsighted merchants cast about for new things to sell, realizing that if they wanted to grow, they would have to offer a fuller line of merchandise.

Many traditionalists opposed this innovation in merchandising. In 1850, a Philadelphia newspaper attacked a dry goods store for "going beyond its proper province" by selling umbrellas, parasols, and canes, and the criticism stirred local clergymen to thunder from their pulpits about the action the way earlier preachers had screamed about adulterers. So-called slop-shops (clothes not made to order were considered slop fit for pigs), which sold ready-made, or "boughten," suits for men, vehemently complained, along with dry goods stores and practically every kind of specialty store from greengrocers to haberdashers.

As the department stores grew, small shopkeepers cried that the "Department Store Octopus" was devouring them. "It is better to have 1000 storekeepers fairly prosperous than two or three millionaires and 997 bankrupt tradesmen," one small store advertised. In Chicago merchants vilified Marshall Field; threats were made on the life of John Wanamaker in Philadelphia, and he had to hire bodyguards. There were even firebombings of department stores across the country. A bill was introduced in Pennsylvania calling for the licensing of department stores as was done with peddlers and the collection of $100,000 in yearly fees from each department store, while a law was actually passed in Missouri levying a tax of $500 on every classification of goods sold in a department store. But bigness here wasn't detrimental to the economy as the giant trusts were. Small single-line shops that satisfied the public's needs, and took advantage of new retailing methods, did as well as they ever

did, and cries that they were being devoured were greatly exaggerated. A Boston study made in 1895, for example, showed that
according to the census there were 3,499 stores of all types in that
year—one store for every 142 people; whereas twenty years previously there had been 2,734 stores of all kinds—one store for 125
people.

Since there was no good reason behind all the criticism, only
unfounded fear and tradition for tradition's sake, department stores
continued to expand, offering a dozen distinct lines of stock and
eagerly reaching out for any item or gimmick that seemed to offer
golden opportunities. Even presents and premiums were tried to
drum up trade: a free pair of suspenders with every suit bought, ten
tickets for free shoeshines with every pair of shoes. Small merchants
who decided to stay small continued to call the big stores rapacious,
devouring monsters from whose greed no trade was safe, but
nothing was to stop the big stores' march forward. Plenty of
customers were in the cities; people had more money than ever
before. By selling large quantities of goods at low prices fortunes
were to be made, and no obstacle proved too great for the new
merchants. High rent in central shopping areas might have proved
a problem, for example, but the department store merchants simply
used the upper floors of the buildings they occupied, which they
were able to secure at lower rentals than the main floor. Thus began
the vertical expansion that led to the skyscraper department stores
of the future, the grand emporiums that would take, in the words of
General Grant, "as much generalship to organize . . . as to organize
an army."

By the late 1860s or early 1870s the department store had a firm
foothold in America. Although the term "department store" isn't
recorded in the language until 1887, when a New York establishment advertised itself as H. H. Heyn's Department Store, the idea
of separate departments in stores can be found in print at least 40
years earlier. At that time an article in *Hunt's Merchandising
Magazine* told of "tubes connecting with each department of a
store, from the garret to the cellar, so that if a person in a
department . . . wishes to communicate with the employer, he can
do so without leaving his station." The author's frequent use of the
word *department* without any explanation of its meaning, suggests

that it probably had been commonly used in this sense ten years or so before the article, this usually being the case with recorded expressions.

Colorful Alexander Turney Stewart, who became America's merchant prince in the mid-nineteenth century, probably founded the first American department store, though several surviving stores also claim that distinction. Stewart, the leading merchant of his era, is surely second in importance only to John Wanamaker in the history of American retailing.

Born near Belfast in Northern Ireland and educated for the ministry at Dublin's Trinity College, A. T. Stewart emigrated at age twenty to New York, where he taught school for two years while hoping for a chance to become a writer. He might have remained a grade-school teacher if a friend of his hadn't borrowed money from him to open a small dry goods store and failed miserably before being able to pay Stewart back. Although he had no retailing experience whatsoever, Stewart accepted the store for his loan in 1823 and boldly proceeded to take the small inheritance his father had left him, all the money he had in the world, and return to Belfast to buy $3,000 worth of Irish linens and laces to freshen his stock. On returning to America he put the following ad in the *New York Advertiser* of September 2, 1823:

NEW DRY GOODS STORE

No. 283 Broadway   Opposite Washington Hall

A. T. Stewart informs his friends and the public, that he has taken the above store, where he offers for sale, wholesale and retail, a general assortment of fresh and seasonable DRY GOODS: a choice assortment of:

Irish linens, lawns,° French cambrics
Damask, Diaper,°° etc.

N.B. The above goods have been carefully selected and bought for cash, and will be sold on reasonable terms to those who will please to favour him with their commands.

°A thin or sheer linen or cotton fabric named after Laon, a French city noted for linens
°°A cotton or linen fabric with a woven pattern of small diamonds

The man who invented the department store, Aristide Boucicaut (1810-1877), founder of Bon Marché in Paris.

The magnificent Bon Marché. Merchants came to visit from all over the world.

A. T. Stewart's Cast Iron Palace in New York in 1898, after it had been purchased by John Wanamaker.

Right: A close-up of the rotunda of the Carson Pirie Scott Chicago store.

Below: The lovely intricate ironwork on the Carson Pirie Scott rotunda.

A reproduction of Daniel Chester French's sculpture "Republic" at the Siegel-Cooper store on Sixth Avenue in New York. The sculpture inspired the store's slogan, "Meet me at the fountain."

Siegel-Cooper had another imposing store five blocks away from the fountain at Sixth Avenue and 14th Street.

Left: Advertising by the noted merchant C. R. Mabley, announcing the opening of what is now Mabley & Carew in Cincinnati.

Below: Many early small-town stores called themselves the New York Store or the Chicago Store after cities famous for sophisticated service.

ELEVATOR COURTESY
A FEW OBSERVATIONS WHICH SHOULD BE READ BY EVERY MEMBER OF THE STORE FAMILY

STORE CHAT regrets to note that notwithstanding several brief references to the matter, there are still some thoughtless abuses of the privilege the Management grants employees of riding on our elevators. We say thoughtless, for we refuse to believe they are intentional.

The cut above, while not a photograph, is, as far as conditions sometimes existing are concerned, quite as accurate as though the scene were caught by the camera.

It is very annoying to patrons to be obliged to push their way out of an elevator through a crowding group of girls, who are endeavoring to wedge each other through the doorway like football players in a flying wedge. It does not speak well for The Store. It is apt to cause customers and visitors to question the sincerity of our claim that this is The Store of Courtesy.

Always stand aside while waiting to take an elevator 'till sure that every one who wishes to alight has done so; then step on promptly, turn about, facing the door, make yourself as inconspicuous and "small" as possible, remembering that customers, in other words, our guests, have first claim upon our facilities of every kind, including the elevators, and that one of your duties, upon the performance of which the Management

insists most emphatically is Elevator Courtesy.

Another elevator fault is that of grouping and talking inside the cars among the younger girl members of The Store Family. To be sure, it is not extremely prevalent, but occurs oftener than it should.

Customers look upon this with great disfavor. In many instances, not thoroughly familiar with locations in the store, they wish to be able to question the elevator operator, without confusion.

Grouping, talking, laughing and giggling in the elevators is to be avoided by all means. And this point is applicable to some of the boys and young men, quite as forcibly as to the girls.

Many stores throughout the country prohibit employees the use of elevators. Others permit the use of only certain cars, which, in many instances, necessitates the use of stairways to a majority of the sections of the building.

Our Management is noted country-wide for its consideration of employees. It has a duty, however, to its patrons. STORE CHAT simply presents this little preachment in the hope that those few guilty of the conduct above referred to, will mend their ways before it becomes necessary to issue restrictive orders regarding the use of our elevators which will work a hardship upon the many who are most punctilious in their elevator courtesy.

Above: Lord & Taylor's steam elevator in its New York Broadway and 20th Street store; one of the first of its kind, it was installed when the store opened in 1873.

Left: Elevators were still novelties in 1910, and several stores saw fit to instruct their employees in "elevator courtesy," as Strawbridge & Clothier did in its store magazine.

The tiny shop, only 22 feet x 30 feet, got off to a good start, and before long Stewart had moved to larger quarters down the block. For the next 23 years he shifted from place to place, always renting larger accommodations with each move. Though his early operation was both wholesale and retail, he probably introduced at the time many of his revolutionary retailing methods, including the fixed prices pioneered by Bon Marché.

Stewart accumulated enough cash by 1848 to build at Broadway and Chambers Street in New York the fabulous Marble Dry Goods Palace that still stands as a block-long office building overlooking City Hall Park. The Marble Palace astounded New Yorkers of the day; it was the first example in America of so large a building devoted to retail trade and soon grew even larger, eventually taking up the entire block frontage on Broadway and a two-hundred-foot frontage on City Hall Park.

A trip to Stewart's Marble Palace in 1850 held a fascination for New Yorkers that can't be compared to a shopping foray to any present day store. Nothing like this huge store had ever been seen, and noted merchants came from as far away as England to study it, including Chicago's Potter Palmer, who would prove such an inspiration to Marshall Field. "Stewart the Great," and "King Stewart," newspapers called the blue-eyed, chin-whiskered Irishman, whose store often took in the then unheard of sum of ten thousand dollars a day.

The Marble Palace catered exclusively to women, but Stewart's merchandising genius was already evident, and some historians see the first American department store emerging in this period of his career. Stewart the single-price pioneer employed dandified floorwalkers and the handsomest young men in the city as clerks to please the ladies. His merchandise was usually imported from Europe and of high quality—except for the distressed and damaged goods he bought up for his "fire sales" and the bolts of cheap cloth he had his clerks cut into pieces for his "remnant sales." In the famous "Ladies' Parlor" on the second floor were full-length mirrors imported from Paris that the ladies could preen in, the first used in an American store. Here were held the first American fashion shows. The customers were always treated courteously and honestly. "Never cheat a customer, even if you can," Stewart told his clerks. "If she pays the full figure, present her with a hair of dress braid, a card of buttons, a pair of shoestrings. You must make her happy so she will come back again."

Important customers like Mrs. Abraham Lincoln the great merchant met personally at the door and escorted through the store. One time he even presented the first lady with an expensive shawl that became the talk of the country. "A love of a shawl," several newspapers headlined. "At the last levee at the White House, Mrs. Lincoln wore a lace shawl, presented her by A. T. Stewart of New York, which cost $2500." Mary Lincoln rewarded him by purchasing many of her clothes at Stewart's—and this compulsive clothes buyer had run up clothing bills amounting to $27,000 at the time of the president's death. She also redecorated the White House with goods entirely from Stewart's store. Mr. Lincoln probably did not object to the source, either, for Stewart had been one of his earliest and most generous supporters, being the first of many American department store owners to dabble in national politics.

Certainly there is a good case for the first American department store emerging from the endless "bargain sales" that A. T. Stewart held at the Marble Palace through the panic of 1857. But if Stewart's didn't become a full-fledged department store in Marble Palace days, it surely did when the merchant decided to move his business farther up Broadway in 1862.

That year Stewart reportedly had an annual income of $4 million from his store, the largest in the city, and hotels, mills, and other enterprises that he owned. He could certainly afford the magnificent Cast Iron Palace he erected on the old Randall Farm at Ninth and Tenth streets. This store, which cost $2,750,000 to build in depression years, was the first example in America, or any other country, of the erection of something resembling a modern department store building. Revolutionary in every way, it remained the largest store in the world for over a decade. Consisting of eight floors of 2½ acres each, Stewart's Cast Iron Palace required over two thousand employees to function properly and stocked an immense variety of merchandise—everything from swaddling clothes to funereal "black goods." The store was the sole American distributor for many European products, including the famed Alexandre kid gloves of the day. One probably exaggerated claim had it doing business of over $50 million one year.

Stewart's was definitely fully departmentalized in the 1860s and probably was in the 1850s. As a visitor noted in 1870:

> The service of this immense establishment is arranged as follows. There is one general superintendant, with nineteen assistants, each of whom is at the head of a department. Nine cashiers receive and pay out money, twenty-five book keepers keep the record of the day; thirty ushers direct purchasers to the department they seek; two hundred cash boys receive the money and bring back the change of purchases; four hundred and seventy clerks, a few of whom are females, make the sales of the day; fifty porters do the heavy work and nine hundred seamstresses are employed in the manufactureing department. Besides these, there are usually about five hundred other persons employed about the establishment in various capacities. . . .

Of the 19 Stewart's departments listed by the writer, "silks" was the biggest money-maker, with "dress goods" second and "carpets" third. Men's and boys' clothing, as well as women's wear, were carried and there were toy and sports departments.

The Cast Iron Palace was one of the first store buildings to employ the cast-iron building façade, a space-saving form of architecture unique to America. Cast iron, molded in local foundries, was used for the façades and occasionally for interiors. Interior cast iron took the form of elegant slender columns that supported the floors and permitted lots of open space inside the building, the open vista that became a characteristic of all department stores. Since each floor took the weight of its own outer wall, the thick masonry traditionally used to support the weight of the upper walls at ground level could be dispensed with and the way was paved for the skyscrapers of the future. Outside, the façade of the Cast Iron Palace, made of many small iron parts bolted together to form an uneven surface, was painted to simulate stone or marble. Inside, the first grand emporium had a central rotunda, with a great glass dome skylight to admit daylight, and an immense double staircase that provided the only access to all floors until six steam-powered elevators were later added. The great dome, or light well, allowed a wide view of the premises, both calling the shoppers' attention to the upper floors and impressing them with the size and unity of the store, the fact that a Baghdad of goods awaited them.

Continuous organ music entertained Stewart's customers while they shopped at his Cast Iron Palace. Over fifty years later John Wanamaker was to say that this store "has never been surpassed in arrangements, facilities, convenience, light, ventilation, and general service for store-keeping." "The Greatest Store in the World" attracted people from all over the world, and "I got it at Stewart's" became a phrase denoting value and satisfaction. Until his death, Stewart took a close personal interest in his greatest creation. One series of prints of the time shows him in the store instructing his employees how to wait on customers and even how to tie a package to save string.

Stewart's name became a magic one in retailing. Marshall Field, who had assiduously studied his methods, was called "the A. T. Stewart of the West." Macy's owed many a debt to the pioneering merchant, and John Wanamaker, whom many considered the greatest merchant of his time, readily admitted that he had expanded on Stewart's methods. Wanamaker did question the wisdom of Stewart attending to the smallest details but he marveled at the older merchant's dedication to the minutiae of his business. "He would go with me over his store and show me his merchandise," the Philadelphia merchant wrote. "One of my strongest memories is going around with him among the stocks. I would hear that he was in the dress goods department . . . and he was saying something like this to the buyers of dress goods: 'I saw these all here yesterday. You have just as many pieces. You haven't sold any of it. I don't want to see it here tomorrow morning.' He talked with a feminine voice—'You haven't sold these goods. I told you to sell them. They have got to be sold. Cut the price in half.' So closely as this Stewart followed the details of his merchandise."

Just before his death in 1876, A. T. Stewart had decided to expand his operation to Chicago, but some adroit maneuvering by Marshall Field ruined his plans for what would have been his first branch store. The merchant prince left an estate of over $50 million, one of the largest fortunes of the day. Opinions vary as to his character. Said to be a mean, miserly man with few real friends, he paid low wages and contributed little to the city where he had made his fortune. "A. T. Stewart was one of the meanest men who ever lived," wrote a contemporary shortly after his death. "He squelched hundreds of smaller dealers without compunction and ground his employees into the very dust of humiliation and impecuniosity." On the other hand, Stewart claimed, "My business has been a matter of principle from the start; that is all there is about it." He did build a nonprofit hotel for working women in New York, in 1869 built the planned community of Garden City, Long Island, as a model city for working people, and gave generously to sufferers in the Civil War, the Franco-Prussian War, and the famine in Ireland. So influential was he in national politics that President Grant appointed him secretary of the treasury in 1869. He was prevented by public opinion from taking office because of his business connections, even though he vowed, "I will sell out my whole store, or give it away if necessary, that I might serve my country."

Stewart remained as colorful after death as he had been in life. In one of the most bizarre crimes of the century his body was stolen from its grave in New York City. Like Charlie Chaplin's body almost a century later, it was eventually recovered, Stewart reburied in the Cathedral of the Incarnation, one of America's most beautiful reproductions of Gothic Architecture, which his wife Cornelia had dedicated to his memory in Garden City. But the A. T. Stewart Company foundered without the merchandising genius at the helm. After a twenty-year decline, during which time it was once known as Dennings, a leading store of the period, it passed into the hands of John Wanamaker, who considered the old name so valuable that he revived it and hung signs on the store reading "Formerly A. T. Stewart & Company." Wanamaker built a new sixteen-story department store alongside the Cast Iron Palace in 1907, connecting the two by subterranean passages and a double-decked "Bridge of Progress." He operated it, until his death in 1922, as part of one of the two largest department stores in the world (the other being Wanamaker's Philadelphia store). When Wanamaker's moved from New York thirty years later, a victim of the northward trend of retailing in the city, the Cast Iron Palace was leased for a while to the federal government as an office building. In 1956 it was already marked for demolition when a raging fire gutted it, the Stewart building going out in a blaze of glory, although the larger iron extension added by Wanamaker still stands today.

Stewart's great success inspired merchants to follow his footsteps in New York and throughout the country. His Cast Iron Palace became the first store on the stretch of lower Broadway between Eighth and Twenty-third streets, bound by Sixth Avenue on the west, that was known as the Ladies Mile in the gentler language of the day. Many early department stores soon lined this elegant cobblestoned stretch, which played host daily to exquisitely clad ladies in flowing gowns and feathered bonnets who alighted from their horse-drawn carriages and floated toward the grand emporiums to buy the latest in furbelows, millinery, shirtwaists, and veils. The merchants who copied Stewart copied him well, and most of the new stores were built in the same cast-iron style as his Palace. On a sunny day the ornately sculptured, shimmering white façades and striped awnings shading the display windows offered one of the most spectacular sights in New York. Ladies promenaded in their best here up until the end of the century, when the shopping district began to move farther uptown. Some of these department stores were among the most beautiful buildings of the period, Lewis Mumford observing that "if the vitality of an institution may be gauged by its architecture the department store was one of the most vital institutions of the era 1880–1914."

Many early stores on the Ladies Mile still remain standing, though all of the merchants who built them have long since gone out of business or have moved on to new locations. The posh Beaux Arts Adams, which didn't bother with price tags, Siegel-Cooper, James McCreery and Company, Ehrich Brothers, Hugh O'Neil, Simpson Crawford, and LeBoutellier Brothers are names forgotten today, but they were once as well known as Gimbels, Saks, or Korvettes. B. Altman's, Stern Brothers, Hearn's, Macy's, Best, Lord & Taylor, Bergdorf Goodman, and Arnold Constable all had stores on the Ladies Mile.

Fortunately, enough of the old cast-iron buildings have escaped catastrophe or the wrecker's ball to permit a "shopping tour" of these phantom emporiums along the Ladies Mile, which should really be declared a federal landmark, so important is it in the history of retailing. Directly opposite Altman's on Sixth Avenue, for instance, was the ornate brick and terra-cotta store of Siegel-Cooper & Company. Henry Siegel, a former peddler, started late, building here in 1896, but his Barnumesque tactics quicky made him one of the leading merchants of this time. The interior of his store was as lavish as the architects could make it. Just past the columned entrance stood a huge fountain, in the center of which was a reproduction of Daniel Chester French's sculpture *Republic*, which had been displayed at the Chicago World Trade Fair of 1893; over 150,000 attended Siegel-Cooper's opening to see it. Siegel's went out of business in 1913, a bad year for department stores, a year in which the Simpson Crawford Company's store also failed.

Stern Brothers Department Store, on Twenty-third Street and Sixth Avenue, was another elegant store, doormen in top hats presiding over the entrance. Since the New York Mercantile Company is now housed in this building, it is one of the best-preserved old department stores in America, its striking white façade and its freestanding colonnettes decorated with leaves, berries, vines, and rosettes kept scrubbed and gleaming.

A few blocks over on Broadway and Twentieth Street is the old Lord & Taylor building erected in 1869, not long after Stewart's Cast Iron Palace. Lord & Taylor's steam elevator proved so popular, customers riding it up and down for fun, that the store added a divan to it along with a plush carpet and gas chandeliers. Now an apartment house, this cast-iron building's mansard roof topped with intricate metalwork and decorated with balustrades is still intact, as is the pyramidal tower over what was once the arched entrance to the store. At Broadway and Nineteenth Street, the architecture of Arnold Constable's old store, built in 1868, is not as frivolous, but the building's white marble façade recalls the store's prosperity.

Of these old New York stores, Macy's, B. Altman's, Lord & Taylor, and Arnold Constable all began to departmentalize not long after Stewart in the late 1860s or early 1870s. Macy's during this period enlarged and varied its merchandise to include men's wear, household goods, ready-to-wear, and many other items in addition to ladies' wear, and was doing a million-dollar business by 1870. The same could be said of other stores around the country, including Wanamaker's, Strawbridge & Clothier, and Marshall Field, which is why there are so many claimants for the title of America's first department store. Aside from Stewart's, Zions in Salt Lake City, Utah, is probably the most deserving of the honor. Zions Co-operative Mercantile Institution, which was founded by Mormon leader Brigham Young in 1868, carries the slogan "America's First Department Store" on all its advertising and in a letter to the author claims that though its right to this title was "thoroughly challenged for quite some time by several Eastern department stores . . . finally one-by-one each of those stores backed down, leaving us with the official title." Joseph Nathan Kane's book *Famous First Facts* does indeed support Zions' contention, citing the store as America's first department store, but the evidence seems to indicate that at least Stewart's earned the title before Zions. The Utah store is, however, America's first *incorporated* department store, having been formed into a corporation in 1870, some years before any other American store.

III

Minding the Store: Early Operations, from Floorwalkers, Drummers, and Cash Children to Pneumatic Tubes

The department stores of late nineteenth-century America were fledgling ones, but already all the important characteristics of today's grand emporiums were evident. The stores were centrally located, strictly departmentalized, appealed to the masses, offered many services, and were big advertisers. They carried a wide variety of merchandise, including even ready-made clothing for men, which seems to have been first manufactured to supply the needs of sailors in New Bedford, Massachusetts, in about 1830 but didn't become popular until the clothing industry mass-produced uniforms for Union soldiers during the Civil War. As for defects, the stores had high operating expenses and low personnel efficiency compared to small shops where the owners worked for themselves or could keep a tighter rein on employees.

In his novel *Au Bonheur des Dames* about an early Parisian department store, Emile Zola noted that the strength of the stores "is increased tenfold by the accumulation of merchandise of different sorts, which all support each other and push each other forward." American merchants found this to be true; sales bred sales, and even the most dissimilar objects placed side by side lent each other mutual support. As someone else observed, department stores both diversified the temptation to buy and at the same time concentrated the opportunity. This was a major reason for the enormous success of the stores in so short a time—a new multi-million-dollar industry created in less than twenty-five years! By the end of the nineteenth century there were nearly one thousand American department stores, the annual business of several ranging from $7 million to $15 million, stores that were visited by up to a hundred thousand shoppers a day.

But no single factor is wholly responsible for the department store's rise. Besides the economic factors previously cited, there was the coming of the electrical age in the 1870s. John Wanamaker, for one, quickly took advantage of Edison's invention of the electric light bulb; he contacted the inventor shortly after its first public demonstration and arranged for his Philadelphia store to be lighted by electricity in 1878. A crowd gathered outside the store waiting for it to explode the first day the lights were turned on, and it was several weeks before many regular customers would venture inside, but Wanamaker's electric lights became commonplace within a year or so.

Electricity permitted the first efficient elevators in department stores—those installed at Wanamaker's and New York's Macy's in the early 1880s—and also made possible highly improved mass-transportation systems—electric trolleys and subways—as well as the fans, air conditioners, and other conveniences that are taken for granted in big stores today. Perhaps most important, electric lighting and elevators gave department-store customers easier access to the upper floors and allowed merchants to fully utilize those areas.

As several early merchants attested, "The profits of the department store are represented by the cash discounts on its bills." That is, the big stores, by virtue of their "no credit" policy and immediate payment by customers, were from the beginning able to pay cash for purchases, instead of buying on "long time," and the 5 percent discount they received from suppliers was their profit. The stores had to turn over their entire stock five or six times a year. Since selling a lot, rather than selling a little at high profits, was their object, they were admirably suited to supply the new democracy. Advertising continually drummed out the theme that so much could be obtained for so little money, as in the ads of North Carolina's Belk Brothers, now a huge chain:

ONE CENT

24 sheets of paper, 2 boxes blacking, cake soap, 25 marbles, 13 pens, 7 pen holders, 25 envelopes, 2 key rings, 12 lead pencils, 2 boxes blueing, 2 fishing lines, 15 fish hooks, paper hooks and eyes, 1 paper, 2 blank books, 4 boxes matches, 2 balls thread, handkerchief, yard ribbon, 200 yards spool cotton, and thousands of other useful articles at same price. *Turn loose the limbs and come in a sweeping gallop to*

BELK BROS.

Cheapest Store on Earth   15 to 21 East Trade St.

Early advertising often consisted of pasting small, narrow posters known as "gutter snipes" on the very high curbstones in the vicinity of a store, or posting pasteboards on the sides of buildings, fences, or mountains, but newspaper ads were always the most important. Ads were crude at first and almost invariably centered on price, whether they were the advertisements of big city stores like Macy's, or rip-roaring ads from the West, such as David May's "PRICES GONE TO——!," or his "OUR PANTS ARE DOWN!" Sophistication would come later, but ads and promotions were essential to department stores from the beginning. "We've got to lure the people inside and keep them here all afternoon," an early department store magnate told his associates. "Spend the day at Field's" the great Chicago store urged early in its career. John Wanamaker made "There's always something doing at Wanamaker's" a familiar slogan in Philadelphia. "A good store is like a big circus," the head of Ohio's F. & R. Lazarus & Company later said. "You can have one ring, or five, or twenty. That is why a department store has it all over others in attracting people to come in and look around."

Some of the pioneer stores even had "pullers-in," persistent young men stationed in the streets who were hired to shout out what goods were being offered for sale and hustle prospective customers inside. Most reputable stores refused to hire these touts, but from the very start the big stores spared no expense to lure customers inside and make them comfortable and happy. None of today's department store attractions is new; in fact, almost all of them—including Santa Clauses, floor shows and free baby sitting services—can be traced, in one form or another, back to the nineteenth century.

Chicago's Chas. A. Stevens Company, which has nineteen stores today, once had a red carpet runner leading to the curb, and when customers alighted from their carriages on snowy days, a liveried doorman welcomed them, whiskbroom in hand to brush the snow-flakes from their cloaks or capes. The young stores boasted many amenities that unfortunately no longer exist today, such as reading and sitting rooms, stools for customers, wheelchairs for old or infirm customers, "dark rooms" lit so women could examine gowns to see exactly how they'd look under dim ballroom gaslight, tables where customers could sit and sample foods, and even "silence rooms" for the "nerve-frazzled shoppers." Several stores displayed no clothing, salesmen instead taking customers to fitting rooms and bringing in merchandise to show them. Back in its early years Belk's Department Store induced customers to come inside in the summertime by keeping a huge barrel of ice water in the foyer with a large sign proclaiming "FREE ICE WATER" on it and five tin cups tied to it by long strings. Another store offered its customers free showers, and Wanamaker's went Belk's several better by becoming the first store in the country to use a ventilation fan system in 1882, which was the ultimate in cooling customers until Rich's of Atlanta became the first store to be completely air-conditioned.

Wanamaker's also provided a free "sick room" for shoppers on the premises, where a doctor was in attendance, and in 1876 became the first department store to provide a restaurant for customers. Their later restaurant, called the Crystal Tea Room and modeled after the house of Robert Morris, the major financier of the Revolution, was equipped with a kitchen designed to serve ten thousand persons at once. Expense was of no concern to John Wanamaker when it came to his restaurants or any of the other services he supplied his customers, for he knew the goodwill he engendered was far more important than any profit he made in this area. "Have only the best mince pies that money will buy," he once told his restaurant manager. "Even if you have to sell at a loss. I can afford to sink $10,000 a year in mince pies rather than have people say I do not give them good pies. The people of Philadelphia can't be fooled on mince pies."

The early stores promised their customers free deliveries by horse, ox, wheelbarrow, or shanks' mare. In 1845, just before the Mexican War, the D. H. Holmes Company of New Orleans, later to become a great department store, agreed to send packages by wagon to the wives of American army officers stationed at a camp outside the city. This new service marked the beginning of free store deliveries, a service long a staple of the grand emporiums. For the remainder of the century most deliveries were made by horse and wagon, although light packages were often carried to the homes of customers nearby in the arms of employees on their way home from work. Marshall Field used delivery boys until 1873; these youngsters were paid two dollars a week to tote package-filled khaki bags to customers within a few miles of the store.

Wheelbarrows, too, were usually confined to nearby city deliveries. John Wanamaker himself once delivered an order by wheelbarrow when wagons weren't available, he and two assistants taking turns trundling the barrow through the streets of Philadelphia. Early retailers relied on the horse and wagon almost exclusively, however, and the animals were often treated inhumanely. "Sales were very poor today; you had better not give the horses any oats tonight," one store superintendent advised his drivers. Horses were often whipped and were flogged to death in at least a few cases until stores like Marshall Field, Wanamaker's, and Strawbridge & Clothier made any act of cruelty to a horse grounds for dismissal. At the latter store horses were rested on the hottest days of summer, when boys carried packages strapped to their backs instead. Marshall Field horses worked only half a day, drivers instructed to leave a horse at a neighborhood stable if it had finished its workday and come back to the store for another horse and wagon to complete the deliveries. Signs in the Field barn constantly reminded drivers "DON'T WHIP THE HORSES!" and over a stable one sign, entitled "The Horses Appeal to his Master," implored as follows:

> Of water stint me not,
> Oh, whip, lash me not.
> And don't forget to blanket me.

Macy's, Field's, Wanamaker's, Strawbridge & Clothier, and

many of the pioneer stores had great fleets of horses and carriages, serving customers at distances up to 500 miles. B. Altman's, prided itself on 500 horses that were hitched in matching pairs to shining delivery carts. Strawbridge & Clothier, whose Isaac H. Clothier, Jr., son of one of the founders, became an internationally known equestrian, had a Race Street stable of 75 wagons and 150 horses, which was supplemented by a like number of horses and wagons in other parts of the city to pick up parcels from substations for suburban deliveries. Three trips a day were made by horses, in single-, double- and three-abreast harness, over an 80-mile radius.

How important horses were to department stores, to all America, for that matter, is emphasized by the great epizootics of the nineteenth century. The animal counterparts of epidemics that afflict people, epizootic diseases include rabies and hoof-and-mouth disease. The great epizootic of 1872, though it is little known, claimed almost a quarter of the nation's horses (some 4 million) and left America without the power it needed to function for three months—most power at the time being, quite literally, horsepower. Scientists never isolated the virus that caused the epizootic, and it only ended its ravages when cold weather killed the mosquitoes that transmitted the deadly virus. By that time the financial losses suffered had helped bring on the Panic of 1873. To a nation wholly dependent on horsepower, the epizootic was indeed nothing short of a tragedy. In cities across the country, homes went without heat, fires blazed unfought, garbage wasn't collected and diseases spread, public transportation ceased, stores closed, unemployment soared. In many cities unemployed men were seen harnessed to carts and even trolleys, pulling them down the street in place of horses. An old Macy's employee once recalled how he had pulled a store delivery cart in place of a horse. In Chicago, where the disease had decimated the city's horses, Field & Leiter solved the problem another way. "We can assure our friends," they advertised, "that there will be no delay in shipping Goods on account of Horse Distemper, as we have secured a large number of Oxen. All Orders will be filled promptly and shipped the same day as received."

Horses were at first favored over motorcars for deliveries because they did better on muddy roads and navigated snowdrifts and other obstacles that would stall a car. They were also thought to make better time along short routes. "When the lines are dropped on the horse's back as he approaches a house, he slows down," a delivery-man explained, "but before he comes to a halt the driver is on the doorstop with the package. The horse recognizes the driver's returning footsteps or the sound of jingling keys or change in his pocket and at once starts off. The driver steps into the wagon while it's in motion, and the run for the next stop is made with hardly any delay."

The stores would deliver anything by horse and wagon. There are even stories of a single spool of thread being delivered—and returned because the customer had called another store that had delivered it faster. But America wasn't yet a decade into the twentieth century when the efficiency experts with their stop-watches and charts found that motorcars could carry as many packages a day as a team, and far more cheaply in an age when gas was only fifteen cents a gallon. Trucks, both gas and electric driven, soon came into their own as delivery vehicles, and it was only a matter of time before the faithful horse disappeared entirely from the scene. The excitement of the automobile was discovered, and store delivery wagons helped to foster it with promotions like the Mercedes horseless carriages that Macy's imported from France and entered in the *Chicago Times Herald* race of 1895, one of them finishing third in the competition.

The next important development in department store deliveries—parcel post service—also came in the first years of the twentieth century. This was largely due to the efforts of John Wanamaker, who served as postmaster general in Benjamin Harrison's administration. Wanamaker, who had first proposed rural free delivery (R.F.D.), among other innovations, during his incumbency, fought hard for a parcel post system after leaving office and deserves much credit for the growth of the mail order business in America.

The parcel post system was used extensively by the early stores, along with their own delivery services, but the more efficient United Parcel Service (UPS), a private concern, began to supplement it right from the start. UPS was founded in 1907 in Seattle by James E. Casey and several associates as the American Messenger Company. By 1929 it had changed its name and spread across the country, its familiar brown vans making deliveries for practically all the big stores in the East except Macy's, which didn't avail itself of the service until 1946. UPS delivers over a billion packages a year today—more than the U.S. Postal Service if special categories like third-class mail are excluded—consistently makes deliveries faster than the U.S. Postal Service, is not much more expensive on the average, and offers free insurance up to $100. "We don't use the post office at all if we can use UPS," says one dispatching manager of a New York department store. UPS is now the largest private package delivery service in the world—and a profitable one, with earnings of $23 million on revenues of $1.7 billion last year, despite a three-month strike on the East Coast. The company is completely owned by seven thousand supervisors and senior staff members, including its founder, the publicity-shy Mr. Casey, who is well into his nineties and still serves UPS as its honorary chairman. It is meant to remain in employee hands, too, for retired staff members must sell their stock back to the company, as must the estates of deceased members.

From the start deliveries were but one of the many facets of department store operations. The department store was always a composition of diverse stores, these "stores" or departments of various importance in relation to the whole. (John Wanamaker's Philadelphia store, for example, consisted of 76 departments by the late 1890s.) At the head of each department was a buyer who was practically autonomous if successful, who ran his bailiwick as if it were his own single store, buying his goods anywhere he wanted, paying whatever he wished, fixing the selling price of goods, and telling the advertising department exactly what he wanted advertised. Usually, he traveled to Europe three or four times a year to study the market and buy accordingly. If sales were high in his department, the rewards were great—a department store buyer commonly made $5,000 to $10,000 a year and was often given a percentage on the yearly sales of his department. In some cases he received as much as $30,000 a year, a tremendous sum in those days, but not much when one considers that big departments frequently sold over a million dollars worth of goods a year. On the other hand, some buyers made only $25 a week with no percentage. It all depended on sales. If profits sank too low, a department might be moved to less-prized space in the store and, finally, the buyer would be fired. But if profits rose year after year, a buyer could

The Kinley Department Store in Upper Sandusky, Ohio, a typical small-town department store in the early 19th century.

The Lamson cash basket system can be seen on overhanging wires in the Levy's Red Star Store, Douglas, Arizona, in about 1908.

Wires running along the top of this J. C. Penney store in about 1915 were part of the Lamson cash basket system, which conveyed all cash taken by sales people to the manager's perch, where change was made.

Above: The pneumatic
tube system at
Strawbridge & Clothier's
in Philadelphia.

Strawbridge & Clothier.
Infants Wear Shop.

Left: Department stores
often advertised their
retail and wholesale
operations on postcards
such as this one in the
early days.

Below: Ladies at the
Strawbridge & Clothier
fountain in the Gay
Nineties.

Above: Like many early stores, G. Fox of Hartford, Connecticut, used to be in the fur and clothing business in addition to retailing.

Right: Hudson's first Detroit delivery wagon.

Below: A heavy-duty Strawbridge & Clothier delivery van from the early 1900s. This one averaged 15 miles per hour on a run from Philadelphia to Atlantic City and back in 1910.

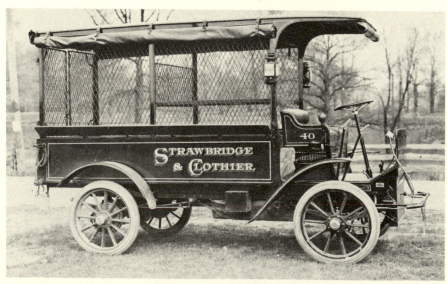

Wanamaker's delivery service in 1913 consisted of Ford trucks, since the Merchant Prince had been an early supporter of Henry Ford—Ford's savior, in fact.

An early Ward truck filled with outgoing mail orders.

The North American.

WEDNESDAY, MAY 2.

THE CASH BOYS.

Those of Strawbridge & Clothier, and the Good Time They Had.

Those wonderfully alert little chaps, the cash boys, that are here, there and everywhere, in the dry goods house of Strawbridge & Clothier, were treated to an entertainment, gotten up expressly for their benefit by their employers, last night, at Wesley Hall, 1018 Arch street. Previous to the entertainment, Mr. Clarkson Clothier addressed the boys. He told them not to think that the house of Strawbridge & Clothier was so great that the individual cash boy was lost in it; that his work was not noticed, or not appreciated. He strongly urged each boy to fit himself for promotion by doing his duty in the place he now was. All the higher positions in the house were filled from the lower grades, and those who did the best work were the ones chosen. He pointed to several of the leading men in the house who had been faithful cash boys in their time. From the ranks of the boys of to-day will come the future successful men. The boy who wishes to succeed must do his best in all cases. He praised the boys for promptness, politeness and attention to business, and encouraged them to lay in the present a good foundation for the future. Several pleasing recitations were given by W. S. Sloan. Professor T. W. Yost mystified them much with strange feats of magic; and then Mr. C. W. Brewster delighted them by his powers of ventriloquism, in which his comical talking figures are introduced.

Left: Strawbridge & Clothier feted its cash boys in Philadelphia in 1882.

Below: Strawbridge & Clothier's newspaper ads in 1890 in the *Philadelphia Record.*

write his own ticket or accept a better offer from another store, for higher-level department store personnel were almost always pirated from rival concerns in those days, employee training programs being a thing of the future. There were fringe benefits, too, including the company of brash, wisecracking "drummers" who always had a risqué story or a new joke to tell when selling their goods, even if most of them were culled from joke books like the popular *Chicago Jokes and Anecdotes for Railroad Travelers and Fun Lovers,* the *Joe Miller's Jest Book* of its day.

A poem by Charles Francis Adams, grandson of John Quincy Adams, summed up many feelings merchants had about the drummer:

Who stops at der best hotel,
Und takes his Oysters in der shell,
Und mit der ladies cuts a swell?
Der Drummer

Who vas it comes into my store,
Throws down his pundles by de floor,
Und never stops to shut de door.
Der Drummer.

Who dakes me by der hand, und say:
"Hans Phiffer, how you vas today."
Und goes for Bisness rite away?
Der Drummer.

Who spreads his goods out in a trice,
Und says: "Just look vonce; see now nice;
You bet, I've got the bottom price?"
Der Drummer.

Who punch my ribs, call me a sport,
My oldest daughter dries to court;
Sells goods cheap, because he's short?
Der Drummer.

Who varrants all de Goods to soot
De customers upon his route,
Und ven dey comes dey ish no goot?
                              Der Drummer.

Who calls by my house ven I'se been oud,
Und drinks my beer, und eads my krout,
Und kisses Kaderiena in der Moud?
                              Der Drummer.

Who ven he comes agin dis vay,
Vill hear vot Phiffer has to say,
And mid a black eye go away.
                              Der Drummer.

Early floorwalkers never enjoyed the popularity of drummers. "Dandified ushers," floorwalkers have been called, and in the 1890s that was exactly what they were. Dressed in either a black frock or a cutaway coat, with gray-striped trousers, a very high collar, and a rose in the buttonhole, the floorwalker was usually a spiffy, smarmy, exceedingly polite living directory who pompously patrolled the aisles and could direct customers to every department in the store. Charlie Chaplin knew the type well and portrayed one in his film *The Floorwalker.* This "floor general" might even wear a button reading, say, "Lazarus—Floorwalker." For his $15 to $40 a week he kept his salespeople "up to the standard of dress, deportment and activity," and acted as a buffer between salespeople and irate customers. One department store manual listed 113 duties of the floorwalker. The *arbiter elegantiarum* of conduct and store etiquette, his word was law on the floor. If, for example, a salesgirl had a friend punch the time clock for her and the floorwalker had her marked "absent" in the timebook he kept to provide a doublecheck on clerks, the salesgirl couldn't collect her pay for the day. If he told a girl to stop chewing gum, she desisted—or was fined or fired.

Floorwalkers never liked their title, which was used as early as the 1870s, preferring "aisle manager" and, later, "floor manager" or "section manager." One of their number, disturbed by the popular misconceptions of his role, published an account of a typical work day in the life of a floorwalker at the turn of the century. "I stand against a booth in the center aisle a few minutes," he wrote, "and answer questions fired at me by the crowd as fast as I can talk. 'Sixth floor for toys, madam, take that elevator!' 'Yes, sir, you'll find shirts in Aisle 2, straight ahead!' 'The rest room is third floor, madam, that elevator!' " He goes on to relate stories about some of the odd customers he came in contact with:

> One woman stopped me in the aisle and held out a parcel.
>
> "Say, mister, I want to exchange this nightgown—it don't fit me right!" she said.
>
> "I'm sorry, madam, but we can't exchange that class of goods," I replied.
>
> "I don't see why not," she answered. "I only slept in it one night, and it ain't hardly messed up at all!"
>
> After some further argument, I finally managed to convince her that there was "nothing doing" on the exchange and she left vowing that she would "never spend another cent in this store as long as I live."

Comparison shoppers were another department store invention. Early price wars saw the birth of the department store comparison shopper, who was at first simply a clerk whom a buyer would send across the street to get an idea of his competitor's prices. Then comparison departments were formed, the average New York department store, for example, employing four or five professional shoppers, "the eyes and ears of the store," to act as "merchandise scouts"—to study the stock, prices, and customers of rival stores and report back to their employers. This was essential to stores like Macy's, with its long-standing policy of selling all merchandise at 6 percent below the prices of other stores in the city. Macy's comparison shoppers sometimes wore disguises and were so persistent, in fact, that Gimbel's once took out an ad apologizing to its customers for the inconveniences caused them by shoppers from the larger store.

The story of department store salesgirls, the beloved shopgirls of O. Henry, who were sometimes forced to sell *themselves* to customers to make a living, is told in another chapter along with that of unions, as is the history of store detectives and the myriad shoplifters, con artists, terrorists, and exhibitionists who still keep them busy. But fixtures of the big stores found only in the early years were the cash children they employed. Though cash registers could be seen in a few stores by the 1880s (National Cash Register sold one model for about $150 at the time), along with other technical innovations like the telephone, which Boston's Jordan Marsh used first in 1876, the department stores generally employed cash children as messengers to run cash that a customer paid for goods to the cashier's office. There the sale was noted and change was made to be returned to the customer. Boys were usually chosen for these positions because it was feared that all the running around, often to deserted areas of a store, might prove dangerous for a young girl. However, when manpower was short during the Civil War, cash girls were hired. In fact, the thrifty founder of Macy's reduced the wages of his cash girls from two dollars a week to one dollar and a half in 1866, telling them that the war was over and that he could no longer afford "high war wages."

Sometimes called "cash" for short, cash children were so named from the way salesmen rapped hard on the counter and yelled "Cash! Come cash!" when they wanted a courier. Almost always children from very poor homes, and ranging in age from ten to sixteen, they were the lowest-paid of department store employees, sometimes making only fifteen cents a day. In a large store, the cash boys might sit on benches at various stations, a monitor in charge of each bench, a boy wearing a round badge if he worked on the first floor and a square one if he worked on the second floor. If a salesman needed a boy, he'd either yell, "Cash!", or reach under the counter and push a button that rang a bell at a connected station, where the bench monitor dispatched a boy to the department. Saleschecks often came in three parts—a stub that remained in the sales book, a voucher, and an itemization of the sale. Taking the check, the money, and the goods, the cash boy rushed them to a wrapping desk, where the cashier tore off the voucher and marked it paid, the cash boy bringing the wrapped goods, receipt, and change back to the department.

Cash children would also be called on to do odd jobs like turning down the awnings or delivering packages on the way home from work—at no extra pay. Often they were laid off as soon as a busy season passed, with no thought given to their welfare. "I always pitied the cash children," Annie Marion MacLean wrote in an exposé of department store labor practices. "Many of them were too young to be working, but the sin was at their parents' door. They placed on file the required affidavits, and the employer asked no questions. One little girl confessed to me that she was *not quite twelve years old,* but she told me not to tell anyone, because her mother told her to say she was fourteen. . . . The little girls frequently responded to the cry of 'Cash! Here cash!' with tears streaming down their faces. They got tired, of course. They were only children, and their instinct for play was strong. *They would kiss the dolls and trundle the carts they were taking to the wrapping room . . .*"

Many stores appeared to have no compassion for the cash children. "When you have commenced work, it means that you have stopped play," the rules manual of one store sternly instructed. "Don't laugh, play, fool or be indolent. . . . If you do not attend to your work, you will regret it in after years. You are to do all work delegated to you, and to obey all commands of your superior."

But other employers took a benevolent or paternalistic attitude toward the cash children and set up programs for their education even before state laws made continuance education mandatory for working children. John Wanamaker's enlisted cash boys and other young workers into a paramiliary Cadet Corps that supervised their education at a store school on the premises and helped train them in merchandising as well. The usual line of advancement in a department store was from cash boy to wrapper to salesman to assistant buyer to buyer—and a number of cash boys traveled even farther along the road to become high-level management. One cash boy who didn't advance farther in department stores was William Claude Dunkenfield. Employed by Strawbridge & Clothier, he quit his job after three months, just before pneumatic tubes took over the cash boy's function. Young Bill, forced to take the job by his grandmother, always considered it a low point in his career: "I had trouble passing the exits with the change box. Sometimes without thinking I'd go out one door and come back in another. It was a difficult time for a self-respecting thief." More appropriately, perhaps, he found work racking balls in a pool parlor. He eventually became better known as W. C. Fields.

Several sources claim that the pneumatic tube systems responsible for the demise of the system of cash children originated at the old R. H. White Store in Boston, but they were probably first used in a department store, or in any commercial establishment for that matter, in 1880 by John Wanamaker, who also introduced them to the U.S. Post Office while postmaster general. Before pneumatic tubes became common many stores used the much simpler Lamson basket cash system. But the tubes were more efficient. They extended from the sales department to the cashier's department in the basement. Called lines and usually 2½ inches in diameter, the tubes transmitted money and papers to the cashier over a distance seldom more than 600 feet. A clerk would take money for a purchase from a customer and put it in a small brass cylinder that could easily be unscrewed at the end. To start the system it was necessary only to insert the cylinder in the receiving end of the tube. Air forced the cylinder through the line to the cashier's office, or main station, the cylinder traveling at a rate varying from 1,000 to 2,500 feet per minute, according to the air current. The current in turn, was produced by a blower system, which was usually operated by an electric engine. To maintain the air current in the tube system the various lines were connected to a main conduit, which led to the engine room and the blowers. These blowers drew the air from the various sending terminals of the lines, expelling it through a conduit, which opened in the engine room or was connected with the street.

The principle involved here was simply the exhaustion of air in the tubes to produce a partial vacuum and the effect was so powerful that, although the carriers and their contents weighed half a pound, they were easily transported. As they sped down the tubes, they were borne by air, with little or no friction against the sides, and reached the cashier's desk unscratched, pressing against the valves at the end of the tubes and dropping onto a receiving table. In a cash transaction the cashier, or "changemaker," glanced over the figures on the sales slip and verified the total. If an error had been made, the slip and money were sent back to the department they came from, and if the slip was correct, it was returned with the change due the customer. In the case of sales that were charged, the slip contained the name of the customer as well as a description of the item and its price. As soon as it was examined, the cashier placed it back in the carrier and inserted it in another tube connected with the bookkeeper's department, where the slip was entered on the books and a duplicate slip was returned to the salesman upstairs.

The pneumatic tube system saved a lot of labor, a transaction usually taking less time than it takes to describe one. In a primitive way the system was the forerunner of many automated and computerized operations in department stores today. Often pneumatic tube systems were huge: Wanamaker's unit had over 250 stations connected by 20 miles of tubes, and Macy's had nearly 24 miles of tubing, the brass cylinders inserted in it traveling a total of over 12,000 miles, or half way around the world, on a busy day. One observer called these tube rooms the pulse of the department stores. The systems were considered engineering marvels of the age, so much glamour attached to them that working in the hot, noisy basement cashier's office was considered a prestigious position, even though it paid no better than most department store jobs.

In the early years, the department stores, with their free services and competitive prices, for the most part managed to disassociate themselves from the small merchants most people disdained, a disdain Napoleon echoed when he contemptuously called the English "a nation of shopkeepers." Actually, Napoleon lifted the term from Adam Smith's *Wealth of Nations* (1776) and his attitude toward merchants can be traced back to Plato, who, though he recognized the importance of trade to public life in the *Republic,* suggested that the "race of shopkeepers" be those "weakest in body and . . . unfit for any other work." Long after Plato, the Roman orator Cicero wrote: "All retail dealing may be described as dishonest and base, for the dealer will gain nothing except by profuse lying and nothing is more disgraceful than untruthful huckstering." It may be significant that Mercury, the Roman God of thieves, was also the god of tradesmen! In any event, this attitude toward small merchants has persisted in America up until recent times, perhaps the most notable example in American literature being Faulkner's Snopses. An eighteenth century writer observed that he didn't trust a single merchant in Connecticut—"damned, ungrateful, cheating, short-weighting fellows," he called them—and another described Boston's merchants as a "pack of deceitful, canting Presbyterian deacons."

As the Mauve Decade ended and the new century neared, department stores had already survived the depressions of 1857,

1873, and 1896; Americans had accepted them with few reserva-
tions. For not only did the big stores offer a wider variety of goods,
and the convenience of being able to buy everything under one
roof, but selling in volume almost invariably meant lower prices.
"Twenty-five years ago," a well-informed shopper wrote in 1892, "a
pair of kid gloves and almost all department store specialties cost
more than they do today. On the contrary, goods which have not
come within the range of the department stores have not changed
in price. Are not the prices of meat, bread, wine and oil, as high or
higher than twenty-five years ago? The principal cause of the stores'
success is the fact that their founders have understood the necessity
of offering to a new democracy, whose needs and habits were being
modified, the means of satisfying in the cheapest possible way a
taste for elegance and comfort unknown to previous generations."

All of the advantages and disadvantages of department stores
could clearly be seen by 1900. In the next fifty years or so their
number would increase to over four thousand, the majority of these
new stores founded in the golden years lasting from 1905 and 1930,
but there would be no radical changes in their composition. Mail-
order stores, chain stores, ownership groups, discounters, and shopping centers were yet to come into their own, and the grand
emporiums would undergo many refinements, but the big department store with its central location, great variety of goods, lower
prices, and free services such as deliveries, liberal credit arrangement, merchandise return privileges, and customer accomodations
remains basically unchanged. Indeed, by World War I the department store had become such a thoroughly American institution that
it began appearing frequently in poems, plays, and novels, was part
of our national literature, including a poem in which the dead of
World War I were lined up in the aisles of the department stores
they had shopped so that their bodies could be "sold again."
Another similar, long forgotten poem, "In a Department Store" by
Charles Hanson Towne, was written about "a great store in New
York turned into a hospital for wounded soldiers":

> Women used to stroll through these aisles,
>   Idly looking at laces,
> Studying the new styles,
>   And the new graces . . .

Now, if they walked these dim defiles
   They would see only faces . . .

These lads have come back—
   Oh, the long aching aisles of them!
They are laid on pain's rack—
   I think there are miles of them . . .

Here are rest and quiet
   Where they never had been;
No "bargain day" riot,
   No bustle and din.
This stuff—you can't buy it!—
   God laid the stock in.

∽ **IV** ∽

The Big Stores: Stories of Famous Full-Line Department Stores and How They Grew

Which was the first American department store? Which is the biggest, the tallest, the most beautiful, the funkiest, the most outré, the most "in," the most profitable, the wealthiest? The following store biographies give some answers to these questions and provide a privileged look into the intricate operations of some of America's best-known stores. The pioneer stores included are far from being the only grand emporiums in America (others are mentioned later), but they do show how the department store developed in different regions of the country and the many diverse ways in which it grew. The store biographies are necessarily brief, and the founding dates note the years when the stores opened (even if in another area), *not* the dates—often much later in time—when they became true full-line department stores. Following chapters will tell the stories of the fabulous specialty department stores, discounters, mail-order houses, the giant chains that dominate the department store industry today, and the ubiquitous shopping center that arose in the years after World War II.

1842

"The World's Largest Store"

R. H. MACY & CO., INC.—*New York, New York*

Whether Macy's was America's first true department store is an academic question that may never be answered satisfactorily—John Wanamaker thought that it was, while other authorities have voted for A. T. Stewart's, Zions, and even Wanamaker's. But there is little doubt that Macy's flagship store in New York City, covering a square city block and containing 2,200,000 square feet of floor space, is the largest in the world under one roof, if not "the world's largest store" as it claims. How large is "largest"? A good-sized house has 2,000 square feet of living space, so you could put 10,100 houses in Macy's, which has as much selling area as many large *shopping centers*. The Herald Square anchor store, with its 168 selling departments and over 11,000 employees handling 45 million yearly transactions and serving three hundred thousand customers a day during the holiday season, is also at this writing the nation's biggest volume department store, its over $200 million in sales edging out Detroit's J. L. Hudson, which held the title itself several years ago.

Macy's is probably the name most American's would give in answer to *department store* on a word association test. Its very bigness, its 120-year history as America's most successful middle-of-the-road store (an image it is aggressively changing today), its 76 branches across the country, and its shrewd promotion over the years have given the store the national prominence it enjoys. Expressions that we owe to Macy's and that are now part of the language include "like a Macy's basement," for any mob scene; "Macy's window," for the ultimate in public exposure; and "Does Macy's tell Gimbels?" Tens of million of American watch the Macy's Thanksgiving Day Parade every year, and even more view television reruns of the film *Miracle on 34th Street* that it inspired, which has become traditional Yuletide television fare. The store's image has also profited by its nationally known executives, who have included notables as varied as former board chairman Beardsley Ruml, who invented the pay-as-you go national income tax, James Mitchell, a Macy's personnel director who became secretary of labor in the Eisenhower administration, and actor Robert Montgomery, a former member of the board of directors.

Part of American folklore by now is the touching story of Macy partner Isidor Straus, the only department store owner to be elected to Congress, and his "darling Mama" Ida, "as good a wife as ever a man was blessed with," in his own words. When in 1912 the White Star liner *Titanic* struck an iceberg and started to sink, another passenger, Hugh Woolner, urged the Strauses to get into a lifeboat. Isidor Straus refused to go before the other men and when Ida was told to get into the boat with the women and children, she too declined, despite her husband's pleas. "We have been together so long," she said, clasping his hand, "please let me stay now." The last time Woolner, a survivor, saw the old couple, they were standing at the rail holding each other close. A bronze plaque at one of the store entrances honors their memory.

No wagering gentleman would have bet on Macy's rise to fame when Rowland Hussey Macy founded his store. This Nantucket Quaker with a bit of P. T. Barnum in him had lived two-thirds of his life when he came to New York in 1858, aged thirty-six, and had failed in no less than six previous retailing efforts. Macy had left home when a boy of fifteen to follow the seafaring tradition of his family, shipping out aboard the famous whaler *Emily Morgan* and spending four years at sea at about the same time Herman Melville was working as a hand aboard the *Acushnet* and gaining experience for his *Moby Dick*. Macy returned with his $500 share in the catch and the red star tattooed on his hand that was to become the symbol of Macy's in the future—though a more romantic account claims that the store's trademark, which Macy's once refused to abandon in the face of cold war criticism that it was a "Communist symbol," represents a guiding star, "a brilliant star of hope" that helped him reach port when he was at the wheel of the ship and trying to make his way through a thick fog. In any case, the money enabled him to start a little Boston thread-and-needle shop, which probably opened in about 1842 and failed within a year or so. Next came a dry goods shop, which did so poorly that he had to abandon it in 1845, writing on the last page of his account book:

> *I have worked Two Years for Nothing.*
> *Damn.*
> *Damn*
> *damn*
> *damn.*

A store that Macy opened the following year also failed miserably, and after working for his brother-in-law a few years in his lace-and-embroidery shop, he decided that the Gold Rush of 1849 would solve all his problems. Leaving his wife and child behind, Macy and his brother Charles sailed to California, where they opened a provisions store for miners at Marysville under the name of Macy & Co. This venture lasted only two months, failing when miners in the town worked out its gold and moved on to another site. Macy was soon back home in Massachusetts, operating a dry goods store in the little town of Haverhill, where he sold for cash only and his trademark was a rooster bearing the motto on his beak, "While I live, I'll crow." Again all of his optimisim did him no good, for the Haverhill store folded within a year. A store he soon started nearby called the New Granite Store did better, lasting three years until it also closed its doors in 1855.

Failures as a stockbroker and real-estate speculator followed before Macy opened his "fancy dry goods" store on Sixth Avenue near Fourteenth Street in New York, but while R.H. could be discouraged enough to curse, he was never discouraged enough to quit. Either exceedingly courageous or supremely stubborn, the bewhiskered, pink-cheeked, cigar-smoking Macy plunged in over his head again. The small store, 60 feet deep with a 20-foot front, was apparently financed by long-term credit for $20,000 from jobbers and wholesalers, a tribute to Macy's nerve, considering his past record. Although he had no cash, Macy brought to the business basic policies he had formulated through all his failures: (1) selling at fixed, marked prices; (2) selling for less than other stores; (3) buying and selling for cash; and (4) advertising vigorously. These policies, not new, but radical enough at the time, would be responsible for Macy's great success in the future. All of them, in fact, still remain in effect, except the Quaker-influenced "cash only" principle, which Macy's abandoned in 1939 when the public trend toward installment buying forced the store to initiate the cash-time accounts that led to Macy's charge cards of today.

On R. H. Macy's first day of business in New York he sold only $11.06 worth of items like ribbons, laces, embroideries, artificial flowers, feathers, handkerchiefs, hosiery, and gloves. But at the end of the first thirteen months of business it was clear that another failure wasn't likely—the store, employing fifteen people, had spent $2,800 for advertising and showed total sales of $90,000. Good times continued and by 1866 Macy's physical expansion began when the founder added to his establishment a store that adjoined the rear of the original premises. More adjoining stores were acquired, and within six years Macy's comprised four stores on Sixth Avenue, two facing Fourteenth Street and one opening on Thirteenth Street. This piecemeal addition continued until Macy's business occupied the ground level of eleven stores. By then the fancy dry goods store with a red star as its emblem had already become a department store, carrying completely stocked departments of clothing for the entire family, drugs, toilet goods, china and glassware, silver, house furnishings, sporting goods, luggage, toys, musical instruments, and books. There was even a soda fountain and a department selling velocipedes, early bicycles.

While Rowland Macy wasn't discouraged by his past failures, they did leave their marks on his personality. His temper was often uncontrollable (at least until he was cured of his rages years later at a Moody and Sankey revival meeting), and he remained a stingy man all his life. Probably the ulcer he developed came from his constant rebuffs as well (ulcers weren't unknown even then to store owners, Justin Strawbridge and Frank Woolworth among others suffering from them). But, despite his scars and eccentricities, Macy never became a cold, withdrawn person. "The old man," as his employees called him, always had an eye for the ladies, whom he flirted with in the store and on buying trips, and he was considered an affable person by his friends and many of his workers. On the other hand, he was extremely disappointed in his son, Rowland, Jr., a "ne'er-do-well" who couldn't be trusted with the business. The older Macy's health began to fail him completely in later years. Up to his death, though, he remained a high-powered merchant, constantly searching for new items to sell and new ideas with which to promote them. Macy always wrote his own advertisements, spending an unheard of 3 percent of sales on advertising, three times more than any of his competitors, and originating several advertising stratagems, including the use of plain white space to attract attention to ads that were traditionally crowded with print. His red delivery wagons, embellished with the same red star they wear today, were a familiar sight to New Yorkers, leading one fire chief to complain, "Them wagons is too damn fast and too damn red—people think it's a hook and ladder roaring up the street!" R. H. also lured people to his store with displays like the singing mechanical bird he had imported from Europe, an attraction that won the envy of his friend P. T. Barnum.

Macy can be counted as the first great store owner to employ a woman in a position of high authority. Margaret Getschell, one of the earliest women executives in merchandising, was a distant relative of Macy's who had taught school in Nantucket until she lost an eye in an accident and could no longer do the close work demanded of a schoolteacher. Beginning as a cashier at Macy's, she was in 1866 promoted to store superintendent, with full responsibility for nearly two hundred employees. Her formula for running a store was, "Be Everywhere, Do Everything, and Never Forget to Astonish the Customer." Macy appreciated her flair for display and publicity—once she spent a week training two cats dressed in doll's clothing to repose peacefully in twin cribs in the toy department as an enticement to customers—and for her Yankee mechanical ability to fix anything with a hairpin. After Margaret Getschell married Abiel La Forge—who had been taken in as a junior partner by the founder along with his nephew Robert Macy Valentine—she moved into an apartment above the store so that she could mind her family as well as Macy's.

The year before Rowland Macy died while hunting for new lines in Paris in 1877, his store had sales of $1,612,788. His partners quickly bought out his heirs, but within three years Abiel La Forge, Margaret Getschell La Forge, and Robert Valentine had all died in rapid succession, leaving the company in the hands of Charles Webster, a handsome former floorwalker Valentine had taken as a partner after the deaths of Macy and La Forge. After a stormy partnership with Jerome Wheeler, who had married Valentine's widow, Webster looked to Isidor and Nathan Straus, who were then running the china department on lease from Macy's, to relieve him of some of the responsibilities of management, and in 1887 he took them in as partners. Eleven years later Webster finally sold his entire interest in the store to the brothers for $1.2 million.

With the ascendancy of the Strauses a new era began at Macy's. They were the sons of Lazarus Straus, a former grain trader who emigrated from Bavaria in 1852, made a fortune as a peddler in the South, and settled in New York after the Civil War. As honest as he was capable—he had astounded his southern creditors by paying back $25,000 in debts they had written off as a total loss because of the war—Lazarus opened a wholesale glassware and china shop on Chambers Street with his sons Isidor and Nathan. In 1874 his sons got the idea of opening a glassware and china department in Macy's basement on a leased basis, and the concession quickly became the most profitable department in the store. Since the elder Straus and his sons joined Macy's 104 years ago, five generations of the family have been associated with the store. Although Macy's offered stock to the public in 1922, three years after its incorporation, and family control is now only partial, two Strauses, Jack I. Straus, who retired as chairman in 1968, and his son Kenneth, remain on the store's board of directors.

Under the Strauses, Macy's moved uptown from Fourteenth Street to its present Herald Square location and began building "the largest store in the world." In 1902, a year that saw Macy's with sales of nearly $11 million, the firm opened its new store on a site that once held, among other enterprises, a few fine brothels, and Koster & Bial's Music Hall, where (a plaque still outside a Macy's entrance informs) "Thomas A. Edison with the 'Vitascope' first projected a motion picture." The new nine-story store contained 33 elevators and four escalators ("moving stairs") capable of accommodating forty thousand customers an hour, and a vast pneumatic tube system used to shoot cash and sales checks from one part of the store to the other. Through a series of building additions in the twenties and early thirties, Macy's grew to encompass the entire block from Broadway to Seventh Avenue and from Thirty-fourth Street to Thirty-fifth Street, with the exception of two small corner plots, one of which the shrewd merchant Henry Siegel

Cooper bought with the intention of selling to Macy's at an exorbitant price and which the Strauses simply built around. The first of the three twenty-story Macy's buildings comprising what is now "The Biggest Store in the World" was completed in 1924.

Macy's became so big under the Strauses and has so long dominated its field that justice can't be done to the store in so brief an account, but several policies were largely responsible for the success of this grand emporium. It's famous "6% less for cash policy" was among the most important of these. Macy's practically guaranteed to sell goods at 6 percent less than they were sold in stores where purchases could be made on credit, and encouraged customers to deposit money in its interest-bearing Depositor's Account System to spare them the inconvenience of carrying cash. Only with the rise of installment selling of big ticket items like washing machines and refrigerators in the late 1930s did the store finally give in and permit credit buying under its Cash-Time plan, which included a 6 percent service charge. Macy's now has a charge card like most stores, but will honor no bank credit cards. Although there were exceptions to the "6% less for cash" policy, as critics often pointed out, the store honestly tried to adhere to it, and its comparison shopping department spent as much as $250,000 a year in competing stores to enable Macy's to cut prices on identical items that it carried, such price reductions having occurred as often as a thousand times a week. The store's often solitary fight against price fixing by manufacturers met with failures, too, but it has been identified as the leader in the battle since the early years of this century, even devoting part of its advertising budget to mobilize consumers against the practice.

Macy's advertising and promotions, treated elsewhere in these pages, have been famous since Rowland Macy's early days in New York. The store's staff has in many ways been just as spectacular. No other store outside Hollywood has served its customers with so many salespeople who went on to become national celebrities. Former New York Mayor Jimmy Walker worked in the Herald Square store, and among movie stars alone, Burgess Meredith, Tom Ewell, Carol Channing, Butterfly McQueen, and Garson Kanin clerked in Macy's at one time or another. Other celebrities-to-be didn't last very long. Author Shirley Jackson once wrote a piece called "My Life with R. H. Macy." It opens on Miss Jackson's first day of work: "I found out my locker number, which was 1773, and my time-clock number, which was 712, and my cash-box number, which was 1336, and my cash register number, which was 253, and my cash-register-drawer number, which was K, and my cash-register-drawer key number, which was 872, and my department number, which was 13." Bemused and bewildered, Miss Jackson couldn't cope with the bigness of the store and finally walked out: "I wrote them a long letter, and I signed it with all my numbers added together and divided by 11,700, which is the number of employees in Macy's. I wonder if they miss me."

Early buyers on Macy's staff earned the reputation of being rough on suppliers, as is witnessed by the old gag about the circus strongman who squeezed a coconut dry and was challenged by a spectator, who squeezed a few more drops of milk from it. "Who are you?" the strongman demanded. "I," the buyer replied, "am a Macy's buyer." One retired domestics buyer used to keep his account books in code lest they fall into the hands of competitors, but few, if any, of the old school remains. Long retired, too, is William Titon, better known as Titon the Taster, who worked nearly sixty years for Macy's and was the store's final authority on all groceries, wines, and liquors. Among other accomplishments, Titon discovered the Idaho potato in 1926 while buying apples for Macy's and promoted it until the spud's name became synonymous with baked potato, for which Idaho's governor wrote a letter of thanks to the store.

Memorable Macy's customers have ranged from Queen Salote of Tonga to the several women who have given birth in the store, one of whom named her child Ann Macy Hettrich. Not all are so satisfied with their deliveries as Mrs. Hettrich, but Macy's has supplied silk to deck the satisfied voluptuaries of a Saudi Arabian harem, a cowboy outfit for the show business chimp Kokomo, who seemed very, very happy about it all, and perfect plumbing for the presidential palace in Liberia.

Statistics and stories abound about Macy's bigness. Consider that even with aid of an excellent protection squad and trained Doberman pinschers that guard the store at night, the flagship store alone loses some $10 million yearly to shoplifters and thieves, about 2 percent of its $480 million in sales. Or that Macy's handles nearly half a million different items of merchandise, uses almost 6,000 miles of twine and ribbon to wrap packages, not to mention 4,000 miles of various tapes, about 7 million folding boxes, and some 21 million sheets of packing tissue paper. The store has attracted well over 300,000 customers in a single day, more than 250,000 children visit its Santas at Christmas time, its products have been tested on scores of machines in its Bureau of Standards, including a shoe tester nicknamed "The Rocky Road to Dublin" and "Iron Man McGinnity," who rides bicycles. Nine million envelopes used annually . . . 3 million paper clips . . . 2 million rubber bands . . . enough pencils to extend 63½ miles—a complete list would fill pages. . . .

After more than a century, Macy's has become the nation's fifth largest full-line department store chain, with 76 stores across the country and sales of over 1.6 billion in 1977. Besides the New York division with 16 branches, these stores include Lasalle's in Ohio (acquired in 1923 and today totaling 7 branches); Davidson's in Georgia (acquired in 1925, 11 branches today); Bamberger's in New Jersey (acquired in 1929, 17 branches); O'Connor Moffat and Company in California (acquired in 1945 and now Macy's California with 13 branches); and John Taylor Dry Goods in Missouri (acquired in 1947 and now Macy's Missouri-Kansas with 11 branches). The corporation also owns five regional shopping centers and has a 50 percent interest in three others.

Under the leadership of chairman Donald B. Smiley, Macy's has been changing its image over the past six years from that of a stolid, relatively conservative retailer to a store with flair that has traded up a notch or so from the middle-income market and is attracting more affluent shoppers.

Macy's California pioneered in the changeover, but since 1974, when Harvard-educated Edward S. Finkelstein, the upbeat, energetic former head of Macy's California, was brought in to head the New York division, the giant has awakened and is now one of the most exciting things in New York retailing. Macy's Herald Square store has gained considerable additional business from its Sunday operations—in effect since spring 1977—and is under attack by Bloomingdale's and other competitors, who are lobbying in Albany for the reinstitution of Sunday blue laws. But the store's new image is far more responsible for its re-emergence as the nation's single biggest volume store.

"Shopping should be comfortable, convenient, and very exciting visually," Finkelstein believes, and the new Macy's certainly is now, having been transformed floor by floor at a cost of $10 million from what was once described as a "grim warehouse" into "New York's ultimate loft." The center aisle on the main floor has been opened up, allowing a greater flow of traffic; the vast book department, triple the size of its predecessor, has replicas of the New York Public Library stone lions at its entrance; and in the children's department on the fifth floor there are seven-foot-high fun house mirrors and riddles with the question on the outside wall and the answer on the inside. Use is being made of the tremendous space in the store, merchandising is being blended with show business. Macy's seems to be introducing new features every week or so in its battle not to win Bloomingdale's customers—many of whom do come down from the East Side now—but to attract shoppers from the suburbs, New York's Upper West Side, and the fashionable new loft areas below Thirty-fourth Street.

Once a Circus Maximus of bargain hunters, Macy's still offers values, but now it projects a fashion image, too. Macy's Cellar, fondly called "our underground street," is the foremost example of the new look at the store. At one time the phrase "I'd rather work in Macy's basement!" meant "I'd rather die!" Today the cavernous dreary bargain basement is gone, replaced by a brick walkway, off which are charming storelike entrances into various subdepartments of a floor devoted mainly to houseware, kitchenware, and gourmet goods. Often the modern "going narrow and deep" technique is used to display products here, one carefully selected product stacked from the floor so that its packaging catches the eye.

At one end of the travertine-floored promenade of the Cellar is a replica of P. J. Clarke's, the fashionable Third Avenue saloon-style eatery where so many celebrities gather, and at another is The Apothecary, a replica of a nineteenth-century pharmacy that carries the famous Caswell-Massey Collection from the oldest drugstore in America, established in 1780. Other attractions include the truly unique Greengrass Gallery, featuring one-of-a-kind "media art" originally commissioned for magazines, record covers, book jackets, posters, and ads, and The Potter's Wheel with a full-time potter for the best of the potter's art. The gourmet food department, headed by buyer Steve Fass, hired away from Bloomingdale's by Macy's, is bested by no department store. It carries everything from hundreds of caviars, cheeses, meats, breads from every country, and epicurean canned goods to out-of-season fresh fruits and vegetables such as raspberries in February at six dollars a half-pint.

The Cellar shopping bags with the big *C* on them are seen increasingly all around Manhattan these days, a sure sign that Macy's is succeeding in its efforts to attract a new breed of affluent and upwardly mobile customers to the Herald Square store. Sales were up 12 percent in 1977—far better than any other New York store. The new Macy's has been called a "people classification store, one that is easy to shop in, that entertains and amuses," and that represents one of the brightest hopes for the big urban department store, which has had so much trouble in recent years. R. H. Macy intends to add 15–20 new stores over the next three or four years at a cost of about $90 million, Sunday openings will continue where permitted. Clearly, Macy's has no intention of becoming like that little store out West which reportedly has a sign in its window advising: "We sell nothing on Sunday and damn little through the week!"

1842

"The Store That Tells The World"

GIMBEL BROTHERS, INC.—*New York, New York*

Gimbels is often regarded as an upstart, Macy's rival in the perennial department store war and a relative newcomer to the retailing field. Actually, Gimbels was founded about the same time that R. H. Macy opened his first little shop and has a history every bit as rich as Macy's.

Bavarian immigrant Adam Gimbel, who began his career here as a pack peddler, founded the original Gimbels as a trading post in what is now Vincennes, Indiana, on the Wabash River. Adam Gimbel's honesty and pioneering fixed-price policy have already been noted—"Fairness and Equality of All Patrons, whether they be Residents of the City, Plainsmen, Traders, or Indians" was another of his early advertisements—and they were major factors in his great success in Vincennes, a location that eventually grew too small even with the three-story Palace of Trade he opened there in the 1870s. Gimbels soon expanded across the country. Its first modern store opened in Milwaukee in 1887, and the first section of the present Philadelphia store was completed seven years later. This last became one of the largest department stores in the country and today is part of a unique urban mall called The Gallery (see Chapter 12).

Gimbels invaded New York in 1910, building its present downtown store a block from Macy's on Herald Square, and the traditional Macy's-Gimbels feud soon began in earnest. Although Macy's first greeted the new store with an ad of welcome, Gimbels started raiding the bigger store's talented staff for executives, and relations have never been the same since. Yet, for all its publicity, the feud has been mainly a good-natured one, with little of the bitterness of Macy's-Hearn's feuds of earlier days, and both stores have profited by it in the way of increased sales over the years. Its history and the stories of slogans like "Does Macy's Tell Gimbels?" "The Store that Tells the World," and "Nobody But Nobody Undersells Gimbels!" are related in Chapter 11.

In the past Macy's large comparison-shopping department made it possible for Gimbels to employ just enough comparison shoppers to check Macy's prices—and at least once in its history the head of Gimbels comparison shopping department was trained in the art at Macy's. But one time Gimbels really got bitter about Macy's comparison shoppers and ran the following ad in the evening papers:

AN APOLOGY BY GIMBELS

We regret that customers in our house furnishing and drug departments have been inconvenienced lately due to aggressive tactics on the part of young women apparently engaged in checking GIMBELS low prices for others. We are confident that the futility of trying to undersell GIMBELS will bring these inconveniences to an end.

Gimbels, with branches on Lexington Avenue and Eighty-sixth Street, is the only New York department store with two major stores. Though its downtown store is only half as large as Macy's, it always featured a bargain basement, unlike its competitor, high-lighting its prices—"Gimbels Basement" was long a synonym for bargain basements in the New York area. Macy's, though richer, is not that much more affluent than its competitor. Gimbels has been a public corporation since 1922, though members of the family were until recently prominent in the organization. This store had 68 units across the country at the end of 1977, including the Saks Fifth Avenue stores acquired in 1923, compared to Macy's 76 units, and annual sales of about $900 million compared to Macy's $1.6 billion—which makes it one of the top 25 department stores in America. Gimbels is now a subsidiary of the Brown & Williamson Tobacco conglomerate, which is in turn owned by the British-American Tobacco Company.

Gimbels was the first American department store to hold a public art auction (New York, 1941) and the first to sell furnished coopera-tive apartments displayed at the store (Philadelphia, 1953). Bad times have befallen Gimbels New York since 1970, with profits falling below their customary levels, but changes made in recent months seem to be turning around the faltering group. Some unproductive departments such as furs and liquor have been elimi-nated, stores have been modernized, and Gimbels now has the first executive development program in its history—in the past the store had done little more than hire people off the street and give them a do-it-yourself training book.

1851

Great Showman and Thinker

F. & R. LAZARUS & COMPANY—*Columbus, Ohio*

America celebrates Thanksgiving on the fourth Thursday in November every year because Fred Lazarus, Jr., former head of the F. & R. Lazarus department store dynasty, thought it would be good for business. Thanksgiving Day had formerly been celebrated on the last Thursday in November and traditionally opened the Christmas shopping season, but in the depression year 1939 the last Thursday in November would have fallen on the very last day of the month, lessening the number of shopping days until Christmas.

Obviously this didn't augur well for department store sales, and Fred Lazarus contacted store owners across the country urging them to lobby for a "fourth Thursday in November Thanksgiving" every year—so that Thanksgiving could fall as early as November 22 and no later than November 28. President Roosevelt responded to their pleas, proclaiming the fourth Thursday as Thanksgiving that year, and Congress enacted the arrangement into law in 1941.

F. & R. Lazarus & Company has pioneered in developing new retailing ideas ever since the store was founded in Columbus, Ohio, by Prussian immigrant Simon Lazarus, who also served as the first rabbi of Temple Israel, the oldest Jewish congregation in the city. Simon's 20 foot × 50 foot shop, started with capital of $3,000, expanded with the help of his wife and his sons Ralph and Fred. The store was the first in Ohio to make deliveries by wagon in 1870, but the founder quickly reverted to hand delivery when his only horse collided with a street car. Wagons weren't tried again until after his death seven years later.

By the 1870s the Lazarus store—which the sons had renamed F. & R. Lazarus—occupied half of Southgate Street in Columbus and was a local landmark known for its clock tower, which was illuminated at night by eight hundred electric light bulbs. Premiums like tickets for free shoe shines with each pair of shoes purchased were offered, and merchandise grew more varied than the men's clothing that had originally been traded.

"Uncle Ralph" Lazarus, as the youngest son was called, handled most of the store's early advertising, penciling ads on brown wrapping paper that proclaimed Lazarus's policies of "It Fits or You Don't Pay," "Strictly One-Price Store," "One Lowest Price," and "Every Article Marked in Plain Figures." Ralph, a confirmed misogynist who never married and even got upset at the thought of a woman secretary or female clerks in the store, left no heirs, but Fred's sons Simon, Fred, Jr., Robert, and Jeffrey came into the business. The store moved to its present location at Town Street in 1909, and its expansion over the years has made it the largest store in central Ohio, about 32 acres of floor space that attract up to a hundred thousand shoppers a day. Oddly, its "basement" is two floors up from some entrances because of the thirty-foot drop in the grade of the store's site, and pedestrians often save themselves a tiring walk up the hill by taking the Lazarus escalators to the High

Street exit. For many years the store had a "weather whistle" that signaled daily forecasts—one toot indicated "fair weather," two "rain," and three "uncertain."

Fred Lazarus, Jr., made his name in retailing with a number of innovative ideas besides "the new Thanksgiving." A trip to the Printemps store in Paris persuaded him to display clothing by size rather than price, and he converted store buyers into department managers with the responsibility of all operating costs of their departments instead of just the buying and selling of merchandising. "Horizontal warehousing," the storing of goods near the department where they are sold, is also his idea. A great showman, he always believed that a store should be like a "big circus" to attract people, and used such gimmicks as a live alligator on exhibit at the store, a blimp to announce a change in store hours, an annual Santa Claus parade, yearly parties for customers over eighty, free trees to school children on Arbor Day, even fashion shows at stockholders meetings. "Everything comes to Lazarus," read a store ad soon after a car crashed through a huge display window.

F. & R. Lazarus purchased Shillito's, Cincinnati's largest store, in 1928 for $2.5 million. The following year it became part of Federated Department Stores, Inc., along with the Brooklyn-based Abraham & Straus and Boston's Filene's, all these firms having been associated since 1916 in the Retail Research Association and the Associated Merchandising Corporation. Federated has since grown into the sixth largest department store group in the country, with sales of over $4.9 billion in 1977 and 135 stores at last report— including such golden names of retailing as Bloomingdale's, I. Magnin, Bullock's, Boston Store, Burdine's and Foley's. Ralph Lazarus, son of Fred, Jr., is currently Federated's chairman of the board.

1861

"The Greatest Merchant in the World"

JOHN WANAMAKER—*Philadelphia, Pennsylvania*

Many years ago someone without the aid of a computer figured that John Wanamaker worked a total of 13,140,000 minutes building what was then the greatest department store in America. This is an odd statistic that might have pleased the Merchant Prince—he certainly believed in filling every moment with work—or might possibly have perplexed him—why would someone waste good time making such calculations when there were so few hours in a day and "so much to do"?

Even John Wanamaker's handshake was hurried; it was as if he had a clock in his head telling him every second counted. Wanamaker was in fact a "workaholic" whose health failed several times in his early years due to overwork. But his will extended his limits, and much like a champion distance runner, he finished the long course at the head of the pack. When he died at eighty-four, still working hard at the end, he was far and away the greatest merchant of his day. Wanamaker could be narrowly righteous, but if this deeply religious man was called "pious John" or "Holy John," it was mainly by jealous rivals, or perhaps because he was so busy that few people got the chance to really know him.

John Wanamaker opened his first store in 1861 after early careers as an errand boy in a publishing house, a store clerk, a helper in his father's brickyards, a paid secretary of the YMCA, and one of the founders of the forerunner of the Red Cross, the Christian Commission, which was established to give aid to the sick and wounded of both sides during the Civil War. With the backing of his wife's brother, Nathan Brown, he operated a boys' clothing store called the Oak Hall Clothing Bazaar on the southeast corner of Philadelphia's Market and Sixth streets, an historic site where George Washington's house once stood. By the time Brown died in 1868, the little 30 foot × 80 foot shop had become the largest retail men's store in the country. The competition dubbed his merchandise "cheap John goods," but such amazing growth in less than a decade must be attributed to Wanamaker's merchandising genius, his tireless work, and his optimistic belief in Emerson's maxim that "America is only another name for opportunity." Buying directly from manufacturers instead of from wholesaler middlemen, advertising widely in ads that he wrote himself, selling goods at fixed, clearly marked prices, and giving his customers "a money-back guarantee" on all goods accounted for his enormous success. Although John Wanamaker did not originate these mercantile virtues, he consistently practiced them, at a time when they were honored more in the breech than the observance. Wanamaker even advertised his store's liberal policies, this 1865 newspaper ad for his famous money-back guarantee a notable example:

> Any article that does not fit well, is not the proper color or quality, does not please the folks at home, or for any reason is not perfectly satisfactory, should be brought back at once, and if it is returned as purchased within ten days, we will refund the money. It is our intention always to give value for value in every sale we make, and those who are not pleased with what they buy do us a positive favor to return the goods and get the money back.

Like all store policies he instituted, the exchange privilege wasn't just a gimmick to Wanamaker. He sincerely believed in it, remembering how as a boy he bought a piece of jewelry for his mother in a local store and the proprietor wouldn't let him exchange it just a few moments later for a broach he liked better. "When I have a store of my own people shall have what they want," he is supposed to have vowed at the time. He would later add to this—"and what they *ought* to have." At any rate, goods could always be exchanged in his store if the customer changed his mind or they didn't "please the folks at home."

Wanamaker's early store was the scene of promotional stunts that won the Merchant Prince the additional title, "The Father of Modern Advertising." Posters 100 feet long were used to stir up business; balloons were sent up from the store and the public was advised that anyone who caught one and returned it could have a free suit of clothes. Once a big gong was set up inside the front door to welcome each customer and make him feel important. This plan backfired, for at the sound of the gong some people were scared out of their wits, while others were embarrassed or annoyed.

Clever promotions and honest storekeeping paid off, and by the mid-1870s Oak Hall, despite several enlargements, was too small for comfort on a busy day. Wanamaker bought the vacant Pennsylvania Railroad Freight Depot on the edge of the city as the site for a new store. Oddly enough, he didn't consider himself a department store operator at the time; in fact, he planned to open a shopping center similar to London's Royal Exchange or the old Halles Central in Paris, where cooperating merchants would operate various shops under one roof. Only when local merchants refused to join him, did he decide to build his historic Grand Depot on the land, and although this was from the beginning among the first of the great department stores, he refused to label it such for many years, calling it simply "The New Kind of Store."

On opening day in 1876 over seventy thousand people entered the handsomely ornamented Grand Depot, which was at three acres "the largest space in the world devoted to retail selling on a single floor," containing 129 counters some two-thirds of a mile in length and 1,400 stools in front of them for the convenience of shoppers, and was lighted by day by stained-glass skylights and by night by great gas chandeliers. The "store of a thousand surprises," as it was called, had an unusual interior design; old prints show the floor plans to represent a series of broken circles extending out from the center. One of the most popular departments was the gaslit "tent" where ladies examined evening gown silks under ballroom conditions, in an elegantly carpeted dark room at the heart of the Grand Depot inside a circular counter 90 feet around. Some of the exhibits shown in the store achieved worldwide newspaper coverage. In 1896, for example, an almost life-size replica of the Rue de la Paix was built by Wanamaker as "a consolation for Americans who couldn't go to Paris."

"All but one solitary man thought I was going to fail," Wanamaker recalled long after opening the Grand Depot, "that one being myself." Friends thought the great merchant had overextended himself; others pointed out that he had started building at 1313 Chestnut Street, an "unlucky" location. Philadelphia's small merchants universally condemned "the new kind of store," which they felt would drive them out of business with its wide variety of merchandise for men, women, and children. Rivals tried to ruin Wanamaker's credit by boycotting his suppliers, he was villified in person and in print, and threats were made on his life. One editorial writer claimed Wanamaker was walking "on the thin crust of a volcano which threatens to blow him and his wigwam sky-high, scattering hats and haberdashery, shoes and chemisettes, collars and cuffs, trunks and teapots, lawns and linens, boots and broadcloth, furs and flannels to the four winds." But the public didn't agree. From the first day on it was apparent that the "new kind of store" was here to stay.

The Merchant Prince enlarged his store over the years and constantly introduced improvements in retailing methods and equipment. Soon the store was being called Wanamaker's by Philadelphians and the designation Grand Depot passed out of use. In 1896 Wanamaker bought the famous A. T. Stewart Cast Iron Palace in New York, later connecting it by a notable double-deck "Bridge of Progress" with an elegant sixteen-story store that he built alongside it. But the high watermark in his career was the 1911 opening of his new store building on the site of the Grand Depot. This twelve-story granite structure, dedicated by William Howard Taft and the only American department store ever to be dedicated by a president, features a Grand Court that soars one hundred and fifty feet high without a break and highlights an interior that is as grandiose as that of any great department store. The immense eagle in the Grand Court is a relic of the 1903 St. Louis World's Fair and has become the rendezvous for tens of thousands of Philadelphians over the years ("Meet me under the eagle at Wanamaker's"). The Grand Court itself is still transformed into the "Christmas Cathedral Square" every year, with displays depicting the life of Christ, fabulous dancing fountains, and a five-story-high cathedral façade.

The great organ in a gallery over Wanamaker's Grand Court is not just the largest organ in any department store, but the second largest organ in the world (only the Auditorium organ in Atlantic City, New Jersey, is bigger). One of the finest organs ever constructed, it was built for the Louisiana Purchase Exposition and purchased by Wanamaker's in 1911. Since then it has been added to, and it now weighs 2½ tons, with 451 stops, 30,067 pipes, 964 controls, and the potential power of 25 brass bands. Great artists from all over the world have come to Wanamaker's to play the immense organ, and it has undoubtedly been heard by more people than any other organ in existence. It has become a store tradition to have daily organ concerts presented by the John Wanamaker organist at 10 A.M., noon, and 5:30 P.M., with occasional guest artists invited to perform.

These pages abound with examples of Wanamaker firsts in the grand Philadelphia emporium, everything from the first "white sale" (adapted from France) held by an American department store to the first restaurant on the premises of a department store.

Wanamaker's was the first, or among the first, to use a pneumatic tube system, the telephone, a ventilation fan system, and U.S. parcel post delivery. In employee relations the Merchant Prince far surpassed his contemporaries. Wanamaker genuinely cared about his workers and went so far as to establish a school in his store where they could complete their grade-school education. From the moment he started at Oak Hall he had made cash payments to employees on completion of their work, a rarity at the time, and in his second year of business he shortened the workday for all employees. Saturday half days off, the hiring of women, bonuses, insurance, pensions, and health and recreation facilities for workers were pioneered by Wanamaker's, and the store's wages were always among the best in the industry. Employee relations were so good that during the depression, when Wanamaker's was failing, Local 9 of the AFL Retail Clerk's International several times spent union funds to advertise and help save the store from going under.

At one time or another Wanamaker's has sold about every kind of merchandise conceivable, including automobiles and airplanes. The store was the first in America to sell an airplane, in 1909, and automobile historians often neglect to mention that Wanamaker's endorsement and advertising of Henry Ford's 1903 car was a major factor in the success of the "infernal machines." Without Wanamaker's protection Ford might well have been forced out of the market by the Association of Licensed Automobile Manufacturers, which had sued him for infringement of the Selden patent.

All his life John Wanamaker immersed himself in the affairs of the Presbyterian Church, its Sunday school and foreign mission, the YMCA, and a number of hospitals. In the realm of politics, he served as postmaster general under Benjamin Harrison, introducing rural free delivery and the parcel post system, not to mention many reforms. He was suggested several times for the vice-presidency, but minding the store took up too much of his time to permit an active candidacy. Though the Merchant Prince turned over many of his responsibilities to his son Rodman in later years, he was deeply involved in store decisions until the end. Ever the autocrat—the chairman of the board who had to be the board—the reins were always in his hands. Two years before his death, for example, he reacted to a post-war-sales slump by slashing all Wanamaker prices by 30 percent, an action that resulted in the first million dollar sales day in department store history on the Saturday after his announcement.

A. T. Stewart had predicted that John Wanamaker would become "the greatest merchant in the world," and before the Merchant Prince died in 1924, his mentor's word had come true. Wanamaker's is not the retailing power it once was, though still a formidable giant. Its big New York branch, too far downtown, had to be abandoned in 1954, and the 15 Wanamaker stores remaining in the East, including the magnificent Philadelphia emporium, which boasts a fine historical museum, now do about $300 million in sales annually. Recently, the Rodman Wanamaker Trust, which owns the store, announced that it had reached a tentative accord with Carter Hawley Hale for the chain to buy Wanamaker's for $45 million in cash and Carter Hawley Hale stock, which would make Wanamaker's the largest stockholder in the giant chain. But no matter who owns his store, John Wanamaker's name will endure as one of the two or three greatest pioneers in department store history. Among the first four merchants elected to the Merchandising Hall of Fame in the Chicago Merchandising Mart, he is remembered not as a flamboyant showman like many of the founding fathers, but as a stolid quiet man, a good man, a kind of George Washington of American retailing who contributed more than anyone else to the development of department stores here and whose record of achievement dominates these pages. Among all our merchants—and there were many like him—he best exemplified the old virtues—deep religious faith, faith in the American dream, hard work—and whether one shares his beliefs or not, it must be conceded that he lived and won by his principles. Among his papers was found an old poem that best sums up his philosophy, Horatio Algeran, moralistic, grist for a Freudian's mill, unlikely to be widely appreciated in an age of instant gratification, but John Wanamaker nevertheless:

> The heights by great men reached and kept
> Were not attained by sudden flight
> But they, while their companions slept—
> Were toiling upward in the night.

1865

"Give the Lady What She Wants"

MARSHALL FIELD & COMPANY—*Chicago, Illinois*

Macy's and Hudson's are probably bigger, but aside from Wanamaker's and New York's Woolworth Building, which is, of course, a company headquarters and not a store, no retailing establishment in America can match the eloquence of the great Marshall Field department store. The grandest of the grand emporiums, in the opinion of many, is a Chicago landmark, its two huge clocks outside a rendezvous point for Chicagoans since the turn of the century, and its interior magnificence has probably attracted as many visitors as any other Chicago showplace. Worth the trip to Field's alone is the magnificent Tiffany Dome in the store's south rotunda. Designed and built by Louis Comfort Tiffany, it is one of the finest examples of glass mosaic to be found anywhere. Fifty men worked two years to install this light well, the biggest glass mosaic ever made, with 1.6 million pieces of iridescent Favrile Glass covering over 6,000 square feet.

Marshall Field, among the four or five greatest merchants in American history, didn't begin his career in this opulent palace of trade, which was completed after his death, in 1906. Field, however, is one of the few store founders who didn't start out with a small cramped shop of his own that he built into a giant. Born in 1835 in Pittsfield, Massachusetts, Field left school at sixteen and clerked in a local dry goods store until 1856 before setting out for Chicago and the unlimited opportunities that the Midwest then offered. He landed a job as a traveling salesman with Cooley, Farwell & Company, wholesale dry goods merchants. A frugal, single-minded person who bought only necessities for himself and slept in the store nights to save paying rent, the earnest young man earned a reputation as a hard worker and by 1864 was offered a partnership in the firm for $15,000, which he managed to raise from loans and his savings. Here he might have remained, but the strong minds of John Farwell and his junior partner often clashed, and

Field moved out on his own the following year when a great opportunity presented itself.

The well-known Potter Palmer, a New York Quaker who had made a fortune in Chicago with his innovative merchandising ideas and real-estate investments, had decided to retire from active business and become a silent partner in his own firm. Palmer operated out of a fine marble-fronted building that had been erected on the site of a Lake Success brothel that had burned to the ground. Known as "The A. T. Stewart of the West," he was an early advocate of one-price, price-tagged merchandise, the policy of sending goods on approval to customers in outlying areas, and the money-back guarantee. The refined atmosphere in his store—quality merchandise, handsome, courteous clerks, and no whiskey barrels or spittoons on the premises—was calculated to please the ladies, and attracted nationwide attention. Palmer boasted, in fact, that Rowland Macy got his best ideas from a representative who visited the Chicago Lake Street store before Macy's opened in New York.

When Palmer put his business on the block, Field and Levi Z. Leiter, a junior partner in his old firm, put up $300,000 they had amassed in savings and shrewd wartime investments, and bought into the company. Capitalizing on Palmer's reputation, they formed a new store, advertised it as "Field, Palmer & Leiter, Successors to P. Palmer," and pledged to carry on the policies initiated by the former owner. If anything, Field outdid his predecessor in service. He took back merchandise no questions asked, even if it was obvious that a lady had worn a gown to a ball before returning it. He hired three women clerks to sell lingerie so ladies would be more comfortable in that department. Low prices, quality merchandise, and honest, pleasant service from clerks like young Montgomery Ward, who worked in the store several weeks before founding the great mail-order house bearing his name, did the trick, and business was so good by 1868 that Field and Leiter bought out Palmer's interest and moved to new quarters in a palatial marble store on State Street that Palmer had built in pursuit of his real-estate interests.

Rented for the then amazing sum of $50,000 a year the new Field & Leiter emporium, "a Dazzling Assemblage of Wealth, Beauty and Fashion," as a newspaper described it, was devoted to both the retail and wholesale trade, its magnificent frescoed walls and walnut counters illuminated by gaslight. Early writers wondered how a Presbyterian farmer's son raised in the stern puritanical atmosphere of repression and frugality could build such a lavish opulent store, but then the store was probably a product of Field's dreams—dreams that rebelled against his upbringing. Here Field toured the aisles every morning, as he would do throughout his retailing career, to insure that his store maintained the "tone" that was already winning him fame. One day he encountered a customer arguing with a clerk, who told the boss he was settling a complaint. "No you're not!" Field snapped. "Give the lady what she wants." His famous words became the store's motto, and years later the title of Lloyd Wendt and Herman Kogan's entertaining and scholarly history of Field's, one of the best books written about any department store.

Field placed great stock in a list he wrote called "12 Things To Remember":

1. The Value of Time
2. The Success of Perseverance
3. The Pleasure of Working
4. The Dignity of Simplicity
5. The Worth of Character
6. The Power of Kindness
7. The Influence of Example
8. The Obligation of Duty
9. The Wisdom of Economy
10. The Virtue of Patience
11. The Improvement of Talent
12. The Joy of Originating

He also conceived the following credo to guide all his employees in running the stores:

To do the right thing at the right time, in the right way; to do some things better than they were ever done before; to eliminate errors; to know both sides of the question; to be courteous; to be an example; to love our work; to anticipate requirements; to develop resources; to recognize no impediments; to master circumstances; to act from reason rather than rule; to be satisfied with nothing less than perfection.

Adhering to these principles over the next decade, Field & Leiter weathered one disaster after another and emerged stronger than ever. Though the store burned to ashes in the legendary 1871 fire that destroyed half of Chicago, most of its $2.5 million in merchandise was covered by insurance. Field led employees in holding back the flames by hanging wet blankets over the windows, while Leiter and others fired the steam elevators and moved goods out of the store to safety. Within two weeks the partners had opened a temporary store in the old horse barns of the Chicago City Railway Company, arranging their $200,000 in salvaged goods on counters built in the horse stalls. Many former employees came back to work here, for Field had won their loyalty with a sign he posted in the ruins of the marble store immediately after the fire: "Call Boys and Work Girls will be Paid what is due them Monday 9 A.M. at 60 Calumet Avenue—Field, Leiter & Company."

It wasn't long before Field was back on State Street, though. Potter Palmer had sold much of his property there to obtain funds to build his magnificent Potter Palmer Hotel, and the Singer Sewing Machine Company had erected an Italian-style five-story store with a huge central glass dome on the land. Field and Leiter were in trouble. Sales began to fall at the horse barn site and at a second temporary location they had moved to on Market and Madison. An epizootic hit Chicago's horses in 1872, and oxen had to be used for a time to draw the firm's delivery wagon. Singer was asking the unheard of annual rent of $75,000 for his new building, but Field and Leiter had no choice. They had to leave their out-of-the-way locations and move into the new store, especially on learning that New York's fabulous A. T. Stewart, eager to expand to Chicago, was considering the same site.

Field & Leiter's grand opening on State Street in 1873 was delayed for two weeks because of a fire that broke out on the roof, and only a month after this the collapse of Jay Cook's corrupt financial empire in New York brought on the panic of 1873 that ruined many businesses across the country. The store survived these crises, as well as a price war with the A. T. Stewart Company, which attempted a short-lived wholesale operation in Chicago. Business was good until fire, which destroyed so many of the old stores, again ravaged the Singer Building in 1877, claiming the store and $750,000 worth of insured merchandise. When Singer rebuilt the building, Field & Leiter bought it outright for $700,000, but delayed in doing so and had to pay Carson, Pirie & Company $100,000 to surrender the lease the company had taken with Singer.

Marshall Field and Levi Leiter parted company in 1881 in a dispute over store policy. Leiter wanted to concentrate on the wholesale end of the business, while Field preferred to develop the retail operation. Since Field already had pledges from key executives that they would leave if he left, the irascible Leiter was forced to sell out for $2.5 million, a surprisingly low figure for a business with annual sales of $25 million. Later, Leiter would lose most of his great fortune in covering $20 million in debts that his son incurred in trying to corner the world wheat market in the winter of 1897. Young Joseph Leiter almost succeeded, but foolishly refused to sell wheat to meat-packer king Philip D. Armour, who promptly hired a fleet of icebreaking tugs and brought back enough wheat from Duluth in his grain boats to fill his own needs and flood the market as well. The elder Leiter sold all his property to meet his son's obligations and was forced to go hat in hand to Marshall Field to sell him the building on State and Madison streets that housed the Schlessinger and Mayer store. This was the first of many real-estate purchases that enabled Field to buy up all of the buildings running north along State Street and make the block his own.

One of the executives who supported Marshall Field and remained to play a key role in the new Marshall Field & Company's growth was Harry Gordon Selfridge. Known as Mile-a-Minute Harry for his restless creative mind as much as for the way he dashed about the store, coattails flapping, Selfridge ranks among the most colorful of department store personalities. Starting as a Field & Leiter stockboy he rose to a junior partnership in the firm and left a stronger imprint on it than any other executive. Selfridge instituted the Field's bargain basement, later known as the Budget Floor, which was the first of its kind and became the world's largest single salesroom, extending six hundred feet from the main store to Field's Store for Men across the street. The store's first restaurant was his idea, too, and it was he who lured window display artist Arthur Fraser away from an Iowa store to make Field's once overcrowded show windows the best in the world. Mile-a-Minute Harry persuaded Field to advertise more and feature less expensive merchandise, writing much of the early advertising copy himself. A great showman, whose office was more magnificent than even Field's, he married a society debutante in a ceremony at the Central Music Hall, where a choir of fifty voices sang in the background. During the Chicago World Trade Fair of 1893, Selfridge enticed the Infanta Eulalia of Spain and other prominent international figures to visit the store.

Selfridge left Field's to open his own Chicago store in 1904, three years after Field's was incorporated and he received fewer shares than the other partners. Failing in Chicago, he emigrated to London, where he founded the giant Selfridge's Ltd. in 1909. The merchandising impresario, who made daily inspections of his store wearing top hat and tails, changed the course of conservative British retailing. He created a flower garden for shoppers on the store's roof; provided an ice rink for skaters; set up a seismograph in the store; exhibited Louis Bleriot's small monoplane, the first plane to cross the English Channel; put famous racing cars on display; commissioned a Hollywood director to decorate the store's façade for the coronation of George VI; devised a large glass panel on which visiting celebrities carved their names with a diamond. . . . Selfridge, who became a British subject, made his department store one of the greatest in England, but his romantic escapades in the years after his wife's death led to his ruin. His affair with Jenny Dolly, one of the famous American Dolly sisters, began in 1926 when he was nearly seventy, and lasted eight years. Over that time he spent a fortune of some two million pounds at the gaming tables, and on most every other extravagance known. By 1939 he had lost control of his store and was reduced to a figurehead, a pathetic old man who still made his daily inspections in top hat and tails down aisles over which he had no real authority. When he died in 1947, he left an estate of $6,000.

Marshall Field's last years were much more renumerative but no happier than those of his protégé. His first wife, long a sick woman, had died in 1892, and just when a second marriage twelve years later was bringing a little happiness into the great merchant's lonely life, his son Marshall Field II was found shot under mysterious circumstances, his death officially called accidental by a coroner's jury but widely believed to be a suicide. Field himself died less than a year later. He had contracted pneumonia while playing golf, a game that had become his only pleasure and which he loved so much that his final match was played in the snow, using red balls. Field left an estate of over $120 million, $8 million of this willed to the Chicago Museum of Natural History, formerly the Field Museum, and most of the rest going to his grandson Marshall Field III in 1945. But his life might best be summarized in the words of his loyal salesman, Pierre Funck, who is said to have died of grief over his employer's death. "Marshall," Funck had once told him, "you have no home, no family, no happiness—nothing but money."

John G. Shedd, a former clerk, succeeded Marshall Field as president of the company, and by 1907 the old store was demolished and the great new 12-story building Field had planned stood in its place on State Street. Marshall Field & Company soon took up the entire square block and seven years later built its famous 20-story Store For Men across the street. For a time the "Great American Store" was the largest in the world, with the largest restaurant, the largest shoe, china, toy, and book departments, and more show windows than any other store on earth. Its elevator operators—future movie actress Dorothy Lamour among them—were sent to charm school. Field's boasted "the biggest indoor Christmas tree in the world" and the world's first personal shopping service, which still averages two thousand purchases a day for confined or busy customers. Just a few of its famous customers over the years include Theodore Roosevelt, William Howard Taft, Prince Henry of Prussia, Isadora Duncan, Grover Cleveland, Shirley Temple, Winston Churchill, Eleanor Roosevelt, Prince Philip of England, Gypsy Rose Lee, Richard Nixon, and Al Capone. The store's information desk from the beginning employed experts who spoke several languages to help foreign visitors and became a trusted, local institution, answering questions about the store and Chicago as well. One man is said to have left an alimony check at the desk every week for his former wife to pick up.

In 1930 Field's completed its huge $28 million Merchandise Mart on Wells Street. Then the largest commercial building in the world, it stood 24 stories high and was to house the company's wholesale and manufacturing division, with the remaining space marked for jobbers and manufacturer's agents. But space was hard to rent during the depression years, and the firm's wholesale operation had already begun to slip before the Mart was built. A failure from the start, this white whale on the Chicago River was sold to Joseph P. Kennedy in 1946 for $18 million and now houses the Retailing Hall of Fame. Field's abandoned its wholesale and manufacturing operations entirely in the 1950s, finally realizing as Wanamaker had long before, that these businesses were quite different from retailing.

Field's has always led Chicago's stores in spectacular promotions. One held in the book department featured Judy the Elephant, who autographed copies of a circus book with a rubber stamp she had been trained to hold in her trunk. When Judy took a liking to the store and refused to leave by freight elevator, a special three-story ramp had to be built to get her out of Field's. The store's annual Christmas celebration features not only its traditional 48-foot balsam fir tree decorated with handmade ornaments, but Uncle Mistletoe, a popular sprite modeled after a Pickwickian character in Dickens. Uncle Mistletoe has only been around since 1948, but many children prefer to visit him rather than the store's Santa Claus.

Field's unrivaled customer services were pioneered by founder Marshall Field, whose battle cry was "Nothing is impossible at Field's!" Some 500 employees, many European craftsmen, now work at services ranging from antique restoration and the dry cleaning of heirloom and antique clothing to the on-the-premises repair of almost all big ticket items the store sells. Field's food service people, who prepare all foods sold in the store's restaurants, use over 5,000 recipes, many of them so treasured that they are locked in the corporate safe.

It would take pages just to note all the wonders past and present of Field's. Merchandise ranging from roller skates to airplanes. The store's soigné "28 Shop" for the Cadillac-and-up trade (so named for the 28 dressing rooms it originally had). A great restaurant called the Cloud Room at the Chicago Airport. Until 1959 the store even owned a 192-acre hunter's farm called Fieldale outside Chicago with thousands of clay pigeons for hunters to shoot at and a huge gun shop on the premises. The firm's immense real-estate holdings, which yielded over $40 million income in 1976, were perhaps the greatest single factor in Chicago's development during the first half of this century.

The trade publication *Clothes Magazine* recently ranked Field's, along with Macy's and Hudson's, as one of America's three greatest stores, but called it "the anomaly of retailing" in doing so, noting that it long dominated both the carriage trade and popular price business, yet made errors in merchandising that prevented it from being bigger still. The Field family, which owns the *Chicago Sun-Times*, no longer has a controlling interest in Marshall Field & Company, and no member of the family has headed the store since the founder. Field's today ranks among America's largest 50 chains, with annual sales of about $600 million. It operates 32 stores, including Seattle's Frederick & Nelson, Cleveland's Halles, and Spokane's Crescent Stores, in addition to its 15 stores in the Chicago area. Although the Carter Hawley Hale chain recently made overtures to acquire Marshall Field, its attempt hasn't thus far proved successful. There have also been rumors that Field's will acquire New York's B. Altman's, but Altman's has denied the report.

In keeping with its tradition of elegance and leadership in retailing, Field's has just opened a new store in the atrium shopping mall of Water Tower Place, a unique urban development including stores, restaurants, a Ritz Carlton Hotel, and a tower of condominium residences in which Field's has a 50 percent interest. This futuristic shopping center on seven levels is an urban retailing hope for tomorrow and makes up for a few disappointing ventures Field's has had in the past. Perhaps the new mall will mark the beginning of a new retailing approach at the store, ending once and for all Field's reputation as "the sleeping giant of retailing," a label it despises. "Field's," writes New York *Times* retailing expert Isadore Barmash, "became perhaps the prototypical carriage trade department store, with numerous special services from candymaking to oil painting restoration to Oriental rug reweaving, in addition to its store fashion offerings. But profit fluctuation in recent years showed that the company's approach needed some updating." One step along these lines was a recent $6 million remodeling of the flagship store's main floor, once considered sacred and untouchable. Another was the overhauling of store advertising and credit policies to appeal to a younger clientele. Finally, Field's hired Angelo R. Arena away from his position as chairman of the Neiman-Marcus store division of Carter Hawley Hale Stores, Inc. in 1977. Mr. Arena was to serve as Field's president, but was appointed chief executive officer as well after the untimely death of chairman Joseph A. Burman, who died less than two weeks after his predecessor, Gerald A. Sivage. Arena, at $300,000 a year, is one of the highest paid store executives in retailing.

Marshall Field hopes to profit by the State Street shopping mall now being built, which will run for nine blocks through Chicago's famed Loop area. The city mall is expected to help not only Field's, but Goldblatt's, a department store that specializes in lower-priced merchandise "for the masses, not the classes"; Carson Pirie Scott, with moderately priced goods; and Wieboldt Stores, strong in medium priced brand name merchandising. These four stores on State Street have recently been feeling the bite of Saks, Lord & Taylor, I. Magnin and other emporiums along Michigan Avenue's tonier Magnificent Mile.

1867

"America's First Department Store"

ZIONS COOPERATIVE MERCANTILE INSTITUTION—
Salt Lake City, Utah

Seeking "a gathering place for Israel," the much-persecuted Mormons followed their leader Brigham Young into the unsettled land they called Deseret ("honey bee") in 1847. Young, one of the ablest leaders and administrators in American history, inspired the Latter Day Saints to make the desolate Salt Lake Valley "blossom like the rose" with the seeds, shrubs, trees, and vines they had brought in their wagons. The story of how the earth was made to yield sustenance and how the state of Utah evolved from the efforts of Young and his followers is a familiar one to most Americans, but it isn't generally known that Young and the Mormons also founded what many consider to be America's first department store.

The store was conceived in 1867 because Young and his people felt that the completion of the transcontinental railroad, only a year or so away, posed a threat to their peace and prosperity. The iron road, it was said, would bring unfriendly "Gentile" merchants who would stifle local enterprises and extract exorbitant prices for their wares, just as traders who followed the wagon trains heading to California had done before. With goods scarce because of the slow, hazardous thousand-mile journey from the Missouri River, Mormon settlers had paid as much as $100 for a sack of sugar, $75 for a hundred pounds of flour, and 75¢ a yard for calico cloth that sold in St. Louis for about 20¢ a yard. Brigham Young vowed that this wouldn't happen again and proposed a cooperative, community-owned merchandising establishment dedicated to supporting the products of home industry. "It is our duty," he said, "to bring goods here and sell them as low as they can possibly be sold and let the profits be divided with the people at large." Mormon merchants were encouraged to combine their stocks and form a new community store in which shares would also be sold to the public generally, each person buying whatever shares he could afford to buy or wished to buy. Dividends, to be divided proportionately, would thus benefit the whole community.

The store was christened Zions Cooperative Mercantile Institution and finally opened on March 1, 1869, in the Eagle Emporium, a handsome two-story store building at the corner of First South and Main streets in Salt Lake City, the still-standing building now occupied by Zion's First National Bank. The first customer was President Brigham Young himself, and though he placed a thousand-dollar order, there is no record of whether or not all his 16 wives accompanied him. Many of the other customers were Zions stockholders; hundreds of their ancestors, it should be noted, still stockholders in Zions, and the Mormon Church owning a one-third interest in the store. From the first day on, Zions was a success, and within a few months two smaller annexes were opened in buildings nearby, all of them constituting Zions Cooperative Mercantile Institution (ZCMI).

It is this store that Zions and many authorities—including Joseph Nathan Kane in his *Famous First Facts*—claim is the first department store in America. Although we've seen that other stores have strong claims to that title, one opinion is as good as another in this instance. At any rate, Zions calls itself "America's First Department Store" in its promotional literature and says that all of "the old

Eastern stores" have relinquished the title to them (something no one of those venerable institutions would acknowledge to this writer). Certainly Zions, incorporated in 1870, was the first *incorporated* department store, and there's no doubt that it was a department store at the time. As distinguished from the typical general store then, Zions was organized with separate department managers for the various classes of merchandise, with central control of credit, record keeping, and store maintenance, and supervised by a general manager—all unmistakable marks of a modern department store.

Zions' original store sold a wide variety of goods, including clothing, shoes, dry goods, drugs, groceries, wagons, machinery, trunks, sewing machines, tools, hardware, crockery, carpets, wallpaper, oil cloth to cover kitchen tables, even fancy notions. Money was scarce, and customers often bartered what they had—a cord of wood, a wagon load of wheat, any home-produced commodity—for what they needed among the half-million dollars worth of merchandise on Zions' shelves. There were no cash registers at the time, and money was dropped into large black kettles under the counters, these carried by clerks to the office at closing time so that their contents could be counted and recorded.

Brigham Young early recognized the sales ability of women. "They can do the trading in the stores better than the men," he said, and thus from Zions first days women clerked behind the counters, freeing Mormon men to work in the fields. Women also managed many of the 146 small branch cooperatives that the store had established in settlements throughout Utah and Idaho by 1870; these retail stores constitute one of the first voluntary chain operations in America, for Zions supplied them but had no other financial stake in the stores. All in all, sales totaled over $1.25 million the first year, an auspicious beginning for a fledgling business that at first made deliveries by wheelbarrow and pushcart. The store sold "Sunday best clothes," ammunition, farm implements, mustache wax, sarsaparilla root and even little "fettle bags" that children of the day wore to ward off measles, mumps, and whooping cough—all the goods made available to the outlying cooperatives at the same price as in Salt Lake.

ZCMI fostered home and cooperative manufacturing among Mormons and served as an outlet for the goods produced. The "Big

Boot," as its shoe factory was called, opened in 1870 and was soon manufacturing 83,000 pairs of footwear a year. In 1872 Zions became the first department store in America to have a clothing factory of its own, a plant that made overalls, housedresses, coats, and many other items. The store also became an exporter of sorts, for on January 11, 1871, it is recorded that ZCMI shipped 60,000 pounds of dried peaches to the eastern states.

Business proved so good that Zions' three main Salt Lake City stores were consolidated into a new three-story brick-and-iron building in 1876. The new building with its unique architecture and colorful striped awnings was called "a veritable merchandise palace" at the time. Completed the year before Brigham Young's death, it has been added to over the years and has become one of the most distinctive of American department stores. A wing was added in 1880, doubling the capacity of the store, and a north wing added eleven years later. In 1902 a two-story addition was built to match the rest of the building, and a classically styled triangular pediment with a wrought-iron façade was erected as a symbol of beauty and stability.

The story of ZCMI's growth in the twentieth century is one of continued progress. Zions moved out into the suburbs in 1961 and now has large modern branches in Cottonwood, Ogden, Valley Fair, Orem, and Logan, Utah, its total sales volume over $70 million in 1976. In 1973 the old downtown store was demolished to make way for the enclosed ZCMI urban shopping center. But the striking cast-iron façade of the old building was saved (duplicated in part) for the new Zions' flagship store that was built on the same site. This new store with the old façade, which has won the Visual Merchandiser of the Year award for the past two years from *Visual Merchandise Magazine* for its stunning displays, remains a "veritable palace of merchandising" with over 368,000 square feet of selling space. Though some critics say the old façade is incongruous on the new building, the store is still a landmark of Salt Lake City architecture. Its ornately romantic façade, gilt edged and gleaming, make it one of the most unusual department store buildings in America.

1867

A Southern Institution

RICH'S—*Atlanta, Georgia*

Some Atlantans contend that Rich's is more a philanthropic institution than a department store. They may be right, too. For instance, who ever heard of a store that takes back *everything,* no questions asked? Rich's does. The store doesn't even have an adjustment bureau; "You make your own adjustment at Rich's" is its policy. Customers simply return any item they don't like (no matter when they bought it) to the appropriate department and get their money back in accord with the founder's policy that Rich's customers have to be contented customers. In the process Rich's has accepted several million dollars in returns every year—including altered shirts and suits, a pair of high-button shoes thirty years old, a dead canary, and even goods from competitors down the street.

Rich's takes back twice as much merchandise as the average American store, almost 12 percent of its annual sales. About the only refusal recorded was to a seven-year-old boy suffering from a bad case of sibling rivalry who wanted to exchange his newborn baby sister (he assumed she came from Rich's like everything else in the house) for a space helmet. The store policy is part of Atlanta folklore by now. One Rich's ad, reprinted in many retailing textbooks as an example of institutional advertising at its best shows a bedridden, blemished moppet moaning, "I wish I had got my measles at Rich's, so I could return 'em." A song made famous in Atlanta by a theatrical group called The Wits End Players is entitled "I Took It Back to Rich's." "It" is the singer's husband Melvin, the lady unable to abide with the man and returning him to Rich's after her every effort to kill him fails. Rich's promptly credits Melvin to her account, though they can't recall selling him. She's so satisfied that she decides to take her mother-in-law back next year.

Rich's philanthropies or PR, depending on the cynicism of the beholder, don't extend merely to exchanges. Rich Foundation benefactions cover a wide range of good causes, including a school of business administration donated to Emory University, a radio station given to the public school system, a computer center for Georgia Tech, a wing for a local hospital, and swimming pools for the city's poor. In times of local tragedies like the great fire of 1917 and the Winicoff Hotel fire of 1946, the store assisted bereaved customers financially, even providing burial clothes for many of the victims. When 130 Atlantans died in a crash of their chartered plane at Paris's Orly Airport, Rich's canceled their scheduled Monday newspaper ads and printed the comforting words of the Twenty-third Psalm instead. It is no wonder that Atlantans tend to regard the store as a member of the family. During the 1920s, when the price of cotton fell disastrously ("Five cents cotton/Ten cents meat/How in Hell/Can a poor man eat"), Rich's announced that it would buy five thousand bales at well above the market price to help farmers dependent upon the crop. In the midst of the Great Depression, when Atlanta was too broke to pay its teachers, the store suggested that the city pay them in scrip, making the scrip redeemable at Rich's for cash with no obligation that the money be spent in the store. The city accepted, and Rich's subsequently doled out $685 thousand, holding the scrip with no collateral until Atlanta repaid it.

For those who think such actions make poor business sense, it should be noted that Rich's had sales of $350 million during 1976, which is about $200 per capita for the 1.8 million people in the store's trading area, quite an increase in volume from the $5,000 Morris Rich took in when he founded his store in 1867. Morris, one of four brothers who emigrated to America from Hungary at the beginning of the Civil War, was working as a peddler of notions when he reached Atlanta, which had been burned to the ground by General Sherman in his march to the sea. Borrowing $500 from his brother William, who owned a store in Albany, Georgia, he opened a retail dry goods shop at what would now be the Peachtree Street end of the Whitehall Street viaduct. The store was only a one-story, rough-hewn lumber building measuring 20 feet × 75 feet, but Morris, thinking of contented customers from the beginning, quickly made improvements. The first thing he did was to put pine planks down over the red clay road so that ladies could alight from their carriages and enter his store without soiling their shoes and skirts in the dust or mud.

Within a few years Morris was joined by his brothers Emanuel and Daniel. M. Rich & Brothers prospered because of Morris's radical ideas about how to treat customers, which might have been called simply "southern hospitality." At a time when "buyer beware" was the rule of the marketplace—when it was standard practice for a customer to ravel a piece of material and chew the thread to make sure it was pure wool—Rich decreed that his customers must always be satisfied or their money would cheerfully be refunded. At a time when customers expected to haggle over the price of an article, Rich set up a one-price policy that made it possible for a child to shop with the assurance of an experienced bargainer. And in an era when credit was virtually unknown, Rich trusted people, permitting a farmer, for example, to buy on his word and the prospect of a crop still in the ground.

Morris Rich remained active in his store until a few years before his death in 1928 at the age of eighty-one, when he was widely eulogized as a "natural aristocrat" who had contributed as much as anyone else to the rebuilding of Atlanta. Other members of the family have headed the family business up until recent times; in fact, when the male line of Rich's ran out in the 1920s Richard Rich, a son of the founder's daughter, legally adopted his mother's maiden name to ensure a third-generation at the store, and his son Michael is a part of high-level management today.

Rich's general managers have also played an important part in making the store what it is. Colorful Lucian W. York, who rose from wrapper to the top of the ladder, often had the store decorated for various sales, filling it on one occasion with wild animals to promote a harvest sale. He instituted Rich's once-famous annual cotton goods sale to mark the anniversary of Eli Whitney's cotton gin, a day on which Rich's invariably sold more cotton goods than any other store anywhere. When York died suddenly of a heart attack in 1924, the astute Rich family hired Frank H. Neely as general manager. Neely, an oddity in the department store world because he had no retailing experience whatsoever, was a nationally known mechanical engineer, an expert on scientific business management who had worked with the noted Frederick W. Taylor and Henry Laurence Gantt in pioneering efficient, time-saving methods in American industry. A good judge of talent, he chose management expert Ben Gordon, later to become president of the Allied Stores Corporation chain, who was hired after he wrote a brilliant college thesis on the store, and Richard Rich to assist him in building Rich's into the biggest department store south of Philadelphia and east of the Mississippi.

Engineer Neely even invented a complex underground conveyor-belt system that not only delivered incoming packages to stock rooms and outgoing packages to delivery trucks, but allowed shoppers to turn in their parking tickets after making a purchase and have their packages delivered to their cars in the store's garage. Under Neely Rich's became the first completely air-conditioned store in America; what he called a "makeshift air-conditioning system" is still in operation today. When he retired as chairman of the board in 1961, Rich's, despite its relatively poor location, was far and away the most modern store in Atlanta. So entrenched was Rich's in the city that Bernard Gimbel is said to have hastily withdrawn his plans for opening a branch there after visiting the town—it would be foolish to "buck competition as efficient and thorough as Rich's" he said.

The "Big Rich's"—as customers call the Atlanta store to distinguish it from its twelve branches and its ten-store Richway discount division—is actually four separate downtown stores in a compact group. The Store For Fashion (1924), the Store For Homes (1946), and the Store For Men (1951) are connected by a four-tier Crystal Bridge spanning Forsyth Street, and there is an underground Basement Store covering over 20 acres. Rich's and all its branches comprise over 5,250,000 square feet and employ over fifteen thousand people. Neely would have been especially proud of the store's unique power management system, which has reduced the store's electric power consumption by about 20 percent per month and has been copyrighted and licensed to IBM for marketing on a worldwide basis.

In 1954 Rich's purchased the S. H. George & Sons department store in Knoxville, Tennessee, marking its first venture outside Georgia, and today Rich's itself has branches in North Carolina and Alabama as well as Georgia. Rich's merged with the Cincinnati-based Federated Department Store chain in 1976, but its close ties with the Atlanta community have continued even though the firm is no longer strictly the "Atlanta-born, Atlanta-owned, Atlanta-managed store" that its slogan proudly proclaimed over the years.

Still known as Atlanta's "Saturday Banker," it cashes millions of dollars in checks on Saturdays when the banks are closed, requiring no more identification than a driver's license or a charge plate, despite the fact that the store loses thousands on bad checks every year. On Labor Day 1945, Rich's even acted as an Army paymaster. The store opened its safe to provide mustering-out pay for servicemen due to be discharged that day from nearby Fort McPherson, the fort's own vaults having been time-locked until after the holiday.

Rich's probably provides easier credit to customers than any store in the South, and it's said that any Atlantan who doesn't owe Rich's at least $300 is a nobody. The store really does serve Atlanta from cradle to grave, as it boasts. A couple might meet while courting under Rich's famous clock, which has the letters RICH'S ATLANTA as its twelve numerals. Their wedding might be planned by Rich's, their wedding clothes purchased there, their wedding cake made by the store's bakery, as hundreds are every year. Their children would certainly receive a card from Rich's at birth, as every child born in a Georgia hospital does, and when the children were old enough to come along shopping, their parents could leave them at one of Rich's two nurseries, where a registered nurse and her staff provide free care for all children from six months to six years of age in soundproof play rooms that efficiency expert Neely even equipped with germicidal lamps.

Atlantans can truthfully find about anything in the Big Rich's, from their nonage until they're nonagenarians. One customer was disappointed that a reproduction of Salzman's famous "Head of Christ" depicted Christ with brown eyes (he had "always thought of Jesus' eyes as being blue"), and the store's art director painted them over in cerulean blue. The store is the big circus that Fred Lazarus, a founder of Federated, said a department store should be. It has several restaurants that serve some forty thousand people more than 15 tons of food a week. Fashion shows, author's autograph luncheons (including one where absolutely nobody but the author's wife came), art shows, flower shows, old-timer reunions where centenarians read poems like "I Ain't Dead Yet!"—Rich's offers almost all of the free entertainment that department stores around the country have invented over the years. Its "Lighting of the Great Tree," an annual event that has opened the Christmas season on Thanksgiving night since 1948, is a great favorite, thousands coming downtown to see the huge Christmas tree, up to 70 feet tall, displayed in the glass-enclosed Crystal Bridge and hear Christmas songs sung by the famous choir.

Rich's seems to have disappointed no one recently, except possibly the mountain man who sent in two dollars asking the store to send him a good wife—"stout, no snuff dipper." No wonder a prominent Georgian has said, "In all Atlanta, there is not a single human being who speaks ill of Rich's." Perhaps this feeling is best summed up in one Ollie Reeves' poem "The Clock on the Corner," a good sample of the many homespun verses that customers have dedicated to the store:

> Very often when a fellow asks his best girl for a date
> They will meet at Rich's corner, where a lot of people wait . . .
> For the homefolks of Atlanta, there is something very dear
> In this old-time institution with its friendly atmosphere.

1868

Principles Before Profits

STRAWBRIDGE & CLOTHIER—*Philadelphia, Pennsylvania*

No department store in America occupies a more historic site than Strawbridge & Clothier on the northeast corner of Market and Eighth streets in downtown Philadelphia. Mapped out by William Penn when he planned his Quaker settlement, the wide thoroughfare now known as Market but called High Street in colonial times, boasted the homes of Washington, Adams, and Jefferson when Philadelphia was the capital of an infant United States. It was on the northeast corner of Market and Eighth that Thomas Jefferson sat behind his desk in the department of state in 1790, and it was in that same three-story brick building that Quakers Justus Clayton Strawbridge and Isaac Hallowell Clothier opened their small dry goods store seventy-eight years later.

The building had previously housed J. Ross Houpe's Cheap Store and is even of some importance in horticultural history, for its original owner—and landlord of the department of state—was David Seckel, who developed the Seckel pear in his garden next door. Six years before Strawbridge & Clothier got together in 1868, Justus Strawbridge himself operated his own little store on the site, so it might be said that today's giant Strawbridge & Clothier, now part of one of three or four most innovative urban malls in America, has occupied the same spot for over 116 years.

The Strawbridge & Clothier partnership is no less remarkable; it is, in fact, the only department store partnership that has lasted so long with members of both families still on the board of directors. From the beginning Mr. Strawbridge and Mr. Clothier—their employees in those days dared not address them in any other way—worked well together. They had much in common. Both were members of the Society of Friends, had had experience in the dry goods world since they were in their teens, and were almost the same age—about thirty—when they went into business together. They were "Friends who stayed friends," as a biographer remarks, and their success from the start was as much due to this as any other factor.

As soon as they went into business the partners moved across the street temporarily until the historic old store could be demolished to make way for a new five-story building on the site. Strawbridge had invested nearly $45,000 in the enterprise and Clothier about $9,000, but they agreed that all profits would be equally divided. The business was to be based on Quaker traditions of honest trading and fair dealing, as one would expect of two idealistic young men. Isaac Clothier, who had marched for abolition and whose idol was Abraham Lincoln—he had once run alongside the president's open barouche down Chestnut Street just to hear the great man's voice—summed it up this way in later years:

The idea in our minds . . . was to build our business on the foundation stones of integrity and character. We greatly desired to acquire fortunes, but that was not the sole and primal idea, for we believed that if we acquired fortune only, our lives would not be successful in the highest sense. . . . The ideal of success as a merchant is to render the best of service to the community, to elevate the condition of em-

ployees, and while doing this to acquire wealth as a natural consequence of a wise, energetic, and prudent management of affairs. . . .

In their new establishment the partners offered all types of dry
goods, foreign and domestic, under one roof, and theirs was the only
store in Philadelphia offering such a wide range of goods. It was
also the first major store in the city to adopt the one-price system,
several years before John Wanamaker, who became far more famous for selling at one price but who had earlier remarked to the
proprietors, "How under the sun can you sell goods at one price. I
don't know how you do it."

A democratic store selling "large amounts of goods" at "a small
percentage of profit," and offering quality and fixed prices as well,
was bound to succeed in Philadelphia. Strawbridge & Clothier
prospered. By 1878 the store had been enlarged to the point where
a New York newspaper described it as "palatial." Lining all sales
counters were stools with wooden revolving seats for customers to
sit on as they examined merchandise. Another interesting feature
was the large mirror that customers encountered at the top of the
stairs leading from the basement. The story is told of a woman
loaded with packages who came upon the mirror and thought her
passage out into the aisle was being blocked by another woman
whichever way she turned. She kept telling her unrelenting reflection, "You go *that way*, I go *this*," until a floorwalker intervened.

Dress for sales help was strictly regulated by the store *Book of
Rules* issued to employees. Women had to wear black dresses all
year, except from May to October, when light-colored dresses were
permissible, "provided good taste is shown." According to an old
employee: "Most of the men came to work arrayed in double-
breasted frock coats and silk hats, and most of them wore a
moustache, short beard or burnsides [sideburns]. A beard was a
symbol of manhood and cash boys looked forward to the day when
they could be so adorned."

W. C. Fields (William Claude Dunkenfield) was one Strawbridge
& Clothier cash boy who didn't wait to grow a beard. It's hard to
imagine Fields, even as a boy, as an Horatio Alger character happy
in a store run by good Quakers who always addressed each other as
"thee," and quite predictably, the thirteen-year-old quit to take a
job in a poolroom racking balls—a position better suited to the

development of his unique character. But despite its Victorian attitudes toward employee dress and behavior, typical of most department stores at the time, Strawbridge & Clothier was a benevolent employer. The firm boasted retailing's first Relief Association, founded in 1880, which paid health and death benefits to its members, had an early Savings Fund Association with interest of 6 percent paid by Strawbridge & Clothier on all money their employees saved, and in 1890 became the first large store in Philadelphia to give its workers a half day off on Saturdays.

Though Strawbridge & Clothier hardly became an American household word like John Wanamaker, the firm is certainly as well known in Philadelphia as its rival. By the twentieth century Market and Eighth streets had large department stores on three corners—Lit's, Gimbels and Strawbridge & Clothier—making it one of the greatest concentrations of department store business anywhere. Both Justus Strawbridge and Isaac Clothier had retired by 1900, but their sons were admitted to the firm, one by one and it remained a family controlled business. Eventually, Morris Clothier became president of the store and his brother Isaac Clothier, Jr., an internationally known horseman who often rode with the horsey set in England, became vice-president. In 1922 general manager Herbert J. Tily was made a partner in the store, and five years later he became its president and Morris Clothier was elevated to chairman of the board. Tily had started as a stock boy—when he began at Strawbridge & Clothier he was so poor he had to walk to work to save the carfare. Among other innovations, he originated the store's Clover Day sale in 1906. This came long before Washington Birthday sales and is one of the first such promotional gambits in department store history, one that Strawbridge & Clothier still holds in its stores today. A retailing genius, and probably the only department store president who was a respected musician as well (he wrote several compositions, was a competent conductor, and had an honorary degree in musicology), Tily was largely responsible for the building of the modern-day Strawbridge & Clothier. Under his presidency, the present store, the first air-conditioned department store in Philadelphia, was built between 1928 and 1932. He also developed Strawbridge & Clothier's first branch stores in Ardmore and Jenkinstown at this time.

Today Strawbridge & Clothier has 17 branches, including those in its discount Clover division, around the state and in Delaware and New Jersey. Annual Clover Day sales alone bring in as much as $3 million, and the store ranked twenty-sixth in the nation among individual department stores last year with a sales volume of over $240 million. Headed now by G. Stockton Strawbridge, chairman of the board, a grandson of the founder, and president Randall E. Copeland, who came to the company from Gimbels, the firm has succeeded in divesting itself of the conservative, rather drab image it had in the past. The strongest evidence of this is The Gallery, a modern urban mall financed by Strawbridge & Clothier and Gimbels and built in 1977 between the two great stores, bringing more business to both and helping to revitalize downtown Philadelphia (see Chapter 10). But Strawbridge & Clothier remains proud of its long colorful history. Its "minimuseum" in the Philadelphia store, created and directed by Vice-President Frank Veale, is one of the few department store museums in America and is open to visitors every day during store hours.

1872

"Bloomies"

BLOOMINGDALE BROTHERS, INC—*New York, New York*

At the height of the hostilities during the 1973 coup in Chile, a reporter found himself chatting with an eighty-year-old resident of the Hotel Carrera, who began reminiscing about past visits to New York. The rumble of rockets almost drowned out her voice as she sighed and said, "I love Bloomies."

There are 80 million stories in New York retailing and sometimes it seems that all were invented by PR people, but one tends to believe that the preceding tale is true. Anybody who knows the Bloomingdale's customer would also believe the lady who moved back to New York from Los Angeles solely because she was too far away from "Bloomies." The lady who offered a Bloomingdale's charge card as proof of citizenship when she returned here from abroad and found her passport missing is another Bloomie belle who rings true—she was allowed back in the country because the immigration officer ruled that only an American would have the nerve to do so.

Bloomingdale's has inspired fanatical loyalty among its customers over the last twenty-five years, and this loyalty has transformed the store from a rather unimaginative, mass-market department store into what many customers and competitors consider to be America's most "with it" store, an adult's Disneyland where "you get hip to the trip" cruising the floor, "slapping the racks," looking for things and people as soigné as you think you are.

"Bloomies," it's called now, the one New York store with a nickname, mother of "Saturday's Generation," yet a store whose customers are on the whole as good a mix of New Yorkers as you'll find anywhere, from Murray Hill matrons and chic young people with a studied insouciance to a few poor souls who look like they've hobbled out of hell and slipped by the security guards.

Standing off to the side near sheets that are supposed to match the color of your lost lover's eyes, an observer whose love's marvelous eyes no matching sheets could mimic asks some Bloomingdale's addicts what they think of the place. "It's where to know what's really happening, what's in," is the gist of a young man's answer, one of many such replies. "Buy something here and you know its not tacky," he adds. A little old lady in leotards and Pumas volunteers that its "hep," and a young woman in a midi (Bloomingdale's was the only New York store where this fashion disaster was a success) calls it "sickeningly pretentious." This last customer is definitely in the minority—the audience rating is 90 percent loyal and favorable—but even she admits to being a Bloomies addict. "After all," she says, "I'm here."

The brothers Bloomingdale—Lyman and Joseph—were incorrigible optimists and might have dreamed of such loyalty back in 1872 when they founded their store only a few blocks away from the present site. Lyman Bloomingdale, who appears to have been the guiding genius of the "Great East Side Bazaar," had been one of a remarkable trio of salesclerks employed by Bettlebeck & Company Dry Goods across the river in Newark, New Jersey, and like his fellow future store owners Benjamin Altman and Abraham Abraham he learned his retailing lessons well. After accumulating enough capital manufacturing the popular Empress dress that international style-setter Empress Eugénie of France had invented to conceal her pregnancy, he and his brother opened their 20 foot × 75 foot store at 938 Third Avenue. Sales were only $3.68 the first day. The large beehive device on the roof meant to symbolize "busyness" within the store seemed quite inappropriate, but Lyman looked to the future. In establishing his store so far uptown, he had made an unusual choice, for New York's shopping district was then located between Fourteenth and Twenty-third streets. But Mr. Bloomingdale felt sure that society was moving uptown and that the shopping district would someday follow and reach up to him. Of all the great department stores in Manhattan only his wouldn't gradually move northward over the years. It would be there waiting.

Time proved Lyman Bloomingdale right. The beehive, which later became the ubiquitous Bloomingdale *B* on the 7 million free shopping bags the store gives away every year, became a very busy one indeed with the construction in 1879 of the Third Avenue elevated, which brought customers from miles away to Bloomingdale's door. Business grew so rapidly that in seven years a move had to be made to larger quarters at the northwest corner of Third Avenue and Fifty-ninth Street, a site that the store has occupied since then, though through expansions in following years it now occupies the entire block from Fifty-ninth to Sixtieth streets and from Third to Lexington avenues. Sales for the first year in the new location were well over a million dollars, and Lyman poured money back into the operation. A buying office was established in Europe, and an unbroken line of display windows was constructed outside the store for window-shoppers. When elevators were installed in the six-story building, the great promotor called them "sky carriages." Finished in plate-glass mirrors and fine mahogany, they had little upholstered seats to carry customers in style from floor to floor. Not content with mere "sky carriages," Lyman soon installed what he called an "Inclined Elevator" from the first to the second floors. This Reno Escalator was one of the greatest attention-getters in New York at the time and almost as well known as the store slogan, "All Cars Transfer to Bloomingdale's," that was visually popularized by famed cartoonist Richard F. Outcault, creator of the Yellow Kid, on walls throughout the city (see Chapter 11).

Bloomingdale's was a major metropolitan enterprise with annual sales of $5 million when its founder died in 1905. Lyman's heirs,

Samuel, Hiram, and Irving, built upon the family business, and in 1929 when it joined Federated Department Stores, the nation's largest department store chain, it had annual sales of about $25 million. Yet Bloomingdale's didn't become "Bloomies" until the late 1950s. Previous to this the store had catered not to the trendy Upper East Side but to a conservative middle-class clientele, offering its customers "the best possible value for the least possible price." Even though Bloomingdale's had early "turned the store around" so that its facade faced Lexington Avenue instead of Third Avenue, it was dominated by the Third Avenue el, beneath which saloons and crowded tenements made for a decidedly unfashionable neighborhood that the carriage trade preferred to avoid. However, another remarkably prescient decision handed down by the store's hierarchy in the late 1940s, when the Bloomingdale family was no longer around, ruled that it was time to trade up Bloomingdale's merchandise quality, displays, and prices.

No one knew that the Third Avenue el would be razed in 1954 and that the neighborhood would change into "the Great Northeast Territory," a colony of career girls, bachelors, and boutiques in New York. But there it was again, the fabulous Bloomingdale break; as the official store biography puts it, "a fairy godmother couldn't have done a better job." The el coming down did as much for Bloomingdale's as did the el going up, and exposed in the new light, the store's fortuitous new trading policy soon attracted the new breed of customer who has been described as "a staunch bulwark against lower middle-class taste."

There is very little elegant or even distinctive about the interior or exterior architecture of Bloomingdale's. But the Bloomingdale's style more than makes up for this to Bloomie customers. "Bloomingdale's is the finest conceptual merchandiser in the country," Neiman-Marcus president Richard Marcus says flatly, and Sears Roebuck and Company is said to have a memo posted in its New York buying office suggesting that its fashion buyers visit Bloomingdale's once a month to get a better idea of what's new and exciting in retailing. The store isn't all things to all people, and many items commonly found in department stores aren't carried. Big ticket items like refrigerators, for example, have been abandoned to the discounters, and you'd be hard put to find a prosaic product like razor blades in Bloomingdale's—but what is offered will usually be the season's height of fashion, and certain shoppers are willing to pay for this.

Bloomingdale's displays, among the cleverest in retailing, are often pure entertainment. Its windows, designed by young Candy Pratts, have featured well-dressed mannequins playing slot machines, a trench-coated girl dragging a body in a handsome rug, and steam-room/bathroom scenes that seemed, to some, to surpass the risqué into the next realm of sex. Displays in the many boutiques throughout the store are just as eye-catching, and the fifth-floor furniture department made famous by Barbara D'Arcy goes to almost any extreme to display its wares. The department is completely renovated twice a year, down to the replacement of floors, and outside the model rooms stand expensive props like the four giant statues from the set of *Cleopatra* that Bloomingdale's bought recently from the Cinecetta movie studio in Rome. Ten million people a year ogle these home-furnishings rooms every year. One ogler was so enchanted by a Bloomingdale's model room that he purchased everything in it, including floor and fireplace, at a cost of over $15,000, and had it shipped home to France.

Other star attractions in the store are the 40 Carrots lunchroom, where diners can order health foods like alfalfa sprouts and the Delicacy Shop, which sells an incredible 146 varieties of bread and 300 different cheeses, among a total of seven thousand goodies. Clearly these are substantial offerings, but Bloomingdale's more often sells "the sizzle not the steak," as one store official puts it. What other department store has the special appeal that makes its plain white T-shirt with the store's name emblazoned across the chest, or its cotton panties with "Bloomies" appliquéd across the seat, hot sellers at six dollars.

The fanatical Bloomies customer, who has made it all possible, is epitomized in the form of the "Bloomingdale Couple" of store ads, a fashionable duo radiating a kind of unisexual chic. To such young materialists Bloomingdale's is a happening rather than a store, attending a carnival rather than shopping. Members of "Saturday's Generation" make dates here for Saturday night; only the Metropolitan Museum is a more popular sexual cruising ground for young people than the aisles of Bloomies. "Bloomingdale's," says its chairman of the board, Marvin Traub, "is in competition not with other stores but with the Guggenheim and Metropolitan museums, restaurants like Maxwell's Plum and Daly's Dandelion, galleries in Soho, and the movie theaters."

Saturday's Generation is of course not more than a fraction of the three hundred thousand people who pass through Bloomingdale's door every week, but the store knows that it had better cater to them, even to the extent of including what strangely resembles a potted marijuana plant in a recent catalog. The Saturday's Generation has immortalized the store and inspired the movie *Meet Me at Bloomies,* which is all about boys and girls meeting and falling in love at the East Side shopping mecca. On the heels of youth have come youth seekers; celebrity shoppers like the international lovebirds Marcello Mastroianni and Catherine Deneuve; Queen Elizabeth, who said before coming here that the one store she wanted to visit in America was Bloomingdale's (which promptly created a special boutique for her); and Queen Sophia of Spain, who bought a denim jumpsuit for the King in Bloomies. After them come all the rest of us, many of whom think we are the Saturday Generation, too—although it may be that that's just what the Saturday Generation is, people who think they are the Saturday Generation.

Bloomingdale's makes its share of mistakes in striving to be and stay "with it." When the store's bakery promoted cakes decorated with the famous G's of the eminent Gucci leather house and icing that read "Gucci Gucci Goo," Gucci wasn't amused and sued. The case was settled out of court. A dispute between Bloomingdale's and Rita Hayworth's daughter the Princess Yasmin Aly Kahn over the identity of a seminude woman on a Bloomies shopping bag was amicably settled with an apology to the princess. The store explained that "due to a name confusion, the name of Princess Yasmin was inadvertently associated with the bag when, in fact, a professional model named Yasmin had in reality posed for the picture."

Some competitors say that Bloomingdale's wouldn't succeed elsewhere, that it owes its special cachet to what amounts to luck—namely its unique location. Sour grapes, replies Bloomies, and points to its thriving branches in 15 other places, including stores in the suburbs of Philadelphia and Boston and a full-line store in Washington, D.C. The Bloomingdale's customer does seem to represent a state of mind rather than a geographic base, but there is no denying that Bloomies is one of the few, if not the only, department store remaining whose flagship store does business equal to the combined volume of its branches. Sales for all stores in 1976 were about $340 million, so the New York store had annual sales of over $170 million, which means that it extracted about $350 per square foot of selling space. This is probably the highest sales per square foot of any store in America—but falls far behind the Marble Arch department store of Marks & Spencer in London, which is the world's most profitable store with an amazing $575 in sales per square foot of selling area.

1877

"Prices Split to Splinters!
Competitors Overwhelmed with Defeat!"

THE MAY DEPARTMENT STORES COMPANY—
St. Louis, Missouri

When fifteen-year-old David May came down the gangplank of New York's Castle Garden in 1863, he had less than a dollar in change in his pocket, little more than *yes* and *no* in his English vocabulary, and hardly any idea of where he would go or what he would do. What this German immigrant did possess was the brash self-confidence of youth and a belief shared by all his fellow passengers that Great Young America was the Land of Opportunity, the Israel of the West, a place of milk, honey, and religious freedom where one could make his fortune without losing his soul.

Still, David May could not possibly have imagined, brash and confident though he was, what his Great Adventure would come to, that he would found the May empire, a billion-dollar business once described by *Fortune* magazine as "the nation's oldest, most prosperous and most successful department store group." The story really began in the West, which was the land of opportunity in America of the early 1870s. David May found a letter from his uncle awaiting him at Castle Garden containing a money order covering the railroad fare to Cincinnati. There he worked at various jobs, attending Nelson College night school for two long years before he learned to speak English passably, and clerked his way up

Macy's New York flagship store—the biggest store in the world.

Gimbel's downtown New York store.

The first Bloomingdale's store on
Third Avenue.

Above: Bloomie's when the trolleys were still running back in 1942.

The original Golden Rule Store in the 1920s.

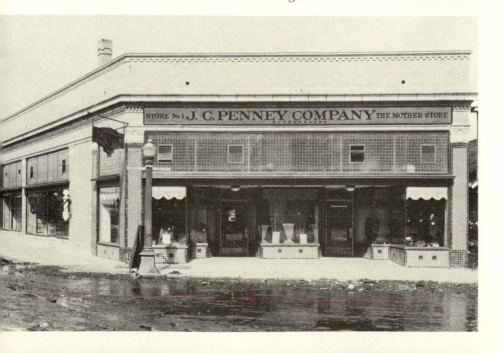

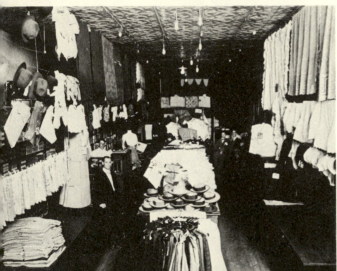

Interiors of J. C. Penney stores, (above) in Preston, Idaho (1919), (left) Roseburg, Oregon (1917), and (below) Wooley, Washington.

A Golden Rule Store delivery team in Great Falls, Montana.

Fabrics, hat, and candy
departments in J. C. Penney's
Seattle store, 1931.

Interior of Hess's first store in 1907.

The Emporium, in downtown San Francisco, its beauty matched by few department stores.

Left: "Meet me under the clock at Rich's"—the store's famous clock.

Below: Bargain hunter's paradise— Filene's celebrated Automatic Bargain Basement, the most famous bargain basement in the world, as shown in 1947.

The First 5 & 10c. Store in the United States. Opened by F. W. Woolworth, June 21st, 1879, at Lancaster, Pa.

Right: Hudson's first store in Detroit.

Below: Hudson's new Briarwood Mall store in Ann Arbor, Michigan.

The old Eagle Emporium, first consolidated unit of Zion's Cooperative Mercantile Institution in Salt Lake City. ZCMI opened for business in this store March 1, 1869. Note the interesting customers who used to come to town in those days. The picture is believed to have been taken in the late 1860s or early 1870s.

Zion's as it looks today in downtown Salt Lake City.

Top: Wanamaker's first great store—the Grand Depot in Philadelphia.

Center: Interior of Wanamaker's Grand Depot.

Bottom: The Grand Court in Wanamaker's, showing the famous eagle and great organ.

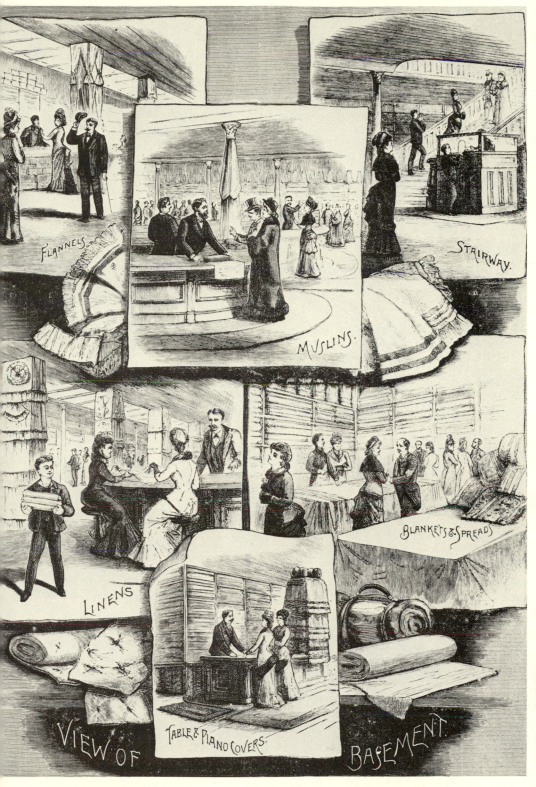

Basement of Strawbridge & Clothier's in the 1880s. Note how even the pillars were covered with fabrics on display.

The "outing goods" department, as sporting goods were called in the 1890s, in Strawbridge & Clothier's basement.

Above: The dress goods main aisle of Strawbridge & Clothier in 1906 was almost 300 feet long, the full length of the Philadelphia store. Stools were for the convenience of the shoppers.

Left: Strawbridge & Clothier's Philadelphia store, as decorated for the Elk's reunion in 1907, won first prize.

to a partnership in a clothing store. May planned to remain there, but one bitterly cold evening in 1876 fire broke out in the store, and he labored from dark to dawn salvaging clothing, saving his stock but losing his health in the process. The pneumonia that resulted left him with a hacking cough; doctors advised that his only hope of avoiding tuberculosis or of not dying from the asthma with which he was afflicted was to leave for a drier climate.

May sold his interest in the store for $25,000 and journeyed to the health resort of Manitou Springs, Colorado, intending to return East when cured. But while on a fishing trip with a party that included Chicago department store magnate Marshall Field, he heard of a silver strike in nearby Leadville. Field later bought an interest in the famed chrysolite mine there, an investment that added materially to his already considerable fortune, but May decided to try his own hand at mining in Leadville. However, after digging a hole deeper and deeper into the ground for about a month without taking a dollar's worth of paydirt from it, he decided to quit and open a clothing store.

May's first store was a muslin and frame tentlike affair where he sold mostly red woolen "longies" (upon which, in later years, he liked to say the May business was founded) and the copper-riveted overalls manufactured by Levi Strauss & Company that were commonly called Levis by the miners but which he advertised as "California Riveted Duck Clothing." His "Levis and longies" soon clothed most of Leadville's prospectors, business prospered, and May wanted to replace the muslin tent with a permanent building, but his two partners refused to go along, fearing that the Leadville boom would soon bust, so he bought the tent site himself and erected a frame store on it. His Great Western Auction House & Clothing Store, which had a false front like most stores of the period to make it appear larger, thrived in a town where millionaires were made overnight and had nowhere to spend the riches pouring from their mines except in the dozen or so stores, 58 saloons, and 118 gambling houses and brothels that lined the quagmire streets. May added sack suits, "hard-boiled" shirts, hard hats, and high-button shoes to his stock. Gentlemen could buy underwear with vertical stripes and pink satin French night robes. For the ladies May once bought out a Chicago store's huge stock of velvet and brocade dresses. The Chicagoans thought Leadville's high altitude had affected his mind. How could dresses so expensive that they didn't sell in the big city find buyers in a town composed largely of log cabins, shacks, and tents? May knew, however, that the newly rich families in those cabins, shacks, and tents were just looking for opportunities to spend their money. Within a week the entire stock of $200 to $400 dresses sold out.

To assist in the Leadville store May hired his former mining and store partner Jake Holcomb, who remained in his employ all his life, and took on Moses Shoenberg, the son of a local merchant, as his partner. Later the founder would marry Shoenberg's sister, Rosa. Since two other Shoenberg brothers, Louis and Joseph, would also become May's partners, and multimillionaires, in years to come, the Shoenberg name is inextricably part of the May story. And the name Beaumont as well! Because of the proximity of the French province of Lorraine to Bavaria, the Shoenberg's native land, French was spoken almost as freely as German. In German "schoenberg" means "beautiful mountain," which in French would be "beaumont." Because of his bitter opposition to the militarism of Germany under Kaiser Wilhelm, Louis Shoenberg changed his name to Beaumont during World War I and thereafter was known as Commodore Beaumont.

David May's clothing shop in rip-roaring Leadville was more like a general store with its potbellied stove and the bearded miners gathered around it ten months of the year swapping stories of big strikes and expounding their cracker-barrel philosophy. The soft-hearted May grubstaked many a miner, winning numerous friends in the area, and was active in the town's civic affairs, helping to maintain Leadville's Tabor Opera House and organizing the Leadville Hebrew Benevolent Association. His store prospered and he soon opened a number of branches in other Colorado mining communities, including the D. May & Company Square Dealing Clothing Room in Irwin, up the street from Old Reasonable Abe's and other small shops. This period marked the birth of his first son, Morton J. May, who would later head the nationwide May operations and is still, at ninety-five a director of the corporation.

From the very beginning David May was an aggressive advertiser who hawked his wares in the no-holds-barred style of the West. An early ad for a fire sale in one of his stores read as follows:

FIRE—FIRE!

but no Small-pox

WATER—SMOKE!

but no Small-pox

COME ALONG AND GET A PIECE OF THE CAKE!

In 1888, when the Leadville mining boom began to peter out, May bought a bankrupt store in Denver and made a thriving business of it by his flamboyant promotions and advertising. On opening day he hired a brass band to parade the streets and to play on a wooden platform built like a marquee over the store entrance. May's ads remained the epitome of extravagant Western advertising, featuring such headlines as COMPETITORS OVERWHELMED WITH DEFEAT! PRICE SPLIT TO SPLINTERS! RED-HANDED CARNAGE! WE'VE GROUND PRICES TO POWDER! In his employ at this time was Colonel Joseph M. Grady, one of America's early advertising geniuses, who even burst into poetry in ads extolling May's merchandise. By 1892 these methods had worked so well that May and the three Shoenberg partners could buy the Famous Company clothing store in Saint Louis, which later became Famous-Barr. Joyfully, he proclaimed victory in the Denver clothier's war with a double-page ad in the *Rocky Mountain News* that has never seen its like for sheer chutzpah in department store history:

WHY WE REJOICE!

It is with a feeling of triumph that we today recall the scenes in the Clothing Arena of Denver of but three years ago, previous to our arrival, when the merciless Clothing Gladiators were feasting at the expense of the masses, asking war-time prices for worthless plunder, holding high carnival over their ill-gotten gains, and compare them with the conditions of today.

As we look down from our lofty positions of Prosperity, Prominence and Popularity into the sunny valley of three short and successful business years, and view with much pride the grand and honorable basis upon which we have placed the clothing business in

Denver, how we have broken the ice of high prices on unreliable apparel, unmasked competition and put them to flight, and opened a new era in the clothing field for the poorest as well as the richest, we rejoice in our title as the CLOTHING MONARCHS OF THE WEST.

As Sheridan, dashing into Winchester, brought victory, for his soldiers, so did THE MAY dash into the competitor's camp with victory for the toilers of the Silver State and open the flood gates of Eastern prices and Metropolitan styles to Western consumers. Our followers' greedy careers must soon draw to a close; they are in a perplexing predicament; they groan in agonizzing tones and their whole frames shake like the tender branches of a leafless elm, as they see themselves through the mirror of chagrin.

With the Famous of St. Louis, which we now own, we are one of the largest consumers of Clothing, Furnishings, Hats and Shoes in the country, with double capacity to work with, with ability, and capital to properly handle it, with hydraulic pressure behind it, we shall forever stand head and shoulders above all competition.

We feel ourselves gaining weight on the scales of the public's confidence; we have won it, and now only ask you to map our matchless methods on your memory, and with our assurance that the grand reward for our past deeds will help strengthen our determination to merit your continued patronage, we now proudly unfurl our banner, upon which is written: Cash, Pluck and Enterprise, the lifeblood which flows freely into the heart of our grand business. Let us shake hands by proxy, and believe us, as ever

Yours for Values

THE MAY COMPANY

Victory in Denver was followed by the May partners moving farther east and laying down $300,000 cash for an old and ailing store in Cleveland, this becoming the nucleus for the May Company operation in that city. The partnership continued until 1910 when it was replaced by the May Department Stores Company, which was incorporated as a prelude to further expansion. Stores were added coast to coast, but success didn't change "hardheaded, softhearted" Dave May, who remained at the helm of the company until his death in 1927, aged seventy-nine. "I started in this business at $5 a week," he once recalled. "Store clerks were on duty from six in the morning till well after dark. It was a period that regarded ten cents an hour sufficient to feed, clothe and house a common laborer and his family. . . . America is the squarest and fairest country on earth, and the only land where every citizen can have as splendid a chance as he dares make or take." May never forgot his old friends and remained a soft touch until the end. Once an "efficiency expert" told him that his old partner Jake Holcomb could "just about draw his weekly paycheck" and advised firing him. "Don't you think," May replied gently, "that for a man of nearly ninety, drawing a paycheck is in itself quite an accomplishment?"

The muslin tent store that Dave May opened in Leadville one hundred years ago has grown into a national chain of over 130 stores, May Company divisions including the Hecht Company, Washington-Baltimore; Famous-Barr Company, Saint Louis; Kaufmann's, Pittsburgh; Meier & Frank, Oregon; and G. Fox & Company, Connecticut—all of these noted stores covered in these pages—as well as the May Company, California (formerly A. Hamburger Son & Company); the May Company, Cleveland; May-D & F (formerly Daniels & Fisher), Colorado; the M. O'Neil Company, Akron; Strauss-Hirshberg, Youngstown; May-Cohens, Florida; and the discount Venture Stores. The company is also involved in building shopping centers. Since 1911 the May Company has paid a continuous quarterly cash dividend every year, longer than any other department store listed on the New York Stock Exchange. Its gross sales of nearly $2.4 billion in 1977 are over six times the value of all men's clothing sold in America the year that the Leadville store was founded.

1879

From Five-and-Ten to Department Store

F. W. WOOLWORTH COMPANY—*Lancaster, Pennsylvania*

Young Frank Winfield Woolworth's first day at work should provide solace for anyone just starting out at anything, no matter how poorly he or she does. It is best described in the homely words of that "boob from the country," as Woolworth called himself at the time:

> When most of the clerks had gone to dinner—lunch as we call it nowadays—in came an old farmer and said to me: "Young man, I want a spool of thread." I didn't know where they kept the thread, so I went over to Mr. Moore, who was busy at his desk, and asked him. "Right in front of your nose, young man," he snapped without looking up from his writing. I pulled out a drawer directly in front of me and, sure enough, found it full of spools of thread. "I want number forty," said the farmer. I never knew till that moment that thread had a number. I fumbled all around the drawer looking for number forty, but could not find it. I appealed to Mr. Moore to know if we kept number 40. "Certainly; right in the drawer in front of you," he said quite sharply. I had to tell him: "I can't find any." "Just as I expected," he said testily as he got down from his desk and showed me the right kind of thread. He immediately returned to his desk. "How much is it, young man?" asked the farmer. I had to turn to Mr. Moore. It was eight cents. The farmer pulled out a ten-cent shinplaster. "Mr. Moore, where do I get change?" I had to ask. "Come right up to the desk and make out a ticket," he ordered me. I picked up one of the blanks and studied it all over to see what I could do with it. But I was stumped. "Mr. Moore, I don't believe I know how to make this out," I had to confess. "Hand it to me; I will show you," he replied. Next I had to ask: "Where do I get my change?" "There's the cashier right there; can't you see him?" he said impatiently. . . .

So it went for the next few years. Woolworth was so poor a salesman that his salary was lowered from ten to eight dollars a week, but the former farm boy who hated it down on the farm survived, the moral of which may be "employers be tolerant"—the most bumbling and inept beginner can go on to become a multimillionaire and *your* employer. At any rate, Frank Woolworth clerked for five years at Moore & Smith's Corner Store in Watertown, New York, and in 1878 helped launch the store's famous "5¢ counter," among the first in the East, which provided the inspiration for his five-and-ten-cent store empire.

The "5¢ counter" had been tried before in Michigan and other places. In fact, a drummer had told Moore and his partner about such a sale in Port Huron. Customers had not only cleaned off that Michigan counter but had bought a lot of higher-priced merchandise as well, and since the Corner Store had a then massive $35,000 surplus of goods that had to be sold to meet payroll obligations, Moore rushed an order to the drummer's company—Spellman Brothers Wholesalers of New York—for $100 worth of "Yankee Notions." Woolworth arranged the tin pans, washbasins, buttonhooks, dippers, and turkey-red napkins on the most prominent counter in the store and sweetened them with "stickers" and "chestnuts," surplus stock that wouldn't move, nailing his home-made sign "Any Article on This Counter–5¢" over the display. "Like magic, the goods faded away," he recalled six years later. This successful sale and others like it over the next four months encouraged him to ask Moore to credit him with $315.41 worth of "Yankee notions" and open his own store in Utica, New York.

The first "Great 5¢ Store," which opened on Washington's birthday in 1879, was a failure from the start due to its poor location, taking in as little as $2.50 a day, but in May the undaunted Woolworth moved to Lancaster, Pennsylvania, where his 14 foot × 35 foot store at 170 North Queen Street, in operation now for a century, became the world's first five-and-ten. "As soon as we added 10¢ goods to the line," Woolworth wrote later, "we took away part of the '5¢ store's charm'—the charm of finding only one price on a counter and only one price in a store. But as long as we kept the 5¢ goods on one side of the store and the 10¢ goods on the other, the 'charm' was not entirely lost. It remained a 'charm' just the same." This was the second great turning point in Woolworth's career. Money flowed into the store's cashbox, and ironically, it wasn't the silver coins normally associated with early five-and-dimes. Silver coins had practically disappeared during the Civil War due to metal shortages, and the government had issued stop-gap fractional currency, contemptuously dubbed "shinplasters," in denominations of 3¢, 5¢, 10¢, 15¢, 25¢, and 50¢. Since the 1875 law enacted by Congress providing for the replacement of fractional currency by silver coins didn't call for its redemption until January 1, 1879, Woolworth's sales were for paper "shinplasters" until about the middle of the next year.

Few people know that in 1884 Woolworth tried a 25¢ store in

Reading, Pennsylvania, a store that he closed when the higher price failed to yield proportionate profits. He had ten red-front stores in the East by 1886, some of these operated by "partner-managers." The bright red fronts, phased out in recent years, were lifted from the older A & P grocery chain, but the famed W or "Diamond W" trademark adopted at the time was Frank Woolworth's own idea. Over the years—and it lasted until 1968 when replaced by a W on a rectangular sign—it became as well known as the MGM lion, the bearded Smith Brothers, the Old English script masthead of *The New York Times*, or the Fisk Tire Company's slogan, "Time to Retire."

Woolworth was soon able to buy for cash in greater quantity and offer his customers "plums" or "corkers," nickel and dime bargains on which he made a profit. These were times of great economic expansion. America's gross national product had increased from $5 billion in 1879 to $9 billion by 1889; in 1860 the country had only been in fourth place among industrial nations and by 1894 would rank first. While bedridden with typhoid fever, Woolworth charted plans to open stores in selected localities at the rate of 10 to 12 a year. He made a buying trip to Europe in 1890, and soon foreign products were flowing into Woolworth stores at nickel and dime prices, including the Christmas tree ornaments he popularized here. Several Woolworth stores became the scenes of riots over these foreign goods, and one paper reported that a policeman sent to calm a crowd battling for bargains in the Syracuse store joined in the melee himself.

Woolworth claimed that the most important turning point in his career came when he was bedridden with a nervous breakdown and realized the importance of delegating authority. "Before that," he said, "although I had several stores, I felt it was up to me to do everything myself. I was sure that there was nothing I couldn't do better than any of my employees—even dressing windows and opening boxes of merchandise. During my long absence, I found things had gone along quite well. After that, I changed my tactics. I let others attend to the ordinary running of the business and devoted myself to working out plans for expansion—and we made much greater progress."

Woolworth's business methods were honest and direct, as would be expected from a big, bluff, and hearty man. He'd buy in great quantities to get the price down.

"Here's a knife that you make," he told one German manufacturer. "If I gave you a big order, at what price would you sell it to me?"

"Sixteen cents," the knife man said.

"If I give you an order sufficient to keep your factory busy night and day, twenty-four hours, for a year, what then?"

The German figured several minutes. "Eight cents," he finally said.

"Done," Woolworth replied.

Similar deals were made thousands of times here and abroad, and no doubt this could be a vicious business practice. By sealing up the entire output of a factory for a year or more, Woolworth was able, by shunting off the manufacturer's former customers, to dictate prices to the manufacturer and reduce him to subservience. This did happen and there was bitter criticism of the practice, but it probably made many more rich men than it did slaves. It is said, in fact, that over one hundred of Woolworth's associates became millionaires.

Woolworth always insisted on knowing the day-to-day operations of all his stores and often made unannounced visits to them, posing as a customer. Like John Wanamaker he believed that "the customer is always right," adding: "He or she is right whether he or she is or not!" He demanded courtesy from his employees and held them to strict accountability, although, for all his demands, he never paid particularly high wages and could by no means be called a pioneer in worker's rights. Often he would send the same telegram to all his stores, one of them reading:

> Good morning. Did you say "Good morning" to each customer this morning?
>
> Frank W. Woolworth

Before Woolworth merged his company with five others in 1911, his keen merchandising ability, dime top price, and "browsers wanted" policy had resulted in 319 Woolworth five-and-dimes throughout the world. Woolworth's sold enough candy alone annually to fill a train 24 miles long. In England, where the stores were called "three and sixes," they were so familiar that many Englishmen believed they were a national institution and on visiting America would comment, "I see our Woolworth's has come over to you, too!" The so-called $65 million merger between F. W. Woolworth & Company, S. H. Knox & Company, F. M. Kirby & Company, E. P. Charlton & Company, and variety stores operated by Frank's brother Charles Woolworth and his old boss W. H. Moore upped the chain's total to 596 stores doing sales of more than $52 million annually. The new million-dollar-a-week corporation was named the F. W. Woolworth Company, the ampersand before "Company" dropped to distinguish it from the old Woolworth's. Along with the A & P it was now one of the two American chain store giants, and it didn't stop growing, inspiring the manager of a Milwaukee unit to pen a parody of Kipling's "L'envoi":

> When earth's last ten-cent store has opened
> And the new-painted red front has dried
> And the oldest clerk has her station
> Down near the register's side,
> We will look to new worlds to sell to
> Perhaps Jupiter, Venus or Mars
> And the master of all the ten-cent stores
> Will put us to work in the stars.

"Woolworth's" had become synonymous with "Five-and-Ten" by 1913 and the completion of New York's fabulous Woolworth Building that year made the name the most recognizable one in American retailing. The Reverend Dr. S. Parker Cadman christened the Gothic-lined building with silvery lacework the "Cathedral of Commerce," and that's just what it looked like. "What shall I say of a city that builds the most beautiful cathedral in the world and calls it an office building," observed British statesman Arthur Balfour, when he visited America. The 50-story "Skyqueen," modeled after London's House of Parliament, was then the world's tallest skyscraper at 792 feet, but was proportioned so gracefully by architect Cass Gilbert that it is still regarded as one of the most majestic buildings in the city of towers. Frank Woolworth's office inside was a replica of the Empire Room of Napoleon Bonaparte's palace in

Compiègne, down to the last detail, for Woolworth liked to think he shared some of the characteristics of the Corsican corporal, a life-size bust of whom stared at visitors from beside his desk. But amid all the superlatives about the building, too myriad to catalog here, perhaps the most amazing is that Woolworth's headquarters was built without a mortgage and without a single dollar's indebtedness. Frank Woolworth just shelled out $13.5 million in cold cash—unique in the history of great buildings in America or anywhere else for that matter.

Seated in his Empire Room, Frank Woolworth, the farm boy who had liked to play "store," was certainly America's "Napoleon of Commerce" at the time. His 30-room marble mansion on Fifth Avenue's Millionaire's Row at Eightieth Street, with its superb organ, a wonder of its time, and luxurious appointments, wasn't bad to go home to either, nor was Winfield Hall, the 62-room, white marble, Italian Renaissance mansion that Cass Gilbert had built for him in Glen Cove on 16½ acres overlooking Long Island Sound. Winfield Hall, which is now partly owned by New York Governor Hugh Carey's brother Martin, and is open to the public, contains numerous panels bearing allegorical representations of Woolworth's life. Among many unusual features, it has a master bedroom modeled on Napoleon's Empire Room; a music room where, as guests heard the strains of a sonata begin, its composer's life-size portrait would slowly emerge from the darkness; and a recessed bench hidden behind the woodwork where a private detective sat spying on Woolworth's houseguests.

But despite his marble mansions and billion-dollar business, Woolworth's last years were miserable ones. Like Marshall Field and Rowland Macy, he was an unhappy man. His wife Jennie had been declared mentally incompetent. His middle daughter, Edna, was found dead in her hotel suite when only thirty-five, leaving her five-year-old daughter Barbara, later to become familiar to millions as the oft-married "Babs" Hutton, "America's Dollar Princess." "Babs" inherited over $40 million as her share of the family fortune when she came of age and once observed, "I won't say my previous husbands thought only of money, but it had a certain fascination for them." When she died in May 1979 she had long since sold her company holdings.

Woolworth himself had suffered several nervous breakdowns and was an ailing man, he and his nurse and Mrs. Woolworth and her nurse often sharing their meals alone together in the vast dining room of Winfield Hall, unable to communicate, with only the thunder and music of the great organ to solace them, a scene hardly the comic one such plutocratic loneliness is often depicted as. It was the American tragedy Dreiser never got around to writing about.

Frank Woolworth's death in 1919 was an ironic one, for the same W. H. Moore who had given him his start was indirectly responsible for his death. Moore had had all his teeth removed by a dentist late in life and died in the dentist's office of a stroke. Woolworth refused all dental care from that day on and subsequently died of septic poisoning.

On Woolworth's death the *New York Sun* observed, "He won a fortune, not showing how little could be sold for much, but how much could be sold for little." His idea had been simplicity itself; it looked simple, that is, after someone else simply had thought of it. Among the greatest of merchant princes, he was one of the first merchants elected to Chicago's Retailing Hall of Fame when it opened in 1953. The billion-dollar empire he left behind totaled 1,081 stores doing business of about $110 million annually, stores in which over a billion people a year browsed and bought things for nickels and dimes.

America's greatest nickel-and-dime romance didn't end until 1932, when the Woolworth board of directors voted that items could be sold in the store for twenty cents. Three years later it became firm policy that there would no longer be any arbitrary price limit in Woolworth stores, and five-and-dime prices have soared upward ever since.

Woolworth's is usually thought of as only a variety store, but the fact is that the company has been in the department store business since 1962, when it entered the field with its first Woolco discount department store in Columbus, Ohio. Today there are 359 Woolcos and 4,840 Woolworths, Kinney shoe stores, and Richman Brothers apparel stores around the world with sales of over $5.5 billion a year in 1977. This makes Woolworth's America's fourth largest chain operation and the chain with the most stores. The company is also the world's largest restaurant chain, serving more than a million meals a day over the two thousand lunch counters in its many units.

Long the epitome of "horizontal" retail distribution with all its branches, Woolworth's has clearly become a full-fledged "vertical" retailer as well—building skyward like most department stores. A store that once relied solely on window and counter advertising now ranks among the largest retail users of newspaper and television advertisements. The trend, says one executive, is for the Woolworth variety store to grow larger and carry more merchandise, including "big ticket" items, with traditional variety lines acting as "sparkplugs." Within another generation, however, it's doubtful that there will be many people around who will still call Woolworth's the five-and-ten. In mid-1979 Woolworth's fought off a $1.1 billion takeover by Brascan, Ltd., a Canadian holding company.

1881

From City to Suburban Giant

THE J. L. HUDSON COMPANY—*Detroit, Michigan*

J. L. Hudson's—along with Macy's and Marshall Field—is one of the three giant stores that emerged in America with the advent of city shopping. Towering 25 stories in the air, it is the world's tallest department store, its 49 acres of floor space exceeded only by Macy's of New York. The block long Brobdingnagian made Detroit virtually a one-store city, entrenching Hudson's among the first ten retailers in America, and although the flagship giant is ailing badly from the urban blight plaguing Detroit, it is now linked with 14 Hudson suburban branches to assure the company a top place among the nation's leading merchants.

If the great flagship store does sink one day in the swamp of the city, its fleet will survive and it will be long remembered, as dreadnoughts always are. The records it holds are part of retailing legend:

• Hudson's downtown in its best years took in as much as $1.5 million a day, was the world's biggest store in sales volume, carrying well over half a million items ranging from antimacassars to zwieback.

• The store is the only one ever to help found a major automotive company—the Hudson Motor Company, which often earned over $20 million a year and later became part of American Motors.

• Hudson's 4-acre, 60-department basement store sold more popular-priced bargain merchandise than any other department store anywhere—exceeding $35 million in sales.

• Hudson's Thanksgiving Day Parade, launched in 1922, two years before Macy's famous pageant, reaches over five hundred thousand people with its dozens of huge floats, bands and thousands of marchers.

• The store's immense 104 foot × 205 foot American flag with stars 5½ feet wide and 12 stripes 8 feet wide is listed in the *Guinness Book of World Records* as the largest flag in the world; displayed every Flag Day since 1949 on the Woodward Avenue side of Hudson's, it needs 6,240 feet of nylon rope to support its 1,500-pound weight.

J. L. Hudson's founder, Joseph Lowthian Hudson, came to America from Newcastle-on-Tyne, England, in 1855 with his father, Richard, a ship supplier and part-time Methodist preacher who had often outfitted ships carrying coals from Newcastle. Richard took his family of eight to Canada first, then crossed over to Michigan, where he became a telegrapher. Young Joseph worked as a telegraph messenger, a four-dollars-a-month clerk and a fruit picker, later opening a small general store in Ionia with his father. He had already been apprenticed at the age of fifteen to Christopher Mabley, a merchant who pioneered in selling men's ready-to-wear clothing, whose empire survives as Cincinnati's Mabley & Carew department store; Mabley was at first a silent, minority partner in the general store venture. This country store flourished for seven years, doing annual sales of $40,000 when the Panic of 1873 all but destroyed the business and Richard Hudson died, a man broken by his failure. His son tried to salvage what remained, but within three years was forced into bankruptcy, the courts ordering him to settle with his creditors for sixty cents on the dollar.

Joining up with Mabley again, Joseph managed his men's clothing store in Detroit, the city's largest at the time, increasing its profits so substantially when Mabley went abroad on vacation that the merchant gave him a quarter interest in the business, plus a $7,500 yearly salary. This generous arrangement would have been more than enough for most clerks, but Hudson was young and aggressive, his ideas clashed with those of the cantankerous Mabley, and he decided to strike out on his own. In 1881, using $60,000 in savings and enticing many salesmen away from his old employer, he launched a men's and boys' clothing store on the ground floor of the Detroit Opera House in downtown Detroit, premises previously occupied by the Newcomb & Endicott Company.

In winning the pitched battle for customers that developed between himself and Mabley, "J. L. Hudson, Clothier" applied many retailing innovations he had dreamed about while clerking, including a "one-price" policy, plain marking of prices and liberal return privileges. These polices made Hudson's store an immediate success. Within ten years, the Detroit Hudson's and seven branches established in Toledo, Saint Louis, Cleveland, Buffalo, Grand Rapids, Saint Paul, and Sandusky had a sales volume of over $2 million annually, and Hudson was the biggest retailer of men's clothing in America. He could now turn his attention to a matter that had been bothering him for some time. Never satisfied with the legal payment of sixty cents on the dollar he had made, Hudson paid his creditors back *in full* all the money they had lost when his first business venture failed. Not only did he fully pay all his "debts" in 1888—he paid in full with compound interest added. This astounding gesture "made business history in his day," according to one chronicler, "and incidentally gave J. L. Hudson an unlimited letter of credit for the rest of his life." Grateful creditors from all over America sent him gifts and letters of thanks, some of which are still in the store's files.

Three years after he paid his creditors, Joseph Hudson built the store on the corner of Gratiot and Farmer streets farther uptown; that was the nucleus for the immense Hudson store that eventually covered an entire block. People said he'd never last there because the eight-story building was too far from what was then the downtown beaten track and, oddly enough, because a commercial building erected on a site previously occupied by a church was considered an "unlucky" one. But Hudson believed that commerce would advance uptown in Detroit, and he wasn't in the least superstitious. His new store was so attractive and its values so enticing that people came. When it did falter, neither poor location nor ill omens had anything to do with its troubles. It was the

Depression of 1893, the second in his business career that Hudson had to weather in order to save his new full-line department store. Hard times were to come, for Joseph had gone heavily into debt building his store, but, fortunately, the branches he had launched in other cities kept the main Detroit store alive through this difficult period. In 1906 the J. L. Hudson Company, incorporated eleven years before, began improving in sales volume again after thirteen years without a gain. "Growing with Detroit!" was the slogan Hudson adopted at this time, and some say his store grew even faster than the city. Other investments also proved immensely profitable, especially his major interest in the Hudson Motor Car Company, where he served as chairman of the board.

When J. L. Hudson died in 1912 at the age of sixty-six, while on vacation in England, his store had sales of over $3.5 million a year and was already a Detroit institution. He had been one of the great old-time merchants, interested in fine quality, durability, serviceability, and value in his goods but having little feeling for style and fashion, which were not yet prime factors in merchandising. A great philanthropist and humanitarian, he was described as "the most completely unselfish man I have ever known" by one writer. Since he died a bachelor, his four nephews—Oscar, Richard, James, and Joseph Webber—took over control of the company. Oscar, who had started as a cash boy in the store, became president within a few years, and Hudson's surged forward. By this time Henry Ford had initiated his profit-sharing plan and five-dollar-day wage for an eight-hour day, and even more workers poured into Detroit; the migration was greater than that of the Gold Rush of 1849, and within a decade the city's population doubled to over a million. Hudson's volume grew until its sales made it one of the largest department stores in the world.

Hudson's under the Webbers helped launch the Associated Merchandising Corporation, the first major cooperative department store buying office in America (see Chapter 9). The Webbers also bought out their largest competitor, Newcomb & Endicott, which was located next door to the store, and in 1928 erected the huge superstructure with a 25-story tower that is today's downtown Hudson's (excluding the 12-story addition made after World War II). Sales volume was $66 million a year with the coming of the Great Depression and the last of the store's branches had been sold or liquidated. All of Hudson's eggs were in one beautiful basket, and that way it remained until 1954 when the Northland Shopping Center was built.

Up until that time Hudson's had been an anomaly among the nation's retailers. The selfless, publicity-shy Webbers and officials like controller Carlos "Pop" Clark—who, incidentally, first proposed that corporations be allowed deductions on their federal tax returns for contributions to charities and suggested the individual "earned income" provision in the tax law—made Detroit practically a one-store town. Hudson's had almost no competition worth mentioning, and in no other market did one store "own" the retail business so completely. Hudson's delivered over a million packages a year in its fleet of delivery trucks, whose drivers in the course of their duties disarmed robbers, saved children from drowning, helped out in family disputes, and even rescued one woman from her burning house after a DC-3 cargo plane crashed into it. The store had a contract with a local taxi company to take home customers who had become ill while shopping. Hudson's was Detroit, even turning its main show window into a voter registration office one year. From its single downtown emporium the store had sales of over $155 million by the early 1950s.

Only in the early 1950s did Hudson's realize that its future was not in Detroit proper. People were already fleeing from a deteriorating city to the suburbs, as Americans were around the country. Detroit's big three auto makers would abandon Detroit for surrounding towns, leaving little local employment. In 1967 would come Detroit's second major race riot, during which federal troops had to be called in to restore peace. Violent crime got so bad that residents were warned not to walk the streets at night. Though attempts were made to revitalize what the media called "Murder City," most of the quality stores folded their tents and left the town to sleazy retail operations. Many of Hudson's traditionally middle-class and upper-middle class customers fled to the suburbs and didn't venture back to the city to shop.

In the early fifties Hudson's management sensed what the future would bring. At that time it became apparent that with the rapidly growing movement of population to the suburbs Hudson's could no longer be conducted primarily as a downtown store if it wanted to expand—or, indeed, to survive. When a *Detroit News* survey showed that 50 percent of the city's suburbanites didn't shop downtown anymore, Hudson executives toured the country to see what was happening in suburban business development and decided that the completely integrated community shopping center was the answer to its problems. In 1954 the store built what was then the largest shopping center in the country, Northland Center, in northwest Detroit, about 13 miles from downtown. This was to be followed by Eastland Center in 1957 and twelve more suburban department stores around the state over the next twenty years in what has been one of the largest expansion programs ever embarked upon by a major retailer. The 14 suburban stores are all modern in design and feature the new "shop within a store," or boutique, retailing concept for their departments. Their combined space is more than four times the size of the mammoth 2.1 million square feet of the Detroit flagship and their five hundred delivery trucks deliver some 8 million packages a year.

The heirs of the Webber family named Joseph L. Hudson, Jr., a grandson of the founder's brother, as president and chief executive officer of Hudson's in 1961, bringing the family name back to the store. But Hudson's merged with the Dayton Corporation in 1969 to become part of Dayton-Hudson, the ninth largest nonfood retailing chain in America, which includes not only Dayton and Hudson stores, but B. Dalton, number one in hardcover sales among the nation's booksellers. No longer was Hudson's a family-owned operation. Joseph L. Hudson, Jr., who had been the youngest department store president in retailing history at age thirty, became chairman of the board and Edwin G. Roberts, a merchandising expert who had turned Franklin Simon into a profitable operation, came to Detroit as president of the store. Under this partnership (Roberts left Hudson's for the May Company in 1978), Hudson's sales volume continued to grow, and more importantly, its dwindling net earnings, or profits, increased greatly.

Today Hudson's has annual sales of close to half a billion dollars and has consistently ranked as either number one or number two in sales among individual stores—not chains—over the past several years. The sad part of the story is that the grand old flagship store downtown—though it is still the buying and administrative center of Hudson's—dropped from $155 million in sales in 1954 to $70 million in 1976, only 14 percent of the store's overall sales, and is barely a profitable operation anymore. In fact, Hudson's North-land—which Joseph Hudson, Jr., doubled in space and made the single largest store in any suburban shopping center—has in essence become the "downtown" store. But the happy ending is that J. L. Hudson's outlying branch stores, constituting 86 percent of sales, have proved beyond doubt that a major department store can be just as profitable in the suburbs as it was in the city.

1881

Bargains and Brainstorms

WILLIAM FILENE'S SONS COMPANY—*Boston, Massachusetts*

In 1940 the greatest bargain basement crush in history occured when Filene's buyers purchased some four hundred expensive dresses by Coco Chanel, Schiaparelli, and other noted European designers as the Nazis advanced on Paris and shipped them to Filene's famous Automatic Bargain Basement in Boston where they were placed on sale for up to $49. Over fifteen thousand women from as far away as Chicago blitzkrieged the basement that morning, but, fortunately for the feet of all concerned, this particular battle of World War II lasted less than a moment, the originals ripped from the plain pipe racks in under 30 seconds.

Filene's Automatic Bargain Basement has been the scene of many similar stampedes over the years. Bargains in Folies Bergères hip-length silk stockings, negligees, and baby carriages have sent women screaming and charging down the aisles. Men have battered and bruised each other for cut-rate suits, overcoats, robes, and pajamas. Reduced watches from Waltham, Saks Fifth Avenue fur coats, even black mourning hankerchiefs from Ireland—there's no end to the variety of distressed or surplus goods that have gone on sale at Filene's. A 1947 sale that attracted 150,000 bargain hunters featured $1.4 million worth of smoke-damaged goods from Neiman-Marcus, including a $190 black brassiere that sold for $8.95, and Stanley Marcus confides in his *Minding the Store* that Filene's Basement is still the biggest, most consistent buyer of his Dallas store's fashion clearances. No wonder the Automatic Basement has been a favorite of such notables as the Kennedy family and has attracted customers from as far away as Pitcairn Island, where all the descendants of the *Bounty* mutineers used to take pencil tracings of their feet every year and dispatch a sailor to Boston to buy their shoes.

Filene's wasn't the first bargain basement in department store history, but it is surely the most successful—it practically carried the store throughout the Great Depression when sales upstairs were abysmal. Established in 1909, and several years later the scene of a silent movie called *One Flight Down*, the first of many films made in a department store, the Automatic Bargain Basement differs in several respects from most bargain floors in department stores. Under the "automatic" scheme merchandise already bargain priced is automatically reduced 25 percent after 12 selling days, slashed by 25 percent more on items remaining after 18 selling days, and reduced by a further 25 percent after 24 days. Theoretically, all items go to Boston charities after this period, but very little merchandise survives shoppers so long. The Automatic Bargain Basement is operated by a staff completely separate from the upper Filene's store, a staff that has included famous help like John Roosevelt, who began his business career here as a clerk when his father was president. Other stores have tried to imitate the operation, but none has succeeded, for Filene's reputation makes the store the first outlet retailers approach when they have distressed, discontinued, or surplus merchandise.

Filene's reputation extends into many areas of retailing, which isn't surprising for a store that has pioneered in every facet of the field. The store was founded by William Filene, a Prussian immigrant, in Lynn, Massachusetts. Within eight years he had prospered enough there and at other locations to move to Boston, opening a dry goods and woman's clothing store at 10 Winter Street. By 1890 business was so good that Filene relocated to Washington Street, where, though suffering from a heart ailment, he made his store the largest of its kind in Boston. He died in 1901, but he left his business to two sons who were to win as much fame as they did fortune.

Edward Albert Filene, the older son, has been described as the greatest merchandising genius in department store history, and Abraham Lincoln Filene (he later dropped his first name) has been called the greatest management and organization expert retailing has ever known. Certainly both rate statues in any retailing Hall of Fame. The brothers turned their father's clothing store into one of America's finest department stores and in doing so made a great many contributions to both retailing and the larger world to which it belongs.

The Filene brothers' business expanded rapidly with their Automatic Bargain Basement, originally a scheme to dispose of surplus merchandise from the upper store, and soon even the larger store on Washington Street didn't provide room enough for their $5 million operation. The brothers engaged architect and city planner Daniel H. Burnham, who had designed Chicago's 20-story Masonic Building, America's first important skeleton sky scraper, the massive Washington Union Passenger Terminal, and both the Flat Iron Building and Wanamaker store in New York, among a host of famous buildings, to design an entirely new contemporary department store. The imposing building at Washington and Summer streets had eight floors above street level and two below, with an underground connection to the subway system, and its basement was the first large area in a department store to be air-conditioned. The new building opened on September 3, 1912, nearly a quarter of a million people passing through its doors that day. It was so well planned that very few changes have had to be made in it since then.

Both Filene brothers, who at first took turns heading the business, believed that "the store would grow only if it had the right people," and with this in mind organized to cope with future development, recruiting college graduates to work at Filene's and instituting some of the earliest systematic department store training programs. Motion study specialist Frank B. Gilbreth, who won wider if not greater fame in his daughter's book *Cheaper by the Dozen* and was portrayed by Clifton Webb in the film of the same name, was only one of many experts who helped formulate these programs. As a result the store functioned smoothly. Filene's clerks were among the best trained in the country—and the most polite or diplomatic. When a customer's feet were badly mismatched, for example—no one has perfectly matched feet, but some pairs of feet are more mismatched than others—clerks were instructed to say not, "One of your feet is bigger than the other," but, "One of your feet is smaller than the other."

The Filene brothers also realized that "to create contentment in front of the counter, we had first to create contentment behind it," and strove to make their employees a part of the "store family." As early as 1899 employees were rewarded for making useful suggestions, one of the first contests for suggestions awarding $25,000 in prizes. By 1903 the store had a profit-sharing plan; in 1912 the store discount for employees was 20 percent, more than in most stores today; and by the following year there were summer Saturday closings. Filene's famous credit union, initiated by Edward Filene after he saw how effectively such organizations functioned in India while on a trip around the world in 1907, has loaned millions of dollars to employees since its inception and served as the model for dozens of department store credit unions in America. Edward Filene also instituted the remarkable Filene Cooperative Association, an employee organization that amounted to a union within the store and did more for Filene employees than any union could have. When the Wagner Act banned it as a "company union" in 1935, he was sorely disappointed, for it was his not-so-secret wish—to the dismay of many colleagues in the department store sphere—that his employees eventually gain at least partial control of the store!

Filene's was the first store in the country to use cycle billing, ending disorderly monthly accounting operations in department stores, and the first to use the Charge-plate or "charge coin" system of credit buying so common before the introduction of bank and store credit cards. The brothers were also among the pioneers in establishing branch stores in suburban areas, their earliest branch opening at Wellesley, Massachussets, in 1925. (The early branches, like those of many stores, were initially established primarily because small towns often stuck Filene's with a bill for a year's taxes even if the store only presented a single fashion show there.) Both brothers wrote a number of books on various aspects of merchandising as well, and one of them, Edward Filene's *The Model Stock Plan* (1930) has been translated into five languages.

Lincoln Filene's organizing genius in merchandising has as its monuments the Retail Research Association and the Associated Merchandising Corporation, the greatest collective buying group in the department store field. It was under his leadership that these organizations were formed, and he was also responsible for Filene's joining F. & R. Lazarus and other stores to form the Federated Department Stores chain in 1929. The story of these organizations and his contribution to them are covered more fully later, but it should be noted here that Lincoln Filene, the grand old man of retailing, remained as Federated's chairman of the board until his death in 1957, aged ninety-two. During his lifetime Federated donated $300,000 to the Harvard Graduate School of Business Administration to create the Lincoln Filene Professorship of Retailing.

Edward Filene was a less likable, far more complex character than his brother, a man who was entirely devoted to his business and his humanitarian interests and who never married. Gerald Johnson, in *Liberal's Progress*, called him aggressive, complicated, tactless, brilliant, and dictatorial. He was all these things, but one should add inventive, energetic, enthusiastic, and humane to this list of adjectives, which could be extended paragraphs. Edward Filene campaigned for many programs of social betterment: social security, the health insurance that became Blue Cross, low-cost housing, even daylight savings time. He invented the term *consumer education*. In international affairs he was a strong and vocal supporter of the League of Nations, for which he helped invent the Filene-Finlay simultaneous translator that is still used by the United Nations for earphone translations of speeches. Filene's own speeches, often ghostwritten by Lincoln Steffens and other noted authors, were given all over the world and would fill a volume. So omnipresent was he in international affairs that H. G. Wells mentions him in *The World of William Clissold*, and at home he was a well-known supporter of FDR and the New Deal.

Edward Filene became probably the best-known person in department store history outside the business world, but at Filene's his then radical ideas and stubbornness created rebellion in the board room. When he was alone in opposing the plan to form Federated Department Stores—remember that he had wished to have the company pass on to his employees after his death—he was ousted as head of the company, brother Lincoln becoming the actual head of the organization while he stayed on with full emoluments as president. Edward Filene died in Paris of pneumonia in 1937, aged seventy-seven, but is still remembered by the two foundations he established in his lifetime. The wealthy Twentieth Century Fund, which he founded in 1919 with securities worth $5 million at the time, aids research and public education on economic questions, while the Edward A. Filene Good Will Fund's objective is to foster the idea of cooperative trading, an idea considered heresy by the department store industry.

Another talented Filene's executive—and there have been scores of them—was Louis Kirstein, who became a partner in the firm. Kirstein, a colorful, dapper man, was active in both merchandising and publicity until his death in 1942. His aphorisms (e.g., "We need more individuality and less straining to be all things to all men") are still quoted in business publications. He always contended that it was wasteful to advertise during holiday seasons such as Christmastime because customers crowded into the store at those times anyway.

Filene's has remained a rich source for new ideas in retailing up to the present day. Boston's best-known store is also virtually a training school not only of leaders for Filene's—which has sales of over $185 million a year today—but for department stores throughout the country. It has been estimated that "graduates" of Filene's have gone on to head over 60 great department stores, including Abraham & Straus, Garfinckel's, Stern Brothers, and Foley Brothers. Quite a tribute to the two Filenes, both of whom have won places in the Retailing Hall of Fame at the Chicago Merchandise Mart.

1885

"A Public Institution"

MILLER & RHOADS—*Richmond, Virginia*

With a stake of only three thousand dollars Linton O. Miller and Webster S. Rhoads came south from Reading, where they had some department store experience, to found their original Richmond store, a 22 foot × 75 foot space on the first floor of a building at 117 East Broad Street. Webster Rhoads, a dignified, conservative man— no one outside his family ever called him by his first name— respected the reserve of his customers, and even the first little store was laid out in a "wide circle design" so that they "wouldn't be crowded." Mr. Rhoads could carry his concern to extremes. He once told the advertising manager of a local newspaper that a

Miller & Rhoads ad was too good, had drawn in too many people. "Customers are being *jostled* in my store," he complained. But his conservatism was balanced by the aggressive policies of his partner, and between the two men the "One Price for All" dry goods store prospered.

After three years Miller & Rhoads expanded to a two-story store at East Broad Street, in the block now occupied by the concern, and over the next twenty years began adding lines until it became a full-fledged department store, the largest in Richmond, with a volume of over $1 million. The East Broad Street store, enlarged over the two decades, pioneered in such innovations as electric lights, installed the first escalator in a Richmond store, and later (1943) became one of the first large stores in America to be completely air-conditioned.

A statement printed on Miller & Rhoads shopping bags and later on the back of its sales tickets summed up the store's philosophy: "Between the patrons and the management there is more to be desired than mere selling; an abiding friendship is valued far above profit." This effort to be part of the community eventually succeeded, but had its minor setbacks along the way. One customer took advantage of the store's liberal exchange policy by charging an expensive opera cape to her account every year and returning it, "unused," as soon as the opera company left Richmond. This continued until the department head, doubling as a detective, trailed her to the opera one night and complimented her in front of friends on how lovely she looked in her Miller & Rhoads cape. This cape was not returned. Another unhappy experience was Miller & Rhoads "free coffee" policy. Small groups of customers gathered outside the doors before the store opened mornings, and they were allowed into the customers' balcony, where coffee was served. After a while some particularly regular early morning "customers" were noticed and a check established that many of the coffee drinkers worked for rival stores in the neighborhood.

The "public institution" character of Miller & Rhoads was well established by 1924, when the store built its five-story Grace Street base, which, combined with a construction five years earlier, gave the firm the complete block on Sixth Street from Broad to Grace— almost one square city block. Miller & Rhoads's sales volume was now over a thousand times more than the stake with which the partners had launched their business. It had the first beauty shop of any store in Richmond, the first book department, and the first tearoom. The latter became famous throughout the state. At the time the fashion was to furnish department store tearooms in the decor of other lands and periods, and Miller & Rhoads provided an Italian tearoom, an English Room, and a Colonial Room. Only when a lady fell into the pool in the Italian Room were these exotic locales abandoned.

When Webster Rhoads died in 1941—his partner had passed away a quarter of a century before him—Miller & Rhoads was Virginia's largest department store and had been recognized as an established part of the community by the distinguished historian Douglas Southall Freeman. Under Rhoads's son, Webster S. Rhoads, Jr., the store continued to expand in size and tripled its volume to $22 million during the World War II boom years. Many widely known public events take place in the store, including the Book and Author Dinner, begun in 1947 with Edward Weeks, editor of the *Atlantic*, as master of ceremonies. Held in the Tearoom to overflow audiences, this annual fall dinner has introduced to the community such outstanding authors and celebrities as Robert Frost, S. J. Perelman, Cornelia Otis Skinner, Fred Allen, and Bennett Cerf.

Miller & Rhoads's Christmas windows, covering the whole Grace Street block, have been devoted entirely to religious subjects since the 1920s and have become part of the store's tradition. The store's Santa Claus has an even longer history, but in 1945 won nationwide fame when Santa was portrayed for the first time by William C. Strother, a stocky, wiry man who had once been the World's Champion Human Fly (see Chapter Eleven).

Miller & Rhoads has never failed to operate at a profit in any year of its existence. Just before Webster Rhoads, Jr., died in 1967, the store merged with Julius Garfinckel & Company, the old Washington, D.C., department store, and the Garfinckel-owned Brooks Brothers, the nation's oldest men's clothing store, supplier of clothes to America's great and famous since 1818—including the Prince Albert coat and trousers President Lincoln was wearing when he was assassinated, which are now reproduced in bronze on many Lincoln statues. In 1976 Miller & Rhoads ranked seventy-second among American department stores, with $80 million in annual sales for its flagship store and its 20 branches in Virginia and North Carolina.

1897

"Barnum of the Boondocks"

HESS'S—*Allentown, Pennsylvania*

From its beginning as a typically conservative nineteenth-century dry goods store, Hess's has become American retailing's "Barnum of the Boondocks," a highly promotional store that is nationally known despite its rather isolated home in the Lehigh Valley. The store was founded by the brothers Charles and Max Hess, German immigrants who came to America when their father died and his widow was left unable to support five children. Charles, the oldest, reached America first and Max, placed in a municipal orphanage when only an infant, joined him in 1877 when he was thirteen years old. After working in various dry goods stores, the brothers opened their own shop in Perth Amboy, New Jersey, in 1889. Seven years later, while he was attending a volunteer fireman's convention in Pennsylvania, Max spotted a location in Allentown on Hamilton Street that he thought was ideal for a branch operation, and in 1897 the Hesses opened there in what had been the storeroom of the Grand Central Hotel.

Business in Allentown proved so good that by the end of the year the brothers sold their Perth Amboy store to concentrate on the branch operation, and by 1902 they had bought the five-story hotel and remodeled it into a department store. Max Hess introduced policies that still guide Hess's today—treating all customers alike, calling all in his employ "coworkers," and having only one marked price for merchandise. The patriarch's leadership was so instrumental to the store's success that when he died in 1922 Hess's floundered for the next decade under the control of various relatives. Then in 1933, the remarkable Max Hess, Jr. took charge. "He added an aura of excitement all his own," says one store executive who worked with Hess. "He had the urge to do things as big as possible. He understood that people wanted to be entertained and invited constantly." Hess was a great showman who sponsored high-wire acts, held a sleeping marathon in a display window, and parachuted Santa Claus into the Allentown fairgrounds to entertain a crowd of twelve thousand children. Another of his ideas was the Hess "Fashion Caravan," which later became the subject of a motion picture. This traveling fashion show in specially designed trucks was only one of the innovations that increased the store's volume over twenty times. In an effort to dissuade shoppers from taking the train to the big department stores in Philadelphia and New York, Max even went so far as to hold fashion shows on trains departing from Allentown.

Max Hess was more an original than any of the designer creations he sold. Refusing an office of his own, he camped at the desks of other executives, spending most of his days roaming his store searching for ideas. Max had two stories added to the old store, and air-conditioned and remodeled it. It was his idea to line the pillars, walls, and staircases with mirrors that reflect and multiply some two hundred glittering silver chandeliers and over a million dollars worth of art works and antiques—all of them for sale, though few customers can afford to buy them. Hess gave his solidly middle-class customers the glamour that they wanted. What difference did it make if they bought relatively few of the designer originals sprinkled through all the ready-to-wear department; shoppers came to see the $1000 to $10,000 haute couture creations, had a good time, and bought the ready-to-wear! Hess's was the first store in America to sell the Rudy Gernreich's topless bathing suit—a great promotional come-on even though only twelve suits sold; and Madame Schiaparelli of Paris personally supervised her first American showing of lingerie at Hess's. One-of-a-kind toys from Europe at up to $5000 could be found in the Hess toy department. About the only Max Hess promotion that didn't work was "the perfume of the week" gambit; Hess rigged the entryways to dispense whiffs of intoxicating perfume as customers entered, but had to dispense with the dispensers when the store began smelling like a perfume factory.

Why Max Hess left the department store business is something of a mystery; one story says he genuinely feared a major social revolution in the turbulent sixties, when there seemed to be utopians and assassins lurking around every corner. In any event, on retiring in 1967, he sold the store for $16 million to a consortium of Hess's executives headed by an outsider, millionaire Philip Berman, who had made his money in trucking. Three odd conditions of the sale were that $4 million be paid in cash, that Hess could keep one of the store's Cadillac limousines, and that he be allowed to buy suits wholesale at Hess's—but he never had much of a chance to enjoy any of these bonuses, as he died four months later when only fifty-seven. Berman, the store's major stockholder, raised more working capital through a public offering of stock and continued along the same promotional course charted by the founder's son. A noted art collector in his own right, he has kept Hess's elegantly decorated with art objects and retained the policy of sprinkling expensive high-fashion items through the store's departments, for he believes that "people would rather buy a $50 dress in a store that carried $1000 dresses than at one that shows nothing higher than $50 dresses."

Amid the store's Tiffany setting, the Barnum-like Hess promotional stunts continue. Not long ago, Hess's offered to sell a one-ounce wafer of gold at a 20 percent discount to the first 50 shoppers in the store; first in line was a man from Staten Island, New York, who had camped outside for eighteen hours only to lose first place in a race to the gold with a fleet-footed woman. Hess's Heritage Days spotlighting various ethnic groups have added exotic excitement to the store. No matter that blacks, Hispanics, and other minority groups are scarce in the Lehigh Valley. To get Filipinos for Filipino Week, for instance, Hess's contacted the Philippine embassy and arranged to pay the transportation for people who had to be bused in from all over the East.

Though the Hess's scene seems less Tiffany-like than ostentatious and garish to some, the great majority of middle-income shoppers in this Pennsylvania Dutch country relish the excitement created by the store, perhaps mainly because it is so unlike the area and lends a little glamour to their lives. "Fantasy is a backdrop for realistic prices customers can afford," Berman says in defending his policy of mixing thrift with a touch of mink. "Hess's is the stage, the Civic Theater for downtown Allentown," adds another store executive. "It's the entertainment center of this country." Hess's doesn't do too badly with out-of-towners either, he could add, for every week at least 20 chartered busloads of eager customers roll into Allentown from as far as 120 miles away.

Philip Berman describes himself as an "impresario," and indeed he is, as were Max Hess and many other department store heads before him. He came into the retailing field with impressive credentials, known not only as a successful businessman and discerning art collector but as a humanitarian who has participated in various missions through the world for the United States and the United Nations. Though he had to learn the department store business from the bargain basement up, he did not blindly follow the path blazed by Max Hess. Not only did he improve upon the ways his predecessor lured customers into the store, he created more stores as well. Max Hess had refused to open branches because he wouldn't change his eccentric management style to suit the demands of a chain department store. Berman realized that Hess's future lay in expansion into new locations and began branching out soon after buying the store. Today there are Hess's in Bethlehem, Allentown, Easton, Whitehall, Quakertown, Capital City, and Dickson City, Pennsylvania, the units in Easton and Allentown located in shopping centers owned by the store. Additionally, Hess's operates the Lancaster Square Factory Outlets, where it sells seconds and closeouts, and a Mary Sachs woman's fashion apparel specialty store in Harrisburg. Expansion has brought annual sales up from $42 million when Berman took over to over $95 million in 1976, sixteenth among independent American department stores, a figure that is certain to increase with the completion of stores to be built in Stroudsburg and Williamsport.

1897

"Organize . . . Harmonize . . . Advertize . . ."

THE EMPORIUM—*San Francisco, California*

The Emporium is actually one of the oldest stores on the Pacific Coast, for it can claim ancestry dating back to gold rush days through an earlier store, the Golden Rule Bazaar, that the Davis Brothers had founded on Kearny Street in 1850. The Golden Rule became one of the leading San Francisco stores during the Gay Nineties and in 1897 its proprietors bought out the Emporium nearby on Market Street, naming this new concern "The Emporium and The Golden Rule Bazaar." The Emporium, erected only a year before, had used only the first two floors for selling, renting out its three remaining floors to the Supreme Court of California. It was a poorly run establishment in which all the departments were leased to vendors, and when the new management took control, it quickly ended this arrangement, making the store profitable and eventually shortening its name back to the Emporium. Its success was indicated by the store slogan: "ORGA-NIZE . . . SYSTEMATIZE . . . CAPITALIZE . . . ECONOMIZE . . . HARMONIZE . . . ADVERTIZE . . ."

The old Emporium was built before the invention of concrete foundations, and during Christmas or other big sales only a limited number of customers were admitted at a time because it was feared that the flooring would collapse under too great a strain. Naturally, the building didn't survive the great earthquake of 1906 that leveled downtown San Francisco. After the earthquake the store was able to remain in business only because of the honesty of its customers, almost all of whom paid their bills, even though it was common knowledge that the firm's accounts payable records had been destroyed in the earthquake and fire. Amazingly enough, the façade of the building remained standing unscathed after the earthquake, and within two years a new Emporium was built behind it. But in the meantime the firm conducted business at the corner of Van Ness and Post streets in the home of one of its stockholders, where the bathroom served as the main office!

The new seven-story store, which is still the Emporium's flagship, was a beautiful structure complete with mahogany fixtures and a glass arcade, the building topped with a magnificent dome almost 50 percent greater in circumference than the dome in the San Francisco City Hall. A grand stairway swept majestically up from the first floor to the wide galleries above, and a glass enclosed roof garden was open to visitors all year. Back in its old restored quarters the Emporium did a thriving business and became renowned enough nationally for Lincoln Filene to invite it to become a founding member of the Retail Research Association in 1916, after which it joined the Associated Merchandising Corporation, an offshoot of the association whose members saved money buying merchandise for their stores in mass quantities. Expansion of the San Francisco store continued, and in 1927 the Emporium purchased Oakland's H. C. Capwell Company, one of northern California's largest stores, becoming the Emporium-Capwell Company. Both stores operated under their own names, and there was no branch store development until 1952 when the Emporium opened a suburban store at Stonestown.

Today the Emporium-Capwell Company is part of the Carter Hawley Hale Stores, Inc., department store chain, which also operates the stores under their own names. The Emporium has 11 department stores in northern California while Capwell has five, though both stores are planning more units in the near future. The Emporium held twenty-fourth place among American stores in 1976 with sales of $225 million and its distinctive *E* is one of the best-known department store trademarks.

1896

A Small Town Department Store

COINER'S DEPARTMENT STORE, INC.—*Berryville, Virginia*

Coiner's is included here because it is as good an example as any of the many little nondescript stores around the country that *haven't* grown much over the years, yet still call themselves department stores. Judging by the wide range of merchandise it carries, this would have to be true of Coiner's, for men's, women's and children's clothing, piece goods, toys, giftwear, furniture, appliances, and floor coverings are all available in the store. Founded by E. G. Coiner in 1896 and operated by him for 50 years, when it was purchased by the present owner, C. A. Hobart, Coiner's serves an area about 20 miles around in all directions in a North Virginia county with a population of about 8,000. Except for delivery by van, little is found here of the services of a big city department store, and the store's physical appearance, as Mr. Hobart advises and a visit shows, hasn't changed much over the last eighty-two years except for the kinds of merchandise crowded on the floor inside. Yet Mr. Hobart says, "In the thirty-one years I have been operating this business we have never had a year that we didn't operate in the black." Some will object to this homespun, relatively minuscule operation being included among all these great giant stores, yet Coiner's is perhaps a grand emporium in another way. At least let's hear two cheers for the things that never change.

1902

Main Street Merchant

J. C. PENNEY COMPANY—*Kemmerer, Wyoming*

He called his first tiny store the Golden Rule, having pledged to do business by the Biblical injunction, "Therefore all things whatsoever ye would that men should do to you, do ye even so to them," that his Baptist preacher father had lived by before him. James Cash Penney had at the time been in "dry goods" for eight years, since he was nineteen, first clerking in the J. M. Hale & Brothers Hamilton, Missouri, general store for $2.27 a month, and had come West (like David May before him), on the orders of his doctor, who warned that he'd become a consumptive if he didn't move to a drier climate. It was with the partial backing of two men he briefly worked for in Colorado that he and his wife opened the Golden Rule Kemmerer store and ran it on a cash basis, believing that it was "immoral" to extend or receive credit.

"My wife worked in the store side by side with me as much of the time as she could," Penney recalled in later years, "wrapping the baby in a blanket and putting him down for naps under the counter while she waited on customers." Their industry and economizing— the young couple had nothing but packing crates for furniture in their attic-apartment above the store—made the Golden Rule a big success in the little town of coal miners and sheepherders. No doubt Penney's altruistic attitude toward his customers helped, too. As the founder once noted:

Whereas the company stores of the mining company treated their customers rather callously, in our store people were quick to notice a different atmosphere, which made them feel welcome and appreciated. They realized that we sold goods at just one price and gave good values. These were people who took the saving of so much as a penny seriously. To save pennies for them we had to save them for ourselves. We threw away no wrapping paper, no short ends of string, no empty boxes, no nails, even though they were bent, because we could straighten them out and use them over again."

Within five years, hard work and the Golden Rule philosophy (which Montgomery Ward had espoused before him) enabled Penney to buy out his silent partners, and by 1913 there were 36 Golden Rule stores, incorporated that year as the J. C. Penney Company. Penney had hit upon what now seems a relatively simple strategy. Let every store manager open a new store and have a quarter of its profits as soon as he has proved himself in his first store and has trained someone to succeed himself. On this foundation one of America's top three chains began to grow, supported by a set of principles that the merchant called "the Penney Idea":

J. C. Penney's business philosophy has been explained in many ways, but never better than in the short citation *Fortune* magazine wrote on his election to the Hall of Fame for Business Leadership in 1976, Penney and A. T. Stewart being the only two retailers elected to this prestigious body. Observing that like most highly successful business leaders Penney got intense joy and ethical satisfaction as well as financial rewards from his career, the magazine noted:

The key event in James Penney's childhood wasn't the time—at age eight—that his father told him he must thenceforth buy his own clothes. Nor was it his father's command two years later that Jim should sell, in a slow market, the smelly pigs he was raising to pay for the clothes. Both these traumas were overshadowed by the awful day when his father was expelled from the Primitive Baptist Church near Hamilton, Missouri, which he served devotedly for twenty years as an unpaid lay preacher while making his living at farming. One of the father's heresies: a conviction that preachers should be paid. Young Penney's lifelong indignation at this injustice determined his position in a theological controversy that has always seethed beneath the surface of Christianity. Some think of religion as above and beyond the concerns of daily life; Penney's religion was intimately bound up with daily life, including business. He developed an organizational

Adopted 1913

◄1►

To serve the public, as nearly as we can, to its
complete satisfaction.

◄2►

To expect for the service we render a fair
remuneration and not all the profit the
traffic will bear.

◄3►

To do all in our power to pack the customer's
dollar full of value, quality and satisfaction.

◄4►

To continue to train ourselves and our
associates so that the service we
give will be more and more intelligently
performed.

◄5►

To improve constantly the human factor in our
business.

◄6►

To reward men and women in our organization
through participation in what the
business produces.

◄7►

To test our every policy, method and act in
this wise: "Does it square with what is right
and just?"

structure into which he could channel his moral passion to help other people. . . . In later years, Penney was much prouder of the people the system produced than of its fabulous commercial success. He loved to be known as "the man with a thousand partners." Before the 1929 crash, Penney was worth $40 million. By 1932 he was insolvent, mainly because he had borrowed on his stock to support philanthropies. Neither his partners nor his faith deserted him. He remained a leader and a power in the company. When he died at ninety-five he had $35 million and the love of thousands his system had helped.

But J. C. Penney wasn't an intense evangelical type. He always had a sense of humor and could appreciate a joke on himself; once, in fact, he wrote an article for *Printers' Ink* telling how as a young salesman in the J. M. Hale & Brothers store he had tried to sell a nursing corset to a young unmarried girl because he didn't bother to read the label on a box he pulled down from the shelf. He was also a frugal man, and some of his strict economies seem humorous today, too, though unintentionally so. One time, for example, he instructed a convention of Penney executives meeting in New York to save money by sleeping seven in a room, three to a double bed and two men each in two three-quarter beds specially added to every room by the hotel. All the executives—several future millionaires among them—complied with the order, no matter what their width.

By 1924, J. C. Penney's had acquired its five hundredth store—the same J. M. Hale & Brothers store that the founder had clerked in for $2.27 a month. Most of these stores were little ones on the main streets of small western communities, catering to a rural blue-collar trade, and their managers were given wide berth in running them. Sometimes the results were amusing, as is indicated by a story told by the former manager of a Penney store in Nampa, Idaho, a tale that, intentionally or not, isn't in the Penney archives:

One year business got a little slow, So I took a piece of plywood, drilled about 50 inch-and-a-half holes in it, randomly numbered them either 10, 20, 30 or 40 percent, nailed mason jar rings to the bottoms, and screwed pint jars into them. The idea was that when a person had something figured out that he wanted to buy, he'd bring it to the mouse board and I'd let out this little mouse and whatever hole the mouse would run down, that is how much discount the person would get. Now the trick is this: a mouse won't go into a hole where no mouse has been, so by taking a few mouse turds and dropping them down the 10 percent holes and say one turd down one of the 40 percent holes, I could provide a little excitement for the customers and a little for myself, as long as I only marked up the goods 15 or 20 percent.

In at least one case, a Penney manager acted as a talent scout. One of America's greatest comedians and mimes, Red Skelton, was discovered at a J. C. Penney's, where he worked after school every day ripping open wooden packing crates. The store manager told the proprietor of a medicine show, "We've got the funniest kid here you've ever seen," and the ten-year-old shortly began his career in show business.

For many years all Penney's stores carried the name J. C. Penney against a yellow panel, but, like Woolworth's red-front stores, this trademark was abandoned as the firm grew in national stature. Traditionally, the chain has done the bulk of its business in men's, women's, and children's clothing, shoes, and men's work clothes, but this hasn't been the case since Penney's introduced full-line department stores in 1962. There are now automatic markdowns at all Penney stores similar to those in Filene's famous Automatic Bargain Basement, though no special areas are reserved for them as in the Boston department store. Legend has it that J. C. Penney himself began the store policy of testing the products it sells when he tested fabric samples with soap and water in his hotel rooms while on buying trips across the country. Testing is now a far more scientific process done at the firm's New York City headquarters in modern laboratories equipped with such odd machines as a Fadeometer (to test for color fastness) and a Perspirometer (to test the effects of perspiration on a garment). The labs even raise their own moths to test moth-resistant fabrics.

J. C. Penney, as would be expected, was one of the first stores to fight the antichain movement that developed in America during the 1920s and claims a large share of credit for defeating the federal legislation that would have destroyed all chain operations. The store's founder led in this battle along with President Earl Sams, who began his career as a company clerk, but Penney became less active in management decisions in his later years. Nevertheless, even when well into his nineties the founding father continued to work a full day. Touring the country, he visited Penney stores and lectured to Rotary Clubs and other organizations on the promise of America. This last was appropriate for a man who is said to have achieved everything he wanted in life except living until one hundred; and he didn't miss that by much, either, dying in 1971 at the age of ninety-five.

The J. C. Penney company was in effect "turned around" in 1958 when the famed "Batten memorandum" issued by then chief executive William Batten, now chairman of the New York Stock Exchange, laid out Penney's first restructuring since it became a retailing power. Soon after, a smooth-running credit operation replaced the store's antiquated cash-only policy and its profitable mail-order catalog business was started from scratch. Penney's also abandoned its practice of paying executives no more than $10,000 a year—a policy that had forced many executives to borrow against the substantial year-end bonuses they were invariably given. Most important the company at this time radically altered its tradition of small soft goods stores by beginning the building of nearly 400 full-line department store units in regional shopping centers that presently yield two-thirds of total sales.

J. C. Penney today employs over 368,000 people—including part-time workers, who constitute 40 percent of all store employees. The company still operates its first "Golden Rule" store in Kemmerer, but now has 3,166 stores—more than any other department store chain, including its 1,442 mail-order catalog units and its 37 The Treasury discount stores. The firm also owns the Thrift-Drug Company, with 271 drug stores; Supermarkets Interstate, which operates 17 supermarkets in Penney's and other stores; and the Great American Reserve Insurance Company. Overseas it operates the 78-store Belgium-based Sarma chain and 5 stores in Italy.

Penney's is presently vying with Montgomery Ward for second place to Sears in mail-order sales, but even with over $9.3 billion in sales in 1977 it was replaced by K mart as the nation's number two retailing chain, and clearly has some catching up to do. Tomorrow's growth, according to Penney's chairman Donald V. Seibert, will come from more new stores and "higher fashion apparel and home furnishings." Whether Penney's which still sells most to the "over-forty housewife" can capture more of a share of the twenty-plus age group that spends the most on fashion items is an interesting question retailers would like to know the answer to. No mass-merchandising chain has ever been able to trade up and break into this market while retaining its traditional customers, but then no chain as powerful as Penney's has ever tried.

V

For the Mass with Class: The High-Fashion or Specialty Department Stores

"If somebody needs something, he doesn't belong here," says Bijan Pakzad, an Iranian who recently opened a store on Rodeo Drive in Beverly Hills, California, that world capital of conspicuous consumption. "If a man comes in and asks for a size 16½ white shirt, he just doesn't belong. But if a man comes in and says 'I'm throwing out 24 white shirts and I'd like to replace them,' then that's my customer."

Mr. Pakzad, whose store boasts a $400,000 brass and glass staircase and about a million dollars worth of expensive fixtures in all, operates on a street lined with one of the richest concentrations of posh emporiums in the world, 60 stores with names well-known to the rich, including Gucci, Hermes, Céline, Bilari, Omega, Ted Lapidus, Battaglia, Saint-Germain, Pierre Deux, Bally, Fred Joaillier, Courrèges, Mille Chemistes, and Lothars of Paris. On this ficus-lined street several stores average up to $1,000 sales per square foot, thanks mainly to media stars who tax their brains trying to figure out what kind of shirt goes with a $2,000 velvet and diamond necktie, American princesses who shop without asking prices, and petro-rich princes, who give their wives $200,000 pin money for Saturday shopping. But Pakzad's words come close to expressing what has long been the unspoken philosophy of grand emporiums ranging from those lining Rome's stylish Via Condotto and Paris's discreet Rue du Faubourg-St. Honoré to those on Manhattan's exciting Fifth Avenue.

For generations America's fabulous luxury or specialty department stores, from Henri Bendel to Neiman-Marcus, and their Tutankhamenian counterparts the world over have been called "the department stores of the rich." Technically, many of these specialty stores aren't true department stores—they don't usually offer a wide enough variety of goods for one thing—but the line between both has grown thin in recent times and has often faded away. Specialty stores are becoming more like department stores and department stores more like specialty stores. Many department stores, for example, have gourmet food sections that rival Houston's Jamail's, generally conceded to be "The Neiman-Marcus of grocery stores," and Zabar's, a favorite of New York's glitterati.

It's no secret that the American department store *is* changing. Many stores have found that they can no longer be all things to all people and are redefining their role, often focusing on the younger, more style-conscious customer. The trend toward specialization is an obvious development, since in the coming decade families headed by younger persons, twenty-five-to-forty-year-olds, will be the dominant consumer buyer groups in America. One result has been the "boutiqueizing" of many stores, which seems to appeal to most but has numerous detractors.

In a recent *New York Times* column John Leonard summarized the minority viewpoint better than anyone else has. "Admittedly, the man hated to shop," he said, writing of himself in the third person, "But if one had to shop, he approved of department stores, where the wares of the world were sensibly organized under one roof. He considered department stores, in fact, to be one of American culture's several triumphs, right up there with plumbing and free public libraries. Bloomingdale's, however, is not a department store. It may once have been ... but it has long since been Bendelized: that is, converted into a fen of boutiques. Boutiques specialize in using up so much of our time that there's not enough left over for what really counts in life, like love and work and professional football. If we are blank, we go to a boutique, whose purpose is ornamental. If we are defined, we go to a department store, whose purpose is convenience. Ornament is a way of purchasing someone else's definition. Ornamented, we are not our own names: we are someone else's labels."

More and more of us do grow less and less "defined" every year, and this is certainly an underlying psychological reason for the popularity of "the fen of boutiques" Leonard describes. But boutiques are more a practical retailing strategy to widen the traditional department store's eroding customer base, to bring back shoppers lured away by specialty stores like Bendel's and The Gap, to mention just two widely disparate fashion stores. On the other hand, specialty department stores can frequently be called true department stores. Many that started as women's specialty stores, for example, have broadened their lines and now feature men's clothing, among other departments.

Other stores seem to be walking a middle line, often off-balance and wavering, ready to fall. The truth is that precise definitions aren't possible at this unsettled time in the history of retailing. It used to be that a store had to sell home furnishings to qualify as a true department store, but many stores have given up marginally profitable lines such as furniture and large appliances. Department stores are really going through a period of transition now and will require a new definition by the end of the century—one that will include the influence of both specialty stores and the supermarket— like the discount department stores such as K mart discussed in the next chapter. Nevertheless, they have proved viable so far, and it is probably safe to predict that most will still offer the fantastic variety of goods, fabulous service, and fantasy fulfillment for which they are so famous throughout the world.

In her novel *Scruples* Judith Krantz creates the Beverly Hills specialty shop Scruples, catering to the wildest fantasies of the wealthy, a haven for what she calls "gratification junkies." Her creation is hardly fictorial, for such stores are all around us today, sometimes as munchkins among the giant chain stores, sometimes chains themselves. Elegant quarters, elegant merchandise, elegant prices, and customers aspiring to elegance are hallmarks of the great specialty stores and specialty department stores. They have an even longer history than true department stores, and the stores briefly examined here are among the oldest and most famous of them. Many others could be added (some writers would list Bloomingdale's and Filene's as specialty department stores rather than as true department stores as I have), but enough are covered to give a good idea of their history and operations. For still more examples see Chapter 14.

1766

America's Oldest Specialty Store— and Only Store-College

GLADDING'S—*Providence, Rhode Island*

Gladding's makes Brooks Brothers—founded in 1818 and the oldest men's apparel store in America—seem like a youngster. But Gladding's isn't just the oldest women's specialty store in the country—it is also the only self-sufficient American store that is a retailing college. Gladding's can be traced back to early 1766, when a *Providence Gazette* advertisement told of the opening of a dry goods store by Benjamin and Edward Thurber "at the sign of the Grapes." Grapes have been the store's trademark ever since, being retained when the Gladding family became involved with the store in 1805, the year that George W. Gladding and Matthew Watson bought it from the Thurbers.

The Gladding family took the store over entirely twenty years later and changed its name to the George W. Gladding Company. Establishing a reputation as the city's finest women's specialty store, Gladding's was once called "the Bonwit Teller of Providence" and remained family-owned until 1968, when it was purchased by the New England Mica Company. But increasing deficits caused the company to close the downtown store in 1973 and three years later it was purchased by Johnson & Wales College, a retailing and fashion merchandising school in Providence. Johnson & Wales converted the upper floors of the five-story building into classrooms and retained the street floor level as space for its unique retailing laboratory/store. Located on Westminster Mall in the heart of the shopping district the store is open to the public daily from 10 A.M. to 5:30 P.M. and until 9:00 P.M. on Thursday evenings. It remains a fine specialty store and has actually spurred sluggish downtown trade since it reopened.

Gladding's is operated entirely by students; all Johnson & Wales sophomores are required to spend an eleven-week trimester in the store, where they put classroom retailing theory into practice. These interns receive and mark incoming merchandise, and learn about comparison shopping, unit control, banking, and, of course, selling. Each student also gets an opportunity to work with a display professional in preparing both window and interior displays throughout the store. Additionally, the internship includes visits to New England area manufacturers and a buying trip to New York, where students learn how to buy, how to write orders, and how a buying office operates. Students are tested on every aspect of their training, which is much more comprehensive and structured than programs in schools that simply place students with outside retailing firms for work experience.

1825

A New York Institution

ARNOLD CONSTABLE & COMPANY—
New York, New York

Like America's first Merchant Prince, A. T. Stewart, Aaron Arnold emigrated from Great Britain to New York, where he founded a small dry goods store on Pine Street, making Arnold Constable—up until its failure a few years ago—the department store with the oldest lineage in the city. Wrote an early store chronicler of the first days:

> They were times of comparative simplicity. Water was obtained at the public pump. Light was supplied by whale oil lamps . . . gas was explosive and people distrusted it. There were no postmen. Mail had to be called for at the post office on Nassau Street. Store windows were shuttered by heavy wooden blinds held in place by iron bars which were taken down when the store was opened in the morning. . . . The getting of merchandise to stock or replenish a store was a slow difficult process, since stage coaches and early vessels were the only modes of transporting freight.

Not more than 180,000 people lived in New York when Aaron Arnold went into business with his nephew George Arnold Hearn, but by the time he parted company with Hearn and took the high-powered salesman James Mansell Constable as a partner in 1842, New York's great increase in population had already inspired some merchants to move farther uptown. Arnold Constable's most important early move came in 1857, when the partners built a beautiful five-story white marble dry goods palace called the Marble House, which is still standing at Canal, Howard, and Mercer streets. During the inflation of the early 1860s, this store became one of the first in the country to render monthly accounts of credit to its customers, its monthly charge bills replacing those that had been sent out every six months. Long an emporium known for its quality merchandise, Arnold Constable quickly outgrew its Marble House and built a cast-iron emporium on Broadway and Nineteenth Street in 1869, still another early Constable building that stands as a landmark today. The "Palace of Trade," as the newspapers called it, was expanded in 1877, a year after the founder died, aged eighty-two, but the new Fifth Avenue façade was not done in the white marble that old Aaron Arnold considered the only material elegant enough for a prosperous emporium.

Arnold Constable was widely departmentalized by the 1880s, long before it built its famous store in 1914 on the site of the old Vanderbilt mansion on Fifth Avenue between Thirty-ninth and Fortieth streets. A century after its founding the venerable store joined with Stewart & Company and came under the presidency of Isaac Liberman, head of that specialty house. Beginning in 1937 with a New Rochelle, New York, store, Liberman went on to build Arnold Constable branches in Hempstead and Manhasset on Long Island, as well as in several New Jersey locations. Only in 1975 did the store succumb to financial problems and close its doors after 150 years in New York, although the firm maintains Manhattan offices for the several boutiques that it still operates in the city.

1826

A Pioneer Fashion Leader

LORD & TAYLOR—*New York, New York*

One of the rules in Samuel Lord and George Washington Taylor's piece goods store was that any article purchased for more than

a dollar should be wrapped in "fancy" store paper—"very accept-
able to housewives for shelving purposes"—while items that cost
less than a dollar had to be wrapped in plain newspaper. Such
frugal measures certainly aren't associated with today's Lord &
Taylor, which has established a reputation as one of the most
fashionable stores in America, but they were to be expected of a
man of Samuel Lord's background.

Samuel Lord, the youngest of nine children who were orphaned
before he turned six years old, had worked in an English iron
foundry since childhood. When he was twenty-one, he married the
owner's daughter and emigrated to America, where he opened his
dry goods store in Catherine Street on the Bowery and eventually
took his wife's cousin, George Washington Taylor, into partnership
with him. Taylor retired and went back to England in 1852, but
Lord stayed on to expand his business, changing his location several
times before he too returned to his native land eight years later.

The early Lord & Taylor buildings were among the most original
and attractive of their day, the store built on the corner of Grand
and Chrystie streets in 1853 being one of the first in the city to use a
large glass-domed central rotunda to light the inside, while the still-
standing building on Grand Street and Broadway is an imposing
five-story palace built of white marble. It was this store that armed
employees barricaded with cases of merchandise and successfully
defended against looting mobs during the Civil War Draft Riots of
1863. Yet none of the early stores compared with the magnificent
cast-iron palace built as Lord & Taylor's home in 1872 (see Chapter
3), a "French Second Empire extravaganza" whose novel steam
elevator carried ten thousand shoppers up and down during the first
three days of business.

Lord & Taylor moved to its present granite and limestone
building on the Thirty-ninth Street corner of Fifth Avenue in 1914.
The store claims many merchandising "firsts": the first electrical
Christmas display; the first quick lunch counter for busy shoppers;
and the first shops catering to short women, teenagers, and college
students. Its executives have ranked among the most progressive in
department store history. Walter Hoving, president from 1936 to
1945, typified them, and under his leadership Lord & Taylor
became one of the most attractive, stylish stores in the world.
Hoving, very much a man of the city and Fifth Avenue, was once

elected Mayor of New York in a *Daily News* poll and founded the USO during World War II. In the heat of the great sales-tax battle of 1943, Mayor Fiorello La Guardia called him "that floorwalker," and Hoving replied, "Yes, and he is 'the little flower' in my buttonhole." Hoving now heads the Hoving Corporation fashion chain, which also owns the legendary Tiffany's jewelry store, founded by Charles Lewis Tiffany in 1837. It was the late William T. Lusk of Tiffany's, not Hoving, who was asked by President Eisenhower whether the president of the United States was entitled to a discount and replied laconically, "We didn't give a discount to Mr. Lincoln." Tiffany's rivals include Cartier, and old firms such as Barthman Jewelers on New York's Broadway and Maiden Lane, in front of which is the only clock inside a sidewalk in America, a clock covered by one-inch-thick plate glass that millions have trod over since 1899.

Dorothy Shaver, who served as president of Lord & Taylor after Hoving until her untimely death in 1959, linked creative art with merchandising, and made the store a fashion leader that pioneered in promoting American designers at a time when the fashion conscious had eyes only for French labels and stores often cut the labels of American designers out of clothes. As one of the first women presidents of a major department store she was often called "America's first lady of retailing."

Today Lord & Taylor, now part of the Associated Dry Goods Corporation chain, is headed by forty-seven-year-old chairman Joseph E. Brooks. Formerly of Filene's, he's one of the highest-paid retailing executives with a salary of $250,000. He plans to recover ground lost by the store since Miss Shaver's death, a period that has seen such stores as Bloomingdale's and the boutiques taking a large chunk of Lord & Taylor's market and a time in which Lord & Taylor lost heavily in the 1970 midiskirt fiasco, when so many women refused to wear the long dresses fashion had foisted upon them.

Lord & Taylor annually presents its Lord & Taylor's Rose Award to "an outstanding individual whose creative mind has brought new beauty and deeper understanding to our lives." Past winners of the award, which is given at a dinner dance in the store's enclosed roof garden include Albert Einstein, Ralph Bunche, Margaret Chase Smith, and Lillian Hellman.

Lord & Taylor spent an estimated $5 million renovating its New York store's main floor in 1977, furnishing it with 65 mirrored columns, travertine marble floors and showcases, and a virtual jungle of green plants. There has been some criticism of all the glittering mirrors spoiling the dignity and graciousness of the floor for the sake of trendiness, but the store is still a very pleasant place in which to shop. The management hopes that the renovation will help "bring uptown downtown" to the Thirty-ninth Street location and greatly improve Lord & Taylor's estimated sales of $51 million. Similar renovations are planned for the store's 22 branches around the country, which brought in an estimated $220 million in sales in 1975. The store's livelier image will feature the promotion of high-fashion merchandise at lower prices, merchandise that appeals "to a mass with class." Retained will be such features as Lord & Taylor's festive Christmas windows, created until 1978 by the late Emil Blasling, which have been seen by millions of people each year and have won a number of visual merchandising awards.

1861

The World's Most Unusual Store

GUMP'S—San Francisco, California

Although Gump's is world famous as a dealer in Orientalia, the store can be included here because it does have many departments, including a fashion salon offering clothes from American designers and imports of Europe and the Orient.

A mecca for lovers of fine art and merchandise, Gump's was founded by Solomon Gump, during California's roaring gold-rush days, at first providing mirrors for San Francisco's ubiquitous saloons and picture frames and gilded cornices for the mansions of the newly rich.

Solomon Gump's son A. Livingston Gump rebuilt the store after it was destroyed in the 1906 San Francisco earthquake, moving it from Market and Second streets to its present location on Post Street. He greatly expanded Gump's, importing many art objects from the Far East. An extraordinary man who was nearly blind for the greater part of his life, A.L. could determine the value of a jade carving by touch and knew the location of every item in his store. To show off the riches in his grand emporium, he imported skilled artisans from China and Japan to construct a series of oriental rooms that are unlike those in any other American store.

Richard Gump, A. L.'s son, broadened the scope of the luxurious store still more, adding the arts and crafts of many unexplored regions, and his book *Good Taste Costs No More* provided Gump's with its familiar slogan. Under him Gump's became widely known as "the world's most unusual store," its buyers combing the globe for things of beauty that range in price from $5 to $5,000 and more. Gump's agents still travel far off the beaten path, from Malaga to Mindanao, from Bergen to Bora-Bora, searching for the unusual. It's said that one time a Gump's buyer waited ten months in Peking just to obtain a pair of rare bowls from the Imperial Palace.

In 1969 the Gump family sold out to Macmillan, Inc., the publishing firm then known as Crowell, Collier & Macmillan. No member of the family is currently involved in the operation, which is run by Executive Director Chris Stritzinger, but the store remains a "must-see" for tourists in San Francisco. Its three treasure-laden floors feature oriental antiques, an art gallery, a contemporary gift department, a fashion salon, a stationery department, a custom lamp studio, and charming rooms featuring expensive furniture, crystal glass, china, jewels, and silver. Perhaps most intriguing is the Jade Room on the third floor where pieces of jade are displayed such as kings of Asia waged wars and ravaged cities to obtain. On the same floor is the only object in the store not for sale, a towering Buddha in the Tibetan style as serene and strikingly impressive as this lovely store itself.

1865

A Stylish Store That's a Charity

B. ALTMAN & COMPANY—*New York, New York*

Since Benjamin Altman's father operated a millinery store on Scranton Street as early as 1853, Altman's history might be traced back to that date. But Benjamin probably founded his own dry goods concern twelve years later, and the store seems to accept

1865 as its founding date. Benjamin had clerked in Newark's remarkable Bettlebeck & Company dry goods store along with Abraham Abraham and Lyman Bloomingdale before opening his first shop on Third Avenue between Eighth and Ninth streets. His brother Morris left the business in 1872, and another early partner, David Frankenberg, was bought out in 1886. By the latter date B. Altman & Company was doing business in a spectacular six-story Palace of Trade opened ten years previously at Sixth Avenue and Nineteenth Street, a stylish store with solid mahogany woodwork and an "elegantly carpeted and upholstered elevator," according to a newspaper of the day. The first department store on Sixth Avenue made deliveries in custom-made wagons with brass side lanterns that were pulled by specially trained matched pairs of "high steppers" kept at Altman's New York stables. Summer auxiliary stables were maintained in Saratoga Springs and the Hamptons just to insure quick deliveries to important customers who vacationed in those posh resorts.

One very important customer was the notorious miser Henrietta ("Hetty") Green, who had a balance of over $31 million in the bank yet was so cheap that her son had to have his leg amputated because he received no medical treatment while she shopped around for a free medical clinic. Hetty, who left an estate of $94 million, was famous for not spending a cent if she didn't have to. She is said to have bought a dress length of fabric at Altman's and found a flaw in the fabric. When she returned it, Benjamin Altman unhesitatingly advised her that his store would gladly replace the fabric or refund her money. This wasn't common business practice at the time, and Hetty was so grateful, the story goes, that she introduced Altman to her bankers and told them that if he ever needed to borrow money, she would guarantee the loan. Though Altman never availed himself of her offer, her promise established him with the financial community.

Constantly searching for new ideas to improve his store, Benjamin Altman was a prodigious worker who scheduled his day so precisely that he often made appointments at odd times like 12:07 or 2:13. In 1888 he made a trip around the world to find new merchandise, establish an office overseas, and add to his already distinguished art collection. His thoroughness can be seen in his account of the trip—an 1100-page diary that records practically everything he did or saw every day without relating a single anecdote or betraying any sense of romance or excitement. Of a camel ride he took, all he could say was that he had "rather a hard seat" and "the cost of the ride was only two shillings."

Though Altman's cast-iron Palace of Trade, which still stands at 627 Sixth Avenue, looked like it "would endure for all time" to one newspaper reporter, the beautiful building with its elegant rotunda proved too small for the store's volume of business after about thirty years. Work on a new store at the present location on Fifth Avenue and Thirty-fourth Street began in 1905. Altman had secretly been buying land for the building for ten years, spending almost $8 million in all for the site, but he didn't live to see his grand vision of "a magnificent whole city block of a store," dying in 1913 shortly before the erection of the 12-story building on Fifth Avenue that completed B. Altman's occupation of the entire block.

Altman left an estate of over $50 million when he died. A bachelor with no family, he bequeathed his renowned art collection to the Metropolitan Museum of Art, a collection in which the Rembrandts alone were worth over $2.3 million at the time. As another memorial he left his $20 million stock in B. Altman & Company to the Altman Foundation, which he had created before his death to "benefit charitable or educational institutions within the state of New York." Thus the foundation owns Altman's today, and millions of dollars in profits over the past fifty years have been used for philanthropic purposes.

On Benjamin Altman's death his friend and relation Michael Friedsam (Altman's mother was born Cecilia Friedsam) became the store's president. In its early years as a department store, Altman's experienced some trouble, all of it minor. One buyer, abroad, for example, tried to surmount the difficulties of price fluctuations in 1917 by investing in foreign currency—unfortunately he chose Russian rubles in the year of the Russian Revolution.

Altman's weathered the depression years under the leadership of John S. Burke, who succeeded Colonel Friedsam on his death in 1931. (It is interesting to note that Colonel Friedsam, like Altman before him and James Hearn before him, left his $10 million art collection to the Metropolitan. The museum owes a large debt of gratitude to New York department store owners.) Mr. Burke more than anyone else molded the modern Altman's. Many new facilities were added, unusual departments such as the Fireplace Shop were opened, and Altman's established the first of its five branches, in Manhasset, Long Island. Oddly enough, its White Plains, New York, store is located on Bloomingdale Road; this never bothered Altman's however, and the store refused to go along with its neighbor Saks Fifth Avenue in trying to have the street name changed.

Mr. Burke established excellent relations with his vendors, once throwing a Waldorf dinner dance for Wamsutta Mills at which the bill of fare was printed on Wamsutta sheet fabric. His reign saw the face lifting of the Fifth Avenue store; in 1935 the building's cracked limestone cornices were beginning to fall to the street and some 5 thousand tons of stone had to be cut away, eventually becoming part of the fill for the West Side Highway.

On his death in 1962, the noted philanthropist John S. Burke was succeeded by his son John S. Burke, Jr., who is now Altman's chairman of the board. Altman's remains a New York City landmark. The store is one of the few places in town that still has a private power plant and has proved a good place to be for many New Yorkers during the city's all-too common blackouts. Another interesting feature is Altman's American flag, first exhibited in 1898, a 100-foot x 65-foot giant with 45 stars. It is second in size only to the J. L. Hudson department store American flag, the largest flag in the world. The flag, which covered almost all of Altman's Fifth Avenue front, was last used in 1945.

B. Altman & Company, with estimated annual sales of $180 million, remains an independent store, having refused a number of merger offers, but there are strong rumors that Chicago's Marshall Field is trying to take it over. Altman's has protested that it is not up for grabs. Just as Field protests the same to Carter Hawley Hale, the chain that has been trying to buy its independence!

1876

The First Store Founded by a Woman

I. MAGNIN—*San Francisco, California*

Mary Ann Magnin, mother of eight, was not, as you might guess from her large brood, a retiring Victorian type who attended kitchen, church, and children. Born in Holland, she had emigrated to America with her English husband Isaac in the early 1870s and headed straight for booming San Francisco with its *nouveau riche* population. Mary Ann was a take-charge lady very much in love with her dreamer of a husband and very fearful that the skilled woodcarver and layer of gold leaf might be hurt at his trade. When Isaac went to work for Gump's, the famous dealers in Orientalia, and his employers put him to work gilding a church ceiling, Mary Ann did some fast thinking. "You'll break your neck yet," she told her husband. "Stay off that scaffold and I'll show you how we'll make do."

Mrs. Magnin did better than "make do"; she became the first woman to found a major American department store. When Isaac came down to earth, she told him her plans for opening a small workshop in their home to make exquisite lingerie for the fashion-starved ladies of Nob Hill. Isaac grumbled, but agreed, and within the week Mary Ann was sewing "nightgowns, chemise, and drawers," adding bridal gowns and baby clothes to her line in a short time. She ordered lace and linen from Europe for her fashions, and since the merchandise came to her in ships around The Horn, her creations were very expensive. But her work was very good as well, and the carriage trade lined up at her door. By 1880 she was able to open a downtown store, which she lovingly named I. Magnin after Isaac, and as she moved from shop to larger shop over the years her exclusive clientele moved with her.

At the turn of the century, Mrs. Magnin's four sons began entering the business. John, Grover, and Sam were to be associated with the store for the rest of their lives, but Joseph, something of a "black sheep," out of necessity founded his own store (see the entry following). Mary Ann had instructed her sons in every facet of the business from childhood, often playing a game with them in which she put between their fingers different types of fine lace that they had to identify by touch. But though they were well prepared for their careers and built the shop into the great specialty store it is today, she inspected the premises every afternoon at three o'clock during her "gradual retirement," even when she was confined to a wheelchair. Her retirement only came in 1943, the last year that the store was family owned—when she died at the age of ninety-five. Mary Ann's motto, "When customers make a purchase, they want something more than a 'thank you,' " still remains store policy, along with son Grover's postscript to his mother's preachment: "Nothing is forgotten as quickly as price, if you back it up with quality and style."

The 1906 earthquake leveled I. Magnin's along with the rest of downtown San Francisco, and the Magnin family found itself keeping store at home again, completely broke until a $50,000 loan without interest from I. W. Hellman, president of Wells Fargo, enabled them to rebuild. Fortunately, the city's reconstruction brought in thousands of workers, whose fantastic wages allowed them to buy luxurious goods at extravagant prices. Magnin's prospered, as it has every year since, except 1932, and moved to attractive quarters downtown at Grant and Geary. Three years later, in 1912, the firm established its first branch in Santa Barbara's exclusive Potter Hotel, eventually opening branches in six posh hotels around the state. E. John Magnin served as president of the company, and he was the only head of a Pacific Coast retail chain who permanently resided in New York City—where he had moved, perhaps to escape the matriarchal domination of Mary Ann.

E. John Magnin discovered some of the great design talents of the century—including Jeane Lanvin, Louise Boularges, Philip Mangone, and Hattie Carnegie—and was the ultimate arbiter of what the "Magnin Woman" should wear. His brother Grover had complete responsibility for the Coast store and became head of the company when John died in 1944. Grover, like many department store magnates, was an esteemed art collector—so devoted to his Renoirs and van Goghs that he never permitted a meal to be cooked in his penthouse apartment in the St. Francis Hotel (which now rents for $1,000 a day), "sending out" for meals from posh restaurants because he was afraid kitchen fumes would damage his paintings. This fastidious man hired America's best architects to design the Magnin stores, which tended to be located wherever the wealthy congregated on the West Coast. The exteriors are of white marble accented by polished black granite—the smooth marble façade chosen, it is said, because Grover didn't want pigeons sullying his storefronts. Inside his two favorite stores—the Los Angeles Wilshire Boulevard store opened in 1939, and the Magnin flagship opened on San Francisco's Union Square in 1948—Grover personally designed the great crystal chandeliers and the display cases of gold bronze, and selected the imported pink beige Rose de Brignoles marble for the walls, as well as the delicately colored draperies, carpets, and furniture. These stores, with their high, silvered ceilings ornamented by sculptured bas-relief motifs, are among the most elegant in America.

In such lovely settings the Magnin Woman over the years purchased the best of everything, from $500 nighties to $5,000 Balenciaga or Dior dresses. Price has never been an object in this bastion of the white-glove, inherited wealth set. One customer orders $25,000 worth of Norells every year *over the phone* and another flies into San Francisco every Christmas to buy about $45,000 worth of clothes. Perhaps the most incredible customer is the lady who visited Magnin's some years ago and had the buyer of fine apparel take her measurements so that in the future every sequined evening gown of Norell's could be sent to her by mail. The buyer complied with her request, of course, and for three years received effusive thank you notes from the lady, but then she suddenly stopped writing. He continued sending her the sequined gowns and her checks always came in the return mail, but he had no idea whether or not she liked his selections. Many years later he bumped into the woman at a dinner party in her hometown and he had the answer. She had put on weight since they had first met and found it much less painful to pay thousands of dollars for the Norells every year than to admit that she was two sizes larger.

I. Magnin's was purchased by Bullock's in 1944, which in turn was bought in 1964 by the great Federated Department Stores chain. No Magnins are in the business anymore, and though the store remains probably the most expensive, fashionable clothing emporium in the West, a liveried doorman still greeting limousines at the door, it is trying to expand its operation and attract a new breed of woman in addition to its wealthy mainstays. A sign of the change was the closing of I. Magnin's exclusive made-to-order salon in the Los Angeles Wiltshire Boulevard store. After attracting no more than 35 customers for dresses that cost as much as $5,000 in recent years, Stella Hanania, or Miss Stella as she is called, retired in 1976, and her haute couture salon closed permanently. This really marked the passing of an era, as it was the last to go of the haute couture design operations in America's high-fashion stores, including those in Saks, Bergdorf Goodman, and Neiman-Marcus.

"People used to feel they needed a pedigree to walk into Magnin's," says the store's president Norman Wechsler. "Let's face it. We're not Bloomingdale's. Bloomingdale's has a greater hold on what they call today's generation than we do. That's what we're trying to build now. That's the future." Fine apparel will still be a mainstay of I. Magnin's, as will fashion firsts—like next year's bathing suits a year before any other store has them—but so will the contemporary and the moderate in designer sportswear and other merchandise. The innovations seem to be working and the store's 22 branches, in virtually every large city on the West Coast and in Chicago and Phoenix as well, are prospering, with sales estimated at about $140 million last year. Insiders say that Magnin's is already planning expansion into the Midwest and other areas of the country.

1890

A Store Built on a Love Affair

JOSEPH MAGNIN—San Francisco, California

In all likelihood Joseph Magnin's is the only department store built on the foundation of a love affair. The Joseph Magnin Company in San Francisco has no connection today with the more renowned, more pricey I. Magnin of the same city, but it is included here because the two stores do spring from the same roots, Joseph Magnin having been the son of Isaac and Mary Ann Magnin, who founded the older I. Magnin store. Joseph, though well trained in the family business, was apparently from the very beginning more devoted to sowing his wild oats than any of his seven siblings, for his grandson, Jerry Magnin, tells the following story about him:

I once heard grandfather, when he was in his eighties, reminiscing to his doctor about working in the Market Street store. The old gentleman smiled and said, "Oh, yes, I remember, there were always a lot of pretty women around there, and the Magnins always loved pretty women. I guess I was bound to get in trouble sooner or later. There was just too much temptation. We made a good many costume dresses then for girls in the Barbary Coast district. Well, one day, my father asked me to deliver a C.O.D. package. When I got to the address, two women in negligees answered the door and asked if I'd like to come in. Well, next thing I knew I was in bed between the two of them and really having a heck of a time. Finally, when I had to leave, I reminded my new found friends that the delivery was C.O.D. They ran me out of that house fast. I didn't have the money to pay my father, and I knew he'd skin me alive. Fortunately, I told my story to a tailor who owned a shop on our block, and he loaned me the cash. But it took two and a half years before I'd saved enough to pay him back for those dresses."

Joseph had more romantic troubles years later when he fell in love with an I. Magnin millinery worker. Too enamoured to pay any heed to the strict company rule forbidding family members from fraternizing with female workers, he broke with the store, married the young lady, and founded his own Joseph Magnin Company store.

For years the store that love built attracted customers who couldn't quite manage I. Magnin's prices, and after World War II Joseph's son, the dynamic Cyril Magnin, directly competed with the older store for the younger woman's market on the West Coast, growing to many branches. The company, which handled the buying of Lynda Bird Johnson's trousseau in 1967, was sold to the Hawaiian-based Ampac, Inc., conglomerate (Liberty House) in 1969 for $30 million, but its 51 stores still bear the Magnin name. Sales at Joseph Magnin were over $83 million in 1976, the flagship Magnin store near Union Square remodeled that year to maintain its attractiveness as a fashion center, as was the Century City store in Los Angeles. "Mr. San Francisco," seventy-eight-year-old Cyril Magnin, still serves as Magnin's chairman of the board. Cyril, incidentally, played a pope in the recent movie *Foul Play*, leading local newspapers to dub him "the first Jewish Pope." Before taking the role, he insisted on consulting the Catholic hierarchy in San Francisco, who thought it was an excellent idea.

1890

Elegance on Fifth Avenue

HENRI BENDEL, INC.—*New York, New York*

Over the years Henri Bendel customers have included some of the most elegant women in America, from New York's Four Hundred to actresses like Geraldine Farrar, who had her own private fitting room in the store. The exclusive fashion house began on East Ninth Street as a fashionable hat store that founder Henri Bendel had gradually expanded to include exclusive dresses, furs, cosmetics, and perfumes by the time he began moving uptown like other farsighted merchants of his day.

After a move to 520 Fifth Avenue, where he introduced ready-to-wear women's clothing to his lines, Bendel opened his present store at 10 West Fifty-seventh Street, then a fashionable residential area. By visiting European salons regularly and bringing back the latest creations of famous Parisian couturiers to be duplicated here for his customers, he attracted a discriminating clientele and became an arbiter of fashion. The founder owed his success mainly to his unerring sense of what women wanted to wear, though he was a hard worker known to participate in all store operations, from decorating windows to wrapping packages with the distinctive brown-and-white striped paper he had designed for Bendel's.

Like most successful stores Bendel's changed with the times, retaining its characteristic cachet of high fashion and personal service while extending its appeal from the carriage trade to a wider range of affluent customers. By the 1950s Bendel's had annual sales of over $5 million. New departments were added and seasonal branches at Palm Beach and Southampton, Long Island, were established even before the giant General Shoe Corporation conglomerate purchased the store in 1957, the year after it bought Bonwit Teller. Under Genesco, Inc., as the Nashville-based parent company is known today, Bendel's progress continued, much of the store's success in recent years due to Jerry Stutz, who became president when Genesco took over. Miss Stutz, one of the smartest fashion experts of her day, had been a model at Marshall Field and on the editorial staff of *Glamour* magazine before coming to Genesco. Under her, Bendel's initiated a wide-ranging program of modernization, including everything from redesigning old departments and opening new ones to completely air-conditioning the old store. Bendel's is now known as one of the two or three poshest stores in New York—"a little jewel box of a store" one writer calls it—and its window displays are renowned in retailing,

1895

Fine Apparel, Past, Present, and Future
BONWIT TELLER—*New York, New York*

Ever since Paul J. Bonwit founded his first store at Sixth Avenue and Eighteenth Street, Bonwit's has been a specialty shop devoted to fine apparel for women. Mr. Bonwit didn't trade long at his first store, however. Taking Edmund D. Teller as a partner in 1897, he moved what was now Bonwit Teller to a new location at Twenty-third Street east of Sixth Avenue. After incorporating in 1907, the thriving concern continued its progress uptown, first moving to a store on the corner of Fifth Avenue and Thirty-Eighth Street in 1911, an advertisement announcing this opening reading: "An uncommon display of wearing apparel from foreign and domestic sources has been assembled which will appeal to those who desire the unusual and exclusive at moderate prices."

Bonwit Teller pioneered in the movement of stores uptown when in 1930 it leased its present quarters, then the Stewart and Company building, on the corner of Fifth Avenue and Fifty-sixth Street. This building, on property that was once part of the John Kemp farm, was erected by William Waldorf Astor in 1897 and had at one time housed the Elysée Restaurant, which catered to a very select clientele and was widely known not only in New York but in the capitals of Europe. Remodeled in 1929 for Stewart and Company, its "daringly modern" interior was the talk of New York, consisting as it did of a series of separate salons—each highly individualistic in feeling and with lighting systems to fit their own schemes of decoration. Each salon was the work of a top designer, but Bonwit Teller, however, had its own ideas about interior architecture and merchandising. Feeling that the store was too beautiful and detracted from the merchandise on display, the firm remodeled the sensationally modern decor to suit its own purposes and installed a uniform system of indirect lighting.

Bonwit Teller was sold to the Atlas Corporation in 1934 when Paul Bonwit retired, and Mrs. Hortense Odlum, the wife of Atlas's president, was elected president of the company a year later, thus becoming the first woman to head a major Fifth Avenue store. A very capable executive, Mrs. Odlum introduced the idea of humanizing the business by injecting "the personal feminine touch" into the store's relationship with its customers. She started a custom of holding teas to which patrons were invited to discuss their merchandise needs with her and she made further changes in the decor of Bonwit Teller. It was under her regime that two more floors were added to the building in 1938 and that a start was made on the 12-story addition on the rear Fifty-sixth Street frontage in 1939.

Mrs. Odlum retired in 1940, a year before Bonwit's first full-time branch in White Plains was completed; as early as 1935 the store had a "season branch" in Palm Beach open only four months a year. Expansion continued when the the Hoving Corporation, which also owned the world-famous Tiffany's adjoining Bonwit Teller, bought out the Atlas Corporation in 1946. Several years later the well-known Walter Hoving became the store's president, bringing to Bonwit Teller one of the finest reputations in retailing. In 1947, the store's Boston branch opened in an historic building that formerly housed the Museum of Natural History, and two years later a third branch opened in Chicago.

Bonwit Teller became part of the General Shoe Corporation in 1956, when the company, now Genesco, Inc., acquired a controlling interest in the Hoving Corporation. The store at present has 14 branches across the country, but is still most noted for the New York emporium, which never evolved into a full-line department store but has long been a leader in women's fashions and now sells men's clothing as well. Recently, Bonwit's held a fashion forecast for 2076, in which leading designers like Bill Blass, Victor Joris, Calvin Klein, and Diane von Furstenberg exhibited clothes they believe will be fashionable one hundred years hence. The clothes, not for sale, were later shipped to Bonwit Teller branches for exhibition, but for anyone "dying to have one of the designs,"

Bonwit's will "make an arrangement." Mr. Blass saw the future as "Silver sequin pants with Dr. Denton's feet, topped by a bloating white poncho," while Diane von Furstenberg simply painted a display mannequin in jungle colors—she believes people won't be wearing clothes by 2076, which would be a big disappointment to Bonwit's unless Genesco merges with Dutch Boy.

Genesco, which also owns Bendel's, Whitehouse and Hardy, I. Miller, and other specialty stores, recently dismissed Bonwit's chairman and chief executive officer John Schumacher, whom they had hired away from I. Magnin less than two years before. One of the highest-paid executives in retailing at a $240,000-a-year salary plus benefits of about $100,000, Mr. Schumacher was reportedly ousted because the corporation objected to a lavish $1 million Park Avenue triplex apartment he allegedly renovated and remodeled with store workers and funds. Mr. Schumacher has filed a suit against Genesco denying these charges, and it should be noted that Genesco has had much trouble keeping top executives at Bonwit Teller, at least five chairmen and presidents having left the company over the last seven years for one reason or another. Mr. Schumacher has taken much kidding in the press, including his nomination by *Forbes* magazine as "Decorator of the year (1978)."

1901

Bergdorf's on the Plaza

BERGDORF GOODMAN—*New York, New York*

Not long ago a woman who felt intimidated by Bergdorf's decided to telephone a order rather than face the sales help in person. "When the store operator answered, 'Bergdorf Goodman,' I was ready," she recalls. "I felt very clever and securely smug. In my most cultured tones, I said, 'Stocking department, please.' 'Oh, yes,' the operator replied. 'Hosiery.'"

Bergdorf Goodman has been a synonym for haughty elegance since the early years of this century. The store began as Bergdorf & Voight, a small ladies' tailoring and furriers shop on lower Fifth Avenue, where a young tailor named Edwin Goodman, the son of a traveling salesman who had once operated a small dry goods store, came to work in 1899. Herman Bergdorf, the proprietor, was noted for adapting men's suits to the female figure and notorious for his drinking during business hours at nearby saloons, his devotion to the world of wine far exceeding his interest in the world of commerce. On the other hand, Edwin Goodman couldn't obtain permission from his parents to marry his sweetheart Belle Lowenstein while a "lowly tailor," and so within two years he saved and borrowed enough money to enter into partnership with his wine-imbibing boss, who sorely needed someone to stand in for him at the store while he sniffed, gargled and swallowed rare vintage, at the café across the street. The partnership lasted only two years, for Goodman bought out Bergdorf as soon as he could, the *bon vivant* returning to his native France, where he enjoyed the life of a Parisian boulevardier the rest of his days.

Ironically, Bergdorf's is rarely called Bergdorf Goodman's by customers today, even though it was Edwin Goodman who made the store the fabulous fashion house that it is. In 1914 Edwin moved the store farther up Fifth Avenue, opposite St. Patrick's Cathedral to a site now part of Rockefeller Center. Here he pioneered in fashionable ready-to-wear clothing for women and took his children Ann and Andrew into the business, Andrew having first served an apprenticeship for a year with the famous house of Jean Patou in Paris. His business quickly outgrew the store, and another move was made to the corner of Fifth Avenue and Fifty-eighth Street, across from Central Park and the posh Plaza Hotel, where the first section of Bergdorf's present marble building was erected by 1928. This building was added to over the years until it comprised the entire Fifth Avenue block between Fifty-seventh and Fifty-eighth streets, most of the property leased to other exclusive shops. The Goodman family lived in the 17-room penthouse above the store, and since Bergdorf Goodman's workrooms were considered "factories" and no part of a factory building may be used for residency except by a janitor under New York City law, the store's wealthy and socially prominent founder had to list his occupation as Bergdorf's janitor.

Edwin Goodman's impeccable taste and shrewd style judgment made his concern one of the world's most renowned stores, an elegant emporium that has employed princesses and countesses, including the Grand Duchess Marie of Russia, as salespeople, not to mention leading dress designers like Ethel Frankau. On his death in 1953, his son Andrew became the store's president and he extended the store's appeal by instituting innovations such as the Miss Bergdorf Shop, where quality apparel in the medium price range is sold—medium-priced, that is, for Bergdorf Goodman. The firm, with stores in New York City and White Plains, was purchased by the Carter Hawley Hale Stores chain in 1972 for $11 million, but the founder's son remained as head of the company. Bergdorf's, which is considered by many to be the leading women's specialty store in America but which in recent years has also introduced a men's clothing department, now has sales estimated at over $45 million a year.

In June 1978, Bergdorf's swanky Fifth Avenue store suffered one of the biggest robbery losses in department store history when three masked, white-gloved thieves hid in a supply room until closing time, overpowered the night guard and made off with $400,000 in jewelry from display cases on the street-floor level. The loss was covered by insurance and the next day business went on as usual, with regular customers like Jacqueline Onassis and Barbra Streisand shopping under the crystal chandelier.

1902

Fashion Firsts from Past to Present

SAKS FIFTH AVENUE—*New York, New York*

Need a cashmere sweater lined with chinchilla? A $20,000 game? How about a teddy bear, one that wears a lorgnette and drinks water or Dom Pérignon? Saks has offered them all at one time or another, in addition to a rich and varied selection of fashionable clothes and accessories for the well-to-do and those of more moderate tastes and means. The emphasis on quality in every part of the store's operation has earned it a nationwide reputation, one that was embodied in the expression "Very Saks Fifth Avenue," common for many years as a synonym for anything fine and fashionable.

It all began with a young boy named Andrew Saks, who sold newspapers and then became a peddler in Washington, D.C., after leaving his home in Philadelphia. Andrew Saks saved until he accumulated enough money to open a men's clothing store in Washington. After adding stores in Richmond and Indianapolis, he finally came to New York at the turn of the century. The specialty store he established on Thirty-fourth Street near Herald Square emphasized quality merchandise and expert service even then, attracting his son Horace, who quit his studies at Princeton to join his father in minding the store. Horace Saks assumed the presidency of Saks and Company when his father died in 1912 and over the next decade bought lavishly and expensively, determined to make its name synonymous with fashionable, gracious living. But to capture the wealthy trade essential to his plan, he knew he had to follow the lead of most of the city's wiser retailers and move farther uptown.

One quite literal obstacle presented itself—the New York Democratic Club. This building stood smack in the middle of the site where Saks wanted to build his uptown store. Horace had rented property on both sides of it, but the price Tammany wanted for their building was far beyond his means. At one point he considered building a U-shaped store around the structure, but gave up the idea as impractical and was on the verge of retreating back to Herald Square when Bernard Gimbel entered the picture. He and Bernard, the grandson of Gimbels's founder, had become good friends, for both had large retail stores in Herald Square and the two men spent many evenings together on the commuting train. One evening Saks mentioned his difficulties, and Gimbel proposed a merger between the two stores. As a result the Saks family was finally bought out by Gimbel Brothers, Inc., in 1923 for $8 million in Gimbel stock, with Horace Saks remaining as president of the smaller store. The Thirty-fourth Street store that Saks was going to close was leased to Gimbels, making it the largest department store anywhere in the world at the time, Gimbels met the price of the Democratic Club, and the construction of Horace Saks's dream store on Fifth Avenue began in earnest.

When Saks Fifth Avenue officially opened on September 15, 1924, the Prince of Wales wasn't in the men's department as was falsely rumored, but Mayor Hyland and Jack Dempsey were on hand to make speeches. The show windows displayed items like a $3,000 pigskin trunk, $1,000 raccon coats, chauffeur's livery, and "foot muffs" for automobile trips. To accommodate its rich customers an electric numbering system (no longer in operation) was installed above the Fiftieth Street marquee so that the chauffeurs waiting across the street could be signaled right on time to pick up weary dowagers. Saks accumulated fifty thousand charge account customers by year's end, most of New York's wealthiest families on their list.

Naming the store Saks Fifth Avenue was a stroke of genius, for by combining the name Saks, already famous for quality, with that of the fashionable avenue on which it stands, the store was given a cachet that embodies the character of its business. The quest for quality continued when Adam Long Gimbel assumed the presidency after Horace Saks's untimely death in 1926. Gimbel, who had studied architecture at Yale and had helped in planning the store, retained Horace Saks's basic idea of a series of specialty shops and opened the first Saks branch, at Palm Beach, in the first year of his presidency. This was followed by stores in Chicago, Miami Beach, and Beverly Hills, all of these branches shunning conventional retailing wisdom in that they were located in mainly residential areas rather than in the heart of the city. Gimbel also redecorated the New York store in the image he felt it needed to attract the socially prominent families living on New York's Fifth and Park avenues. The interior was redone in a more lavish and opulent style, with Art Moderne interior furnishings and window displays adopted from the 1925 Paris Exposition.

Adam Gimbel headed Saks until his death in 1969, and he and F. Raymond Johnson, once described as his alter ego, really made the store what it is today. Adam Gimbel liked expensive goods and had an instinctive sense about their reception in the store. Wanting Saks to become known for exclusive, unique merchandise, as well as to be able to sell luxury items in volume, he spent much time traveling throughout the world looking for special things to intrigue Saks customers. Despite criticism, he bought lavishly, not only to establish Saks's reputation, but because beautiful things appealed to him. Two unique shopping services he established during the store's first decade were the Executive Club and the International Shopping Service. The Executive Club, exclusively operated for harried businessmen who couldn't take the time to shop and whose members joined by invitation only, entitled members to turn their annual gift lists over to the store with notations for special birthdays, anniversaries, and the like. The club assumed full responsibility for reminding the gentleman of each date as it arrived, as well as for doing the actual shopping. The International Shopping Service, run by multilingual sales personnel, helped non-English-speaking customers find just what they were looking for in the store.

Saks can also boast the first full-time designer employed exclusively by a major retail store. "Sophie," Adam Gimbel's wife, produced two complete collections three times a year for Saks—one for the ready-to-wear trade throughout the country and the other for the exclusive made-to-order business featured in the Salon Moderne, where society leaders and entertainers often bought their entire season's wardrobe. Over the years, the creations of European designers gave way more and more in the store to the styles created by Sophie Gimbel, who was a legend in her own time when she retired in 1969.

Today Saks Fifth Avenue is headed by chairman of the board Allan Johnson, son of Adam Gimbel's former second-in-command. Though Gimbels, and thus Saks, is now a subsidiary of Brown & Williamson Industries, Inc., and financial data isn't available for publication, it is estimated that all Gimbels units, including the 32 Saks stores, have annual sales of close to a billion dollars, with Saks contributing about $435 million of this. Saks Fifth Avenue remains a suave, urbane store that specializes in the extraordinary and the highbrow, although it has most of the departments found in a department store, excluding furniture for the home. Louis Vuitton luggage, Baccarat crystal, Fauchon foods from Paris, shoes by Ungaro, Revillon furs, Ralph Laurent's clothes for men, the great name boutiques of Dior, Adolfo, Pucci, St. Laurent, Rive Gauche, Chlöe, Bill Blass, Oscar de la Renta, Cerruti—these are only a few of the expensive attractions throughout the store.

One fascinating item offered by Saks that resists overlooking is the new simulation game, Petropolis, created by Baron Arnaud de Rosnay and marketed to 70 top stores throughout the world in 1975. When the baron decided to have his game made in a luxury edition he had Van Cleef & Arpels jewelers outfit it with playing pieces so exquisite that they can be worn as jewels by themselves. All of these pieces, including the derricks and oil rigs, the tanker, refinery, airplane, barrel, gas pump, and dagger, were made in solid 18-karat gold. Three $20,000 "super editions" of the game were offered, and for that price it hardly mattered that the playing board and the Petropolis accessories that come with the lower-priced version were included.

Another interesting Saks promotion was a collaborative effort with the International Design Conference (IDCA) in Aspen, Colorado, the world's leading forum for the exchange of design ideas. In 1976, as part of its bicentennial celebration, Saks invited a number of individual members of the IDCA to collaborate with many of the store's fashion designers on projects in apparel or accessories design. Famous architects, industrial designers, graphic designers, interior designers, psychologists, and environmental planners teamed up with the world's foremost fashion designers to create new fashions. These ranged from the "Creative Couture Kit" of architect Julian Beinart and Florentine designer Giorgio Sant'Angelo—a do-it-yourself fashion design kit including a standard T-square muslin dress, paints, stencils, and studs—to the "Paradox" apparel of psychologist Richard Farson and design luminary Adolfo—clothing that challenges you with questions such as, "Is it a bathing suit or is it lingerie?" All of these "cross-fertilization" creations, some reproduced in these pages, were featured in a Saks's street-floor boutique and displayed in store windows.

Saks's window displays have always been crowd stoppers. In 1976, for example, the store converted the entire bank of its Fifth Avenue windows into one giant glamorous New York apartment. Each window had a certain degree of animation: mechanical marvels such as snow falling, or a jet on its way to Tangier, or a moon rising behind feathery clouds. Inside, on the street floor, one hundred decorated blue spruce trees four to five feet high greeted Saks customers.

Saks spares no expense in its 32 branches, either. Whenever a new branch is opened there is a gala celebration, the ribbon cut by the same pair of gold scissors that have been used for this purpose since the 1930s. One interesting branch feature is the huge mechanical tiger guarding the Hackensack store's children's gallery that winks its eyes and wags its tail. Still another is the great "Madame Pompadour" bathtub with gold-plated "claw feet" in the linen department at the Bal Harbour, Florida store. This store, when opened in 1976, introduced possibly the most extraordinary international collection of display mannequins ever assembled, many especially sculpted by Mary Brosnan, one of New York's most talented sculptors, her creations in the likenesses of some of America's best-known beauties.

Brown & Williamson is said to have earmarked over $100 million dollars for the building of 20 new Saks stores over the next decade and hopes to make the specialty chain itself, which employs 10,000 people, a billion-dollar operation by that time.

1904

Fashion for the Big Beautiful Woman

LANE BRYANT—*New York, New York*

No store founder in America had to overcome more misfortunes than Lena Himmelstein, who established the Lane Bryant chain of specialty shops. Ten days after Lena was born in 1879, her mother died and she was raised by grandparents in her native Lithuania. When she emigrated to America with distant relatives, the sixteen-year-old wasn't told that she had been brought along as a bride for their rather homely son, and upon landing, she refused to marry the young man, staying with a sister instead and taking a job as a seamstress in a sweatshop making "beautiful lingerie for fast women," as she once put it. Lena gave up this life to marry David Bryant, a Brooklyn jeweler who died of tuberculosis soon after their first child was born, his illness consuming all the store's assets and all of their possessions as well, except for a pair of diamond earrings he had given her as a wedding gift.

Pawning the diamond earrings to make a down payment on a sewing machine, Lena moved in with her sister again and began making negligees and tea gowns until she had saved enough to open a tiny shop on upper Fifth Avenue near Mount Morris Park. Though the sign on the shop read "Bridle Shop," thanks to an illiterate signpainter, and the store specialized in bridal gowns, it was Lena's maternity gowns that made her famous. The Empress Eugénie had worn a maternity dress in Europe, but such gowns were unknown in America when on the request of a customer Lena fashioned a tea gown with an accordion-pleated skirt attached to the bodice by an elastic band. This stylish maternity garment attracted so many customers to the store that new quarters had to be erected at 19 West Thirty-eighth Street. The store was called Lane Bryant instead of Lena Bryant because Lena had transposed two letters of her name in the excitement of making out a deposit slip at the bank one day, the deposit having been the $300 her brother-in-law had loaned her to expand the business. Timidity prevented her from correcting the misspelling at first, but she eventually decided she liked the euphonious "Lane Bryant" better than her own name and put it above her store.

Though the diamond earrings saw Lena through rough times at least once more in the early days, her maternity gown eventually made her shop's name a synonym for maternity clothes throughout the world—in later years an envelope from Poland addressed only to "Maternity Dress, size 32, Amerika" actually reached the store. Lane Bryant's rise to the top would have been even quicker if newspapers hadn't prudishly refused all advertising for maternity clothes until 1911, when the *New York Herald* first accepted a Lane Bryant ad and sales doubled within the year. The ad read in part: "It is no longer the fashion nor the practice for expectant mothers to stay in seclusion. Doctors, nurses and psychologists agree that at this time a woman should think and live as normally as possible. To do this, she must go about among other people, she must look like other people. Lane Bryant has originated maternity apparel in which the expectant mother may feel as other women feel because she looks as other women look."

In 1909 Lena Bryant married a second time, this time to Albert Malsin, an engineer who assumed management of the business. Malsin convinced dress manufacturers to make popular-priced maternity dresses for street wear from design patterns and materials Lane Bryant supplied, and he built the store's mail-order catalogue business, which became one of the largest in America. But his major contribution was in making Lane Bryant a pioneer in ready-made clothes for "women of larger proportions," as advertisements put it. By studying insurance company reports and making studies of over 4,500 Lane Bryant customers with a special yardstick he invented that conformed to the angles of the body, engineer Malsin established that some 40 percent of American women required larger sizes than the perfect 36 figure that designers of the day idealized. Lane Bryant pioneered in these larger sizes, later adding clothes for tall women to their line, and this business soon made maternity clothing but a fraction of the store's total sales. In 1916, when the store was incorporated, sales were about $1 million. By the time Malsin died in 1923, "larger size" sales alone were $5 million a year. The store once sponsored a "Chubby Club" for young customers and is still most noted for its "larger sizes for fuller figures," or "fashions for big beautiful women."

After Malsin's death, Harry Liverman, his long-time assistant, who had in his youth served as the mayor of an Australian town, became the store's president. Lena's first son, Raphael Malsin, a Phi Beta Kappa member, succeeded him as president in 1938, when Liverman became chairman of the board. Today the firm is headed by Raphael's younger brother, Arthur, an accomplished architect. Lena Malsin died in 1951, leaving an estate of nearly $2 million in Lane Bryant stock and the diamond earrings that started it all. The firm that she founded now has sales approaching $300 million and operates 175 units throughout the country besides its main store across from the New York Public Library. These include its mail order stores, 20 Town and Country discount department stores, 14 Coward shoe stores and 9 Neiman-Benton stores.

1907

The World's Most Outré Retailer

NEIMAN-MARCUS—*Dallas, Texas*

It would be illogical for Texas not to be home to Neiman-Marcus, as unfair as the fact that Barnum wasn't born within its borders. Neiman-Marcus simply belongs in a land that is America exaggerated, where ranches are as big as republics, where oil wells ornament front lawns and rivers are dyed green on Saint Patrick's Day.

No store anywhere has the outré pizzazz of the Neiman-Marcus emporium with its his/her airplanes and miniature submarines ("the ultimate in togetherness"), its $300 mink slings for ladies with broken arms and its 24-karat-gold hard hats for affluent conservatives. To the opulent list of Christmas catalogue items that the store has featured over the years can be added the following: his and her genuine Greek volcanic craters exported legally from Greece,

$5,000 each; a silver-plated "mouse ranch" with pet mice, $3,500; a silver "gravy train" designed to chug around the dinner table delivering gravy, salt, and pepper, condiments, sugar, and lemon; and a "Saurian Safari," a $29,995 scientific expedition into Utah to search for the remains of *Allocarus,* the giant carnivorous dinosaur that preyed upon its more benign contemporaries. Other Neiman-Marcus catalogue entries in the lavish gift market have included a pair of his/her camels, $16,000; energy-saving his/her windmills, $11,500 (exclusive of installation); Chinese junks; his/her bathtubs like Casanova's; a bejeweled chess set for $165,000; an emerald ring for $150,000; a $150,000 mink coat; a pair of rose colored glasses and a clock that runs backward for the nostalgic person yearning for "the good old days"; diamond-studded pipes; and a catalogue page explaining "how to spend $1,000,000 at Neiman-Marcus" quite easily.

While it's true that such offerings were conceived as a publicity stunt to stimulate sales of the hundreds of items ranging from $10 and up that Neiman-Marcus features in its catalogue, an average of one to twenty of them have been sold every Yuletide—including the camels, junks, bathtubs, chess set, and even $1600 Egyptian mummy cases ... just about everything but items like the store's $800,000 "think tank," its $588,247 Noah's Ark, and the Saurian Safari, which were a bit exorbitant for even oil-rich Texans.

By no means are expensive items limited to the Neiman-Marcus Christmas catalogue, either. The Dallas store is a large, airy emporium designed as a showplace for fashionable, disintinctive merchandise. Texan land and cattle heiress Electra Waggoner Wharton Bailey Gilmore once spent $20,000 in the store and returned the next day to buy $20,000 worth of merchandise she'd forgotten to mark on her shopping list. The famous customer who reportedly purchased six mink coats in the store's fur salon for his wife and five daughters and a $50,000 sable coat for his mistress is a public relations invention, but very real is the mail order customer who has spent more than half a million dollars at Neiman-Marcus over the past ten years without ever visiting the store.

One could echo the Texas cattleman who visited Neiman-Marcus and observed, "In all my time I never saw so many things a body kin get along without as I have here," or Billy Rose's observation that the store gets only a small fraction—"say 6/5ths"—of the value of certain items it sells. But most people realize that spectacular items like $50,000 mink coats and $150,000 necklaces constitute only a small percentage of Neiman-Marcus sales. Obviously no big store could survive offering its customers a steady diet of "whipped cream," and Neiman-Marcus sells far more moderately priced articles for both women and men in all its departments than it does glitter merchandise. There is no denying, however, that style and quality are Neiman-Marcus trademarks and that the store's fantastic offerings spectacularly advertise this fact. The store's ability to promote itself, to make news, accounts largely for its great success.

Neiman-Marcus was founded as a superior fashion store in Dallas by Herbert Marcus, his sister Carrie, and her husband Abraham Lincoln (Al) Neiman. Herbert had quit his job as boys' department buyer for Sanger Brothers when he didn't get the raise he wanted and had migrated to Atlanta with Neiman, a department store sales promoter, to open an advertising agency. This operation proved so successful after two years that the young men were offered a chance to sell out for $25,000 or the equivalent in Coca-Cola stock and the Missouri Coca-Cola franchise. They rejected the latter offer, which could have made them millionaires many times over and went back to Dallas to open their specialty store—leading Stanley Marcus to comment much later in the store's biography that it was "founded on poor business judgment." Neiman, who put up most of the $30,000 capital, was always the financial wizard of the enterprise, while his wife Carrie brought her excellent taste and style judgment to the store and Marcus contributed his considerable merchandising know-how. The store on Elm and Murphy streets that they rented and decorated was an elegant one for a town with 222 saloons serving a population of only eighty-six thousand; the store was stocked with "tailored suits, evening gowns and wraps, furs, dime-costumes, coats, dresses, modish waists, dress and walking skirts, and petticoats and millinery," as initial advertisements put it. From the beginning, the proprietors proudly proclaimed in ads that theirs was the "most elegantly equipped storeroom in the South" and promised that it would be "the policy of Neiman-Marcus ... to give buyers in Texas something out of the commonplace ... exclusive lines which have never been offered to the buyers of Dallas. ..."

Opening day found Carrie Neiman in the hospital recovering

from a miscarriage and Herbert Marcus recuperating from typhoid fever. But despite their absence and the panic of 1907, which affected even oil-rich Texas to some extent, the store sold out its stock in a few weeks and was well on its way to becoming a success. Within several years, with Herbert and Carrie recovered and back at the helm, the firm had added accessories, and children's, infants', and men's wear to their line. The great fire that destroyed the store in 1913 proved only a temporary setback, for a new four-story Neiman-Marcus arose within a year at Main and Ervay, a far more elaborate emporium that cost over $192,000 to build.

One of the manufacturers that Al Neiman persuaded to buy a $10,000 block of stock in Neiman-Marcus to raise money for the new store saw his investment increase to $700,000 before he finally sold out years later. The store grew with the Texas oilfields, supplying the newly rich with everything they wanted. By 1929 the Neiman-Marcus name was known throughout America, the downtown store had been enlarged to twice its original size, and sales were over $3.6 million. At this time, Al and Carrie Neiman were divorced, Carrie remaining with the firm and her former husband selling his interest to Marcus. Herbert Marcus took his four sons—Stanley, Edward, Herbert, Jr., and Lawrence—into the business over the years, but until his death in 1950 he remained active, even after he became blind in later years. "An old Jewish story might very well pertain to him," Stanley Marcus writes in his book about Neiman-Marcus. "It is about a merchant who was very ill, and his four sons gathered at his bedside in filial solicitude. He glanced around at all of them and said, 'I appreciate your interest in the state of my health, but who's minding the store?' "

Stanley Marcus joined the store in 1926 after earning a master's degree in business administration at Harvard. Although he didn't become president of Neiman-Marcus until his father's death, he very early assumed a leading role in the business. "Mr. Stanley" was instrumental in introducing lower-priced merchandise at Neiman-Marcus during depression years, making the store attractive to people of moderate incomes and the "upper masses" as well as the upper classes. He also created a national image for Neiman-Marcus, beginning by placing ads in national fashion magazines, an unusual practice at the time.

It would be hard to find a more colorful figure in retailing today than Stanley Marcus. A hard-driving perfectionist with a great sense of style, and a flair for promotion unmatched anywhere outside a three-ring circus, the bearded Marcus is completely devoted to his store. So furious was he when Neiman-Marcus models and salespeople were charged with acts of moral turpitude in the book *U.S.A. Confidential* (1952) that he sued the authors and publishers on their behalf for $7.5 million. This was the first single libel suit in history that incorporated three charges of damage: damage against individuals, an entire class, and a corporation. In an out-of-court settlement the authors and publishers agreed to pay Neiman-Marcus $10,000, place half-page ads of retraction in newspapers across the country, and write letters of apology to each of the individuals listed as plaintiffs.

Stanley Marcus served as chief of the Clothing Section of the War Production Board during World War II, and his book about Neiman-Marcus, *Minding the Store,* is probably the most delightful history of a department store yet written, but he is also something of a Renaissance man, with many interests outside of retailing. A noted collector of primitive and modern art like his father before him, he is also a typography expert and is active in community and political affairs. As a collector he is rarely fooled, but a great practical joke was played on him one Christmas by business associates. Marcus had a large oil of a standing nude figure, back facing, hanging in his home at the head of a stair landing. His friends commissioned the artist Saul Schary to do a front view of the same nude and hung the picture in the original's place. That Christmas Eve, Stanley Marcus passed by the painting as he went upstairs, but only when he got to his bedroom did he realize that "something was unusual." Making his way back to the painting, he began studying it—"flabbergasted, for I had never heard of a painting turning around"—when his wife and friends burst out laughing.

As much an original as any of the promotions he creates, Stanley Marcus is largely responsible for Neiman-Marcus' modern image as "the world's most fabulous store." Marcus learned early that specialty store retailing "consisted of a mass of minutiae." "You made and kept your customers," he once observed, "by your ability to remember small details; such as anniversary dates or birthdays, a promise to get a certain evening bag for a specific social occasion . . . a promise that the dress bought for a girlfriend would be billed to the Mr., not the Mrs. account. . . . None of this was trivia; it's

Haute Couture Salon in I. Magnin's Los Angeles store, one of the *haute*st" in America.

The exterior and interior of Gump's Market and Second Street store in 1874.

Above: A view of the Modern Gifts department in Gump's beautiful new store.

Right and below: Early interiors of the elegant B. Altman store.

CARRIAGE CHECK
THIRTY-FIFTH ST. ENTRANCE
231
B. ALTMAN & CO.

Left: Chauffeurs waited for their numbers to come on the Altman carriage check to know that Madame had finished shopping.

Below: Saks Fifth Avenue's New York flagship store today.

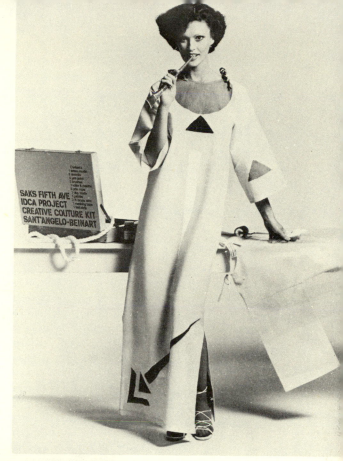

Fascinating Saks Fifth Avenue
offerings created by distinguished
designers in various fields at the
International Design Conference
in Aspen.

Left: A Neiman-Marcus Christmas catalogue cover by noted artist Bjørn Wiiblad.

Below: From the Neiman-Marcus Christmas catalogue, "His and Her Hoverbugs, two passenger crafts that move or hover on a cushion of air six to eight inches off the ground or water, cruising at an average speed of 35-45 mph, depending on the surface. Red or white—$3,640 when first offered.

Above: *Haute couture* salon in Neiman-Marcus' Dallas store. Below: Neiman-Marcus' main floor elevators decorated as the Hall of Mirrors for a "French Fortnight."

A typical Kresge 5 & 10¢ store toward the end of last century, long before the day of K marts.

Interior of a K mart.

Many traditional department stores now have discount operations like this typical Strawbridge & Clothier discount Clover store.

The original Neiman-Marcus store.

what specialty store retailing is all about." With this in mind, he made Neiman-Marcus "the store that can get you anything." Neiman-Marcus has supplied a wig for a stuffed lion after moths had gotten into its mane and an electric blanket for a living pet lion residing in cold climes. Neiman-Marcus once delivered a pair of ducks to a customer by chauffeur and limousine because Railway Express would not deliver livestock. One customer, arrested for drunkenness and disorderly conduct at a football game, was allowed to pay his bail with his Neiman-Marcus credit card. When another customer wanted to send a pair of nylon stockings to Queen Elizabeth for her birthday, the store discreetly found out her size. Only on rare occasions has Neiman-Marcus thrown up its hands in surrender. Nothing could be done for the lady who wrote a "male order" for "a companion—between seventy and seventy-five—who is completely and absolutely finished with sex."

Neiman-Marcus operates on the premise that "if we can please the 5% of our customers who are the most discriminating, we will never have any difficulty in satisfying the other 95% who are less critical." The store's style shows even in its gift wrapping, which was made famous by designers like Alma Shon, a young Korean-American woman whose packages have become nationally imitated. Many customers across the country have ordered widely available items from Neiman-Marcus just to get the gift wrapping. The store reports that when a busy employee accidentally gift wrapped her lunch instead of a luxurious gift and sent it on to a customer, the package was never returned.

The Neiman-Marcus look in clothes was famous back in the days of Carrie Neiman, who was noted for "caliper eyes" that could detect the slightest mistake in a garment. Moira Cullen, another early store buyer with near infallible taste, invented the "step-in" dress when she convinced a manufacturer that women needed a garment they could get into without messing up their hair. Neiman-Marcus style is also reflected in its store restaurant, The Zodiac, "a Balenciaga of food," its Christmas catalogs, whose covers have been done by such eminent artists as Ben Shahn, Robert Indiana, and Ronald Searle, and its store display windows, one of which a Texan oilman bought entire on the promise that the store would reproduce it—plate glass, ermine evening wrap and all—in his playroom along with a large display card reading "Merry Christmas to Mary from Dick."

Stanley Marcus's astute promotion of vicuna coats, made from the wool of the *Lama vicugna* of the Andes, led many people to believe that Neiman-Marcus had invented the precious material, which was prized by the ancient Incas. The store's successful cookbook, *A Taste of Texas,* which has gone through seven editions, was another clever promotion. Various VIPs were advised that Neiman-Marcus was planning a cookbook and would be pleased to have them contribute their favorite recipes. Many did so, but author Paul Gallico replied saying he was "planning to start a store" and would appreciate Neiman-Marcus sending him free "your favorite . . . pieces of merchandise," especially "a fur evening wrap for my wife . . . solid gold cuff links . . . a pair of diamond and sapphire clips . . . and a complete set of Sèvres or Copeland china to serve twelve."

One Neiman-Marcus creative effort that failed was a novelty wristwatch on which the hour numerals were replaced with Chinese characters that spelled out a Chinese adage. The watches were ordered from an American manufacturer soon after trade restrictions on China were lifted—at about the time Stanley Marcus visited the Canton Trade Fair in 1972 with the first group of American merchants to visit the country after President Nixon's historic journey there. Unfortunately, the "Chinese adage" turned out to be the message "We shall take over America by force." The manufacturers claimed that this happened by chance when an assistant randomly cut Chinese characters out of a newspaper and pasted them on the face of the prototype watch, but the store immediately withdrew all the watches from sale.

In the way of ongoing promotions Neiman-Marcus is justly famous for its Fortnights, introduced in the 1950s and inspired by similar shows at Nordiska, Stockholm's leading department store. These are two weeks in the fall of every year when the downtown Dallas flagship store is decorated in the style of another country and merchandise is displayed in this setting. Some 20 countries, from France to the mythical Ruritania, have been portrayed thus far, and the Fortnights have been called one of the outstanding merchandising devices of the postwar era.

Neiman-Marcus remained a family operation until 1968 when it was bought for $40 million by Broadway-Hale, Inc., the Los Angeles chain that later became Carter Hawley Hale Stores, Inc. The chain promised autonomy to Neiman-Marcus, and today Richard Marcus is president of the store, while his father Stanley takes an active role in its operation as executive vice-president of Carter Hawley Hale. About the only stipulation made by the chain in the merger was that Neiman-Marcus build more stores, and now there are nine branches in Dallas, Fort Worth, Houston, Atlanta, Bal Harbour, Saint Louis, and Chicago, with plans on the drawing board for three others in San Francisco, Beverly Hills, and Newport Beach, California. The store also runs the Neiman-Marcus Greenhouse, a luxurious spa in Arlington, Texas, that draws socialites from all over the world, charging them up to $1,000 a week to help them lose weight and get in shape with scientific exercises, the ultimate in beauty products and "500-calorie daily diets that look like banquets."

✑ VI ✑
Everybody Loves a Bargain: From Shlock Shops to Discount Department Stores

The story is told of a writer who tried New York's Lower East Side for some long black socks he needed, the wages of writing being insufficient for shopping regular retail stores. "But don't bother showing me the kind that fall down," he told one merchant. "I've seen enough of those here." "Fall down? Not *my* socks!" the merchant cried indignantly. "Look!" he said, hoisting up his pants legs—but there were the sloppy black socks, bunched up around his ankles. Unabashed, this Filene of the future continued: "These socks don't *fall* down, mister. I had to *push* them down to get them like this!"

From the wit, wisdom, and chutzpah of such inspiring salesmen will surely come the grand emporiums of tomorrow, but these stores will not necessarily be the fashionable ones usually associated with the name. More likely the peddlers and shlock store operators will create giant discount department stores, which are grand emporiums in their own way. Discount department stores are still light years removed from éclat stores like Neiman-Marcus, I. Magnin, Macy's, and Marshall Field, but the discounters have achieved respectability in recent years and are no longer regarded as grubby little shops run by shifty-eyed peddlers behind the Chicago stockyards where they slaughter the cows—an impression frequently fortified if not fostered by traditional department stores over the past few decades. One discounter, K mart, has in fact become the nation's second largest retailer after Sears, with sales of more than $10 billion a year. Successful merchants don't argue with success, and so today more department stores are emulating the discount houses than disparaging them.

Discounters made their first appearance during the Great Depression, when times were hard and price was everything. It was then, in 1937, that Steven Masters borrowed $500 and opened his first Masters discount store in a vacant New York City warehouse, selling radios and other appliances at discount prices and building his little store into a multimillion dollar chain. It wasn't until the postwar years, however, that discount houses came into their own. This was the era when Masters himself told a U.S. Senate subcommittee that discounting was "a revolution in retailing spreading like wildfire through this country." The fire had been sparked by small New England outlet stores like Ann & Hope, founded in Cumberland, Rhode Island, in 1953, that were housed in old mills or warehouses and had little to offer but low-priced irregulars, seconds, and discounted merchandise. These stores, emphasizing hard goods like appliances, stayed open every night and on Sundays— becoming the first in the field to challenge Sunday blue laws, which led to the repeal of these laws by some state legislatures and to today's Sunday openings of traditional department stores like Macy's. They gradually expanded from hard goods to soft goods (merchandise with a short life such as clothes and accessories), took on more and more lines, and prided themselves on being undersold by no one, this last being their only virtue, for their interiors were usually plain pipe racks at best, and almost all were self-service operations where it seemed you got 10 percent off for rudeness and it was hard if not impossible to get your money back.

Spreading out across the country, the discount houses did best in the growing suburbs, where department stores had neglected to include their traditional bargain basements in suburban branches. Suburbanites, of course, both needed and wanted bargains as much as city dwellers did, and the discounters filled this huge retailing void. The physical appearance of the stores improved greatly, and although few became luxuriously appointed emporiums, most were soon clean, well-lighted places quick and easy to shop in. Many became more like department stores. They featured "one-stop shopping," adding leased departments or establishing departments on their own for the convenience of customers. Everything from hot-pretzel vendors outside the stores (some of whom now pay up to $1,000 a month rent for their locations) to beauty parlors and supermarkets inside were added. By the late 1960s, according to one source, nearly 2,500 discount stores could be called "rigidly defined, true full-line discount department stores." Discount stores of all types and sizes probably number close to 10,000 today and account for sales of some $50 billion, though these are no more than rough estimates.

The discounters typically mark up merchandise 30 to 35 percent, compared with the department store's average 45 percent; turn over their stock four times a year, often twice the rate of department stores; and have payroll costs about half those of department stores. Thus a discount house might be defined as "any store which operates on a low-expense, low-markup basis and which emphasizes competitive pricing as a main attraction to win customers," in the words of one retailing consultant. Ironically, however, this definition would encompass many department stores that didn't start out as discount houses. The truth is that discount stores weren't created out of a vacuum during the depression or after World War II. As a business philosophy the low-profit, high-volume approach of discounters is as old as the Industrial Revolution. All of the precedents were there for discount stores. These included frontier western stores like Old Reasonable Abe's and the Square Deal Clothing Room, not to mention the pushcart dealers on Hester and Orchard streets in New York, where anyone who accepted a price without haggling was regarded as some kind of American boob. Then there was Macy's old "save 6% for cash" policy, Gimbels' slogan, "Nobody but nobody undersells Gimbels," and the early discount prices of May's, Alexander's, and many other stores. One discount store critic even traces discount house origins to the earliest native peddlers. "Loss-leader selling," Walter Henry Nelson writes in *The Great Discount Delusion*, "probably goes back to the days of the American pack-peddler who preyed on frontier housewives a hundred or more years ago. Carrying a few brands of merchandise of known quality, he unloaded tons of junk on families too far away from the stores to be able to say no."

Though pack peddlers probably preyed on people no more than

did other merchants in the past, "loss-leader" selling has long been condemned on the grounds that it is deceptive. Supreme Court Justice Louis D. Brandeis had this to say about it in a *Harper's Weekly* article of November 15, 1913: "When a trademarked article is advertised to be sold at less than the standard price, it is generally done to attract persons to the particular store by the offer of an obviously extraordinary bargain. It is a *bait*—called by the dealers a 'leader.' But the cut-price article would more appropriately be termed a 'mis-leader', because ordinarily the very purpose of cut-price is to create a false impression." Yet if discounters don't bait and switch—that is, advertise "loss leaders" and attempt to sell customers other, more expensive products when they come to the store, using the excuse that they are all out of the advertised special—loss-leader selling is perfectly legal. And if consumers bought the genuine loss leaders advertised, and were careful about the rest of the merchandise in a store, they would be well off indeed.

Discounters are also often accused of "cherry-picking" or "creaming"—"selling a great volume of a small selection of high-turnover merchandise," or, as *Fortune* magazine puts it, a policy that "offers consumers little choice and that concentrates only on fast-moving high-profit goods that are constantly in demand by an overwhelming majority of consumers." Discounters reply that they are only giving the public what it wants.

The shadier discounters even have a special jargon of their own. The following is a brief glossary of some common terms:

Borax—cheap goods, especially furniture

Cherry-Picking—selling a great volume of a small selection of high-turnover merchandise

In-and-Outers—goods strategically placed to be bought on impulse on the way in and out of the store

Kickers—merchandise used for loss-leader purposes

Nail-downers—bait goods that are "nailed to the floor"; though they are advertised as loss leaders, salesmen are instructed not to sell these goods, to switch customers on to more profitable products

Putting Them on the Elevator—the practice of switching customers from loss leaders to higher priced goods

Slotting—another name for the above

Spiffs—bonuses paid to salesmen for switching customers from loss
leader merchandise

The discounters of the future may come from the ranks of the
surplus stores, or shlock stores as they're often called. These have
been around for years, at least since the end of World War I, but
something new has been happening to them in recent times. Many
shlock stores now seem to be trading in a gray area between the
surplus and discount store. The more fortunate of them will go on
to become discount store chains, some will remain essentially the
way they are, and others will fall by the wayside. In any case,
shlock store shopping is a pleasure no one should miss. One area
famous for the stores is New York City's Canal Street, where in
emporiums like the City Dump and the P. & A. you never know
what you're going to find for sale.

Shlock, a Yiddish word that derives from the German *schlag,*
"blow," means shoddy, cheaply made articles—merchandise that
has been knocked around, that has received more than one blow in
its time. To be sure, enough shlock goods are available on Canal
Street, but there are also real bargains like bins of brand-name
sneakers for $5.95, Yardley soap for 34 cents, factory-second toilet
paper at four rolls for 69 cents. Even more intriguing are the bins of
books for a dime (rock bottom for an author to be remaindered on
Canal Street for a dime but you *are* out there with people who
never before bought a book), king-sized tank wrenches, twenty-five-
year-old yellowing white shirts with French cuffs, second hand
bowling trophies, and, yes, cardboard boxes filled with thousands
upon thousands of slides and photos—*somebody else's* family
snapshots selling at "25 for $1," and, according to the proprietor,
selling well!

Donald Dayton of the Dayton-Hudson chain has written that the
discounting revolution of today "will end with two successful
operations at opposite ends of the spectrum, the quality, fashion-
right stores at one end, the discounter at the other end and trouble
for the merchant in between." Whether this happens remains to be
seen, but it can't be denied that discounting has had a great impact
on department stores, especially in improving their merchandising.
"Thanks to the discount houses," says one marketing consultant,
"we are coming close to matching mass distribution to mass manufacturing for the first time."

Perhaps the greatest tribute to the discounters is the fact that so many department stores now have discount divisions. Just a short list of these includes Dayton-Hudson's Target and Lehmere stores; Federated Department Stores' Gold Circle, Gold Key, and Gold Triangle stores; May's Venture stores; Rich's Richway stores; Penney's The Treasury stores; Woolworth's Woolco stores; J. H. Newberry's Britt stores; Allied Stores' J. B. Hunter and Almart stores; and Gamble's Tempo-Buckeye stores. Following are the stories of several prominent discounters and how they grew. The proprietors of the first grand emporiums—Marshall Field, John Wanamaker, Grover Magnin—would have let peddlers into their stores before addressing them so, but they are nevertheless called "discount department stores."

1897

America's Second Biggest Retailer—Thus Far

K MART, INC. (formerly S. S. KRESGE COMPANY)—*Troy, Michigan*

This is a story about money pure and simple, no other considerations or pretenses here. There it is: a blue overhead light begins blinking. Customers stop their carts dead in the aisles as the PA system crackles: "Attention, K mart shoppers! In footware for the next ten minutes—and for ten minutes *only*—boys' sneakers will be priced at only $2 instead of $3.97 a pair!" Shoppers immediately begin wheeling down the bare aisles toward the shoe department with all the intensity of drivers at Indianapolis, carts colliding, feet assaulted—maybe this is why K mart has gone into the insurance business in addition to its retailing operation! At any rate, the "blue light special" will flash every hour on the hour all day long, so more "buys" and more collisions are inevitable.

Nothing resembling a boutique in this store or any of the myriad K marts across the land. No decor here, either, unless it is Barren Economical. There are snack bars, and customers can get charge cards, but otherwise these are discount stores pure and simple, each one an identical twin of the other, stores that buy in big lots— recently K mart placed the largest book order in history, two *million* copies of an Elvis Presley biography—and feature REAL

BARGAINS. Critics say that the stores, the hottest thing today in retailing, contribute nothing to the communities they adorn—but REAL BARGAINS *are* their contribution to the community. The three out of four Americans who are reached by K marts aren't complaining, either, and neither is K mart, which has grown rich beyond all dreams of upgrading in helping its mostly working-class customer save a few pennies and live a little higher on the hog civilization.

Thanks to its K marts, S. S. Kresge changed over a period of only 15 years from a diminishing chain of variety stores to the chief rival of Sears Roebuck for the title of America's biggest retailer. The experts say that the store—now named K mart—will reach a saturation point and never surpass Sears, but then the experts never thought K mart would become number two—and number two here translates to over $10 billion in annual sales.

Kresge's or K mart—more later about the name change—has touched about every base in the retailing game since it was founded at the turn of the century. Sebastian S. Kresge entered the dime-store business in 1897 when he took his lifetime savings and bought a half interest with J. G. McCrory, another prominent retailing figure, in a Memphis, Tennessee, dime store. A year passed and the partners opened a second store on Woodward Avenue near Shelby in Detroit, but in 1899 Kresge traded his half of the Memphis store and three thousand dollars for full ownership of the Detroit store, taking a brother-in-law into partnership with him but buying him out eight years later.

Kresge, of course, had the example of Frank Woolworth before him and, in fact, acknowledged his debt to the dime-store pioneer years later when he closed all of his stores for an hour on the day Woolworth died. In any event, he followed Frank Woolworth's example faithfully. By 1917 his firm was incorporated, had 150 dime stores with annual sales of over $12 million, and next to Woolworth's, was the largest variety chain in the world. Kresge had become one of the most successful American merchants and had experimented in almost every phase of retailing, from a mail-order catalogue business carrying only a stock of items selling for a dime or less, to the department store field, which he entered when he bought Chicago's The Fair, a store Kresge's operated along with several branches until Mongomery Ward purchased it in 1957.

When the end of the true dime-store era came (except for Wool-worth's) in 1917, stores everywhere trapped in the World War I inflation, S.S. raised some items to fifteen cents in his stores and then upped others to a quarter. Within four years his so-called Kresge green-front stores, abutting Kresge dime stores and patterned after Woolworth "red fronts," were selling items for from twenty-five cents to a dollar, this marking the birth of the "dollar store" in America.

By the time S. S. Kresge stepped down as president in 1929, retaining his post as chairman of the company, Kresge's had a Canadian subsidiary, a total of almost six hundred stores and annual sales of about $156 million. The firm reached its dollar store peak during the Great Depression, phasing out the green-front division by physically joining their green-front stores and dime stores to make Kresge variety stores, but continued to grow, and by the end of World War II had nearly seven hundred stores. In postwar years Kresge's began converting their variety stores to a checkout counter operation, opened stores in shopping centers, and expanded into the South and West. But the next milestone in its history came with the appointment of Harry B. Cunningham as president in 1959.

Cunningham, a former Harrisburg, Pennsylvania, cub newspaper reporter who had risen from a lowly store manager to the company presidency, gambled $80 million on his beliefs about the modern shopper when in 1962 he built the first Kresge K mart in a Detroit suburb. These Kresge discount department stores were generally based on the premise that grocery supermarket shopping has taught people to *like* self-service, and that a self-service department store chain with discount prices can succeed if quality merchandise is offered rather than the house brands, seconds, and irregulars that most discounters push. In other words, many shoppers don't care if decor is almost nonexistent and the ambience is Bargain-Basement American so long as there are bona fide bargains. Cunningham was right, for enough shoppers "didn't care," making Kresge the number-two retailer in the nation.

By 1966, when founder Kresge died at the grand old age of ninety-nine, Kresge sales had topped the magic billion-dollar mark for the first time in its history, thanks mainly to the K mart, which constituted 162 of their 915 stores. The following year Cunningham became chairman of the board, and over the next decade an average of more than a hundred K marts a year were built in the United States, Canada, Puerto Rico and Australia, Kresge operating in the land down under in partnership with G. J. Coles and Coy Ltd. The company also acquired Schiller Millinery Stores of Detroit, which had operated fashion accessories departments in the United States' K marts, and the Dallas-based Planned Marketing Associates, which designs and mass markets life, accident and health, property, casualty, and other insurance policies.

Harry B. Cunningham retired from Kresge management in 1973, continuing as a director and honorary chairman of the board, with president Robert E. Dewar succeeding him as chairman. In 1975 he was elected Man of the Half Century in a nationwide poll of discount department store merchants. Clearly, the company he molded has hopes of passing Sears in the future. The venture into insurance is evidence of plans to compete with Sears's Allstate and, perhaps not coincidentally, the store's sales goal for 1980 is $12 billion—a figure very close to Sears's annual sales volume at the time the projection was made. The firm is well on its way to its goal, having passed J. C. Penney as the country's number-two retailer in 1977; some 1,700 stores have thus far turned S. S. Kresge's original $8,000 investment into almost $10.1 billion in annual sales. So much of this phenomenal success story is due to the 1,300 economical K marts, which carry fifteen thousand items ranging from cheap underwear to color televisions, that in 1977 the eighty-year-old Kresge's became a relic of the past when the company changed its name to the K mart Corporation, requesting that the name always be printed with "a capital *K*, space, no hyphen and a small 'mart'—K mart," a store that doesn't want to settle for second place to anyone.

1914

"We're Big on People"

FISHER'S BIG WHEEL, INC.—*New Castle, Pennsylvania*

From a modest dry goods store serving the small western Pennsylvania town of New Castle, Fisher Brothers Dry Goods Company first developed into a statewide chain of clothing stores offering economy clothing for the family. Initially, the company frankly "imitated the strategy of J. C. Penney," which at that time was the giant of the industry, carrying the same quality merchandise, price lines and selling at the same markup as Penney. Operating in end-of-town, low-rent locations Fisher prospered until the 1950s, when the discount idea swept the nation. Giant new discount stores, offering the same economy clothing and many more departments than Fisher, became tough competition, and a major corporate decision was made to join an enemy that couldn't be beaten.

In the early 1960s Fisher joined the ranks of the fast-growing discount stores, but there were a number of problems to overcome. Fisher's major mistake was that it attempted to sell high-quality nationally branded clothing in the first large discount department store the company opened in New Brighton, Pennsylvania, while discounting all other goods in the store. Customers didn't understand that the other merchandise was actually discounted when they saw it displayed side by side with branded clothing being sold at full price. The company found it had a definite identification problem with the public. It finally decided to discard the branded soft goods department and develop department stores that sold only discounted merchandise.

Going into the discount store business full force proved an immediate success. Fisher developed its new image to the utmost and communicated it to customers through sophisticated advertising techniques. Checkouts were installed at the front of the stores for all departments, and the names of the discount department stores were changed to Fisher's Big Wheel to distinguish them from the company's remaining traditional clothing stores. The discount department stores were 45,000 square feet in selling area, six times the size of the older stores, and contained over eighty departments featuring clothing, and items for the home, outdoors and auto.

Under the new plan Fisher's sales volume increased from $6 million in 1967 to over $100 million today, which inspired the company to change its name to Fisher's Big Wheel, Inc. The chain, which operates under the slogan, "We're Big on People," has grown to 34 stores in the tri-state area, New York, and New England and 18 to 24 new stores are planned for the next three years as part of an accelerated expansion plan. Fisher's Big Wheels are fast becoming one of the great success stories in the "discounting revolution," whereas only three units are left of the original Fisher's Clothing Stores.

1947

"Those Two from Harrison"

TWO GUYS—*Garfield, New Jersey*

Soon after the Hubschman brothers, Herbert and Sidney, opened their first discount store in an empty 20 foot x 40 foot diner in Harrison, New Jersey, they called it Two Guys from Harrison. The name was suggested by a rival merchant, who discovered that the Hubschmans were underselling him by offering TVs and other appliances for only $5 or so above cost and roundly cursed out "Those two bastards from Harrison." The brothers considered his anger a tribute to their merchandising skills and adopted the name, though they had to launder it with a euphemism, leaving the world to wonder forever whether a store prefixed "Two Bastards" would have succeeded.

"Two Guys" did succeed. Customers wrote out their own orders in the first little store, for there were only six in help, but business boomed. Expanding from hard to soft goods, the brothers added stores throughout New Jersey and then branched out into neighboring states, shortening their corporate name to Two Guys when they closed the original Harrison store. The Hubschmans were innovative merchants, advertising widely and even using buses as mobile showrooms. Tremendous volume made up for their low prices, and service contracts brought in more profits. By 1959 Two Guys was big enough to merge with the O. A. Sutton Appliance Corporation and took the corporate name Vornado after a brand that Sutton manufactured.

The Hubschmans are no longer connected with Vornado—Sidney left the company in 1963 after a policy dispute and Herbert died a year later—but Vornado has become a discounting giant, with overall sales of close to $1 billion, making it the twenty-first largest general merchandising chain in the country, ahead of such giants as Gimbels, Korvettes, and Marshall Field. However, poor earnings forced the company to sell 22 of its West Coast Two Guys stores to the Fed-Mart Corporation in 1978 for $65 million, leaving it with sixty Two Guys stores in the East. Vornado also sold its 59-unit Builders Emporium home improvement center to Wickes Corporation for $70 million in 1978 and began phasing out of its supermarket business.

1948

The Store That Made Discounting Respectable

KORVETTES—*New York, New York*

Eugene Ferkauf, the founder of Korvettes, first named his store E. J. Korvette—the *E* taken from his forename, *J* for his early business associate Joseph Zwillenberg, and *Korvette* after the small World War II Canadian subchasers called Corvettes. The Brooklyn-born and reared Ferkauf, who had worked in his father's luggage shop before serving as a Signal Corps sergeant during the war, and learned the old proverb, "If you're good to a store, it will be good to you," opened his first store in a second floor walkup on Manhattan's East Forty-Sixth Street. With only four thousand dollars capital, part of it borrowed from his father, who also secretly underwrote all his losses, he began by selling luggage at a mere 20 percent markup, half that of the customary profit. Soon he hit upon the idea of selling scarce appliances and jewelry as loss leaders to attract customers to his store, and when he found that the tail was wagging the dog, he concentrated on the appliances and jewelry, selling them at a small profit.

What followed amounts to one of the great success stories in retailing history, "a bags to riches" story as it has been called. Within just two years Ferkauf was doing over $2 million in sales; by 1955 eight Korvettes had sales of $36 million. In 1964 Korvettes, with sales of $622 million, was called "the fastest-growing retailer in the modern history of retailing" by one expert. Ferkauf himself was dubbed "the Duke of Discounting" and was quoted as saying that "all we hope for this company is that it should do all the merchandising business in the United States." The chain now carried all lines, hard and soft, and no one could say it wasn't a true department store. It typically operated stores with about 200,000 square feet of selling space in suburban shopping centers around the country, doing sales of up to $300 a square foot, but it proved that discounters can do business in luxurious settings as well when it opened a unit in the crystal-chandeliered palace where W. & J. Sloane, America's best-known carriage-trade furniture store, had formerly done business there on New York's Fifth Avenue. Six years later, in 1968, it would launch another attractive New York store on the site of the old Saks premises between Macy's and Gimbels on Thirty-fourth Street.

Ferkauf frequently went to great lengths to get quality merchandise for his upgraded chain, which he now preferred to call a "promotional department store" rather than a discount store. "Back door buying" was often necessary, for traditional department stores often threatened to boycott manufacturers that sold to Korvettes. Sometimes cloak-and-dagger maneuvers had to be resorted to. One time, for example, Korvettes managed to offer its customers high-fashion Pringle fur-trimmed cashmere cardigans for only twenty-five dollars. How did Korvettes get the sweaters? "Pringle tried to hold the price to nearly twice as much by refusing to sell to discounters," an observer explained. "Pringle tracked the cardigans Korvettes was selling back through at least two intermediaries. Pringle had sold them to a manufacturer of sweater linings, who had sold them to a manufacturer of fur collars, who then presumably sold them to Korvettes."

Korvettes had organizational problems in the mid-sixties, mainly because of their fast, vast expansion, and Ferkauf left these to Charles Bassine, the chairman of Spartan Industries, an apparel manufacturer that Korvettes had merged with in 1966 after a slump in sales and profits. The unorthodox Ferkauf, whose name means "sell" in Yiddish, rarely wore a tie, had no office or secretary, never dictated a letter, for many years had no official title at Korvettes, and relied on his own judgment rather than a consensus of "experts." A rare bird who seemed to have no patience for the more prosaic workings of a large corporation, he severed all connections with Korvettes two years after the Spartan merger. When he left, at the age of only forty-seven, many knowledgeable observers regarded him as one of the greatest merchants in the history of retailing. He has been active in several ventures over the past decade, the latest being the consulting firm Pennfield Retail Services, Inc. (see the Plaza Exchange store biography following), but none has brought him anywhere near the national prominence that Korvettes did. The maverick merchant believes that a retailer needs "no special mental processes" and that his great contribution to society was that he "stretched the buck" for the consumer "more than anyone in American distribution." The only American merchant to be featured on a *Time* magazine cover in recent memory, he has been rated by Malcolm McNair, professor of retailing at the Harvard Business School, as "one of the six greatest merchants in U.S. history," his exalted companions being Frank Woolworth, General Robert Wood of Sears, and supermarket pioneer Michael Cullen.

Spartan Industries merged with Arlen Realty and Development Corporation in 1971, three years after Ferkauf's departure, and Korvettes became a division of America's biggest publicly held real-estate company, which owns 27 of Korvettes' 52 store locations. Korvettes has always courted trouble whenever it departs from its discount policy of value for low prices—as when it features fashion rather than savings—but Arlen seems to have wanted it both ways. Although there are still promotions like 10 percent off for senior citizen days, management has been trying for the past four years to draw bargain hunters into the store by promoting loss leaders (what it calls "traffic appliances") and then get them to shop Korvettes for higher fashion apparel such as that featured in the boutique-like "Other Korvettes" while they're in the store. Many critics doubt that this can be done. "If you've gotten people into your store under the impression that you're a cheap store, and then you try to sell them stuff that's higher priced, higher quality, they're not going to buy it," one veteran retailer says. "Consistency of image is very important. But Korvette's doesn't feel that it must correct an image problem like the much smaller Fisher's Big Wheel did and contends that their plan just needs more time. Meanwhile, the store that made discounting respectable has been steadily losing money on sales of about $600 million annually over the past few years, although it earned a profit of $1 million in 1977 from day-to-day operations. Generally speaking, most New York Korvettes are profitable, while the company stores outside New York are losing money or just breaking even. Early in 1979 the Agache Willot Group, the French retailing and manufacturing concern that owns Bon Marché, acquired Korvettes from Arlen Realty for over $55 million.

1970

"So what's the storieeee, Jerry?"

JGE STORES—*Bayside, New York*

Television viewers in the metropolitan New York area will recall more than enough of the 309 irritating commercials that Jerry Rosenberg appeared in every week for his JGE discount stores, which sold appliances and other merchansdise. Jerry made national news with the hard hat he wore and the great belly that popped out from under his shirt as he leaned way back arms outstretched and in fine New Yorkese answered his own question by telling viewers that the story was that there were bargains galore for "union members, civil service employees, and their families" at JGE. Actually, you could get in the store without any trouble if you just knew what a union member was and Jerry's business prospered, growing to 51 franchises at its peak.

Then disaster struck in the form of a lawsuit by the Consumer Affairs Department of New York City charging JGE with violation of consumer regulations. Jerry Rosenberg, who had been drawing a $5,000 a week salary and had been driven around in a chauffeured limo, suffered a heart attack, lost all his stores due to the unfavorable publicity, and in his own words "was a pauper ready to go on welfare." Fully recovered now, he owns a dance hall in Queens. Jerry has a $161 million defamation of character lawsuit against the city, which dropped its suit against JGE, and expects to prove malice. He blames bigger stores for ganging up on him because they opposed his circumvention of the fair trade laws prohibiting discounting of name-brand products—laws that have since been repealed. The man who originated the "irritating but memorable" commercial technique—inspiring others like Crazy Eddie and Frank Perdue—may be back with us again. And that's the story so far . . .

1977

America's Newest Department Store

THE PLAZA EXCHANGE—*Brooklyn, New York*

Bedford-Stuyvesant is one of America's largest black communities and one of her poorest, a section with unemployment and crime rates among the highest in the nation. After the Bedford-Stuyvesant Restoration Corporation tried to persuade six department store chains to open a branch in the area's shopping center on Fulton Street, and all refused for one reason or another, the corporation went ahead and opened its own store in June 1977.

The small store's ten-man staff was trained over a period of six weeks by Pennfield Retail Services, Inc., a consulting firm headed by Eugene Ferkauf, founder and former head of Korvettes. Ferkauf, who has also organized company-owned employee stores for Citibank and the New York City teachers union, as well as several minidepartment stores around the country, describes all his stores as academies, "which will give experience to young people so they may have the opportunity to become a businessman or businesswoman." The "store doctor" is assisted by Vice-President Louis Wachtel, a former executive at the Allied Stores Corporation, and a staff of 18.

Consisting of eight departments, established on the basis of a consumer survey to determine what local customers wanted most, the Plaza Exchange minidepartment store was started on an initial investment of $90,000 and a bank loan of $74,000 for stock. Plaza Exchange sells goods "at the lowest prices possible, the lowest in the city," operating at only a 22 percent markup, half that of most department stores. High volume, fast turnover, and relatively low operational costs will hopefully give the store a 5 percent profit on a first-year volume of $750,000, one executive predicts.

Plaza Exchange has been promoted with personal appearances by prominent blacks like Knick basketball star Earl "The Pearl" Monroe, radio ads, leaflets, even church announcements and T-shirts—everything but TV spots, which the store can't at present afford. Three departments have been added since opening day, including a toy department, to attract more shoppers, and items like button-down collar shirts that don't sell at all in the area have been discontinued. The major problem is still "to get the name of the store to the people so that they know it's here."

Plaza Exchange's pilot store may well move into a larger 28,000 square foot store in the near future, as its founders hope. Certainly there is great potential for development in a section with a 400,000 population, not to mention hundreds of thousands more shoppers who could be pulled in from the New York metropolitan area and suburbs. Over the past 150 years, as noted so often in these pages, many American stores have started with far less and are now grand emporiums or giant full-line department store chains.

✑ **VII** ✑

Hurry, Hurry, Hurry . . .
Send No Money . . .
Satisfaction Guaranteed:
The Mail-Order
Department Stores

"Dear Montgomery Ward," one Minnesota mail-order customer wrote at the turn of the century. "Do you still sell embalming fluid? I saw it in your old catalogue but not the new one. If you do, send me enough for my husband, who is five foot eleven inches tall and weighs 165 pounds when in good health. Henry has been laying around the house looking mighty peaked lately and I expect him to kick off any time now. He liked to have gone last night. When you send the stuff please send instructions with it. Must I pour it down his throat just before he dies, or must I rub it on after he is dead? Please rush."

"Can you send me a 'love powder' from your drugstore?" a correspondent more recently asked Sears Roebuck. "I can't keep my man home nights. I've tried everything from buying a television to hiding his pants. It's no use. Please help me. P.S. I do not want to buy in this town. . . ."

"I have been looking for a book on how to get started with a girl . . ." a young man wrote "Monkey Ward." "I need to know what to say the first time or how to get on with it the first time. . . . Please send me information along this line."

Another time a Montana rancher ordered a wife from Sears—and she was supplied, in a fashion, when an order clerk took a fancy to the young man, quit her job, and went West to wed him. Similarly a

Ward customer spotted a drawing of a model wearing a fetching dress and ordered #1242 for a wife—he wasn't successful, merely the first of many men and women who have ordered playmates by number from various mail-order catalogues. There have been cases of mail-order houses tracking down errant husbands for customers (through their orders), locating a missing daughter who had "decamped for parts unknown with a low-down, no-account bum" (he turned out to be all right), and sending a tombstone catalogue to a lady who complained that her husband had "kicked the bucket" because of the "snake oil" cure he had bought from the firm's patent medicine catalogue pages!

It is obvious that mail-order is as American as cherry pie or chewing gum, a business that is largely indigenous to this country and has affected every aspect of American life from love and birth to loneliness and dying. Our earliest ancestors, with no manufacturers of their own in a virgin land, first used mail-orders to obtain supplies from the mother country. George Washington ordered goods from England and France, as did Thomas Jefferson and, most likely, all the rest of the Founding Fathers. Benjamin Franklin, as a matter of fact, has been called "the father of the mail-order catalogue" because he issued a list in 1744 of six hundred books he would sell by mail.

It's hard to establish who was the first native mail-order merchant, but among the first to sell through the mails on a large scale was a thirteen-year-old boy named Charley Thompson of Bridgewater, Connecticut, who made a fortune from an initial investment of seventy-five cents. Young Thompson purchased some large mailing envelopes with his meager savings, bought a supply of stationery on credit, and borrowed enough money to run an ad in the *New York Tribune* on July 4, 1866. His "Trust Scheme" offered people a chance to "get something for nothing." On receipt of a quarter, Charley promised, he would send anyone a package of stationery, a pencil, and ABSOLUTELY FREE, a piece of unusual jewelry. Within two years, the youngster was doing so well that he was able to branch out into Grandma's Wonder Healing and Complexion Cream. This he made at home with the aid of grown-up employees and mailed to "agents" who sold it for him in exchange for premiums like mandolins and lace curtains. Charley pioneered in the extension of credit; "Send no money" was a mainstay of his advertising. His catalogue pictured four pages of dolls alone, in addition to premiums like watches, rifles, alarm clocks, furs, petticoats, even 31-piece dinner sets. In his best years he employed over a hundred workers, a New York newspaper observing, "There is not a wreck-strewn shore on the Seven Seas that does not have at least one packing case board marked Chas. B. Thompson."

Thompson, who opened a country store and dropped out of the mail-order business before World War I, mainly due to big-city competition, died in 1942 aged eighty-nine. He may or may not have been the first American mail-order merchant. No authority seems to award him this honor, but it is interesting to note that at least no one succeeded on such a large scale before him and that the expression "mail-order" is first recorded in the language in 1867, a year after the thirteen-year-old went into business. Some authorities say that selling goods by mail was common by the end of the Civil War, when the ads of many firms offering merchandise like seed, farm implements, sewing machines, dry goods, books, and medicines frequently appeared in rural magazines. Most of these firms, however sold only a single line of products.

Aside from Thompson's Premium House, the earliest entrepreneur to offer a wide variety of items by mail was E. C. Allen of Augusta, Maine, who nationally advertised a selection of specialty items including everything from washing powder to novelties in a magazine he founded in 1869 called the *People's Literary Companion*. Allen's success—his fifty cent magazine sold or was distributed free to five hundred thousand people a year—inspired many imitators, and in a few years Maine became the direct-mail capital of America, pioneering in this American institution as it had in the chewing gum industry a few decades before. Soon there were P. O. Vickery's *Fireside Visitor,* True and Company's *Our Fireside Journal* and a score more mail-order magazines or papers with a combined circulation in the millions. Augusta didn't last long as the mail-order capital, though—not when city firms, complete with their own magazines, sprang up in New York, Chicago, and other urban areas. Mail-order was now a national craze.

Aaron Montgomery Ward, a former country storekeeper and a clerk for Field, Palmer & Leiter, the predecessor of the great Marshall Field department store, founded the first large firm to sell a wide variety of products by mail in 1872. While working as a traveling salesman in rural areas for Chicago dry goods stores, Ward found that farmers were objecting bitterly to the prices they paid for goods at the traditional but obsolescent country stores. Ward probably also heard stories like the one about the "devout" Yankee storekeeper who enjoined his clerk to "come to the prayers after you have sanded the sugar and watered the molasses." Not only were prices high and storekeepers often dishonest, but the choice of goods was frequently small at the inefficient general store, and if the farmer complained, the storekeeper—honestly or not— advised that he had to buy what his wholesaler offered at his wholesaler's prices. The farmer could take it or leave it and he usually had to take it, for the country store was almost always the *only* store in small towns.

The prevailing system put the farmer in the local merchant's power, especially since he usually bought a year's supply of goods on credit, counting on his next crops for payment. Ward knew that these economic inequities had been partly responsible for farmers forming the Grange in 1867. Oliver H. Kelley of the Federal Bureau of Agriculture had organized the National Grange of the Patrons of Husbandry in the belief that farmers could obtain a better life by associating in a fraternal order, but the Grange had quickly become a political organization, electing a large number of representatives to state legislatures, where they succeeded in passing laws regulating railroad rates and unfair practices—freight rates were often so high that it took the entire value of one bushel of wheat to pay the freight for two bushels, and big corporations were frequently charged much less to ship freight than farmers. These "Grange laws" mark the first attempt by government in America to limit the power of businessmen (the railroads in this case) to manage their businesses any way they wanted. The Grange also set up hundreds of small cooperative stores in an attempt to cut prices by eliminating the middleman and by buying goods in quantity, an effort that eventually failed but that worked for a time and encouraged Ward to try a similar idea.

Ward figured that he too could eliminate the middleman—the wholesaler, jobber and retailer—by selling direct to country people by mail from offices in Chicago. As Victor Hugo said, "Nothing in this world is so powerful as an idea whose time has come," and it was Ward's luck that mail-order's time was here. American industry had already moved into the mass-production era, inspired by Eli Whitney's development of interchangeable parts in his musket factory, and suppliers would be willing to cut prices on large orders—savings Ward could pass on to his customers. Though far from satisfactory, transportation was improving throughout America, and there was a ready market among the dissatisfied customers of the country store, rural dwellers who accounted for nearly 70 percent of America's population at the time, only a dozen or so cities then having two hundred thousand or more residents. Perhaps most importantly, Ward believed he could obtain the business of the Grange.

In August 1872 Montgomery Ward, with capital of $1,600 in savings, founded what was to become the world's first great mail-order business. His original partners, George S. Drake and Robert P. Caulfield, sold out their interest in the firm after a year, seeing "no future in it." Later Ward would write that his business was "ridiculed by retail merchants, doubted by manufacturers and predicted a short life by all." His first catalogue, if it can be called that, was a simple, one-page price list measuring 8 inches x 12 inches, which his wife helped him address and which he sent mainly to the Granges, now boasting about a half-million members. Ward himself wasn't so optimistic about the business. While they were addressing the circulars, he upset the inkwell on Elizabeth's marble-topped table, her favorite wedding present, and she came close to tears. "Never mind, dear," Ward said. "Maybe I can make enough out of this to buy you a new table."

Judging by his first year in business Ward must have figured that he'd never make enough to buy red ink, much less another table. His post-office box was often empty that first year and through most of the following year, when the panic of 1873 made life difficult for even established businesses. But by the end of 1874 sales had reached $100,000, three years later they were triple this, and after ten years of business Ward sales exceeded $1 million. How Ward succeeded—by being appointed the official supply house for the Grange, by his "Satisfaction Guaranteed or Your Money Back" offer and other policies—is shown more fully in the following company biographies, which include the stories of Sears, Butler Brothers, L.L. Bean, and other famous mail-order houses. But it shouldn't be forgotten that conventional department stores also played an important part in the development of the mail-order business, though after 1910 most of them decided to cultivate their "home markets" rather than range far afield via the mails. Appropriately, a specialized book entitled *How Department Stores Are Carried On* published in 1901 devoted 8 of its 34 chapters to department store mail-order operations. R.H. Macy ran a mail-order department as early as 1874, and its 1881 catalogue contained 127 pages. Although Macy's later stole ideas from the master copywriter Richard Sears to use in its own wish book, the store never catered to the rural dwellers who were the backbone of mail-order, amusing its city customers instead with derogatory references to country Rubes.

The main reason that most department store direct-mail operations failed is best expressed in an ad Ward's published in 1892:

> We started this mail-order business and made it such a success that there is scarcely a department store in the land which has not tried it too. They, all, without exception, imitate our methods as far as they can find them out; they all want to know: "How does Montgomery Ward & Company do it." We will tell you. We carry the goods in stock and are the only firm who can honestly say so. We attend to the mail-order business alone. It is not a side issue with us, but our entire business. We have no retail trade to bother us and delay us. We study methods of improving our business as we would a science. We imitate no one.

No doubt the most important of the hundreds of department stores that experimented with mail-order was Philadelphia's John Wanamaker, which started advertising a mail-order service in 1872 and did try to reach rural customers. Wanamaker's founder, who served as postmaster general in Benjamin Harrison's administration, first proposed the idea of rural free delivery (R.F.D.) in 1891, at a time when three-quarters of Americans had to go the post office (often the country store) to get their mail. The Wanamaker system, under which the post office hired carriers to deliver the mail at no charge from town to roadside letter boxes, became a reality in 1896 under another administration, taking so long because Congress had to save the $30,000 needed to implement the plan. But John Wanamaker deserves full credit for recognizing the broad popular demand for R.F.D. and supporting it. Its effect on the direct-mail business can't be exaggerated, for now rural customers could receive their mail-order catalogues at home and place their orders without leaving the house.

All that remained was for the government to do something about delivering mail-order packages from town to the old homestead itself. Wanamaker, aided by the lobbying of the Populist Grangers, continued to work hard for such a parcel post system long after he left office as postmaster general. Surprisingly, Ward's, Sears, and the other large mail-order companies had mixed feelings about parcel post. They knew that their catalogues couldn't be shipped any cheaper than they were under third-class mail via R.F.D., but they also believed it possible that parcel post would lead to many small purchases that would increase handling costs. Wanamaker was more farsighted and fought the small merchants, chambers of commerce, retail associations, and private express companies that testified against parcel post delivery in hearings that Congress held from 1910 to 1912. It is said that his clever reply when asked to give the reasons why America didn't have a parcel post system—"There are four main reasons: The Adams Express Company, The American Express Company, The United States Express Company, and the Southern Express Company"—crystallized public sentiment for the national parcel post system and made it a reality in the Taft administration.

At any rate, Wanamaker personally mailed the first package under the U.S. Parcel Post System on January 1, 1913, commenting that "the nation was chained twenty years to the express companies," but failing to add that his department store's direct-mail operation would benefit greatly by the new law. The first free delivery by parcel post was made on the next day, and it marked the beginning of the golden age of mail-order, helping the direct mail companies far more than it did most department stores. Not only would shopping by mail be speedier and more convenient, but the parcel post system raised the four-pound limit on mail parcels. No longer would mail-order companies have to cut a heavy item like an overcoat into halves, and ship it in separate parcels along with a needle and thread as Ward's frequently did in the 1870s. More important, Wanamaker's R.F.D. combined with parcel post would help change the face of the nation. Roads had previously been in a deplorable state. In the early days of the U.S. mail system two West Virginians who had a government contract to deliver mail across the mountains failed to make it several times and received a nasty reprimand from the Post Office Department. Back went their reply: "Dear Sirs; if you knocked the gable end out of hell and rained fire and brimstone on Cheat Mountain for 40 days and 40 nights, you wouldn't melt the snow enough to get your damned mail through. Yours truly, Trotter Brothers." Vastly increased traffic under R.F.D. and parcel post helped inspire the building of better roads throughout the country, ending such conditions and literally paving the way for the automobile and the social revolution it wrought in America.

Soon after the introduction of parcel post, Sears alone was handling twenty thousand mail orders a day from customers. Business increased so dramatically for all the companies that shipping departments had to be completely reorganized along modern lines in order to cope with the flood of new orders. Once this problem was solved, the only obstacle the mail-order giants had to overcome was the continued resistance of small merchants to their enterprise. From the very beginning small storekeepers, especially those in rural areas, fought the mail-order companies just as furiously as they waged war on the department stores. Only a year after Montgomery Ward went into business the *Chicago Tribune*, instigated by small merchants, published an "exposé" headed "GRANGERS BEWARE. *Don't Patronize Montgomery Ward & Company—They are Dead-Beats.*" The article ridiculed the "swindling firm's" low prices as "utopian figures." This first recorded attack on the mail-order business went on to say: "The firm boasts that they make 'no display,' in fact, they keep altogether retired from the public gaze, and are to be reached through correspondence sent to a certain box in the Post Office. . . . There is probably only one man composing it, and he wants to have all the money the gulls send for himself . . . for the trash sent to his dupes, if, in fact, anything at all is sent." The *Tribune* soon retracted this statement, saying it was "grossly unjust" after a thorough investigation prompted by the threat of a law suit, but the harm had already been done.

Urged on by the storekeepers, the country press went on a rampage, and bankers, public officials, lecturers on the Chautauqua and Lyceum circuits, even ministers from their pulpits, damned the mail-order firms with slander and invective unmatched in business history until the great war against the chain stores a few decades later. The mail-order companies were called "trusts" that sold inferior merchandise. In an attempt to arouse unions and workers as well as customers against the mail-order merchants, the lie was spread that their "shoddy goods" were made by prison workers and always arrived damaged and late. One newspaper printed a joke that "Rears and Soreback" offered a watch that was not only half the price but ran twice as fast as any watch that could be purchased from any local jeweler. Names like Rears and Soreback, Shears and Rawback, Shears Sawbuck, Monkey Ward, and similar derogatory epithets were spawned in poetry contests sponsored by local merchants to denounce the mail-order houses, but in the case of "Monkey Ward," at least, this tactic backfired, for the name became an endearing one to Ward customers and was used in many letters still in the company files.

As with power looms and the sewing machine before it, people wanted to destroy the mail-order business because they honestly thought it would put men out of work, not realizing that every cost-saving device eventually adds to the wealth of the community. Many country newspapers refused ads from mail-order companies and condemned them in news columns as well as in editorials and editorial cartoons—though rural mail-order customers were often faithful, one editorial calling Ward's "a dealer in trashy merchandise" resulting in a small-town Kansas newspaper losing nearly half of its subscribers. Mail order was even equated with adultery in a rural paper, Ed Howe, a columnist on the *Atchison Globe,* writing: "Ben Bradford, known to be a little gay, says the first time he kissed a woman other than his wife, he felt as sneaky as he did when he first began buying of Montgomery Ward. But Ben gradually became hardened, and many say he now trades with Sears, Roebuck, too."

Mail-order buying was considered "downright treasonable" by many. Politicians denounced locals for "sending off money to the Chicago millionaires," and a mayoral candidate in Warsaw, Iowa, pledged that he would fire any municipal worker caught buying from a mail-order catalogue. In the South, where the wounds of the Civil War still weren't healed, politicians and storekeepers spread the rumor that Richard Sears, Alvah Roebuck, and Montgomery Ward were blacks. Montgomery Ward actually ran an ad in 1898 headed "An Infamous Lie" that offered a hundred dollars for the name of the person who started the rumor that Ward was "a mulatto Negro." Later, when Julius Rosenwald became Sears's partner, anti-Semitic stories were spread about Sears Roebuck. These were among the most shameful episodes in the mail-order war—Sears even printed photos of its founders to prove they weren't "colored"—and were only rivaled by the book burnings of mail-order catalogues that were arranged by country merchants and newspapers.

The term "book burner" itself, meaning "self-appointed censor," didn't arrive until 1933 when thousands of pro-Nazi students ended a torchlight parade at the University of Berlin by burning a pile of twenty thousand books while Nazi Propaganda Minister Joseph Goebbels proclaimed: "The soul of the German people can express itself. These flames . . . illuminate the . . . end of an old era and light up the new." But the first mass book-burners in American history were the anti-mail-order people at the turn of the century who burned mail-order catalogues to censor not the free expression of ideas, but free enterprise. Local merchants persuaded or arm-twisted people into tossing their catalogues into a bonfire in the public square every Saturday night. Prizes up to fifty dollars were offered to those who collected and brought in the greatest number of catalogues to be burned. This practice seemingly reached its nadir in a small Montana town where a movie theater gave free admission or ten cents to any child who turned over a catalogue to town authorities for public burning. Yet the Montana orgy of destruction was repeated in other states, all in the name of insuring a continuance of "freedom of opportunity in America."

The mail-order companies for their part took to the offensive as soon as the war began. Ward's, number one at the time, ran an ad in the *Farmer's Voice* in 1892 claiming that all the vilification served the company well. "P. T. Barnum," the ad reminded its customers, "once said that he did not care what was said about him so long as they did not forget to mention Barnum. We feel the same. Slander has proved cheap and good advertising for us, doing not the slightest injury. We are honorable, and we know we are. So do over three million of our customers. Thus are curses turned to blessings."

A Ward catalogue editorial asserted: "Trusts. Every day in

country towns little trusts are formed by the merchants who stand by each other and dictate to you what you should pay for sugar, coffee, groceries, etc., and when you come to sell, you will almost always find they all pay the same price for your butter, your eggs, your produce and your stock. . . . We belong to no trust. . . ."

Another Ward ad "sympathized" with the country merchant and his "high overhead," making more points for Ward's: "Many an honest dealer has to charge you more for goods simply because he has paid too much for them himself. Ignorance is less provoking than dishonesty, but it costs you just as much." Richard Sears took the same tack in a sarcastic catalogue editorial entitled "Our Compliments to the Retail Merchants," in which he charmingly conceded that store owners weren't making an "excessive profit" from their high prices; it was just that they couldn't buy in large lots like Sears Roebuck could—they were incompetent.

Words weren't the only ammunition the mail-order giants fired at the opposition. Although its money-back guarantee convinced most people that Ward's didn't offer inferior merchandise, the firm invited one group of farmers to inspect its warehouse after an editorial in a rural newspaper savagely attacked its goods. A committee of three farmers and their wives chosen by the Farmers Institute tested the quality of Ward merchandise by opening boxes, cans, bottles, and packages of all kinds, weighing and measuring the contents. They even applied acid to underwear, men's clothing, and fabrics. Said the committee in conclusion: " . . . the quality of the goods is the same or better than the qualities that the usual stores sell and no attack on their quality is justified by the facts. . . . The committee destroyed enough groceries in this test to start a small store. We were trying to find something that was short in weight or quality or in some manner inferior, or worthy of criticism, and we failed to find it. . . ."

Both Sears and Ward's took to sending goods and catalogues in unmarked packages—the famous "plain brown wrapper" later used by other companies for explicit sexual material—just to protect customers from the wrath of local merchants and neighbors. Sears Roebuck soon claimed that country stores themselves could and did secretly buy from their company. Ward's went so far as to send a Kansas lady three hundred catalogues after she wrote to them admitting that she had collected that many from neighbors to win a fifty-dollar prize in a catalogue-burning contest and had promised to return the three hundred catalogues to her neighbors. As for Sears, it once gave a village committee a donation to help build a local church, despite the fact that a local merchant had tricked the committee into addressing the letter appealing for the contribution to "Rears and Soreback."

Public relations played an important part in the victory of the mail-order houses. Montgomery Ward advertised with signs painted on barns and fences and used street entertainment. Its advertising crew not only traveled the country with brushes, paint pots, and magic lantern shows, but organized a road company that barnstormed in a Pullman Palace railroad car and gave minstrel shows similar to those staged by the "snake-oil" salesman of the day. Ward's also bought one of the new buggylike "horseless carriages," going on tour with it in 17 states and giving free rides to spectators adventurous enough to ride in the "Young Man's Special." But Richard Sears was the real master of public relations. When a visitor to his Chicago plant lost a five-dollar bill, Sears gave him another one—he didn't want it said that anyone ever lost money at Sears Roebuck. On another occasion the brake on a Sear's bicycle failed to work and an Ohio youngster crashed into a tree, breaking his leg, which a local doctor set improperly, leaving the boy a cripple. Richard Sears brought the youngster to Chicago, and had his leg reset at company expense by a noted surgeon, and the boy finally recovered. Probably the most famous PR story, possibly apocryphal, concerned a conductor who helped a lady off a streetcar and broke his Sears watch when it dropped on the pavement. Richard Sears, who happened to be aboard the car, brought the conductor to his plant and presented him with a new watch, telling him: "We guarantee our watches not to fall out of people's pockets and break."

Such stories, true or not, were worth thousands of dollars in publicity, but the direct-mail companies won the war when the smoke finally cleared, primarily because mail order was something the people wanted—many of the book burners threw their catalogues in the Saturday night village bonfires and then went home and ordered new ones. The small country storekeepers and urban shopkeepers lost their fight against the mail-order companies for the same reason they had lost the war against the new department stores—you can't beat an idea whose time has come; eventually, usually sooner than later, it prevails. Yet it shouldn't be assumed that there wasn't some truth in certain of the country merchants' charges. In fact, many of the frauds perpetrated on mail-order customers today were invented well over a century ago. Examples abound:

•*Double your money—just send in ten cents and we'll show you how.* (Those who reply are still sent simple instructions: *Fold it.*)

•*A complete sewing machine for only $1!* (From early days the "sewing machine" has been a needle and a spool of thread.)

•*Send $1 for information on how to keep your bills down. (The "information" still sent in reply: Place your bills on a flat surface and put a weight on them.)*

Though it seems that no one with an IQ exceeding .001 would fall for such obvious examples of low-level chicanery, thousands have for a century and more. People still respond to the ancient ad, "Send a dollar," *when absolutely nothing is offered them,* perhaps expecting some surprise! A writer in the *Atlantic Monthly* of September 1904 perhaps explained in part the American attitude toward such fraudulent mail-order advertising. "The Americans," he wrote, "have a curious indolence and toleration of a fraud or an injustice. Nowhere is this seen more plainly than in the average man's attitude toward the ingenious humbug and adroit swindler. To be good-naturedly imposed upon is a positive pleasure provided the cost of it is not too great. This explains the vast number of trifling frauds carried on year after year in the advertising columns of magazines and newspapers." How else can one explain the rascal who made a fortune advertising in numerous agricultural newspapers that he would mail an "infallible Potato Bug Eradicator" to anyone sending him ten cents—he sent back two pieces of whittled pine with the instructions, "Place the potato bug between them and press together." Or the New York man who in 1896 advertised a sure way to prevent any bugs from destroying crops—for one dollar the buyer received the simple direction, "Don't plant any crops." Or the Portland, Maine, mail-order man who for fifty cents guaranteed a sure way to cure horses from slobbering: "Teach your horse to spit!"

While "Snake-Oil Sams" of yore originated most such schemes, don't for a moment think that today's respectable mail-order firms weren't involved in similar ploys. Several early magazines, including the *Ladies Home Journal*, refused to run ads for any mail-order companies because of their often wild claims. At the turn of the century, for example, it was a common practice to send unordered merchandise to customers in the hope that a certain percentage would keep it. (Today, under federal law, people have no obligation even to return unordered merchandise and in certain states it is considered an outright gift.) Richard Sears himself got started in the mail-order watch business when a Chicago company shipped some unordered gold-plated watches to a Minnesota jeweler and he returned them to the railway station where Sears worked as freight agent. The company, following what was considered standard business practice in those days, then put part two of their ploy into play. They wrote Sears asking him to buy the watches at a discount for resale and he did so, starting the business that was to become the world's largest mail-order firm. Sears, and all the mail-order mavens of his day, used the same trick, and many more, never considering themselves dishonest. Sears's 1900 catalogue actually claimed that 24 fifty-cent medicines offered on one page could "cure" 24 diseases ranging from "nervous troubles" to "pleurisy" and "pimples." Until the passage of the Food and Drug Act in 1906 almost any claim at all could be made for patent medicines in the mail-order catalogues—little wonder that the average American only lived until forty-eight at the time!

One of Sears Roebuck's biggest sellers was an "electric belt" a device recommended for nervous diseases, headaches, and backaches and vaguely suggested as a sexual panacea. Over a period of seven years beginning in 1898 Sears sold at least a half-million dollars worth of these contraptions (possibly well over a million dollars worth, as records of sales for the early years are missing), taking in profits of more than a thousand dollars a day on them at one time. Yet in an unpublished manuscript about the firm Alvah Roebuck tells why he refused to take over the electric belt department in 1899 when Richard Sears asked him to: "I tried one of the belts . . . and found that while it developed a strong current of electricity and produced a tingling sensation, *it was so strong that if the battery cells became uncovered and touched the flesh it would burn and cauterize it, and as I did not have faith in it as a curative agent, I declined the offer.*" (Italics mine.) Richard Sears, of course, went on selling the belts.

Today, although Americans are still taken for over half a billion dollars yearly by mail-order fraud, Sears, Montgomery Ward, Penney's, and all the American mail-order giants go to great lengths to avoid even the suggestion of fraud in their operations. This has been general company policy since the early 1900s, probably just as much for good business reasons as for moral commitment—as Richard Sears reportedly said, "Honesty is the best policy. I know, because I've tried it both ways." About the only taint on any of the big companies recently was the accusation by the Federal Trade Commission in 1974 that Sears used "bait and switch" tactics—advertising low-priced appliances to lure customers into its retail stores and then pressuring them to buy more expensive appliances. In an out-of-court settlement Sears agreed not to use such tactics in the future and vowed, "Incidents which came to light in the recent FTC hearings were violations of Sears' policy as well as FTC standards."

Neither can one say with any fairness that the mail-order giants were ever the worst offenders among mail-order companies or retailers in general. Quite the opposite is true. At a time when the mottoes, "Never give the sucker an even break" and Caveat Emptor("Let the buyer beware") were supported by most merchants, "Monkey Ward" and Sears, Roebuck, beloved of rural dwellers, built their businesses on trust, actually owed their existence in great part to the distrust farmers had of small-town merchants, as we've seen. The great mail-order companies were "family" or "friendly neighbors" to their customers from the beginning, and the relationship, carefully cultivated, has persisted to this day. In the case of Sears this bond is perhaps best illustrated by the remarks of two politicians very familiar with the feelings of their constituents. "Your only friends are Jesus Christ; Sears, Roebuck; and Gene Talmadge," the governor of Georgia used to say to groups of farmers during his many successful campaigns. Today Senate Majority leader Robert Byrd merely extends this remark a few powers. Says Byrd: "I always tell the people of West Virginia that they always had five friends; God Almighty; Sears, Roebuck; Carter's Little Liver Pills: the Democratic Party; and Robert C. Byrd." Proof that others share his faith is the town of Seroco, North Dakota, a blend name that honors Sears, Roebuck probably because a Sears' catalogue was the first piece of mail to reach the village post office.

As regards Montgomery Ward, its founder from the beginning established himself with his customers as a source of unlimited information, an adviser, a personal friend, and an entrepreneur who always put the customer first in matters of dissatisfaction. In 1875 his catalogue gave the American consumer one of the earliest, and certainly the strongest, pledges of consumer protection by a mail-order company. Ward went so far as to advise customers about the claims of manufacturers in his copy, even when selling ordinary wares such as pots and pans, which he often cautioned: "Will not hold as much as represented," or "Manufacturer's measure, will not hold quite as much as represented." As seen in the following biographies, his "fatherly advice" really set the tone for Sears and other firms to follow, marking the beginning of the great revolution that made mail-order houses figure so largely in the American way of life. That revolution is over now, and these biographies clearly show that the mail-order giants have for many years been making their biggest profits in the department store field, but though it is not the force it once was in the American economy, mail-order is far from dead. The newest mail-order approach is the small catalogue display operation (offering 18 items) being tested by Safeway Stores, America's biggest supermarket chain. But the other major mail-order merchants—Sears, Ward's, Penney's, Spiegel, and Alden's, in that order—along with smaller specialty houses like L.L. Bean of Maine, already give the mail-order business a healthy 1 percent of all retail sales in America, compared to the 8 percent claimed by department stores, and direct-mail selling at present provides an impressive one-third of the revenues of the U.S. Postal Service.

1872

The First Great Wish Book

MONTGOMERY WARD & COMPANY—*Chicago, Illinois*

Aaron Montgomery Ward (he never used his first name) was born in Chatham, New Jersey, in 1844, the son of a cobbler, and by the time he founded his mail-order company in what was then known as "the Mudhole of the Prairies," he had labored in a barrel factory for twenty-five cents a day, stacked bricks for a nickel more daily, and, as noted, worked at the various salesman's jobs where he conceived the idea of selling to farm Grange societies by mail.

Ward's first quarters were in a dingy 12 foot x 14 foot room on the fourteenth floor of a building located at 825 North Clark Street, and his earliest surviving catalogue—a single sheet listing 163 items mostly priced at one dollar—described the firm as Montgomery, Ward & Company, the gremlin coma in the name not excised until ten catalogues later. Ward's first order was for $14 worth of goods. The early years weren't easy ones. The young merchant was forced to work for C.W. & E. Pardridge Company, a dry goods concern, and handle his business in his spare time, he lost his original partners after a year in business, and the panic of 1873 brought business to a virtual standstill. But Ward whistled his way past the graveyard. The following year he took as a partner George Robinson Thorne, his brother-in-law and close friend, and moved to West Hubbard Street, this the first of five moves the company would make to larger quarters over the next twenty-six years.

On first starting in business Ward had been appointed the official purchasing agent of the Illinois Grange, after he had satisfied the secretary of the organization, who had come to Chicago in August 1872 looking for "an honest man." Honesty was always Montgomery Ward's policy; in fact, he advertised a Golden Rule philosophy years before J.C. Penney. "Honest treatment of customers is the foundation of our business," he wrote in an early catalogue. "The Golden Rule has always been and is sacred to us and we have always put ourselves in the place of those who buy from us."

Ward went all out to get the business of other Granges, identifying his firm as "The Original Grange Supply House" in every early circular catalogue and including a Granger hat as one of the first illustrations in his initial bound catalogue, which was printed in 1875. This catalogue, one of the best-read books of its time, consisted of 32 pages and was pocket-size, only 3 inches x 5 inches. Ward, who prepared all the copy, explained on the inside cover how he could sell high-quality goods at such low prices. "We don't pay $40,000 a year rent," he wrote. "We don't employ high-priced salesmen. . . . We don't sell goods to country retailers on six months time. We buy for cash and sell for cash. Our goods are bought direct from manufacturers. . . . By purchasing from us you save from 40 to 100 percent, which are the profits of middlemen. . . . We therefore decline to pay commissions or employ agents on the grand Grange principle, 'Do away with the middleman as far as possible.' "

The following year's spring-summer catalogue was the first in mail-order history to contain a money-back guarantee, though similar pledges had been made earlier by department store merchants like A.T. Stewart, John Wanamaker. Potter Palmer, and Marshall Field:

☞ We Guarantee All of Our Goods. ☜

If any of them are not satisfactory after due inspection, we will take them back, pay all expenses, and refund the money paid for them. When in the city please call and see us.

MONTGOMERY WARD & CO.

Ward persisted in his money-back policy even when his friends told him, "They're going to rob you blind." Obviously he was helped by his victory in the war small-town merchants waged against him and by the great advantage that rural free delivery and the parcel post system gave the mail-order business in general, but the satisfaction-guaranteed credo was probably the major reason for his success, if any one factor can be singled out. Ward's became the official supply house for many Granges, granting Grangers special privileges such as a ten-day grace period in which to pay, and these farmers became the bedrock for his business. Yet his money-back policy won him customers who made lasting success possible long after the Grange had ceased to be effective as a major rural political force. In fact, Ward's 1876 catalogue reminded Grangers that the company could not "for prudential reasons refuse the patronage of any person. The more goods we handle the cheaper we can sell them. . . . We sell our goods to any person of whatsoever occupation, color or race, provided they conform to our rules."

The Montgomery Ward catalogue along with the products the founder wisely chose for it and the homey style in which he wrote its copy, was another element vital to Ward's success. The importance of the catalogue in inducing customers to buy from afar can hardly be overestimated, but the Ward wish book is far more important than this in American history. In 1946 the esteemed

Grolier Club, a New York society of book lovers, chose the Montgomery Ward catalogue as one of the hundred books most influential on American life. Said the selection committee:

> No idea ever mushroomed so far from so small a beginning, or had so profound an influence on the economics of a continent, as the concept, original to America, of direct selling by mail, for cash. . . . The mail-order catalogue has been perhaps the greatest single influence in increasing the standard of American middle-class living. It brought the benefit of wholesale prices to city and hamlet, to the crossroads and the prairies: it inculcated cash payment as against crippling credit; it urged millions of housewives to bring into their homes and place upon their backs and on their shelves and on their floors creature comforts which otherwise they could never have hoped for, and above all, it substituted sound quality for shoddy. . . .

Ward's catalogue was called "the great wish book" long before Sears's, which, incidentally, gives that name today to its Christmas catalogue. In preparing it Montgomery Ward successfully identified himself as the personal friend of his customers, a friend who would quickly point out to them any exaggerated claims that even his suppliers made. Ward also led in establishing test laboratories to make sure his clients were getting their money's worth. Sometimes he even babied his customers. "In writing your name and address, do not endeavor to show us a sample of spread-eagle, but rather affect the plain and perfectly legible signature of John Hancock," he reminded in one catalogue. In another instance he wrote: "If you don't receive postal from us saying your order has been received, see if order is not in your other coat pocket. Perhaps it is still in your post office without any stamp. Maybe you forgot to sign your name to the order."

By 1890 the slogan, "You Can't Go Wrong When You Deal With Montgomery Ward," had become country-famous, and the Ward catalogue was being used in rural schools as a reference for nearly every subject. The wish book, which cost fifteen cents up until 1904 when the catalogue was provided free for the first time, grew in size from the little 24-page pocket booklet issued in 1874 to the huge 2 pound, 544-page catalogue issued during the 1893 Columbian Exposition. "When I was a child," one old-time Ward customer recalled, "the arrival of Ward catalogues was like having Christmas come three or four times a year."

Montgomery Ward was the forerunner in offering several grades in each class of goods, giving "a range of prices and qualities to meet the requirements of every purse." Though generally a shrewd buyer, sometimes the lure of a bargain trapped him, as when he bought so many buttons at rock-bottom prices that it took five years to sell them. It's said that the short, stocky Ward and tall, distinguished-looking George R. Thorne perfectly complemented each other. "Mr. Ward had the characteristics of a setter dog," Thorne's son once recalled. "That is, he was here, there and everywhere and saw everything and wanted to buy everything. GRT had the opposite characteristics. He never would have found anything, but he knew what to do with it when he got it. . . . It is doubtful if either one of them could have successfully conducted the business alone, but together their success was great." It is ironic to note that while Thorne, a Civil War veteran who had served with General Custer in the Indian campaigns, was far more instrumental to Ward's success than Roebuck was to Sears's, and later bought the business from Ward, making far more money from mail-order than Alvah Roebuck ever did, his name is still relatively unknown in the mail-order field, whereas Roebuck's is immortalized for all time as part of Sears Roebuck & Company.

The Montgomery Ward catalogue always provided country folk with the exciting game of "You think of it, Ward's has it." From the 163 products in the first circular catalogue the items listed grew to 3,899 in the 1876 wish book and were added to by the hundreds every year. There were fabrics like red flannel and calico—one bolt often used to make shirts and dresses for an entire pioneer family. Ward's had hoop skirts, corsets, bosums, perfume, ostrich feathers, and a hundred other things for the ladies. Groceries included everything but liquor, which was tried briefly in 1875 but brought such violent protests from the Prohibitionists that it was dropped (only recently have mail-order houses even dared to list such items as cocktail glasses). Pianos and other musical instruments made life more bearable for the hardy settlers on the treeless plains, whom the government gave 160 acres and bet they couldn't live on it six months. At first these pioneers lived in dugouts or the sod houses described in a contemporary song: "My house is constructed of natural soil;/ The walls are erected according to Hoyle;/the roof has no pitch but is level and plain./ And I never get wet till it happens to rain." But as the settlers prospered, "luxuries" like cast-iron stoves and iceboxes, Seth Thomas clocks, rugs, and silverware were wanted, and "Monkey Ward" supplied them, too.

By 1900 America was still largely rural, with 11 million of its 76 million people employed in farming, and although the average hourly wage was only twenty-two cents, people paid the lowest prices for goods and services that the country would ever see. In the Ward's catalogue could be found everything anyone needed to exist in rural or urban America of the period, from swaddling clothes and baby carriages to guns, bullets, and tombstones. Steam engines, windmills, cream separators, traps, and barbed wire were but a few items of farm equipment offered for sale. There were even exotic farmer's aids like "Adjustable Animal Power": a treadmill that could be operated by one or two animals (dogs, horses, sheep, goats, or cattle) and which supplied enough power for a churn, cream separator, or grindstone.

Ward's advertised a popular water filter after one disgusted Chicago inspector filed the following slightly exaggerated report: "The appearance and quality of the public water supply here were such that the poor used it for soup, the middle class dyed their clothes in it, and the rich used it for top-dressing their lawns. Those who drank it filtered it through a ladder, disinfected it with chloride of lime, then lifted out the dangerous germs that survived and killed them with a club in the back yard." The company, whether dealing with rural or urban customers, from the early years gave bilingual directions for all complicated equipment to aid the immigrants flowing into the country. Later, instructions in 12 languages were printed for filling out an order and customers were urged to use their native language in making orders if they preferred.

In 1878 Ward's ran the first fashion illustration for a woman's dress to appear in a mail-order catalogue. Men's ready-made suits were sold even earlier. By keeping track of the sizes of uniforms and noting that certain combinations of measurements were more common than others, the makers of Civil War uniforms had found that if they made many different sizes, they could provide almost everyone with a reasonably good fit. Ward's helped civilian ready-to-wear replace the old custom-made suit by selling thousands through the mails. Its catalogue instructed: "In ordering clothing, be particular to send your size. Measure for coat around the chest, just under the arms; for pants, take size around waist and length of leg, inside seat. Give your age and describe your general build, and we will, nine times out of ten, give you a fit."

Montgomery Ward's catalogue was first with just about everything. In 1892 George Thorne introduced a smaller catalogue typeface that reduced printing costs and saved on postage. R.R. Donnelley Sons Company, the catalogue's printer, introduced the first rotary press to be used in commercial printing, presses that Donnelley later adapted for what was to become its huge telephone directory printing business. The first half-tone photographs used in a catalogue, featuring a baby as a live model, appeared in the 1896 wish book, and color photos, showing carpets and other merchandise, first appeared in 1901, the catalogue containing over a thousand pages that year. Ward's latched on to every new product that appeared. In the 1890s during the cycling craze, bicycles and "the newest and nobbiest line of bicycle clothing ever brought out" were featured. The company later offered its own car, the Modoc, "the car without a weakness" that was made from parts manufactured by 15 leading suppliers—all the best in their particular field—and assembled for Ward's by an expert automobile maker. Introduced in 1912, the Modoc proved a failure only because there was a lack of Modoc dealers to service them—one thing even the Ward wish book couldn't do.

Certainly the mail-order catalogue ranks with the railroad train, automobile, and airplane as one of the great unifying forces in American life. But people weren't thinking of that when they read their catalogues, ordered from them, reread them in place of literature on cold winter nights, used them in schools along with McGuffey readers, and—after the new catalogue came—put them to good use in the outhouse. Its great wish book made Ward's a $10 million business by 1900, at which time the 25-story Ward Tower on Michigan Avenue, with its famous nude "Spirit of Progress" statue atop it, was the tallest commercial building in the world, and Ward's was by far the biggest customer of the U.S. Post Office.

Founder Montgomery Ward had sold his controlling interest in the company to George Thorne in 1893 and, though he remained president, was not active in management. Ward devoted the rest of his life to good works, notably a crusade against widespread opposition to preserve Chicago's open lakefront, which thanks largely to his efforts is today a magnificent "front yard" for all Chicagoans. He died of pulmonary edema, a form of pneumonia, in 1913, age sixty-nine, believing that his environmental victory, a fight "for the poor people of Chicago, not the millionaires," was his greatest accomplishment, one that far overshadowed his pioneering in mail-order. History has thought otherwise, ranking him as one of the great merchants of all time for giving the nation a new method of shopping, and he is one of the handful of men whose bust is on display in the Chicago Merchandising Mart's Retailing Hall of Fame.

At the beginning of the new century Montgomery Ward & Company lost first place in the mail-order field to Sears, Roebuck, which had countered Ward's slogan, "The Cheapest Cash House in America," with its own, "The Cheapest Supply House on Earth— Our Trade Reaches Around The World." Sears held first place from then on, but only after World War I did the younger company achieve the tremendous lead it enjoys today. The battle for leadership was highly competitive at first, with Ward's coming within striking range of Sears several times. Ward's had its problems. Labor troubles with the United Garment Workers Union in 1902 led to a sympathy strike by the Teamsters Union, which called out the few Teamster drivers on Ward's payroll. While the company managed to continue in business with few disruptions, the strike mushroomed against other large shippers, and by the time it ended in 1905—after Ward's and the garment workers were no longer principals—14 persons had been killed and 312 injured. The strike inspired Ward's to do more for its employees, and it provided overtime pay, paid vacations, and medical attention. In 1912 Montgomery Ward became the first major American company to provide life insurance for its employees, under a landmark Equitable Life plan that also covered sickness, accidents, and old age.

The year before George R. Thorne died in 1918, Ward's directors approved the selling of goods on time payment for the first time, breaking with the founder's policy of cash sales. In 1919 the company became a public corporation and took the name Thorne Brothers, Inc., headed by George Thorne's sons Robert and Charles, though it reinstated its original name within a few weeks. The firm had sales exceeding $100 million the following year, but was in a loss position for the first time in its history because of the postwar inflation and poor management, and the Thornes had to arrange for new capital. Whelan Drugstores, owned by United Cigar Stores, purchased an issue of common stock that gave them control of the company, which finally passed out of the hands of the Thorne and Ward families. But through their own business reverses Whelan lost control soon after and J.P. Morgan & Co. bought the controlling stock.

Perhaps Montgomery Ward would be the leading mail-order company in America today if General Robert E. Wood had remained with the company. Wood, who had worked for a decade on ths Panama Canal under General George Goethals and was a master of supply operations, became Ward's vice-president in charge of merchandising in 1919. Wood's hobby was population shifts, and it is said that his favorite reading was the *Statistical Abstract of the United States.* He was quick to see how the movement of people from rural to urban areas, wrought by the increasing number of automobiles (there were over 8 million registered cars by 1920) and new improved roads like the recently completed Lincoln Highway, would influence the selling of goods in years to come, and he urged the establishment of Ward retail stores that farmers could drive to. Chain stores, especially J.C. Penney with their stores in county seats, were already on the scene with their advantages of larger volume, purchasing power, cheaper operation and what Wood considered the great asset "of allowing the customer to see what he buys." Those mail-order companies that would survive, the general knew, would do so by dropping many of their convenience staple lines, transferring their merchandising to the growing suburban market and establishing department store chains.

Realizing that the golden age of mail-order was over, Wood wrote a memorandum stating, "We can beat the chain stores at their own game. We can easily and profitably engage in the chain store business ourselves with a relatively small amount of capital . . . adding $20 million to business." But Ward's directors could not see the tremendous advantages Ward's respected name, its well-organized purchasing system, and its large distribution plants throughout the country would give the company in operating retail stores. President Theodore Merseles held that decreasing rural population would mean that those farmers who remained would have a larger slice of the agricultural pie and thus be better Ward customers. These differences forced Wood to leave Ward's in 1924 and join the Sears operation, where he instituted his retail store scheme a full two years before Ward's finally saw the light. Both Ward's and Sears had been doing badly in the early 1920s. By failing to realize soon enough that the golden era of mail-order had passed when the steam age yielded to the gasoline age and that Ward's future lay in a chain of retail stores, the company lost its chance to pass Sears, in fact, fell so far behind that it would never catch up again.

Ward's actually had to be *forced* into opening its first retail store. Its first three catalogue stores—where articles were displayed for catalogue ordering but weren't sold—had opened in 1926. The catalogue store in Plymouth, Indiana, had the good fortune to attract an adamant carpenter who noticed a saw on display seventy-five cents cheaper than any he had seen elsewhere, and he demanded the right to buy it on the spot. He was told that this saw was rusty, that a new one would be specially delivered to him from Chicago the next day, but the combative carpenter persisted, and the manager finally let him have the saw on display. As soon as locals discovered that the carpenter had been accorded this service, they demanded the same privilege. People stormed the store buying everything in sight, even the caged canaries, potted plants, and wicker furniture in the reception room! Within a few days the entire stock plus two loads of replacement goods from Chicago sold out. Called up on the carpet by President Merseles, a Morgan man, the manager simply showed him the sales figures and soon Merseles himself was a convert preaching the new gospel of the retail store. By year's end there were 10 Ward retail stores, and by 1928 retail expansion had accelerated to the point where there were 244 chain stores, including Ward's first full-line department store in Birmingham, Alabama.

The changeover wasn't painless. "In setting up basic lists of merchandise to be shipped to new stores," recalls one longtime Ward's executive, "mail-order thinking led to some amazing and expensive incidents. Stores in the South received toboggans, snowshoes and ice skates. A Florida store got a shipment of skis; a Nebraska store far from the water got a 35-foot motor boat. The prize of all was a Memorial Day window display. That department overlooked the fact that Memorial Day is not celebrated in the South." Nevertheless, the new program worked. By 1930 Ward's had 556 retail stores and well over $200 million in sales. Expansion was only halted by the Great Depression, Ward's closing its books in 1931 with an $8.7 million loss, the greatest in its history, at which time Sewell Lee Avery, former president of the U.S. Gypsum Company, became Ward's chairman of the board.

Sewell Avery surely ranks as one of the most colorful, controversial characters in retailing history. He made his share of mistakes in the beginning, as when a notice in the catalogue seeking to add names to Ward's mailing list offered children "a nice little present" for filling out a coupon with papa's name and address—nearly 3 million children responded and $280,000 had to be spent on penny balloons to send them. But Avery did bring the company through the depression in relatively good shape. Ward's showed a profit in every year but 1932; it started its first telephone ordering service, new retail stores were opened, and catalogue sales passed their 1926 peak. Ward's also designated items as Good, Better, and Best for the first time under Avery, and in 1939 a writer in the advertising department, Robert L. May, prepared a Christmas giveaway for Ward's featuring a red-nosed character called Rollo, then Reginald, and finally Rudolph—the same famous reindeer that has become part of American folklore.

Ward's has contributed four things of varying worth to American folklore: the mail-order idea, the great wish book, Rudolph, and the famous photograph of Sewell Avery being carried from his office by the United States Army that made the front page of practically every major newspaper in the country on April 28, 1944. Ward's had prospered during the war, but again there were labor troubles and when Avery refused to renew a union contract in 1944, President Roosevelt ordered the company seized under wartime powers, and Avery was forcibly ejected from his office, earning a national reputation as a "Neanderthal" in the process. Yet that incident was really insignificant compared with what was to follow. Avery's deserved or undeserved reputation as a dodo bird—the mythical dodo bird with eyes in the back of its head that knows where it has been but not where it is going—might have been forgotten, or even glamorized, if it hadn't been for his leadership backwards in the postwar years.

Ward's came out of World War II with a huge cash reserve and was within sight of Sears, with annual sales of over a billion dollars. Here was a second chance for the company to catch its traditional rival, but instead of expanding as Sears did, Avery sat on his nest egg during the postwar boom, expecting another depression. He was sure it would come—why, he could point it out on the elaborate chart in his office showing the fall in the economy after every war since Napoleon! These were known as the "lost years," or the "do-nothing period," in the words of later Ward officials. Not only did Avery decline to expand, but he refused to modernize, air-condition, or even paint the company's dowdy old stores. Although models like Lauren Bacall, Susan Hayward, Mona Freeman, and Suzy Parker graced Ward catalogues, the 1951 catalogue used mannequins instead of live models to display items like brassieres and panties. The prudish Avery even vetoed hosiery on shapely *leg forms*, insisting that it be illustrated folded. One could go on and on. Perhaps equating S.L. Avery with "slavery," Avery's top executives quit on him right and left when he refused to delegate even minor authority to them.

The American Institute of Management summarized a report on Ward's by stating, "Here is a fine company, led by brilliant businessmen, but it is a one-man company and in this lies all its troubles." Avery was called a "dictator" and Montgomery Ward, with a $650 million nest egg by 1954, including real-estate holdings, was dubbed "the bank with the store front." Yet Avery suffered from a grossly unfair characterization; he was hardly the incompetent fool he had been pictured as. Though he was no Wanamaker or Filene, up until the postwar years he had led the company well, a traditional merchant who insisted on quality goods and operated on sound business principles. Even Avery's resistance to the War Labor Board in 1944 had its basis in reason, as another chapter will show, and his action did ultimately save Ward's more than a million dollars. What transpired after World War II was a tragedy. As Booton Herndon wrote in his modern-day Ward's biography *Satisfaction Guaranteed*: "In 1950 Avery nearly died with pneumonia, and suffered a severe stroke. He was 77 years old, and his brush with death brought on a psychopathic fear of being old. He had seen his father retire and wither away with nothing to do, and he now lived in terror of the senility which had already seized him. He refused to retire. . . . Martinets emerged to toady to him and make life miserable for others. . . . Avery stayed on."

The curtain came down on the tragedy in 1955 when corporate raider Louis Wolfson, a highly intelligent, aggressive man who had once played tackle for Georgia University's football team, made a spectacular bid for control of Montgomery Ward. Wolfson launched a nationwide campaign to gain the proxy votes of enough stockholders to oust Avery and win control of the board of directors, a sorry group including one member who regularly slept through meetings. This was one of the great proxy fights in corporate history, but turned into a "pitiful sight," according to Herndon, when "Avery, badgered by Wolfson and his lieutenants, cracked up and became incoherent." Wolfson failed to win control of the board, though he and two associates won seats, but the battle finished the eighty-one-year-old Avery, who resigned in 1955 at the urging of his friends. As for Wolfson, he ultimately went to jail for selling unregistered stock in another company and for perjury. Wolfson indirectly brought down Abe Fortas, who resigned under fire from the Supreme Court when it was alleged that he had been involved financially with Wolfson while the latter was under investigation by the Securities and Exchange Commission.

Montgomery Ward was "a socially and spiritually bankrupt" firm after Avery's reign ended, says one company official, but the new management under chairman John A. Barr began to expand and modernize Ward's retail stores and create a healthier working atmosphere for employees on all levels. With the coming of the 1960s all of Ward's excess cash was fully invested in the business. The Sixties have been labelled the "Turnaround Years" at Ward's. Robert E. Brooker, a former Sears' executive who became Ward's president and then chairman, on Barr's retirement in 1965, led the firm in closing many old stores, building new ones and modernizing and mechanizing many operations. Ward's introduced Charg-all, its revolving credit plan in 1961 and two years later developed its store "cluster concept" in metropolitan areas, where all stores were ordered to carry the same goods and take part in coordinated promotion and advertising campaigns. The Sixties also marked

Ward's entry into the banking and insurance business with the purchase of Pioneer Trust & Savings of Chicago and the formation of the Montgomery Ward Life Insurance Company. Just before the decade ended, in late 1968, Ward's and the Container Corporation of America, the nation's largest manufacturer of folding cartons and shipping containers, merged into a new holding company called Marcor, annual sales in the following year surpassing the $2 billion mark for the first time in Ward's history.

Today, Montgomery Ward remains a fast-moving, growing organization that shows no signs of decline. In 1974, the year in which the company's new 26-story headquarters building was erected across the street from its historic location on Chicago Avenue, the Mobil Oil Corporation acquired a controlling interest in Marcor. Two years later the merger of Marcor into the Mobil Oil Corporation became effective, both Montgomery Ward and its partner, the Container Corporation of America, becoming wholly owned by Mobil. Led by its new chairman Edward S. Donnell, formerly Ward's president in the Brooker administration, the company opened its Chicago Ford City retail stores, the largest ever constructed by the company, and made national news again with a $1 million donation to the 1976 U.S. Olympic team in the following year. Ward's now operates 433 retail and 474 catalogue stores, which have annual sales of about $5 billion making it the fifth largest general merchandise retailer in America. Its major problem is in becoming a truly national company like Sears or Penney, a problem that now has first priority. Like Sears, another public-spirited company, which gives away some $19 million a year to good causes, Ward's is proud of its affirmative action plan under which there have been large increases in black, Hispanic, and women employees over the last few years, but in neither company do members of minorities yet hold positions of real power.

Mail-order (a lot of it really telephone orders) still accounts for almost one-quarter of Montgomery Ward's business, and its $1 billion in catalogue sales puts Wards in second place behind Sears, though J.C. Penney is hotly contesting the company for this position. Ward's wish book is now printed twelve times a year—two big basic books running around 1,300 pages each and weighing about five pounds brought out in the fall and spring, and ten special books, including the Christmas catalogue published at other times.

A few statistics about this great wish book shows just how big mail-order remains in America:

• 900,000 trees are harvested to produce the 50,000 tons of paper for the Ward catalogue, enough paper to circle the globe four times.

• 2 million gallons of ink and 125 tons of glue are required to print the catalogues and hold them together.

• 750,000 worker-hours are needed to produce a year's worth of wish books, a task that would take one person more that four centuries.

• The free catalogues, taken together, would cost well over $100 a set if sold by a book publisher.

• Over 100,000 items are listed in the wish books—about three times more items than are carried by most large department stores.

• 86 million copies of the 12 catalogues, containing a total of 28 billion pages, are distributed to customers from Ward's name file of more than 10 million people.

1877

The World's First Wholesale Mail-Order House
BUTLER BROTHERS—*Boston, Massachusetts*

The year after America's centennial, George and Edward Butler scraped together about three thousand dollars and founded Butler Brothers at No. 9 Arch Street in Boston, their little wholesale store occupying a space no larger than 16 feet x 40 feet. The world's greatest jobbing business grew from that seed. Because of their limited capitalization and inability to offer wide selections, the brothers conceived the idea of offering a number of specialties at a uniform retail price of five cents each. They put together an assorted case of goods (tacks and pins, screwdrivers, corkscrews, etc.) containing 50 dozen five-cent items, which they offered to merchants for twenty dollars. The contents were not itemized, though a few "leaders" or bargains were mentioned, and included with each assortment, at no charge, was a printed sign reading: "ANYTHING ON THIS TABLE—5¢." Jason Bailey, a Boston merchant, was so enthusiastic when he saw the success of a Butler Brothers five-cent counter in a local store that he brought $800 worth of their merchandise and opened Boston's first all variety store in 1878, a full year before Frank Woolworth had his first success in New York. In years to come, after being called Racket Stores and Rummage Stores, the name Variety Stores was given to such enterprises; in fact, it was at Butler Brother's suggestion that Dun & Bradstreet first established Variety Stores as a classification in their audit rating books.

In January 1879 Butler Brothers initiated the practice of selling wholesale by mail, offering their $20 assortment of 5¢ goods to the trade via a penny post card. In doing this they were forsaking bartering and their secret codes for plain prices that all merchants could see. Within a few years their post cards became their famous wholesale catalogue, *The Drummer*, drummers in the late nineteenth century being salesmen sent out to "drum up" business.

Butler Brothers lasted exclusively as wholesalers much longer than Carson, Pirie Scott, Marshall Field, and other present-day retailers who began as wholesalers or had early wholesale divisions. In the 1920s, the company entered the retail field, under the voluntary chain idea, but it remained primarily a wholesale operation until 1951, when it began serving only company-owned variety and department stores and its Ben Franklin franchises. Butler Brothers–Ben Franklin was purchased in 1960 by the City Products Company, now owned by the Household Finance Corporation. The former wholesale mail-order company that began with capital of three thousand dollars is now a retailing giant with over 2,500 stores and annual sales of close to a billion dollars.

1882

"We Trust the People—Everywhere"

SPIEGEL, INC.—*Chicago, Illinois*

Spiegel's began as a retail furniture store called Spiegel, May, Stern Company, but went into mail order in 1904, pioneering in installment credit selling. The Spiegels, who were the major force in the firm, descended from Marcus Spiegel, a rabbi who had fled Germany to America in 1848 like so many liberals and revolutionists, supported himself and his family here by peddling needles and thread, and later commanded combat troops as a captain in the Union Army. The firm's first catalogue, issued in 1904, was a modest 24-page affair that offered credit terms as liberal as 15 percent down and ten months to pay, and its slogan was "We Trust the People—Everywhere." Though Spiegel's credit policy ran counter to the early "cash only" policies of Ward's and most other houses, the firm prospered and became one of America's mail-order giants— despite the undesirable publicity it got one year when a U.S. senator was convicted of taking a bribe from a Spiegel official to vote for a postal law designed to help Spiegel sales.

In 1961 Spiegel's built an automated 12-story warehouse considered by *Business Week* to be "the first fundamental change in mail-order warehousing in 50 years." According to another account, the new warehouse inspired the larger mail-order firms to upgrade their facilities.

Spiegel's was acquired in 1955 by the Midwest Mail-order Company, a subsidiary of Beneficial Finance, this merger probably necessary because of Spiegel's constant need for capital. Spiegel's now does about $420 million in sales annually, making it number four in the mail-order field, but the company recently closed all its catalogue stores, calling them "less and less profitable" every year.

1886

The World's Number One Retailer

SEARS, ROEBUCK AND COMPANY—*Chicago, Illinois*

If, as the Montgomery Ward people say, it would take four centuries for one person to produce Ward's annual catalogues, it would take the same superhuman almost as much time just to count Sears, Roebuck's money. Montgomery Ward is giant enough to satisfy the wildest longings of any fledgling storekeeper; Sears is simply beyond the comprehension of all but the computers among us. Sears, Roebuck and Company, if anyone doesn't know it by now, is the world's largest retailer, with annual sales of over $22 billion, almost half the sales of General Motors, which has the largest annual sales of any company in the world. The $22 billion comes from all its varied operations, which include everything from catalogue and department store sales to its insurance and banking businesses. That's enough dollar bills to circle the globe at the equator more than 75 times, or to make a stack over 1300 miles high that will reach to the moon if Sears continues making merely the same annual sales for the next two centuries or so.

Right now Sears has the most stores, the most customers, the most sales, the most profits of any retailer anywhere. Three out of every four Americans shop at a Sears store at least once a year; half of all American households read the Sears mail-order catalogue. Sears's Allstate insurance company alone is almost as big as its two biggest rivals, Ward and Penney's. Sears is not only the world's largest retailer but it is the seventh largest American company, employing one out of every 204 workers in the country. As the world's biggest advertiser it spends nearly half a billion dollars a year, including $125 million for its catalogues, and keeps 40 ad agencies busy creating $378 million worth of retail ads every year, an expenditure greater than the annual sales of all but a handful of department stores. Sears was even the recipient of the largest check ever issued by a bank or business concern—one for $960,242,000 issued in 1961 by the Continental Illinois Bank & Trust Company of Chicago. In 1976 the company had 858 retail stores and more than three thousand catalogue, retail, and telephone sales offices and independent catalogue merchants in 15 countries. Its total assets are valued at nearly $23 billion. Operating out of the 110-story Sears Tower in Chicago, very appropriately the world's tallest building, Sears's annual sales represent over one percent of America's GNP (gross national product), which is $2 trillion; that is, about one percent of all the goods and services sold in this country. No other retailer in history has been as prosperous.

Sears's unsurpassed success can be attributed to three great merchants: Richard Warren Sears, the company founder and a "Barnum of merchandising" who "could sell a breath of air"; Julius Rosenwald, who saved the company in later years; and General Robert Elkington Wood, who led Sears into its retail stores operation, which far overshadows its mail-order business today. The company's second eponym, Alvah C. Roebuck, had comparatively little to do with Sears, Roebuck's success.

Richard Sears was the son of a Minnesota farmer-blacksmith of

English descent who had prospected in vain for gold with the Forty-niners, served in the Civil War, suffering a serious wound, and finally lost all his money in an ill-fated stock-farm venture. He died a bitter man when Richard was only fourteen, blaming his failures on "politicians," and the boy became the family breadwinner, learning telegraphy and eventually becoming freight agent of the Minneapolis and Saint Louis Railroad station in North Redwood, Minnesota. His six dollar-a-week paycheck inspired him to find other ways to make extra money, and so he sold lumber and coal to local residents in his spare time. A few years later a shipment of five hundred unordered gold-filled watches refused by a Redwood Falls jeweler was returned to the railroad office and Sears bought them from their Chicago maker for resale. When the watches sold out quickly to neighbors and train crews, he ordered more, selling these to other station agents up and down the line at a profit of about $2 apiece. (Sears bought the watches for $12, sold them for $14 and his station agent salesmen, operating on a smaller scale, hawked them for up to $20.) Since he was bonded as a station agent and didn't have to pay for the watches on delivery, the enterprising young man took no risk at all. By sending watches to fictitious names in towns up and down the line, like the unscrupulous Chicago wholesalers did, more watches were returned to railroad stations and Sears recruited still more station agent–salesmen. In six months he netted about five thousand dollars and decided to quit railroading, moving to Minneapolis, where he founded the R. W. Sears Watch Company in 1886.

The little business did so well, thanks mainly to the sparkling copy Sears wrote for his low-priced watches in newspaper ads, that it outgrew Minneapolis within a few months and its founder moved it to Chicago to take advantage of better shipping facilities. There Sears found that he could increase profits by buying watch movements and cases separately and doing his own assembling. Knowing nothing about watchmaking himself, he put an ad in *Chicago Daily News* of April 1, 1887 seeking an experienced helper:

WANTED: *Watchmaker with reference who can furnish tools. State age, experience and salary required.* ADDRESS T39, *Daily News.*

Alvah Curtis Roebuck, a young watchmaker who read the ad, put it aside and woke up in the middle of the night to answer it, got the job when he brought Sears a sample of his best repair work. First, Sears examined the timepiece as if he were an expert himself. Probably noting that Roebuck wasn't in the least disturbed, he finally said, as Roebuck later recalled: "I don't know anything about watchmaking, but I presume this is good, otherwise you wouldn't have submitted it to me. You look all right and you may have the position."

No doubt Sears was impressed with this tall, almost emaciated young man who usually dressed in high collars and black suits and reminded some of a distinguished Methodist minister. The incredibly energetic, aggressive Sears, handsome, mustached, and dressed to the nines, probably also saw that he could easily control the gentle, retiring Roebuck. Roebuck, who had been operating a watch-repair shop in the corner of a Hammond, Indiana, delicatessen before Sears hired him, always remained a simple farm boy far less complicated than the watches he had loved to tinker with since childhood. Certainly he was easily led by his employer—according to one biography, "Persuading Roebuck seems to have been among Sears' most easily come-by accomplishments. . . ." At any rate, Roebuck organized an assembly line, something few manufacturers utilized at the time, to make cheaper Sears watches from wheels, springs, and other parts, but he contributed little else to the development of the company. It was Richard Sears who conceived the idea of a small Sears catalogue and wrote all copy for it. Sears added jewelry and diamonds to the company's line, instituted installment payments, advertised a money-back guarantee, and established a Toronto branch. Finally, it was Richard Sears alone who made the decision to sell his United States operation in 1889 to what became the Moore and Evans Company. He did not consult his partner at all, but nevertheless managed to sell Roebuck and another employee the firm's Toronto branch.

Sears invested most of the $72,000 he got for the R. W. Sears Watch Company in Iowa farm mortgages and bragged about becoming an Iowa banker, but in a few months returned to the mail-order business in Minneapolis. At first he called his new firm the Warren Company, using his middle name because his sales agreement with Moore and Evans stipulated that he wouldn't use the name Sears commercially for three years. In 1890, however, he talked Roebuck into buying Warren and retired again, only to come back within a week and persuade the gentle Roebuck to sell him a half-interest in what was now A.C. Roebuck, Inc., and make him president to boot! By September 1893, when the three-year name-ban expired, the firm became Sears, Roebuck and Company for the first time, Sears now owning a two-thirds interest in it, and was well on its way to becoming the colossus known throughout the world today. An enlarged catalogue of 196 pages appeared at this time, featuring men's and boys' clothing, bicycles, sewing machines, wagons, furniture, musical instruments, and other products in addition to watches and jewelry. Sales topped $400,000 in 1893 and kept growing. By 1895, the year the firm moved back to Chicago, sales were $750,000 and the catalogue, its cover already proclaiming Sears, "The Cheapest Supply House on Earth," numbered 507 pages, all in the face of a severe business depression.

Alvah Roebuck's nerves, stomach, and perhaps his conscience couldn't cope with the company's growth, or the ways Richard Sears made the company grow. While he admired Sears for being everything he would never be, Roebuck found it hard to abide with some of the skittish tricks his partner devised to catch customers. Farmers were urged for example, to send ninety-five cents "to pay expenses, boxing, packing, advertising, etc." for a "beautiful miniature UPHOLSTERED PARLOR SET of three pieces." The furniture, handsomely pictured in the ad, turned out to be "miniature" all right—farmers on opening the package found that it contained doll-sized chairs and tables. Sears was also back to his old trick of sending unordered watches to businessmen in the vicinity of each of the twenty thousand railroad express offices in the country. And he'd advertise whatever came into his mind to keep his rural customer interested, even if the company didn't have the item in stock. One time he cut the picture of an impressive swagger suit from a newspaper and pasted it in a catalogue on its way to the printer. It's said that five thousand orders piled up before poor Roebuck could find an adequate supply of suits.

"To make room for the next mail delivery every now and then," one biographer writes, "Richard Sears would carry a bundle of unfilled orders to the furnace. He had a merry time of it." Not

Roebuck. Roebuck worried. His constitution couldn't take the twelve-hour-a-day, seven-day-a-week schedule Sears seemed to thrive on. Neither was he a gambler. Sears, Roebuck sales were growing greater each year and every sign indicated a fantastic future, but profits were not yet increasing and the firm's debts were $75,000 by 1895. Roebuck insisted on selling his one-third interest, and Sears bought him out for $25,000, only a fraction of the millions Roebuck would have received had he waited just a few more years, and about as much as Sears takes in every ten seconds of a working day at present.

Roebuck allowed the company to continue to use his name and worked for several years as the head of the watch and jewelry department. Later, he formed a company that developed stereopticons, projectors, and other equipment for motion pictures and accumulated a moderate fortune that he eventually lost in Florida real estate during the crash of 1929. Broken by the Great Depression, he came back hat in hand to the company bearing his name and was given a low-paying job answering letters about patents held by the firm. Sears, Roebuck and Company finally sent him on a tour of its stores as a kind of "full-time travelling exhibit of what a co-founder looks like." When he was made a Kentucky colonel by Kentucky governor Ruby Laffoon, he was billed as such and placed at a desk near store entrances under a sign reading, "Meet Colonel A. C. Roebuck, Co-Founder." This sideshow rather smacked of the Barnumesque showmanship of Richard Sears, but Roebuck didn't seem to mind, probably enjoyed it all. Whenever anyone mentioned his "failures" he'd say, "Sears made $25 million—he's dead. Skinner [the first merchandising manager] made a million and a quarter— he's dead. Rosenwald made a hundred million—he's dead. Me, I never felt better!" He died in 1948, aged eighty-four, knowing full well that Richard Sears had died when only fifty.

After Roebuck left the company, Richard Sears scouted around for a new partner and found one immediately in the person of Aaron E. Nusbaum, who walked in one day to try and sell him a pneumatic tube system. Nusbaum, who had made $150,000 from the ice-cream and soda-pop concession at the Chicago's World's Fair before getting into the pneumatic tube business, failed to sell Sears one of his money carriers. Instead, Sears talked him into buying a partnership in Sears, Roebuck. Nusbaum then brought in his brother-in-law, Julius Rosenwald, a suit manufacturer who had done business with Sears and didn't have to be sold on the company's bright prospects. By 1898 the three men each owned five hundred shares of the firm, Richard Sears able to concentrate on promotions and selling while his partners ably administrated the business.

With sales of over $11 million in 1900, Sears, Roebuck entered the new century leading Montgomery Ward for the first time in its history, a lead it was never again to relinquish. The horizon seemed bright to Richard Sears, except for the figure of Aaron Nusbaum, a compulsive fault finder, who constantly went around criticizing employees (in contrast to Sears, who believed praise got more work done), and whose favorite phrase was a smug "I told you so" that grated on everybody's nerves. The personality clash ended with Sears demanding that Rosenwald and he buy out Nusbaum, or that the two brothers-in-law buy him out. Rosenwald decided to stick with Sears, realizing he was the only one of the partners who really understood the American farmer, and agreed to join in buying out his sister's husband, a decision he knew was right when Nusbaum at the last minute raised his selling price from $1 million to $1.25 million dollars.

Sears, Roebuck's early history is very similar to Montgomery Ward's, with Sears passing the older company because Richard Sears was a better promoter and Julius Rosenwald a better administrator than anyone at Ward's. The two men working in tandem were unbeatable. There were no longer any unfilled orders under Rosenwald; Rosenwald organized the Sears shipping operation so well that Henry Ford studied it before setting up his famous automobile assembly line in Detroit. Then there was Richard Sears's great promotion called "Iowaization," which began in 1905. Sears encouraged Iowa customers to make customers of their neighbors by offering them premiums in return for personally distributing catalogues to 24 friends. The plan did so well in Iowa that all of America was eventually "Iowaized" by Sears.

Sears, Roebuck went public in 1906, with Sears and Rosenwald receiving $4.5 million each in exchange for their previous stock on the company's incorporation. But when a national business panic followed the next year, Richard Sears and Rosenwald were at odds about what to do. Sears argued that more money should be spent on advertising, while Rosenwald was for a general belt tightening. After the board supported Rosenwald's strategy, Richard Sears stepped down as president. Though he continued as a company director and as board chairman for a time, he took no further active part in Sears's affairs.

Richard Sears's health had been poor for close to a decade due to the torrid pace he had set for himself in building the company, and upon retirement it failed him entirely. He died in 1914, leaving an estate of $25 million, but the evidence indicates that he hadn't been interested in making money so much as in making his mail-order business grow. Schemer though he was, Richard Sears "was born, lived, died, in an age of schemes . . . the grand era of the unfettered entrepreneur." His business was his whole life and he would have appreciated the tribute paid to him in *Printer's Ink*, the journal of the advertising business, soon after his death:

> R.W. Sears was a mail-order man, had the mail-order view point, knew how to use advertising space, knew the value of copy, knew the conditions surrounding mail-order publications, and he succeeded in a big way because he possessed those qualities to a greater degree than any other mail-order man who ever lived.

The great huckster of mail order was the last of a breed, and his passing from Sears marked an end to the company's days of bold aggressive promotion, the cautious, systematic merchandising of Julius Rosenwald prevailing in its place. Under Rosenwald, Sears Roebuck catalogue advertising changed from the flamboyant to the factual, patent medicines, for example, being dropped altogether in 1913. The company began a period of steady growth that saw the development of manufacturing facilities and the introduction of a testing laboratory. Rosenwald was a great organizer, not a great innovator. The son of a Jewish pack peddler who had experienced much prejudice and many hard times on the road, he was also a renowned public benefactor whose philanthropies alone would be a story in itself—when he died in 1932 he left only $17 million of the $200 million fortune he had made over the years, most of the rest having gone to charities or causes he supported. Although he generally separated his philanthropic from his business life and his standing with labor wasn't extraordinary, Rosenwald did introduce

Sears's profit-sharing plan in 1916, at a time when critics were charging that low wages at Sears and other concerns were forcing working girls into prostitution. Sears's plan was the second such scheme in the history of large U.S. corporations and perhaps the most generous—one low-level worker employed by the firm for forty years retired in the 1950s with over half a million dollars from the plan. It has often been credited with attracting talented people to the company and holding on to them.

Rosenwald has been called the greatest pioneer in the history of corporate management, a more gifted administrator than Alfred Sloan of General Motors, who created the modern corporation. He was not without fault and made ludicrous mistakes—once he tried to bribe a Republican candidate for the Senate, offering the man $500,000 in Sears stock if he would withdraw in favor of a reform candidate! But "General Merchandise," as he once called himself, is still regarded as a saint at Sears for dramatically rescuing the company in the midst of the 1921 business recession, when the firm lost over $16 million and was in danger of failing as many small mail-order companies had. Rosenwald pledged $20 million of his personal fortune to help Sears meet its debts and continue business as usual, an act that restored public confidence in Sears and saved the company. This inspired the praise of business leaders and public officials throughout America, who observed that it was the first time in the history of American business that the leader of a giant corporation had rescued that company with his own assets. Later, during the stock market crash of 1929, Rosenwald would do something similar, personally guaranteeing the stock trading accounts of all Sears employees and borrowing $7 million to do so.

Rosenwald, despite the huge fortune he made as head of Sears, had some unorthodox views about wealth and intelligence. "I never could understand the popular belief that because a man makes a lot of money he has a lot of brains," he once said. "Some very rich men who made their own fortunes have been among the stupidest men I have ever met in my life. Rich men are not smart because they are rich. They didn't get rich because they were smart. Don't ever confuse wealth with brains."

Albert Loeb, Rosenwald's righthand man, might have succeeded to the presidency of Sears when Rosenwald began a search for a successor, but the kindly Loeb, known as "a prince among men," never recovered from the shock of the Leopold-Loeb murder case, dying soon after his son Richard and Nathan Leopold, Jr. confessed to the "thrill killing" of thirteen-year-old Bobby Franks and were sentenced to life imprisonment. The next great leader to guide Sears was General Robert Elkington Wood, a retired Army general with whom Rosenwald had been friendly when he served as a dollar-a-year man in Washington during World War I as head of a committee for the purchase of noncombat supplies. As noted, Rosenwald hired Wood away from Montgomery Ward in 1924, after the older company refused to go along with the general's plans for expanding into retail stores. Wood promptly began Sears's retail store chain, which is now the largest in the world.

General Wood made sure the company lived by the so-called Rosenwald Creed:

Sell for less by buying for less. Sell for less by cutting the cost of sales. Make less profit on each individual item and increase your aggregate profit by selling more items. But always maintain the quality.

He also recognized the fact that most department stores did 80 percent of their business with women at the time and made sure that Sears stores were "family stores," catering to men as well. Wood not only expanded Sears's retail store operation over the years, but decentralized it in every area but buying to make it more effective.

"The General," as he was widely called, became president of Sears in 1928 and chairman of the board eleven years later. His quarter-century leading the company—he retired in 1954 and died fifteen years later, aged ninety—marked a period of growth the likes of which is unprecedented in retailing history. Though hardly the infallible man that early biographers make him—his politics included purblind isolationism, support of the fascistic America First, and support of McCarthyism and union busting—he does deserve most of the credit for molding the Sears of today. Incidentally, this might very well have been a Sears that included Montgomery Ward, for in 1931 the two companies come close to merging, the informal negotiations breaking down when Sears would only offer one share of its stock for three of Wards, while Ward insisted on a one for two exchange.

Sears's gargantuan business, aside from its store and catalogue operations, now includes the Allstate Insurance Company, which dates back to 1931, when automobile insurance was first sold through the mail. Allstate takes its name from the Sears Allstate tire, named by the winning entry from over 900,000 names submitted in a $25,000 contest held in 1925. The company's familiar slogan, "You're in Good Hands When You're with Allstate," is said to have originated when Dave Ellis, an Allstate executive, told Sears admen how he had been concerned about his daughter's condition when she was hospitalized with hepatitis and his wife had reassured him, "The hospital says not to worry. We're in good hands with Dr.———." Ellis also suggested the company logo, a pair of hands cradling a car, that has been used for over twenty-five years now.

Sears, Roebuck has had its share of failures through the years. A notable example is the *Encyclopaedia Britannica*, originally purchased by Rosenwald in 1920, sold back to its original proprietors at a loss of $1,848,000 only a year later, and purchased yet again by the company in 1928. Sears tried for fifteen years to make a success of the great EB, but it proved too expensive and sophisticated for its customers and the company finally donated it to the University of Chicago, its present publisher. Sears's grocery business never made money, either, and after many years was abandoned in 1929. The most humorous of failures was a line of high-fashion dresses created by the noted American designer Lady Duff-Cooper and featured in the 1916 catalogue. One such dress was dubbed the "I'll Come Back to You," by its creator and it did exactly that for Sears— two dresses were sold, the same two being returned.

Sears's manufacturing ventures began with Richard Sears's cream separator, which he contracted to have manufactured for the company at fifty dollars when all other separators on the market sold for three times the price. Stoves, pianos, and many other items followed, until today suppliers in which Sears is a part owner manufacture about 30 percent of the products the company sells, partly Sears-owned firms operating some 278 plants with total sales of about $4 billion a year.

Sears could very well become "America's Banker" as well as a leading manufacturer and the place "Where America Shops." The company presently operates 45 savings and loan branches in California through its Allstate Enterprises, which includes its insurance company and now brings Sears 26 percent of its total revenues. A proposed merger with the 39-branch Security and Loan Association in California, yet to be approved by federal and state regulating agencies, would make Sears the fourteenth largest of the more than five thousand savings and loan associations in America. One observer reports that modern-day electronic funds transfer (E.F.T.) technology could be used in Sears's banking operations "to create fundamental changes in the way dollars travel through the American economy by eliminating many of the billions of checks written each year to pay bills." E.F.T. has already given birth to a new kind of retailing establishment where the customer chooses merchandise and instead of writing a check, using cash or credit, hands the clerk a plastic card similar to a credit card. Using a countertop terminal linked by the telephone lines to the customer's bank, the clerk can transfer money from the customer's account to the store's account. Similarly, customers can deposit money with a retailer and bypass conventional financial institutions. No one yet knows what the future holds for E.F.T., but Sears entry into the field in a big way will no doubt influence the outcome.

Through concessionaires Sears has since 1970 broadened its operations into a dozen new fields besides banking, including driver education, commercial photography, frozen foods, floral shops, income-tax preparation, and optometry. The newest service, initiated in an El Monte, California, store early in 1977, is a dental clinic open during store hours to treat members of California's Denti-Care Plan. This is the very latest addition to the department store "shop under one roof" idea—now the Sears shopper can buy a new set of teeth in addition to clothing, furniture, and hardware.

With total sales of over $22 billion, from all its operations, Sears Roebuck is more than twice as big as its nearest retailing competitor, K mart, and has the combined sales volume of both K mart and J. C. Penney, which occupies the third place in retail sales. The company is at present headed by Edward R. Telling, Jr., who in 1977 was elected chairman and chief executive officer on the retirement of Arthur M. Wood, no relation to the general. The mild-mannered Telling, noted for a phenomenal memory that still stores stock numbers of items Sears carried twenty years ago, came up through the ranks and had directed Sears's field operation as senior executive vice president. Back in 1974, when Sears's profits tumbled because the company sought a fashion image and began stocking and advertising higher priced goods (just as a recession hit America), Telling urged a return to the company's traditional niche—between the fashion shops and the low-priced stores, a position that discounter K mart was successfully invading. The move back to the middle market was a huge success. "We are not Bloomingdale's or K mart," Telling said. "We are once again back to where people feel comfortable with us."

Sears stores are divided into four classes: "A" stores, carrying every Sears line; "B" stores, about one-half to three-quarters the size of the former and carrying about 60 lines; "C" or hardline stores, carrying mostly appliances, sporting goods, and automobile supplies; and "D" stores, carrying only appliances. Buying is a centralized operation, but five regional divisions otherwise control the stores in their areas, the divisions in turn, being responsible to the main office in Chicago's Sears Tower.

Though Sears company headquarters, opened in 1973, is no architectural masterpiece, its very bigness and efficiency makes it typical of Sears. The tallest building in the world, some 100 feet higher than New York's World Trade Center at 1454 feet, Sears Towers has 4.5 million square feet of space. It is a bundle of nine tubes, each rising to a different height—like a bunch of straws of different lengths set in a glass. These separate structures form a living profile, but, unfortunately, the building's liveliness is limited to the top, its lower part being flat and dull. Outside, automatic unmanned machines clean the building, while high-speed elevators inside travel at 1,800 feet a minute, and robot carts glide over invisible tracks sprayed onto the carpets to carry communications from office to office. In the lobby is the sculpture *Universe* by the late Alexander Calder, the inventor of kinetic art and perhaps the most "American" of all contemporary artists. The total composition spreads over a massive 55-foot-long by 33-foot-high wall and weighs in excess of eight tons. This mechanized mural sums up Calder's life work as it revolves, swings, turns as if on a spit, and generally activates itself in the full brilliance of the artist's favorite colors. The tower itself does not equal Calder's sculpture, but it has become one of Chicago's icons—in fact, local souvenir shops sell models of the building.

Cover of Sears' famous 1894 catalogue.

GRANGERS BEWARE

Don't Patronize "Montgomery, Ward & Co."—They Are Dead-Beats.

Saturday, November 8, 1873

Another attempt at swindling has come to light. This time it is a firm, Montgomery, Ward & Co. by name, and the parties specially aimed at by the project are no less important a body than the Grangers. This swindling firm, in a bill headed "Grangers Supplied by the Cheapest Cash House in America," sets forth that, at the "earnest solicitation of many Grangers," they have consented to open a house devoted to furnishing farmers and mechanics throughout the Northwest with all kinds of merchandise at wholesale prices. Then comes the list of Utopian figures, such as gold locket for $1.50; 10 yards poplin, $1.75; gentlemen's toilet set, containing Westenholm razor, toothbrush, nail-brush, combs, hair-brush, lather-brush, razor-strop, shaving-box, and soap for $1; 1 secretary writing-desk with implements complete for $1; 1 hoop-skirt, 1 bustle, and 1 hair-braid for $1, and the balance of 200 articles or lots, all at the same figures. The firm boast that they "make no display;" in fact, they keep altogether retired from the public gaze, and are only to be reached through correspondence sent to a certain box in the Post-Office. They are prepared to make purchases for customers of all kinds of merchandise they do not keep, and do it "simply as an accommodation to customers," who are charged only 5 per cent commission on the net cost. The firm employ no agents. There is probably only one man composing it, and he wants to have all the money the gulls send him for himself. He gets all the letters, with the 10 cents inclosed for sample, the occasional sums sent to make purchases on commission, and all the remittances for the trash sent to his dupes, if, in fact, anything at all is sent. On the letters asking for samples merely, the profits amount to something worth while, for it is known that a certain proportion of the multitudes of circulars issued fall into the hands of credulous fools, who place boundless faith in anything which is set up in type and printed. If such fools would only consider how easy a thing it is to start a swindle of this kind, the dead-beats who got them up would be driven to hard work, or still better, perhaps, starvation. After sending out a couple of hundred thousand circulars, at a cost of a couple of hundred dollars or less, the victimizer sits in his room and awaits responses, which, strange to say, in "tight times" particularly, come in in such numbers that in a fortnight he has his $200 back, together with a very handsome margin of profit. Then he starts another huge benevolent scheme, with a different Post-Office box as his headquarters, addresses a different class of people to those previously tempted, and cleans out its fools of their spare funds; and so on until wealth brings renown, and, finally, he becomes the successful candidate for aldermanic or higher honors on the ticket of a bummer party. The safety of these operators lies in the fact that out of a thousand men who have been duped in it is hard to find one who cares to expose the swindle, and necessarily his own stupidity at the same time.

Alvah Roebuck wanted nothing to do with Richard Sears' electric belts, which were, quite frankly, a rip-off.

The *Chicago Daily Tribune* later retracted this anti-mail order article, which was "planted" by hostile retail merchants.

Single Dog Power.

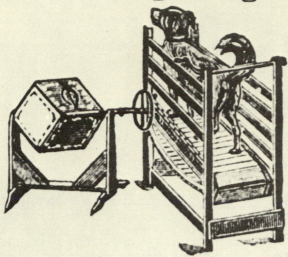

No. 78855 This power can be operated by a dog, goat or sheep; **yields 25 per cent. more** power from a given weight of animal than any other, and **with adjustable bridge,** to regulate the required power and motion, a 30-pound animal will do the churning; if you keep a dog, make him "work his passage." The power can be connected to any churn sold by us.

Price. $14.70

Double Dog Power.

No. 78856 Double Dog Power. The illustration above shows how the double dog power can be used in operating a cream separator. When the separator is not in use and you desire to churn, connect it to tumbling rod sent with ma-

Even the dogs put in a full day's work back in 1898! The Sears, Roebuck & Co. catalogue of that year listed both single dog power and double dog power treadmills, which would be connected to a cream separator, corn sheller, fan mill or sawing machine. Catalogue copy for the item also pointed out that this treadmill "can also be operated by goats and sheep; yields 25 per cent more power from a given weight of animal."

Mail order catalogue medicines could cure you of anything. . . .

Or mail order catalogues could take care of you if they didn't.

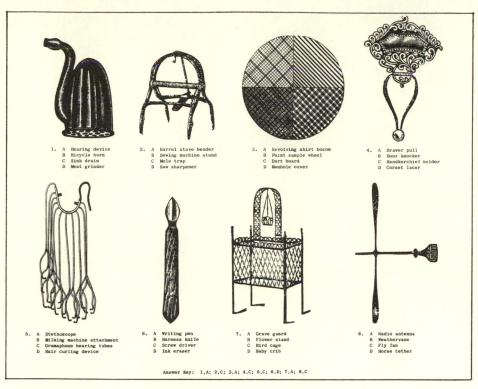

1. A Hearing device
    B Bicycle horn
    C Sink drain
    D Meat grinder

2. A Barrel stave bender
    B Sewing machine stand
    C Mole trap
    D Saw sharpener

3. A Revolving shirt bosom
    B Paint sample wheel
    C Dart board
    D Manhole cover

4. A Drawer pull
    B Door knocker
    C Handkerchief holder
    D Corset lacer

5. A Stethoscope
    B Milking machine attachment
    C Gramaphone hearing tubes
    D Hair curling device

6. A Writing pen
    B Harness knife
    C Screw driver
    D Ink eraser

7. A Grave guard
    B Flower stand
    C Bird cage
    D Baby crib

8. A Radio antenna
    B Weathervane
    C Fly fan
    D Horse tether

Answer Key: 1,A; 2,C; 3,A; 4,C; 5,C; 6,D; 7,A; 8,C

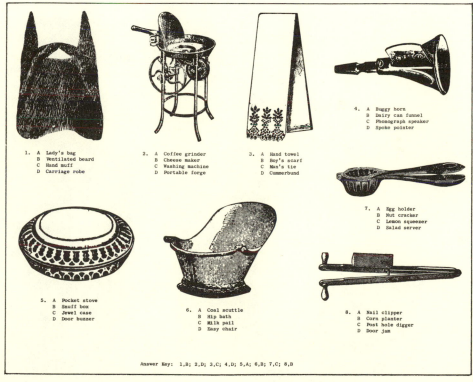

1. A Lady's bag
    B Ventilated beard
    C Hand muff
    D Carriage robe

2. A Coffee grinder
    B Cheese maker
    C Washing machine
    D Portable forge

3. A Hand towel
    B Boy's scarf
    C Man's tie
    D Cummerbund

4. A Buggy horn
    B Dairy can funnel
    C Phonograph speaker
    D Spoke pointer

5. A Pocket stove
    B Snuff box
    C Jewel case
    D Door buzzer

6. A Coal scuttle
    B Hip bath
    C Milk pail
    D Easy chair

7. A Egg holder
    B Nut cracker
    C Lemon squeezer
    D Salad server

8. A Nail clipper
    B Corn planter
    C Post hole digger
    D Door jam

Answer Key: 1,B; 2,D; 3,C; 4,D; 5,A; 6,B; 7,C; 8,B

Try your skill at identifying these items from early Sears' mail order catalogue. Odd today, such merchandise was commonplace in the early 1900s. Answers below.

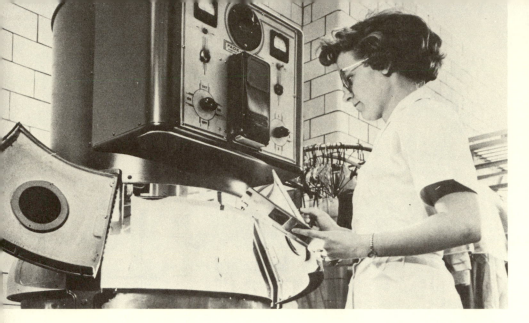

The sunburn you get at the beach can never be as severe as the sunburn being given the fabric in this "fadeometer" in Sears Merchandise Development and Testing Laboratory. Upholstery, drapes, wearing apparel, carpeting, fabrics—all can fade from the sun. Using high intensity arclights, the fadeometer subjects fabrics to the equivalent of hundreds of hours of sunlight.

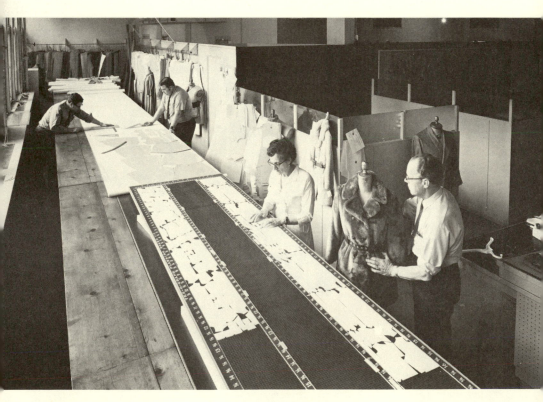

Miniature layouts (foreground) help pattern designers in the Sears Merchandise Development and Testing Laboratory to use fabric efficiently, thereby cutting clothing costs while maintaining proper fit.

Ward's 72-page Catalogue No. 13 was the third to be bound and contained the company's first strong statement of consumer protection on the inside cover.

Mail orders being filled and shipped in the early days of Montgomery Ward.

Ward's 1896 catalogue featured the first live model to be used in a mail order catalogue.

Montgomery Ward & Co.'s Improved Western Star Washing Machine.

(Note Reduced Price)

57191 The Western Star Washer is acknowledged by all the best and most perfect machine on the market. No nails or iron of any kind are used in its construction which can come in contact with the clothes, causing iron rust on the linen, as is the case with other machines; this, together with other improvements that have been made in this machine and not contained in any other, are of the greatest importance and must be seen to be appreciated. If you desire a more complete description of this machine send for descriptive circular, which will be mailed on application. Price...$2.75 Weight, 65 lbs.

Interesting products from the early mail order catalogues.

When ordering be sure to state size and color.

Left: Mail order companies even sold their own brand of automobile.

Below: Homes were offered in early mail order catalogues. Some of these houses still stand today.

To fill orders promptly, Montgomery Ward clerks in St. Paul rollerskated around the warehouse.

Small-town merchants' reactions to catalogue competition were typified by these 1916 cartoons, which appeared as newspaper ads in Calvin, North Dakota, and Billings, Montana.

Next Time Buy at Home

WHEN YOU BUY AT HOME:---

YOU SEE WHAT YOU BUY "BEFORE" YOU PAY OUT YOUR MONEY.

YOU ARE SURE OF GETTING KNOWN "RELI-ABLE" BRANDS OF GOODS.

YOU HAVE NO "FREIGHT" TO PAY.

AND WE ARE HEAR 365 DAYS OUT OF THE YEAR TO "MAKE GOOD" ON WHAT WE SAY AND SELL.

BUY AT HOME---BUT ONLY BECAUSE YOU CAN BUY FOR LESS.

PORTER & HENDERSON

NO MORE MAIL ORDER GOODS FOR US WEVE BEEN STUNG

I'LL JUST BURN THIS THING UP

I'LL BUY AT HOME AND SEE WHAT I GET

What's the use of sending money east when we can buy just as cheap at THE POPULAR STORE.

Men's, Women's and Children's Ready-to-Wear

Agents for W. L. Douglas Shoes

The Popular Store

Aaron Lipsker, Proprietor

Second door East Corner 27th street and Montana avenue

"One Price to All."

When mail order firms began to win the country stores' customers, the country stores fought back futilely.

Mall entrance of a typical Ward store.

The 1920 Spiegel catalogue shows the company as the greatest source of buying power for the American family.

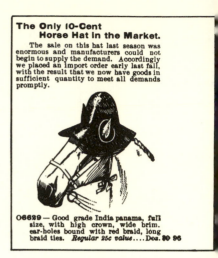

A hat for horses from the Butler Brothers catalogue.

"Accusing Fingers"—a typical cartoon from *Truth*, a propaganda publication published by small southern merchants in the early 1920s and directed against the chain store system.

Sears, Roebuck still leads the world in catalogue sales as well as in retail store sales. This has been the case since Richard Sears made the Sears, Roebuck catalogue famous with his early slogans, "Send No Money" and "We Guarantee Satisfaction and Safe Delivery on Everything You Order," which evolved into the company's present "Satisfaction Guaranteed or Your Money Back." Sears's genius for flamboyant yet folksy advertising copy and his "Iowaization" scheme eventually made "the farmer's friend," as he called his creation, even more popular than the earlier Ward wish book. Farmers did consider Sears, Roebuck a friend. They bought everything from "centrifugal cream spreaders" ($24) to "Stradivarius model" violins ($6.10). Some returned coats worn threadbare, plows with which entire farms had been tilled, but other customers were honest enough to correct and pay for mistakes Sears made in billing—several after as long as twenty years.

By the time Julius Rosenwald had cleaned up its advertising, the Sears wish book was an American institution. Edgar Guest wrote a poem entitled "The Catalogue" for the 1934 edition and the long-running play *Finian's Rainbow* made reference to the catalogue of "Shears, Robust and Company." Notable models who have appeared in the "big book" include Gloria Swanson, Norma Shearer, Joan Caulfield, Ginger Rogers, Lauren Bacall, Jean Arthur, Anita Louise, Elyse Knox, and Frederic March. The catalogue is genuine Americana because it faithfully reflects life-styles over the past century—space to items always having been allotted on the basis of sales. Many writers and film makers have thus used it as a reference tool in authenticating the fashion and furnishings of a particular period. Using the catalogue, for example, one can establish that bosom boards were widely used by women during the Gay Nineties, that pyjamas weren't popular here until about 1908, that twin beds were almost unheard of until 1921, and that the frontier lasted longer than most people think in American history—judging by the fact that the last covered wagon was sold as recently as 1924! No wonder a fifteen-dollar edition of the 1897 Sears Catalog recently brought out by a book publisher sold 150,000 copies.

Franklin D. Roosevelt once said that the best way to convince Communists of the superiority of the American way of life would be to bomb Russia with Sears catalogues, and Associated Press Moscow correspondent Eddy Gilmore later reported that the catalogue, with its over eighty thousand items, is the most effective weapon in the American propaganda arsenal. Julian Louis Watkins included the Sears catalogue in his book *The 100 Greatest Advertisements in History,* calling it the "most famous of all salesmen in print," while still another writer has called the Sears's wish book the greatest invention "in the interest of pure fantasy since the discovery of hard-core pornography." More than 315 million copies of Sears catalogues—using 175,000 tons of paper and 3 million gallons of ink—are printed a year, making the company the biggest private publisher in the United States.

Sears catalogues generate sales of over $3 billion a year from 28 million customers, and do so at a cost of only 5 percent of total sales, far below the figure for Sears's retail store advertising. The wish books have made the company far and away America's leader in mail-order sales, and none of its competitors seriously thinks of claiming the crown in the near future. The major challenger in the field today, aside from Ward, is J. C. Penney, which only entered the mail-order business twenty years ago. Penney, which came close to merging with Sears in the 1920s now has 1,363 catalogue sales centers and should soon hit $1 billion in sales, neck in neck with the 104-year-old Ward's. Right now, however, the top five are Sears, Ward's, Penney, Spiegel, and Alden's—with Sears larger than all its major rivals combined.

1888

Old Pioneers

NATIONAL BELLA HESS COMPANY—Chicago, Illinois

National Bella Hess ranked behind Sears and Ward as the third largest U.S. mail-order house up until 1932, when it was liquidated although it had annual earnings of about $5 million. The company had allowed its mail-order techniques to hamper retail stores it operated and had compounded its troubles by overcirculating its catalogue, distributing some 5 million books in its last year. National Bella Hess had begun life as a 1927 merger of two Chicago mail-order firms—the National Cloak & Suit Company and the Bella Hess Company—the former of the two houses established in

1888 by Maurice Rosenbaum and David Hartman. The year after the merger Brooklyn's old Charles Williams Stores mail-order concern was added to the business.

Though it long ago fell to the wayside, National Bella Hess deserves mention as one of the mail-order pioneers. Other old companies no longer prominent, include New York's H.F.C. Moch Company, and Buffalo's Larkin Company. The latter began as a soap manufacturer and expanded into other mail-order lines in 1885. Larkin, famous for its early slogan, "Thirty days' trial and pay if pleased," later established a chain of retail food stores and a department store. It also formed consumer clubs called Clubs of Ten to promote sales; these groups of ten housewives paid a dollar or so each month to obtain Larkin mail-order products.

1902

America's Number Three Mail-Order Merchant

J. C. PENNEY—Kemmerer, Wyoming

(See Chapter 4)

1913

The World's Best Known Specialty Mail-Order House

L. L. BEAN—*Freeport, Maine*

Among the thousands of specialty mail-order houses, trading in everything from food to clothing, the most famous is probably Maine's L. L. Bean, Inc., founded in Freeport in 1913. Its founder, Leon Leonwood Bean, who liked to hunt and fish more than he liked to work, was a failure as a clothing store operator, but he made his fortune when he invented his famous Maine Hunting Shoe and began selling it through the mails. The waterproof shoe, leather on top and rubber on the bottom, did very poorly at first—Bean made and sold a hundred pairs and ninety were returned because the bottoms had come off—but he honored his "100 percent money back guarantee," perfected the boot, and today sells a hundred thousand pairs a year. The lightweight Maine Hunting Shoe, which, according to Bean, saves an outdoorsman from lifting 2,310 extra pounds in the average seven miles or 18,480 steps he takes a day, led to a catalogue featuring hundreds of items for sportsmen, including the famous Bean chamois shirt (in which a Playboy Playmate once posed), down vests, and North Maine Woods shirts. There have been instances of sportsmen ordering the entire catalog and orders addressed merely "Bean, someplace in Maine" reach the company.

L. L. Bean died in 1967, aged ninety-four, and his grandson Leon A. Gorman runs the completely family-owned firm today. Under Gorman, who started as a Bean's buyer, the company's sales have increased 120 percent over the last ten years and net profits have risen from 2 percent of sales to 5 percent of sales—J. C. Penney, by way of comparison, has only a 2.7 percent profit margin. Over 5 million copies of the 128-page color catalog are sent out every year now, Bean's six hundred loyal and well-paid employees filling over a million worldwide orders annually for total sales of nearly $60 million. These orders go out to all 50 states and 70 foreign countries within 48 hours after being received. Service is so efficient that when Israel's desert troops needed a rush order of boots and heavy shirts for duty on the Golan Heights in 1973, they bypassed regular military suppliers and ordered direct from Bean.

The L. L. Bean store in Freeport is open 24 hours a day, 365 days a year to accommodate the thousands of customers who visit Bean's every year—one motel in the area says it puts up over five hundred people a year who come to town solely to shop at the store. Famous customers have included Supreme Court Justice William O. Douglas, General Matthew Ridgeway, Eleanor Roosevelt, Jack Dempsey, John Wayne, Gregorey Peck, Lowell Thomas, Robert MacNamara, Walter Cronkite, Ethel Kennedy, Amy Vanderbilt, and astronaut Alan Bean, who is no relation and didn't wear Maine Hunting Boots when he walked on the moon. The company now spends half a million dollars annually on advertising and rents mail-order lists from other firms—radical departures from crusty old L. L. Bean's day—but Gorman routinely rejects all acquisition and franchise offers. "That would be growth for growth's sake," he says. "We're better off sticking to our traditional distribution methods." Gorman feels that Abercrombie & Fitch Company, the famous New York sporting goods company that recently filed for bankruptcy after eighty-five years in business, "didn't define their role in the recreation market and focus on it," and is determined that Bean's won't make the same mistake. The company should reach the $100-million a year sales mark by the early 1980s and that, he feels, may be "an optimum size for this company, beyond which we can't offer significantly greater service." Such thinking is in line with Bean's image as the embodiment of Yankee virtue—good value and plain dealing.

✍ VIII ✍

The Urge to Merge and "The Chain Store Menace": American Chain Store Development

They are often called children of the twentieth century, but chain stores really go back even farther in time than the mail-order idea. The first recorded seems to have been a chain distribution system involving a large number of stores established by a Chinese merchant named Los Kass some two hundred years before Christ. Centuries later, in 1643, the Japanese Mitsui group formed a drugstore chain that held leadership in the field until World War II, and at about the same time in Europe, Germany's immensely wealthy Fugger family and England's Merchant Adventurers carried on important mercantile operations of a chain character.

In the New World early chain operations would have to include the trading posts of Canada's venerable Hudson's Bay Company, still a major retailer, and John Jacob Astor's fur trading posts in the American West. The Singer Sewing Machine Company, which in 1856 became the first company anywhere to offer a true installment buying payment plan, also qualifies as an early chain. Apparently chains weren't regarded as big business in early America, for even that fierce man of the people Andrew Jackson was a chain store operator. The president was a partner in Jackson and Hutchings, which ran a small chain of retail stores in Tennessee about 150 years ago.

Merchant-peddler Thomas Danforth of Rocky Hill, Connecticut

is generally credited with the first true retail chain stores in America. Danforth started his main store in Rocky Hill, now Stepheny, in 1778 and dispatched peddlers around the country to sell the many articles of hardware he carried, most of which he or his brothers manufactured. He established his sons in strategic branch stores along the East Coast as far south as Savannah, and they sold his goods in these shops or outfitted local peddlers.

Another early chain was that of John Meeker, a Hinsdale, Massachusetts, entrepreneur who operated at least 15 stores in upstate New York at the beginning of the nineteenth century. Meeker stocked about eight thousand dollars worth of merchandise in each of his stores and commonly sent out wagons laden with goods to trade with farmers for wheat, potash, and other products. An interesting advertising flyer for Meeker's store in Delphi, New York, shows thousands of customers rushing toward the store for bargains and "goods received daily," arriving at the front door on foot, horseback, carriage, train, via balloon (Thaddeus Sobriski Coulincourt Lowe had recently made a pioneering balloon flight from Cincinnati to South Carolina), and even with wings attached to their backs like science-fiction travelers of the future. One of Meeker's protégés, Jedediah Barber, opened the Great Western Store in Homer, New York, and is said to be the original for wise old "David Harum" of the novel and radio soap opera of that name.

The oldest American chain organization still in operation is the Great Atlantic & Pacific Tea Company, or A & P, which had its beginnings as a little tea store opened in 1859 by George F. Gilman and George Huntington Hartford on Vesey Street in New York City. Originally, the proprietors simply wanted to import tea directly from the Orient, cutting out some of the middleman's profit and making it less expensive to the public. But the company had 25 stores by the time it took the name A & P six years later, when it also added a line of groceries at reduced prices. In ten more years there would be 67 stores, and the time would come when the firm would open an average of 50 stores a week for an entire year.

A & P became the symbol for a chain operation and remains so today, though Sears took its place as the world's leading retailer in 1964 and Safeway Stores has surpassed it in sales and number of stores to become the leading supermarket chain. Yet, contrary to what might be supposed, the A & P operation was not the first supermarket, which was opened by Michael Cullen in Jamaica, New York, in 1930; the King Kullen chain was composed of 15 large stores within six years. Neither King Kullen nor the A & P invented the revolutionary self-service concept in retailing that supermarkets and many discount department stores—notably K mart—have adopted over the years. This was the idea of Clarence Saunders, a Memphis, Tennessee, merchant who introduced the novel Piggly Wiggly chain of small grocery stores in 1916. Piggly Wiggly stores were set up so that customers passed through a turnstile and followed a predetermined course exposing them to the appeal of all the merchandise displayed on the shelves. They, in turn, may have been suggested by the Horn & Hardart self-service cafeterias, which were opened in 1902 and were a Swedish invention. Clarence Saunders's fertile, playful mind also conceived the intriguing Keedoozle stores, the first of which he opened in 1937. *Keedoozle* is a coined word for "key-does-all." Goods in the store were displayed behind rows of tiny glass windows like those in a Horn & Hardart. Customers made purchases by inserting a notched rod into a keyhole beside the merchandise wanted. The merchandise was automatically recorded, collected, and finally wrapped after the insertion of a key in another slot released the contents to a conveyor belt that transported it to the wrapping department.

After the A & P, scores of national chains, including Woolworth's, McCrory, and Kresge (now K mart) variety stores, appeared on the scene; at least a dozen chains in the drugstore field alone can trace their origins back to the late nineteenth century. Department stores, owing to their late development, were among the last businesses to organize into chains, although many had branches from their earliest days as dry goods stores—notably Carson Pirie Scott, which had four stores as early as 1858. Most department stores today are both vertical and horizontal distributors; that is, they have at least one unit that is a huge, departmentalized emporium under one roof—their vertical aspect—and a number of branch or chain stores—their horizontal operation.

The obvious advantage of chains is their buying power, their large-scale purchases direct from manufacturers making it possible for them to sell at lower prices than independent stores, which often depend on a middleman today and almost always did in the past. In other words, chains correct the outstanding inherent defects of the old wholesaler-retailer system by combining the whole-sale and retail functions instead of having them performed by separate independent factors. With stores in many areas the chains are also less likely to be catastrophically affected by local conditions, such as a long period of low employment in a community, than if they had all their eggs in one basket. Their bigness and greater profits also permit fashion merchandise, better stores in superior locations, and more money for advertising and promotions.

On the other hand, chains are managed by employees rather than their owners and don't usually inspire local loyalty the way independent stores do. This, however, depends on the type of chain a store is and, of course, on the store itself. *Chain store* is a loosely used term that means different things to different people. Strictly speaking, some 85 percent of all department stores are chains, or multistore organizations, but there are two main types of chains. First are the *regular retail chains* with centrally owned and operated stores in several states, one of the first of which was the J. C. Penney Company. Other examples are the amazing K mart, Woolworth, Montgomery Ward, R. H. Macy, Belk Brothers, Gimbel Brothers, Korvettes, and Marshall Field. Their stories and the histories of other regular retail chains are recorded throughout this book.

The second type are the *ownership groups,* chains that have grown by purchasing established stores and usually retaining the original stores' names, identities, and operating policies. Ownership groups are a later development than regular retail chains, becoming common only in the mid-1920s, though there are earlier examples like the May Company (see Chapter 4). The evidence seems to indicate that they were influenced by cooperative buying groups, the first of which was the Associated Merchandising Corporation. The AMC came to life in 1918 as a creation of the Retail Research Association, which was formed at the suggestion of that retailing genius Lincoln Filene. In 1916 Filene had invited eighteen prominent department stores, including F. & R. Lazarus, J. L. Hudson, L. S. Ayres, the Dayton Company, and the Rike-Kumler Company, to form an organization for the scientific study of store and merchandising operations. The Retail Research Association established a uniform system of records so that member stores could compare figures accurately, and instituted studies to determine how department stores could operate more efficiently. One study led to the formation of the AMC, which was established for the mass buying of goods sold by all the group's members. Today the AMC, which has taken over the functions of the Retail Research Association as well, is a multibillion-dollar organization that is financed by and services 31 U.S. department store chains. It operates from buying offices here and abroad and saves its member stores millions of dollars through mass purchases. AMC is still the biggest of the cooperative buying groups, though there are other giants now like Frederick Atkins, Inc., which handles 40 stores with a total volume of over a billion dollars.

Among the first ownership group chains in the department store field were Federated Department Stores, Inc., and the Allied Stores Corporation. Allied began as Hahn Department Stores, a promotion headed by Lew Hahn, former head of the National Retail Dry Goods Association, who in 1928 began taking over established stores and running them under their own names. Later, under B. Early Puckett, it became for a time the largest department store ownership group, its principal unit Boston's Jordan Marsh Company.

Federated Department Stores is now the biggest ownership group among department store chains. This chain was formed in 1929 by Louis Kirstein, general manager of Boston's Filene's, Fred Lazarus, Jr., of Ohio's F. & R. Lazarus & Company, and Walter Rothschild, president of Brooklyn's Abraham & Straus. At a meeting aboard Rothschild's yacht in Long Island Sound the three men, well known to each other from AMC, laid the groundwork for the company, which was incorporated several months later and joined by Bloomingdale's the following year. At first, each of the stores existed as a separate corporation, with Federated as the controlling holding company, but, subsequently, the individual corporations were dissolved, each store becoming a division of Federated. The company was long headed by Fred Lazarus, Jr., and the chairman of the board is now his son Ralph. Federated owns some of the most prestigious stores in the country.

Ownership groups would probably rather be called collections than chains and do try to be a part of the communities they serve. Another important ownership group is Carter Hawley Hale Stores, Inc., prominent in the news recently for its attempted takeover of

Chicago's Marshall Field. In terms of sales the top five department store ownership groups are the following, in order: Federated; May Department Stores Company; Allied; Associated Dry Goods Corporation; and Carter Hawley Hale. However, the ownership groups aren't even among the first 5 of the top 28 department store chains, as the following listing shows, these positions all held by regular retail chains. More on these leading chains and the individual stores they own can be found under the store biographies in other chapters, but the basic information about them is noted on this chart (though these 1977 rankings, sales figures and numbers of stores will doubtless change even before this book goes to press):

AMERICA'S TOP CHAINS

Sears, Roebuck and Co.—Chicago, Illinois: $22 billion sales; 3,858 retail and catalog stores

K mart (formerly S. S. Kresge)—Troy, Michigan: $10 billion sales; 1,700 stores

J. C. Penney Co.—New York, New York: $9.3 billion sales; 3,000 stores

F. W. Woolworth Co.—New York, New York: $5.5 billion sales; 5,200 variety and department stores

Montgomery Ward and Co. (division of Mobil Oil)—Chicago, Illinois: $5 billion sales; 907 retail and catalogue stores

Federated Department Stores—Cincinnati, Ohio: $4.9 billion sales; 134 department and specialty stores

Winn-Dixie Stores—Jacksonville, Florida: $4 billion sales; discount stores

Lucky Stores—Dublin, California: $3.9 billion sales; discount department stores

American Stores—Wilmington, Delaware: $3.5 billion sales; discount department stores

May Department Stores—Saint Louis, Missouri: $2.3 billion sales; 129 store

Dayton-Hudson Corp.—Minneapolis, Minnesota: $2.1 billion sales; 339 department and specialty stores

Rapid American—New York, New York: $2 billion sales

Allied Stores Corp.—New York, New York: $1.9 billion sales; 165 stores

R. H. Macy and Co.—New York, New York: $1.6 billion sales; 76 stores

Gamble-Skogmo Inc.—Minneapolis, Minnesota: $1.6 billion sales; 680 stores

Carter Hawley Hale Stores—Los Angeles California: $1.5 billion sales; 96 stores

Associated Dry Goods—New York, New York: $1.4 billion sales; 158 stores

McCrory Corp.—New York, New York: $1.35 billion sales; 1600 department and variety stores

Zayre Corp.—Framingham, Massachusetts: $1.2 billion sales; 524 department and specialty stores, gas stations

Gimbel Brothers (subsidiary of British-American Tobacco Co.)— New York, New York: $1 billion sales; 69 stores

Vornado Inc.—Garfield, New Jersey: $1 billion sales; 60 Two Guys discount stores

Genesco—New York, New York: $1 billion sales; specialty stores

Mercantile Stores Co.—New York, New York: $789 million sales; 81 stores

Wal-Mart Stores—Bentonville, Arkansas: $734 million sales; discount stores

SCOA Industries—Columbus, Ohio: $685 million sales; discount stores

Zale Corporation—Dallas, Texas: $678 million sales; discount stores

Marshall Field and Co.—Chicago, Illinois: $611 million sales; 36 stores

Korvettes (unit of the French Agache Willot Group)—New York, New York: $600 million sales; 52 stores.

Though department stores chains can be traced back to the early 1900s in America, the largest chain store gains here were made after 1920. By 1929 more than 60 percent of the 4,221 department stores in this country were chain stores. These stores accounted for only 15 percent of all department stores sales at the time, but they would grow over the next fifty years to the point where they are responsible today for over 92 percent of department store sales and constitute 85 percent of all department stores.

Their path wasn't easy. Chains began to flourish here in the time of the trustbusters, when all American big business was suspect. An anonymous untitled poem printed in the *Chicago News* humorously summed up a common attitude about the ubiquitous efficiency experts, who made big business successful—but made it too machinelike for the taste of most Americans:

> The devil opened the furnace door
>   and heaved in a shovel of coal,
> When out there popped on the scorching floor
>   A truculent half-baked soul
> "Look here, good devil," it said, "I pray
>   You will pardon my seeming haste,
> I am—you must listen to what I say—
>   appalled at your awful waste!
>
> "Two thirds of your heat goes up the flue,
>   Your coal is but half consumed;
> If a modern plant should compete with you
>   This business were surely doomed.
> Your times and motions, I've studied well
>   As you hustle the sinners in,
> And I find you have here but a third-rate hell,
>   For the way it is run is a sin!"
>
> The devil grabbed up that critic then
>   With an angry shake and a flirt,
> And said: "Go back to the world of men,
>   You efficiency expert!
> If you stay down here you will get my job!"
>   (Here he uttered a dismal groan),
> "But if you go" (here he gave a sob),
>   "You will fix up a hell of your own!"

America wasn't the only country where efficiency and bigness were considered hells on earth. Antichain laws in Italy, for example, were so severe that by as late as 1930 only one chain had as many as a hundred stores. In Germany, one of the 25 points Hitler presented to a mass meeting in a Munich beer hall on February 24, 1920, when he was first becoming widely known, called for the immediate socialization of the great (often Jewish-owned) depart-ment stores and their branches, which would be leased at low rates to small middle-class merchants. Yet American opposition to the chain operations was more vehement and better organized than anywhere else; it was, as one writer points out, "a latter-day manifestation of the same opposition which had fought mail-order so bitterly in its early days," only the small merchants fighting the chains were far more sophisticated than they had been during the mail-order wars, and they were helped by the agents of wholesalers, who were losing money because of the chains.

Chain store opposition in America grew through the 1920s until there were over 260 local or national organizations with more than 8 million members—nearly 7 percent of the population of the United States—arrayed against the chains by the end of the decade. Seventeen senators and congressmen had come out strongly against chains, and seven governors were hostile to such operations, includ-ing Huey P. Long, who once said he would rather have thieves and gangsters in Louisiana than chain store operators. Hundreds of state officials ran for office on anti-chain-store platforms, and thousands of newspapers, magazines and radio stations supported them.

Sometimes broadcasting con men profited by the antichain move-ment. They would approach wholesalers, demanding a "contribu-tion." A quarter of the wholesaler's business might have come from chains and the rest from independents. If he contributed to the antichain fight, that fact could be broadcast and hurt him with chain customers. If he refused to contribute, that fact could be broadcast and hurt him with his independent customers. There is one way out, the con man would suggest: "If your contribution is sufficiently large, it may not be necessary to mention your name at all."

Anti-chain-store lobbying reached its heights or depths during the depression when chain store opponents ranted about chains siphoning money out of the community, paying less taxes because they kept fast-moving minimum inventories, using big city banks and insurance agencies, taking kickbacks disguised as "advertising appropriations" from manufacturers, and deserting communities when hard times hit "because they have no more roots than a toadstool." The chains were even accused of hiring low-salaried "plodders" at the expense of intelligent local workers because "exceptional intelligence is a handicap in their operations." Their critics, however, had little more than emotions on their side—the mistrust most Americans have of overweening bigness whether in government or private industry.

It is true that the early chains were no angels. But the federal Robinson-Patman Act of 1936 effectively legislated against kickbacks, as did state and federal fair-trade acts like the federal Miller-Tydings law, which encouraged manufacturers of trademarked items to set retail prices at one level so small retailers could sell them at a profit. Most of the other antichain criticism was pure fantasy. Economist A. A. Berle pointed out that it was the small-town retailer who was most often America's rank monopolist, his customers forced to buy from him at his prices. Other economists exploded the myth about chains "taking money out of town."

About the only good that resulted from the antichain agitation, aside from laws that helped encourage honesty, was the growth of voluntary chains in America. In these combinations ownership of individual stores is retained, but wholesaler and retailer bind themselves into an organization that can do most of the things the chain does: buy in quantity, standardize methods, exchange ideas, and improve advertising. By 1930 there were five hundred such groups with outlets estimated as high as sixty-five thousand. One of the first of them in the variety and department store field was Butler Brothers, formerly a Boston mail-order wholesaler (see Chapter 7), which went into the voluntary chain field in 1927, forming the highly successful "Ben Franklin League" of independent variety stores. Certainly the voluntary chains didn't come onto the scene until after the big chain stores made their appearances, and were formed as a reaction against chain store domination of the marketplace. But they perform the same function as their rivals; that is, voluntary chains also combine both the wholesale and retail functions of business instead of leaving them to separate factors—the wholesaler and the retailer.

Voluntary cooperative chains, incidentally, should not be confused with cooperative stores or trading societies. In England and other countries, cooperative trading societies played an important role in the early development of department stores, but in America a stronger belief in the principals of private enterprise worked against the creation of such cooperative ventures. England had and still has a score of multimillion dollar cooperative stores that were great influences in department store development, while not a single outstanding cooperative department store has arisen in America. The efforts of the Grange to form cooperative stores failed in the late nineteenth century (see Chapter 7). Not even the Common Distribution Corporation set up by the eminent head of Filene's could change this. Edward Filene was called "a traitor to his class" for forming and liberally endorsing this organization, which was supposed to foster the idea of cooperative trading. Two cooperative department stores opened with Filene's money failed miserably, and his corporation has yet to yield successful results. It would be interesting to know all the reasons for the failure of organizations in America to obtain merchandise at basic cost for consumers, but the main one seems to have been an ingrained dislike of anything smacking of socialism.

Unfortunately, voluntary chains weren't the answer for most independent merchants and wholesalers. Most of them concentrated their efforts on getting anti-chain-store laws passed in state legislatures. Discriminating tax laws were passed as early as 1927. Within ten years over 50 such laws were on the books in various states, and no doubt there would have been far more if the chains themselves hadn't lobbied effectively—for fully *one thousand* such bills were introduced to fight "the chain store menace." Supreme Court decisions consistently upheld these local laws, and this, along with the success of the federal Robinson-Patman Act, inspired Congressman Wright Patman of Texarkana, Texas, to go beyond the negative intention of restricting and punishing chain stores and propose to put chains out of business altogether.

In 1938 Patman introduced a bill (H.R. 9464) in the House of Representatives that was popularly called "the chain death sentence bill," frankly stating at the time that it was his intention to drive the large chains into bankruptcy. To quote a scholarly study on the involved proposal:

The proposed statute provided for a tax of $50 per store on chains having 9 to 15 units; a tax of $100 per store on chains having 16 to 25 units; $200 per store on 26 to 50 unit chains, and so on up to a maximum levy of $1000 on each store of a chain having more than 500 units. In addition to the foregoing, the bill provided for the complete extermination of all large chains of national scope by an additional section which requires a chain operating in more than one state to multiply the applicable tax by the number of states in which the chain operates!

Needless to say, the Patman bill would have put all the national chains out of business—J. C. Penney alone would have been taxed $64 million on earnings of about $14 million in 1940, the year the bill came up for final vote in Congress. The chains naturally fought for their lives, employing the best public relations experts money could buy and bombarding the country with prochain propaganda. In testifying on behalf of all chains before a congressional subcommittee condemning the Patman bill, Earl Corder Sams, president of J. C. Penney, warned that the elimination of national chains would "add to the cost of living for every American family and destroy small towns for the benefit of the larger cities." Sams pointed out that, contrary to the propaganda of wholesalers, chains paid more local taxes than independent merchants, paid better wages and higher rents, contributed to local charities as much as independents, increased real-estate values, and were either locally or publically owned in most cases, not controlled by Wall Street financial interests. Sams concluded with a plea for progress. "No law, no human mandate can breathe life back in the very small trading center which formerly supported a couple of general stores," he warned. "Those stores existed only because without automobiles or good roads the customer couldn't get to the city. Because of horse-and-buggy transportation and because of mud roads the customer bought what the general store offered at its own price. . . ."

The committee heard scores of witnesses condemn the Patman bill and considered a 35-volume Federal Trade Commission report made in 1934, which showed that customers benefited from the chains and recommended not taxing them. The Patman bill was finally killed in committee, the members agreeing with Dr. Caroline Ware, who summed up the matter as follows:

The evidence seems conclusive that chain stores . . . have brought real advantages to American consumers: *First,* by savings in price, partly through allowing people to avoid paying for services they do not want or cannot afford, and partly through economies in wholesale handling, standardized displays, advertising and so forth; *secondly*, by bringing greater variety of merchandise and more sanitary and attractive stores, especially to remoter places; and, *thirdly*, by inducing better merchandising methods in nonchain stores and thus affecting the whole system of distribution with which consumers deal.

When department stores first appeared, small merchants tried to outlaw them; then they tried the same thing with mail-order houses and house-to-house selling (as they had previously with peddlers); and finally they ganged up on the chains—only to be defeated in all cases by the consumer's instinct for getting the most for his or her money. Most shoppers just don't care whether they are buying from a chain or an independent—or from a peddler in front of Bloomingdale's, for that matter—if the price is right. But the chains did far more for department stores and their customers than lower prices. Even those independent retailers who didn't join voluntary chains responded directly to trends introduced by the corporate chains. Independents modernized store appearances and layout to match or exceed chain standards. The success of the chains was such a shock to competitors that it caused a revitalization of the competitors' management operations and marketing outlook as well as their price policies. "This revitalization," says one authority, "was one of the most progressive aspects of retailing history in the second quarter of the 20th century."

No antichain legislation has been enacted on state or federal level since the defeat of the Patman bill, and several states have replaced earlier repressive measures. Even fair-trade laws are now on the demise in America; the national statute aimed at protecting small businessmen from "unfair competition" by authorizing minimum prices on brand-name merchandise expired in 1976, and many states have since repealed their fair-trade acts.

Chains remain a powerful force in the American economy, especially in the department store industry. Chain department store divisions encompass more territory than ever today, with their branches taking in 68 percent of revenues. No longer is the territory of a division limited by the size of a newspaper coverage area, the rule of thumb formerly accepted by the industry. Federated's New York-based Bloomingdale's, for example, has a store in Washington, D.C., now; the same chain's F. & R. Lazarus division has a store 171 miles from Columbus in Indianapolis; and Detroit's J. L. Hudson has a department store 153 miles away in Grand Rapids. The chains are branching out to new markets everywhere and have learned that the images of local department stores can be transferred to other areas just like those of specialty stores such as Saks Fifth Avenue and Lord & Taylor have been exported in the past.

Today the chains are still busy acquiring, or trying to acquire, new stores to add to their retailing empires. But not only retailers are in the market; giant corporations like Mobil Oil, the British-American Tobacco Company, and the chemicals company W. R. Grace, which controls Herman's Sporting Goods and other stores— are all storekeepers today. Frequently, bids for control of independent stores by chains or large corporations become bitter affairs. The apparel and shoe manufacturers, Genesco, Inc., for example, tried to buy Garfinckel's in 1966 and when management refused made what is called a "tender offer" directly to the company's stockholders. This particular attempt failed, but others have succeeded.

One amusing takeover battle was the unsuccessful 1978 attempt by Carter Hawley Hale to merge with Marshall Field, which almost reached the "tender offer" stage. Not only did Field's management reject Carter Hawley's offer, finding it "illegal, inadequate and not in the best interest of Marshall Field, its stockholders and communities which it serves," but it filed an antitrust suit against Carter Hawley Hale. This complicated antitrust suit ironically charges that the two firms are potential competitors in several cities. The ultimate irony is that Field's itself, while admittedly a Chicago institution, is hardly a local independent store, considering its Frederick & Nelson stores in Seattle, its Halle's stores in Cleveland, Spokane's Crescent discount stores, and the many stores it operates elsewhere under its own name. There have, in fact, been recent rumors that Field's is trying to buy New York's Altman's much against Altman's will! By anyone's definition Field's is a regular retail chain—one that is trying to expand itself—Carter Hawley Hale differing only in that it is an ownership group chain. It seems that chain expansion has come to the point where the whales have run out of little fishes and are swallowing, or gagging on, other whales.

⚭ IX ⚭
The Malling
of Main Street:
Suburban and City
Shopping Centers

They have replaced the movies, baseball and football games, eating out, Sunday driving, and lovers lanes as the favorite haunts of most people. Americans of all ages spend more time in them than anywhere else except at home or work, if we are to believe a 1973 *U.S. News and World Report* poll. Rather than replacing the old neighborhood drugstores or candy stores as hangouts for kids, they are replacing villages and towns themselves. Often containing one or two department stores to anchor them, yet resembling huge department stores, they have become a major force in shaping American society and according to Vance Packard in *A Nation of Strangers,* are "the only focal point in sight" in the social, community, and cultural life of suburban America. This last may be a bit extreme, but many people in both the country and city do identify with the great American shopping centers as they used to identify with local schools, churches, and other institutions.

Just how big are shopping centers today? Less than thirty years ago there were fewer than one hundred in America. At the end of 1977, there were almost twenty thousand centers serving over 85 million suburbanites, taking in over $300 billion in gross sales and accounting for about half of all retail sales in America, as well as for some 50 percent of the total U. S. retail market for most personal and household items.

The shopping center has been called "the quintessential American place" of today, even "the Acropolis of modern America." Not

[268]

long ago the Chicago Symphony Orchestra gave a free performance in a suburban Chicago shopping center and over forty thousand people from miles around attended, the largest live audience ever to hear the orchestra. A recent five-day performing arts festival in a New Jersey mall featuring local performers drew capacity crowds every night. At a health fair held in a Brooklyn mall over two thousand women received free Pap tests, mammography, and thermography to detect cancer. In a Texas "vertical shopping center" an ecumenical counseling agency regularly provides help for hundreds of troubled residents.

Shopping centers certainly are "the Tivoli Gardens of America . . . safe, often glassed in, weather-proofed, verdant, sculptured, myriad, timeless pleasure grounds where every day's a holiday and tomorrow never comes. . . ." Malls all over the country attract shoppers with plays, movies, operas, concerts, restaurants, snack bars, miniamusement parks, flea markets, art shows, fashion shows, antique shows, puppet shows, roller skating, ice skating, swimming, athletic events, schools, libraries, decorating seminars, cooking classes, consumer education programs, square dances, belly dancing instruction—even traveling zoos and circuses. One mall actually contains the local city hall, where marriages are performed, others contain non-denominational churches. All of the traditional services and promotions of the department store are now offered by malls—only more of them and on a larger scale.

Shopping centers as we know them today are a relatively recent American invention, dating back only to the years after World War II. But rude examples of their kind can be found farther back in American history, and they have their deepest roots in many age-old institutions, including the bazaars of Persia, the agoras of ancient Greece, the forums of Rome, and the fairs and marketplaces of medieval Europe. Bazaars like those in Persia originated even before the beginning of civilization, in the form of bartering between primitive people. They came to full flower when the first nomads of Asia settled down in permanent towns that were usually located along rivers or on caravan routes and contained open marketplaces where craftsmen traded metal tools, baskets, pottery, and other goods for the hides and grains of hunters and farmers. Such marketplaces go back to the most primitive tribes who gathered together to trade and developed in China, Egypt, India—

wherever people were free to exchange their goods under peaceful, secure conditions.

Athens's famed Agora was one of the first important marketplaces, as was the Roman Forum, the hub of Rome's great marketplace, which was the first of the great European shopping centers. Like the agoras in each Greek city, the Forum served not only as a market place, but for civic, political, judicial, and festive activities—a similarity that is becoming more pronounced every year in today's malls. After it came marketplaces that formed around the great cathedrals and castles of medieval times, each centered by a huddle of craftsmen's huts, where farmers and hunters came to barter, and later there were stalls of opticians, shoemakers, tailors, and incidental sidewalk vendors.

Medieval shopping centers also included marketplaces on bridges, where shops of all descriptions were located. The most famous of these was the Old London Bridge, which survived into the 1600s with its four stories of residences lining the outer edges of the wide stone span, and shops of drapers, milliners, and dressmakers facing the roadway down the middle. Bridge shopping centers were common until vehicular traffic increased and new spans were built for transportation only. The Ponte Vecchio, spanning the Arno River in Florence, Italy, remains as a relic of such centers, but is now a bridge containing only jewelry shops.

Ancient marketplaces gave birth not only to the little shops of merchants and craftsmen that began to appear in cities even before Grecian times (see Chapter 2), but to the great medieval fairs that somewhat resemble today's shopping center. The fairs of Europe date back to the tenth or eleventh century, when they attracted merchants from all over the world, long caravans from exotic places like Arabia, Egypt, and Byzantium winding their way to the hundreds of towns where they were held. Chartered by the crown in England and most countries, the fairs were strictly supervised and went on for weeks. "Amongst the crowd of eager buyers and sellers," one early writer noted, "were Venetian and Genoese merchants with their rich stuffs, their silks and velvets; the Flemish weavers with their linens; the Spaniard with his stock of iron; the Norwegian with his tar and pitch; the Garcon and his wines; the Hanse merchants with their furs and amber." The fairs were spectacles to behold, especially London's Saint Bartholomew Fair, originally chartered by Henry I to a worldly churchman, "which enable him to fleece the pilgrims during these three days festival of his patron saint." Wordsworth writes about Saint Bartholomew Fair merchants with hurdy-gurdies, monkeys, wild beasts, equestrians, tumblers, dwarfs, giants, albinos, painted Indians, magicians, ventriloquists, fire swallowers, stone eaters, and myriad more entertainments to help them pitch their wares. Not even the Puritans could outlaw the amusements and dissipations that accompanied all the selling, buying, and haggling.

In the early years of the Renaissance, shopping centers became the working places of artists, actors, singers, poets, and storytellers as well as merchants. Plays were performed in the marketplace, paintings and sculpture were made and sold, music was sung there—indeed, it is said that Italian opera developed from the strong, earthy, emotional cries of street vendors in these early shopping centers.

During the Industrial Revolution, architects tried to revive blighted urban areas with shopping centers, just as they are doing today. Probably the most famous attempt was the famed Galleria Vittorio Emmanuele in Milan, Italy, which was the winner of an 1867 contest organized by the city fathers for the best plan to revive the heart of the city.

Designed by traveling salesman Guiseppi Mungone, who had no architectural training whatsoever, the Galleria consisted of a large glass dome covering two city streets and their intersection, the streets lined by buildings housing shops and restaurants. Although private British investors provided the capital for the dome, the streets it covered remained city property. The Galleria wasn't Europe's first enclosed shopping center by any means. The Pardis des Femmes in Paris, a building holding many shops, dates back to 1300, and London's Royal Exchange, another huge building with many shops inside, was built by Sir Thomas Gresham in 1566. But from the moment the Galleria opened its doors in 1867 it became a wonder of Europe, celebrated in song and story. Destroyed by bombing in World War II, it was rebuilt and remains a great attraction today. It has inspired a number of American imitations, including The Old Arcade in Cleveland, built in 1936. Only seven years ago the Galleria of Houston, Texas, a modern adaptation of the Italian Galleria, opened its doors. This is a 600,000-square-foot, three-level enclosed mall, with a 65-foot-high glass dome 550 feet × 40 feet wide. On the first level is a huge skating rink and both escalators and elevators transport shoppers from level to level, a bridge crossing the open center on the second level to permit transverse access.

America's first shopping centers were born with the unrestricted freedom of movement that came with mass-produced automobiles and a growing highway network. Something like a shopping center was created back in 1907 when the landlord owning Roland Park Center, north of Balitmore's central business district, provided an offstreet area where shoppers patronizing any of the six stores could hitch their buggies or park their cars. Then there were the unplanned neighborhood shopping centers, collections of stores that sprang up in the suburbs in the late nineteenth century and reached their peak in the 1920s, when clusters of stores formed around Sears and Montgomery Ward outlets and the branches of other large stores.

The first *planned* American shopping center appears to have been built in 1922, when the J. C. Nichols Company opened Country Club Plaza on a 40-acre site five miles south of Kansas City to serve a new real-estate development of fine homes on the outskirts of town. This center predates Suburban Square, the Ardmore, Pennsylvania, shopping center listed in the *Guinness Book of World Records* as the world's first, by over six years. Country Club Plaza was the forerunner of the fully planned mall with unified architecture, management, landscaping, and adequate parking for customers. Here for the first time the needs of shoppers were carefully analyzed. Based originally on the small locally owned store, it did not accept chain stores or branches from downtown department stores until much later, being basically a small-town business section reproduced in more orderly and coherent fashion. Country Club Plaza became the prototype for other small centers, but grew itself from 14,000 square feet of selling space to its present size of over 1.4 million square feet.

It wasn't until after World War II that truly controlled regional shopping centers, with one large branch department store dominating or anchoring shops around it, began to appear on the scene. The first was the Town and Country Shopping Center in Columbus, Ohio, which opened in 1949 and was under construction in 1947.

Town and Country, on a tract of 45.7 acres, was also the site of the
first suburban stores for J. C. Penney, Kresge (now K mart), and
other chains, and was the first center to keep its stores open at
night. A year later came Allied Stores' $12 million Northgate
Shopping Center in Seattle, Washington, with its 80 or more stores.
By this time demographic conditions were ideal for the flowering of
shopping centers around the country, because of the postwar baby
boom and one of the great migrations in American history—the
exodus from city to suburbs. At the time, says Leonard Farber, the
first president of the International Council of Shopping Centers,
"the demand for shopping centers was so great, a developer could
pick his site simply by using a map of the United States as a dart
board." Soon the first planned *enclosed* shopping center opened—
Southdale Shopping Center in Edina, Minneapolis, which, like
Houston's Galleria after it, was inspired by Milan's La Galleria and
London's Burlington Arcade. This idea caught on so fast that
virtually all of the malls built since then have been covered ones,
with many older centers becoming enclosed as part of an upgrading
process that is still going on.

Spectacular promotions heralded the big shopping centers born
after the war. At Town and Country's 1947 opening, for example,
Grandma Ella Carver dove into a burning pool from atop a high
tower while a huge crowd watched. The Don M. Casto Organization's Great Western Shoppers Mart, which opened in Columbus,
Ohio, in 1955, featured a miniature "Wonders of the World"
exhibit in the parking lot. The display was called Walk-O-Wonders
and formed a central motif of the huge center, connecting the north
and south wings. Over 700 feet long and 60 feet wide, it took the
"traveler" on a journey to the Taj Mahal, the Eiffel Tower, Niagara
Falls, the Parthenon, Carlsbad Caverns, the Grand Canyon, the
Leaning Tower of Pisa, the Pyramid of Cheops, and Rome's magnificent Trevi Fountain. Of these nine wonders, designed by artist
Ivan Pusecher and sculptor Louis Mori, only the Eiffel Tower
remains today. At the time, promotional stunts were designed to
attract crowds, irrespective of whether the spectators shopped in
the center, while nowadays events are planned to draw shoppers,
not gapers.

Adequate parking facilities are necessary for all malls. This has
been worked into a precise formula by builders; there must be 2 to

3 square feet of parking for every square foot of marketing area, or 400 square feet for every car. Today's malls are variations of four basic types. The smallest is the so-called *neighborhood center*, typically covering three acres or so and ranging in gross leasable area from 30,000 to 100,000 square feet. The neighborhood center has as its leading tenant a supermarket or drugstore, and needs anywhere from 2,500 to 40,000 people in a surrounding area to support it. About two-thirds of all shopping centers fall into this category.

One out of five shopping centers are of the *community center* type. These larger centers feature a variety, discount, or small department store as chief tenant, are built on 10 acres or more, range from 100,000 to 300,000 square feet in rentable area and must be supported by 40,000 to 150,000 people. The average-sized shopping center—133,437 square feet—falls within the bounds of the community center and does about $93 a square foot in gross sales.

Regional centers, the third type of shopping center, have one or more large full-line department stores as their leading tenants, occupy 30 to 50 acres, and range from 300,000 to 750,000 square feet of gross leasable area, needing the support of 150,000 or more people. Eight or nine percent of all shopping centers are regionals.

The giants of the shopping center world are the *super regionals*, which comprise only about 2 percent of American malls. Super regionals usually have three or more large department stores as their chief tenants, are built on over 50 acres of land, consist of 750,000 to 2,450,000 square feet of rentable space and need the support of millions of people. The world's biggest shopping centers obviously fall in this category, those malls of which it has been said jokingly that "the time zone changes in the middle." Which is the biggest mall of all is a tricky question. For many years everyone gave the title to the multilevel Woodfield Mall near O'Hare Airport in Schaumburg, Illinois, a center erected on 191 acres owned by western country singer Bob Atcher, the mayor of Schaumburg. But today the *Guinness Book of World Records* ranks Lakewood Center in Lakewood, California, as number one, and others pick Randall Park in Cleveland, Ohio. Lakewood is chosen because its 2,230,000 square feet of gross leasable space—available selling area—is greater than that of any other center. Woodfield remains the choice of many because it has far greater sales than any competitor—$136 per square foot—and occupies a greater *total area* than any of the others. Randall Park gets the nod because it has more stores—250—and more full-line department stores—than any other mall.

Another giant is New York's Roosevelt Field, which was internationally known as the cradle of aviation even before Lindbergh took off from the airport in 1927 to make his epic transatlantic flight in *The Spirit of St. Louis.* Opened in 1956 on the site of the 110-acre airfield, the mall was enclosed in 1968 and contains four major department stores among its 150 shops. For anyone who wants to tour America's biggest shopping centers, here is a list of the top seven—so far as can be determined from often conflicting figures. Any one of the top three or four centers could justifiably be called the biggest of all:

CENTER	*BUILDER*
Lakewood Center Lakewood, California	Macerich Real Estate Co.
Woodfield Mall Schaumburg, Illinois	The Taubman Company & Homart Development
Randall Park Cleveland, Ohio	Edward J. DeBartolo Company
Roosevelt Field Mall Garden City, New York	Roosevelt Nassau Operating Company
Cinderella City Englewood, Colorado	Von Frellick Assoc.
Metrocenter Phoenix, Arizona	Westcor Inc. Phoenix & Homart Development
Yorktown Shopping Center Lombard, Illinois	E. D. Pehrson Assoc.

Other notable shopping centers include Dayton-Hudson's $25 million Northland, opened in 1954, which was the first mall to have underground truck delivery; Bergen Mall in Paramus, New Jersey; Eastlake Square in Tampa, Florida; and Shopper's World in Framington, Massachusetts. The last center started off on the wrong foot not only in financing—substantial repayment of the principal was called for only 17 months after opening in 1951—but in planning, including routing of customer traffic. After the center went bankrupt in 1957, it was taken over by Allied Stores, which owns Jordan Marsh, the principal store in the mall, was reorganized, and is doing well today.

Successful shopping centers don't have to be super regionals erected by giant developers. Historic Murray Hill Square, a quaint shopping and office center built by local contractor Natale G. Conti in New Providence, New Jersey, is a striking example of what can be achieved on a smaller scale. This charming complex consists of shops housed in faithfully restored buildings that are reproductions of structures that once dotted the eighteenth-century streets of the northern New Jersey town. Mr. Conti selected buildings to be reproduced at the square for their historic significance, architectural style, or unusual masonry and millwork, he and his architect Alexander Bol paying strict attention to detail and scouring the countryside for materials like weathered wood siding from barns, hand-hewn beams, hand-forged hardware, and old brick to be used in their construction. The 19 replicas completed thus far include the old New Providence Academy, the Elkwood Train Station, Burnett's Cider Mill, a church, civic buildings, and other local landmarks, all set in a square complete with brick walks, colonial gardens, formal courtyards and antique street lamps.

More American shopping centers are located in the Northeast than any other area, but California (2,044), Texas (1,470), Florida (988), New York (868), Ohio (737), Pennsylvania (730), and Illinois (628) are the seven state leaders. Even Alaska has 30 shopping centers, with sales of $250 million yearly—six more than does Wyoming, which has the fewest in the nation. The American institution has been adopted by at least 30 other countries, including Russia, where Frenchman Jean-Louis Solal, the European "King of the Mall," is building a vast enclosed mall near Moscow to open in time for the 1980 Summer Olympics. A spectacular sight is the $40 million Helicoid in Caracas, Venezuela, a shopping center 492 feet above sea level consisting of over 300 stores built on the great Tarpeya Rock, the center reached by a road winding a mile and a quarter to the summit.

An early shopping center in 1928. This one, in Columbus, Ohio, had thirty stores and parking for 400 cars.

The parking lot of the Great Western Shopping Center in Columbus, Ohio, was the site of replicas of the "Wonders of the Modern World," including the Taj Mahal. Of the nine wonders presented, only the Eiffel Tower replica remains standing today.

Randall Park Mall in Cleveland, Ohio, one of the three largest shopping centers in America. In the background is Thistledown Race Track.

The huge Woodfield Mall outside Chicago is one of the world's three largest and generates more sales than any other shopping center.

Chicago's Water Tower Place is designed for today's urban lifestyle, featuring a vertical shopping center built around a soaring seven-story mall, the posh Ritz-Carlton Hotel and a tower of luxury condominium residences.

Charming Murray Hill Square shopping center in Murray Hill, New Jersey. (Courtesy of Murray Hill Square)

Shopping centers are sound, profitable investments, and life insurance companies, traditionally very conservative in their investment and loan portfolios, annually provide nearly 70 percent of the total capital for their long-term mortgages. A recent survey of 21 insurance companies showed that only seven times in a period of 29 years was foreclosure on mall loans necessary. Under 15 percent of shopping centers built over the last twenty years have been sold by their original developers. These developers include a number of great department store chains, among them: Sears, Dayton-Hudson, Allied, May, Macy's, Federated, Marshall Field, and Carter Hawley Hale.

Center owners have taken a lot of unwarranted criticism over the years by uninformed critics because of their high visibility, but they have generally been socially responsive members of the community. Shopping centers are not, for example, large users of energy as critics charge, despite their well-lighted parking lots and malls. The entire retailing industry, for that matter, accounts for only a minor portion of total energy consumption, according to a study made by the Federal Energy Administration—less than 1 percent (0.62%) of the total energy used in the United States is consumed by retailers other than supermarkets.

In 1973 the Environmental Protection Administration announced that it considered shopping centers to be indirect sources of air pollution, and directed states to control their future growth, but tests commissioned by the International Commission of Shopping Centers indicated that the planned center produces less road congestion and pollution than the proliferation of retail stores along surburban highways and streets. Another study made by the U.S. Department of Transportation showed that the use of the automobile for shopping center trips accounted for very little of the total miles driven by an average family—only 7.6 percent of the total vehicle miles for a year, the average round trip to a shopping center being just 4.4. miles.

Perhaps the ultimate tribute to shopping centers is the new Monopoly-like amusement called "The Mall Game" on the market today, a game complete with paper money and cards reading "You've been caught shoplifting—lose two turns," and "You've tripped on melted ice-cream—collect $200 damages," etc. One writer says that shopping center theory is the Marxism of America and that "the simple act of attracting customers to patronize your center requires more planning and strategy that any Communist five year plan." A story is told about "Big Al" Taubman of the Taubman Company, which built the behemoth Woodfield Mall, that shows to what lengths a developer will go to keep his mall functioning smoothly. It seems that a shopper slipped on ice cream that had fallen out of a cone and onto the floor of one of his malls. Taubman had the ice cream analyzed to establish what store it came from and had the vendor evicted on the grounds that he should have prepared his ice-cream cones better.

Although shopping centers may be "the one thing that typify civilization in the United States in the twentieth century," as a mall expert puts it, this isn't to say that they are without detractors. Some claim that in order to be successful malls must cater to what might be called the Me/Me Too Generation, which makes selfishness and acquisitiveness major virtues. Others predict that malls are the first step toward a real Orwellian world, an attempt to reduce and enclose the universe physically and spiritually. Arguments here range from the profound to the sophomoric, but it can't be denied that malls have frequently destroyed the towns around them. "Malls succeeded because they approached shopping as an idea, but now they have become too successful in the way the automobile became too successful," says Cesar Pelli, who used to design shopping centers and is now dean of Yale's School of Architecture. "They are so powerful that they overwhelm everything else—there is nothing strong enough to balance them." Aurora, Illinois and Plattsburgh, New York, are only two of many communities that saw their business centers virtually wiped out by shopping centers. Today the city fathers of Burlington, Vermont are fighting a proposed mall that will be bigger than all downtown Burlington. "Our position is that rural areas don't want to become suburbs, suburbs don't want to become cities and cities don't want to become wastelands," says Frank Keefe, Vermont's state planning director.

Critics have charged that malls are far from crime free. It is true that there have been muggings, rapes, pickpocketing, car theft, vandalism, kidnappings, and acts of political terrorism in malls. The unhinged aren't unknown at the malls, either. "Dr. Dirty," a Minneapolis salesman, used to call women recently discharged from maternity wards and pose as a gynecologist, advising them of his formula to make sure their milk didn't dry up. Cut the legs off a pair of panty hose, he told them, pull it on over your chest, making holes for your breasts, and go to the shopping center and expose yourself. Fifty women followed Dr. Dirty's advice before he was caught. Then there was David Berkowitz, "the .44 calibre killer" who wandered a Yonker's mall wishing he had a machine gun, and the political terrorists who bombed a South African mall in 1977. But statistics show that the crime rate in shopping malls is much lower than that in the country as a whole. Mall owners realize that one of the major reasons people shop in malls is to get off crime-ridden city streets and they plan their shopping centers and police them accordingly. If malls are "the feudal castles of contemporary America," as one writer puts it—"aloof, inviting, separate and powerful"—they are as well-protected as feudal castles.

Besides providing service, safety, and fun and diversion for people, shopping centers create jobs and pay taxes that contribute significantly to the well-being of the communities they serve. It is estimated that a shopping center creates one full-time job for every 500 square feet of center selling space—which translates into about 5 million jobs provided by shopping centers and their tenants nationwide. This is not to mention part-time jobs and jobs created by shopping center construction. As for taxes, the centers collected $8.3 billion in sales taxes last year—almost 35 percent of all state sales tax revenues. Center real-estate taxes bring in as much as 90 percent of some towns' real-estate tax revenues; for example, one town's large regional center, with an assessed valuation of $20 million, pays $160,000 a year to the community, which has a tax rate of 80 cents per $100 assessed valuation. Since most centers are self-sufficient—using private police, sanitation services, and so forth—and require few community services, a great profit is made on them locally. One investigation of the major regional center in Oak Brook, Illinois, reveals that the center generated $1.8 million in revenues for the village and cost the local government $210,000 in municipal services, yielding the community a benefit of $1,590,000 for the year.

Shopping center department store branches take in about $77 of every $100 spent in department stores throughout America. While they are often outnumbered 50 to 1 in a mall, they still get many more visits per shopping center shopper than any other kind of store—three visits compared to less than two for their nearest competitor, specialty stores—and their average visitor spends $27. What's more, shoppers rate the department stores in a mall, the mall's proximity to their home, and the overall variety of stores in a mall almost equally in importance as factors that attract them to a shopping center. Most observers anticipate that the big full-line stores will continue to be part of the centers, but there is one major problem—keeping building and land costs down. It costs up to $60 a square foot exclusive of land to build a department store in a shopping center—$75 a square foot for a really posh store trying to create an atmosphere to match its higher prices. This makes it necessary for a department store to generate yearly sales of at least $85 a square foot to get the necessary returns on its investment. Here the mall palls for department store management. Since the average mall department store brings in something closer to $75 a square foot at first, the stores must take losses for a few years— something no retailer likes.

The shopping center of the future will most likely be a smaller one, according to Albert Sussman, executive director of the International Council of Shopping Centers. Malls probably have reached their maximum efficient size, there are fewer large suburban marketing areas left for major mall development, and land is becoming more difficult to acquire than when the shopping centers boom started a quarter of a century ago. "Our industry has reached a stage of maturity," Sussman says. "The perimeters of most metropolitan areas are now mostly covered or will be soon. I don't believe the population centers will expand rapidly beyond their present perimeters. There will be exceptions. There are population shifts to the Sun Belt. Some areas will boom. But I believe the coming years will see developers checking back through present population centers to find gaps that somehow were left during the big boom of the past 25 years. New centers will fill these gaps, but they are likely to be of limited size."

Everyone seems to agree that there will be more shopping centers in the future—up to 25,000 more by the year 2000—and many observers believe that the malls will become entertainment centers for suburbanites who prefer to enjoy their leisure time near home. According to this last theory, an increasing number of bowling alleys, skating rinks, billiard parlors, theatres, and even

amusement parks will become parts of malls, thus making it unnecessary for the suburban family to go downtown at night for its
recreation, and drawing customers into the mall stores at the same
time. A skating rink, for example, can bring as many as 300,000
adults to a shopping center every year, including parents who drop
off their children.

But the cities aren't going to be standing by helplessly while all
this is going on, so it seems likely that some sort of compromise will
be reached. For many years suburban shopping centers drained
business from city department stores, but today the cities are
fighting back with urban malls of various kinds. The largest of the
conventional types is Lloyd Center in Portland, Oregon, a city
within a city with three department stores, a hundred smaller
shops, a Sheraton Hotel, and parking for nearly ten thousand cars—
parking facilities being as important in the city malls as it is in
suburban centers.

Another exciting city center to visit is Boston's Faneuil Hall
Marketplace, among the most successful of downtown retail resto-
rations. Here, in addition to stores, one of selling's oldest con-
veyances—the pushcart—has been put to work in a market
originally built 150 years ago and reopened during the Bicentennial. Twenty-eight carts, filled with unusual crafts, gifts, food, and
original creations serve the more than a million shoppers who visit
Faneuil Hall each month, more people than Disney World draws.

The Rowse Company, builder of the Faneuil Hall Marketplace
and one of America's largest developers and mortgage banking
firms, also built the Gallery at Market East in downtown Philadelphia. The Gallery is a strikingly modern four-level enclosed mall
with 125 stylish shops and restaurants that connects Strawbridge &
Clothier's modernized department store with the dazzlingly new
Gimbels department store, the largest built on the East Coast in
fifty years. Occupying 205,000 square feet of leasable space and
200,000 square feet of public area, it has as its focal point a skylit
court with fountains and plantings. Twenty merchants in the Gallery sell a variety of international and local foods, and there is even
an old Philadelphia Marketplace section featuring pushcart vendors. Though it is located at the hub of Philadelphia's mass transit
system, space has been provided for 1,700 cars in two parking
garages, and there are 4,000 additional spaces within a five-minute

walk, which assures a flow of business from the outlying suburbs to the inner city. The Gallery, developed by Philadelphia's City Planning Commission, is urban renewal at its best and has proved a great success for both its two department stores and smaller tenants since opening in 1977, its sales of $250 a square foot being more than double the national average for malls.

Another approach to the urban shopping center is the vertical mall. Critics say that vertical shopping centers don't work because their layout interrupts the "flow" that true shoppers enjoy, but the success of high-rise city department stores and multilevel suburban malls show that vertical centers can be workable, too. Chicago's 74-story Water Tower Place, which is the world's tallest reinforced concrete building at 859 feet, is the biggest vertical shopping center, featuring an eight-level shopping mall, a 1,300-seat stage, a theater, a bank, corporate and professional offices, an elegant 20-floor Ritz-Carlton Hotel, and 40 floors of luxury condominium apartments. A coventure of the Aetna Life & Casualty Company and Marshall Field that was built at a cost of over $100 million, Water Tower Place was planned as a part of Chicago's Magnificent Mile on North Michigan and is bisected at ground level by a two way street. This "omnicenter" has parking in four underground garages, and each component of Water Tower Place—hotel, business offices, apartments, and shopping units—has its own separate transportation system. Included in the 600,000-square-foot atrium mall shopping center are two major department stores, Marshall Field and Lord & Taylor, over 100 specialty stores, four cinemas, and numerous restaurants. Similar to it, on a smaller scale, is the seven-story tree-dotted atrium mall in New York's new sliding-pond-roofed Citicorp Building, which first opened in 1977. Scores of exciting shops and restaurants fill this glittering glass-walled mall, even "the World's most beautiful newsstand." There is a magnificent modern high-vaulted church—St. Peter's Lutheran—on the first level that serves as the center's "spiritual anchor."

Cities have even tried underground shopping centers to save the inner city, notably in Atlanta, Georgia. But American underground centers haven't usually been as successful as foreign ones, with the exception of prestigious developments like Rockefeller Center. This is probably due to poor planning more than any innate dislike of them by Americans. A vast multilevel underground mall was recently completed beneath the Arco Towers in Los Angeles, and New York's Grand Central Station has been suggested as the site of an underground mall by August Heckscher, the city's former commissioner of parks. In other countries, however, the underground mall is a national institution. In Montreal it has been popular for over a decade, perhaps because of those cold Canadian winters, and today there is a four-mile network of underground walkways beneath Montreal's streets. The Japanese have more than 70 shopping complexes in the depths of their larger cities, shopping centers that are earthquakeproof, weatherproof, less expensive to heat and air-condition because of their natural insulation, cheaper to build in a land where real estate above ground is sky-high, and completely free of air pollution. These "buried malls" are active 24 hours a day, and the largest one, in Osaka, is said to have a daytime population greater than that of Seattle and Denver combined. The Osaka Mall, owned primarily by the city, contains some 200 stores on over four acres, including 55 restaurants where hawkers banging tambourines urge passersby to try their food. This almost surreal "shopping center of the future" is serviced by a railroad and two subway lines and is among the few "cities" in the world that never sleeps, a place where people buy day and night.

❦ X ❦

Does Macy's
Tell Gimbels: Ads,
Displays, Dummies, Parades,
Santas, Reindeer and
All Manner of Promotions
Past and Present

```
COME, COME, TIME, TIME
   COME, COME, TIME, TIME
   THE TIME HAS COME!
WHAT IS TO BE DONE? IS THE QUESTION
WHAT IS TO BE DONE? IS THE QUESTION
   WHAT SHALL BE DONE?
   WHAT SHALL BE DONE?
MARK EVERY ARTICLE
                          WAY
WAY
   WAY DOWN!
```

This rather hysterical old ad, written by R. H. Macy himself, was actually a refreshing change in the 1880s, when department store advertisements were generally crowded single columns that used little white space to break the monotony and attract attention. But although ads in the early days were usually cramped and stodgy, pioneering merchants had already made use of drawings of pretty girls, humor, and primitive forms of all the latest selling techniques. Most stores advertised from earliest times, too; in fact, the large volume of department store advertising over the years was a major factor in the development of great metropolitan newspapers, providing them with much of the money they needed to expand from four- or five-sheet journals to the 9-pound Sunday editions that we lug home today.

While the British abhorred the idea of advertising—"Let us be a nation of shopkeepers as much as we please," *Punch* pleaded in 1848, "but there is no necessity we should become a nation of *advertisers*"—Americans had no prejudice against advertising ad infinitum or ad nauseam, there perhaps being a national tolerance to it fostered by the tall tales of our literature, even a belief in it born of the promise beyond reality America has always held to her children, the wild exaggeration of this country itself with its seemingly limitless land and golden opportunities.

The first full-page department store ad in an American newspaper is said to have been placed by John Wanamaker in the *Philadelphia Record* in December 1878, but San Francisco's White House also claimed this distinction. John Wanamaker, known as "the Father of Modern Advertising," definitely was the first department store owner to copyright an advertisement, in 1874, an expedient the merchant prince found necessary because other stores were stealing his ad ideas. This was his famous "long ad" (over 2,500 words of text) guaranteeing both "one-price" and "money-back." At the time "Pious John" was spending $1,000 a day on newspaper ads, twice as much as most stores in an era when the top advertising man in the country was making a relatively modest $15,000 a year. His credo was that "continuous advertising, like continuous work" is most effective. "If there is any enterprise in the world that a 'quitter' should leave alone," he wrote, "it is advertising. Advertising does not jerk, it pulls. It begins very gently at first, but the pull is steady. It increases day by day, year by year, until it exerts an irresistible power. To discontinue your advertisement is the same thing as taking down your sign. . . . I would as soon think of doing business without clerks as without advertising."

As early as 1861 John Wanamaker had distributed clocks bearing the legend "Wanamaker & Brown" and perfumed picture cards to be used with stored clothes to keep them smelling fresh. One early stunt he pulled had six employees dressed in the height of fashion driving a fine coach drawn by six white horses and distributing handbills whenever a "tally-ho" was sounded. In another, balloons twenty feet high, bearing store ads, were released, and a free suit of clothes was given to each person who returned one.

Early ads were often exaggerated, enough hypes printed to prompt a few satires by newspapers and magazines. The *Philadelphia Sunday Gazette,* for example, ran a mock ad ridiculing the great Wanamaker's in 1877, an ad that seems to have been suggested by the small shopowners of Philadelphia, who were still railing against the big stores. Leading off it read:

> *Billions of millions, more or less, of Ladies and Gentlemen, Boys and Girls, Spitzdogs and Poodles, have visited our Immense Emporium during the first week of its existence and the mammoth headquarters of Monopoly is now an established fact, and must remain a monument to the Gullibility of the Public as long as there is a Public to be gulled. All of our Departments are thoroughly stocked with miscellaneous merchandise for Culinary Purposes and our attendants are constantly prepared to wait on customers. . . .*

The ad went on to offer several culinary "bargains," including:

TRAINED OYSTERS

> *At an enormous outlay we have secured several large beds of thoroughly trained oysters. These bivalves may be kept in cold cellars for any length of time. When wanted, the cook has but to whistle for them as though they were pet dogs. On hearing the familiar sound the educated bivalves come into the kitchen by the dozens, open themselves, and jump into the stewing pan, or into the frying pan, as may be desired. . . .*

Nowhere in America were store ads more colorful than in the West, where there were no holds barred in the all-out price wars of the late nineteenth century.

One Denver store had the slogan, "OUR PANTS ARE DOWN," appropriately illustrated, painted on the outside brick wall of the establishment. Under a picture of the devil a May newspaper advertisement carried the screamer: "PRICES GONE TO———!"

The May Company, inspired by its ad manager Colonel Joseph

M. Grady, one of America's early advertising geniuses, led all western competition in its promotions and advertisements. With every child's suit purchased, the store gave a baseball and bat or a whistle. It raffled off Shetland ponies to its young customers and gave away pug dogs with each five-dollar purchase so that "the magic of childhood's happy laugh will resound through our houses."

Some May Company ads were such gems they should be preserved permanently somewhere. Often they emphasized bargains:

WE'LL TOE THE SCRATCH AND FACE THE MUSIC WITHOUT A WHIMPER

OUR BARGAIN HORN OF PLENTY TIPS DOWN TODAY!

WE ARE NOT CONTENT TO SIT AND SUCK OUR THUMBS WAITING FOR SUNSHINE AND ROSES

Or they played on customer vanity:

TOLERATE NOT ANTIQUITY IN HEADWEAR

O, but for a peep into the brains of the thousands and thousands of heads our Headwear has covered; what volume of massive intellect, what ambitions, noble aspirations, and ever-reaching fame could here be compiled.

Or put down their competitors:

The Exponents of Bogus Telegrams and Liberal Producers of Prison-made Goods are Left Far, Far Behind!

THE CHEAPEST HOUSE IN AMERICA!

Still other May ads praised the store's courage:

Where on God's Good Green Earth outside of our House will you find men morally brave enough to place on sale, on the very threshold of the busy season, our Sixteen Hundred, tailor-made, figured, seasonable and stylish suits at TEN DOLLARS FOR THE CHOICE?

And resorted to still more name calling:

THE HIGH-PRICERS' WAIL OF WOE

The boom is busted and the Bloom is off the Rye! The Rip van Winkle's razzle-dazzle won't work! Their camphorated clothing exhumed from the catacombs of a bygone style, affronts the intelligence of sensible people everywhere.

And made an attempt at humor:

Spring is likely to return before you know it, and you don't want to stick to long underwear until it begins to stick to you!

Colonel Grady even wrote a lengthy poem entitled "Idyl of the Rockies—Machine-made poetry by the May Shoe and Clothing Company":

> What are thy dreams, O maiden fair
>   With wondrous, azure eyes?
> What are thy thoughts so sweet and rare
>   As thou gazest at the skies?
>
> "O! sir," she said, "I do not dream
>   of days gone long ago,
> But I'm wondering how in Dicken's name
>   The May Company sells so low.
>
> My Brother's clothes were nigh worn out;
>   He went there for a suit,
> He now struts like a dude about,
>   They made him look so cute.
>
> I went there for my Seal Plush Sacque
>   That's so very much admired;
> Now all the girls are furious
>   And say I make them tired. . . .

Meanwhile back in the East, Macy's rivalry with Hearn's, which predated the famous Macy's-Gimbels feud by some thirty years, resulted in many memorable ads. One noted exchange took place when Macy's put down Hearn's weekly bargain sale in the following ad:

Selling goods at exorbitant prices five days in the week and pretending to sell bargains on one particular day is not and never has been our practice. We have six bargain days every week as we always aim to give greater value than any other house.

Angered, Hearn's directed no fewer than five vitriolic ads against Macy's, concluding with:

SOME FOLKS

are so wrapped up in their own conceit that they think the world is made for them and them only. They want the earth and all of it. In this free country there is room enough for all who do not want all of this free country. We were born here and expect to stay if some who are in the crockery business have no objections [a reference to the Strauses, who started their association with Macy's as the proprietors of a leased china department in the store]. . . .

The better-known Macy's–Gimbels rivalry was never as bitter as the Macy's–Hearn's feud. The by-now proverbial expression "Does Macy's tell Gimbels?" arose from this friendly, well-publicized war, possibly originating as a publicity gag, possibly as a line in an Eddie Cantor comedy skit when a stooge asked Cantor to reveal some dark secret and the comedian replied, "Does Macy tell Gimbels?" Actually, Macy's has often told Gimbles and vice versa. One time Gimbels ran an ad calling attention to Macy's flower show, heading it, "Does Gimbels tell Macy's? No, Gimbels tells the world!" On another occasion, in 1955, both stores posted signs on their buildings directing shoppers to the other's store.

Gimbels slogan, *Nobody But Nobody Undersells Gimbels,* was invented by the irrepressible Bernice Fitz-Gibbon, a former English teacher and star in the Macy's omniverse before Gimbels shoplifted her from the bigger store. (She had coined their famous *It's Smart to be Thrifty* slogan—not to mention a legendary ad featuring a voluptuous woman in a strapless evening gown that was captioned "How do you keep it up night after night?") Gimbels slogan became world famous, Winston Churchill once asking his friend Bernard Baruch, if it was "really true that nobody, but nobody, undersells Gimbels?" When the William Randolph Hearst art collection was sold at Gimbels in 1943 the slogan "Nobody but nobody, undersells Gimbels," got a boost—a complete Spanish monastery with a total weight of 10,000 tons, which had cost Hearst half a million dollars, went for the bargain-basement price of only $19,000.

The Gimbels-Macy's rivalry was further publicized in the film *Miracle on 34th Street,* in which Macy's directs customers to Gimbels when it doesn't have a particular item in stock and flustered Gimbels executives, realizing their store has been made to look like a "profiteering money grubber," have to adopt the same PR policy. But it was best summarized in an ad written by former Gimbels president Bernard F. Gimbel:

> We congratulate Macy's on their 100th birthday. (They certainly don't look it.) Our public recognizes that the "battling for business" in mid-town New York, good natured in the main, has helped build the most varied, the most accessible and most patronized shopping area in the greatest city on earth. Sometimes it has been a little rough on the contestants, but it has never been unpopular with the crowd. If the manners look a little better, it does not mean that the battle is less real. (Neither store ever takes its eye off the other. What it sees, it quickly translates into action.) This is the kind of competition the customer loves; and we have always believed that the customer is the boss.

Macy's most durable ad is the store's slogan, "It's Smart To Be Thrifty," which Bernice Fitz-Gibbon coined in 1938 and which is even painted on the store roof for air travelers to view. Macy's advertising manager at the time claimed that when he visited Bernice in the hospital the day after she gave birth to her son, Peter, she smiled at him and whispered, "Well, I've done it!" Until she pressed a piece of paper into his hands bearing the new slogan, he thought she was referring to the birth of her child.

Two of the four department store ads chosen by advertising expert Julian Louis Watkins for his book *The 100 Greatest Advertisements* are Macy's ads. The most celebrated of these was the

1948 Christmas effort headed, "Oh, Darling—You Shouldn't Have!" and showing an attractive woman embracing her husband after opening her Christmas gift from Macy's. Watkins notes that the ad, written by Macy's Barbara Collyer, drew more letters, calls, and personal visits from customers than any before or since. His other Macy's winner was a cartoon showing a man and woman sitting in a crowded football stadium in the midst of a driving rainstorm. The caption, written by Macy's Margaret Fishback, has the woman saying: "We could be just as crowded at Macy's, and not get wet!"

Watkins's advice to all copywriters is "to get a file of Macy advertisements of the Fishback era and read them like the Bible." Margaret Fishback, a noted writer of light verse, was responsible for a great number of classic ads, including a series about Macy's delivery service illustrating how widely the drivers and their helpers traveled to bring customers Macy merchandise. One was a cartoon showing a cannibal and his wife seated by a bubbling cauldron. A Macy driver's cap lay on the ground beside them, and the husband, gnawing contentedly on a bone, says to his wife: "Put a little more salt on the helper, dear." Another in the same series shows a Macy's truck delivering palm trees to a tent of an Arab sheik in the middle of the scorching Sahara. The sheik's sentry calls within: "Say Hassan—did you order an oasis from Macy's?" Macy's trucks have never seen Africa or the Sahara, although they've traveled to many unlikely places, including a nudist colony, but the ads made their point. So did Miss Fishback's ad entitled, "6 Easy Ways to Save Money," which showed Mom and Dad in overalls pushing their naked children in a soapbox on wheels. Recommending such economies as "Sell your furniture and stand up," and "Give up wearing clothes," this one concluded that the best solution was to be thrifty by shopping in the World's Largest Store.

The prosaic Sears Roebuck catalog is called "the most famous of all salesmen in print" by Watkins, who points out that "advertising containing 10 facts as against 4 facts is 44% more effective." But the only other traditional department store ad chosen for *The World's 100 Greatest Advertisments* is a B. Altman ad from 1934. Written by Ruth Packard, this ad simply pictures a $2.50 bouquet of flowers, the copy beneath reading: "*We believe there are at least* 500 MEN IN NEW YORK WHO LOVE THEIR WIVES . . . (and want to give them flowers for Easter) . . ." In about three hours after the ad appeared the entire 500 bouquets the New York store placed on sale were gone.

Oddly enough, department stores' ads have produced no symbols for stores like the White Rock Girl or Borden's Elsie, or the Man in the Hathaway Shirt. Macy's, to be sure, is known for its Red Star, theirs long before the USSR adopted it, Boston's Filene's is known for its *f*, and San Francisco's Emporium for its *E*, but no store has its equivalent of the Jolly Green Giant or the Smith Bros. Some stores have come close. For example, the Lilliputian Bazaar, the forerunner of the late Best's, had as its trademark a hand of Gulliver's on which children were playing. Korvettes recently tried to develop a mythical "Mayor of Korvettes" patterned on New York's Little Flower, Fiorello La Guardia, but the Mayor was withdrawn when he irritated too many television viewers.

Bloomingdale's, Lane Bryant, Rich's, Penney's, and many other stores, all conceived notable early ads, with Penney's "The Penney Idea" probably the most famous of them all. Lyman Bloomingdale's promotional savvy was responsible for one of the first and foremost publicity campaigns ever to come out of New York retailing. At the turn of the century he dotted elevated trains and trolley cars with the slogan, "All Cars Transfer to Bloomingdales," and in 1902 Richard F. Outcault, who fathered the comic strip with his "The Yellow Kid" and "Buster Brown" strips, was commissioned to visually popularize this slogan. The result was an umbrella design that unfolded on walls all around town (several faded examples can still be seen, including one at Lexington Avenue and 116th Street). Songs and vaudeville sketches featured the slogan. Actual umbrellas carrying the words shielded drivers of early Bloomingdale's delivery wagons. Gaily colored sunshades bearing the phrase were distributed free. Within a few years the five words were known to virtually every New Yorker.

Lane Bryant's World War I ad explaining the strategy behind their styles for stout women is a masterpiece of copywriting and euphemism.

Today stout clothing is taken for granted by shoppers, but it took many such "Appearing Stout is Merely A Matter of Clothes" ads to educate the public when Lane Bryant first introduced the new line.

Stores are not legally obliged to honor typographical errors in their ads, as is often believed. Nevertheless, as a matter of good public relations, many stores have sold $495 coats for $4.95 and $15 hats for $1.50. Since 87 percent of all women and 51 percent of all men read newspaper department store ads, such typos can prove very costly. Sometimes a store will lodge a claim against the newspaper responsible for the typographical error, but newspapers have no legal obligation for such errors, either.

During the Great Depression, stores cut down on their ads considerably, but the excess profits tax inspired heavy advertising during World War II, which carried over into present times. One would be hard put to find a store that doesn't advertise today, that depends on word of mouth to sell its wares as many did in the past (Tiffany's used to print just its name in its ads—nothing else, not even an address!). If there is a trend at present, it is toward more risqué advertisements. Bloomingdale's, for instance, regularly advertises a "hipster panty" with "Bloomies" written across the rear as "the best seat in the house," and not long ago published a sexy lingerie supplement in the New York Times that became a collectors item, selling for six dollars in one bookstore. Page 602 of Sears's 1975 winter catalogue is also something of a collector's item. Though Sear's catalogue illustrations are definitely sexier than ever, this particular catalogue picture was not intentionally so. A mistake in the printing process did, however, make it seem like a model for men's underwear was "indecently exposed," as one newspaper report put it.

If ads are getting sexier, today's "new-wave" store window displays have become a kind of street theater featuring comedy and violence as well as sex. Traditional window displays date back to the early 1880s, when the use of plate glass on a wide scale in America made display windows a standard feature of department stores. Macy's Fourteenth Street store in New York was famous for its Christmas window, featuring a collection of toys revolving on a belt, as far back as the mid-1800s. Marshall Field's Arthur Fraser was world renowned as a window display artist in the early 1900s, and he advanced from merchandise-dominated windows to symbolism and abstract designs to catch the passerby's eye. Ignoring complaints that "the public doesn't understand," Fraser designed windows to "make people think," and he was so powerful at Field's that if goods offered for display by buyers were out of harmony with his designs, he simply refused to feature them.

Another early expert at window display was L. Frank Baum, who later wrote *The Wonderful Wizard of Oz,* but whose first book was *The Art of Decorating Dry Goods Stores Windows and Interiors* (1900).Window displays were in fact so familiar to the public before the turn of the century that they possibly inspired the expression, a stuffed shirt. It seems that in the absence of mannequins, department store decorators simply stuffed new shirts to be displayed with tissue paper, these bloated figures reminding window shoppers of pompous people like the floorwalkers inside. Window dressing, manipulation to show more exaggerated value, is another expression that has its origins in the store windows.

Display windows have been used for every purpose from showing goods and educating people (Filene's once had a window illustrating how an atomic bomb was contructed) to arenas for contests like sleeping marathons. Recently a nude couple, discreetly covered with blankets, settled down for a night's sleep in a New York shop window to demonstrate the heating qualities of a down comforter. Many stores believe, "It's what's up front that counts," that a store is in great part its windows, and spend millions a year decorating them. Macy's even has telephone connections from the sidewalk to its store windows so that designers can direct workers from outside at the proper artistic distance. But in the last decade traditional display windows have been disappointing, which is probably why the so-called new-wave windows (they really owe a large debt to Fraser and other pioneer display artists) are getting so much attention today. These avant-garde windows are spreading out across the country but are still most popular in New York, where one Park Avenue hostess reportedly takes her guests on window-hopping tours in the family limousine. Some new-wave windows are tasteless, others preciously trendy, a few stupid, but most are original and will give an energy transfusion to an art form that badly needs it.

Described as "situation-comedy and melodrama for the acquisitive class," the most innovative windows are to be found at fashionable or trendy stores such as Bloomingdale's, Bendel's, and Halston's. The "kinkiest commercials in town" almost always utilize the shock technique. "When you do store windows," one display artist explains, "you have to use a shock manner to call

attention to the display. There's so much visual pollution everywhere that it keeps people from really seeing what's in the windows." Strolling around Manhattan, window shoppers have
happened upon the following displays in the last year or so:

• Well-dressed Bendel mannequins surrounded by mounds of
garbage—a comment on a New York City garbage strike.
   • Bendel mannequins drinking at what is obviously a lesbian bar.
   • A high-fashion Bendel corpse apparently dead on the floor with
a bottle of sleeping pills nearby—a comment on the sleeping pill
syndrome.
   • A "suicide mannequin" hanging in a Bloomingdale's window.
   • A nude Bloomingdale's mannequin, covered by sponges, leaning back sensuously in a bathtub.
   • A peek at a Bloomies male mannequin making his toilette in a
bathroom.
   • An "after the explosion" scene in a Halston's window inspired
by the terrible LaGuardia airport bombing.
   • A Bendel's window decorated by artist-writer Edward Gorey,
who designed the set and costumes for the Broadway hit *Dracula*,
with a sack of Gorey-made frogs, bats and unborn creatures called
Pheetus Pairdew sown among the mannequins, or resting on their
arms and shoulders.
   • A Halston's window that ran like a serialized soap opera for a
week, the stomach of a pregnant mannequin in a hospital bed
growing larger every day—until a baby was born on the seventh
day.

Two top new-wave display artists (never call them "window
dressers") are twenty-nine-year-old Bob Currie, display director at
Bendel's until recently, and twenty-seven-year-old Candy Pratts of
Bloomingdale's. Currie once planned to do a window funeral
complete with coffin to display some somber jersey dresses, but
Bendel's president Geraldine Stutz told him, "Over my dead body."
The outspoken Pratts, who says, "I'm giving Bloomingdale's hump
and pump and excitement," is also in charge of Bloomies' interior
design. For a recent Christmas toy display she purchased a $5,000
talking mannequin—a zoo keeper. With eyes that wink and lips that

move, he recited a two-minute script describing some of the stuffed animals for sale: "Here comes the grizzly bear. He eats honey and sweets. He likes kids, too, Generally for breakfast."

Automated mannequins are used by many stores, including Hess's, which was first with the Audio Visual Mannequin introduced during the Bicentennial. Created by Duane A. Machtig and produced by AVM, Inc., of Washington, D.C., this automated mannequin has remarkable synchronization and articulation of movement and speech. Models of George Washington, Benjamin Franklin, Patrick Henry, and Betsy Ross were on display at Hess's, each telling the story of an important revolutionary event. The extremely realistic mannequins have only been surpassed by the mime recently hired by a New York store to portray a mannequin on the sidewalk outside; a price tag on his coat, he stood stock still for 45 minutes at a time, suffering pokes, kicks, kisses, and tickling from passersby who wanted to see if he was real.

Department store mannequins are no longer glassy-eyed dummies made of wax whose chins often sagged to their chests on hot days when the sun beat down on display windows. The new breed of mannequins, introduced by Seigel of Paris in 1925 and brought to America by Macy's that year, is made of nonmelting fiberglass, or plaster, or papier-mâché and is much slimmer and curvier than her ancestors—she wears a size eight dress, is about six feet tall, and has measurements of 32-24-34. A decent mannequin can't be bought for under $350 today, and most of them average $450—except for the "real dummies" with chipped fingers and ghostly faces found in dime stores. A decade ago it was the fashion to create mannequins to resemble society figures like Baby Jane Holtzer, Babe Paley, and Wendy Vanderbilt, but the most popular mannequins today are modeled for by professional fashion models like Sara Kapp, a particular favorite because of her interesting, rather than perfect, face.

At Adele Rootstein, a mannequin house considered to be one of the best in the industry, a company sculptor measures the mannequin model's head with calipers to get the proportions exactly right. The mannequin is first molded in clay by a sculptor from the live subject, then cast in plaster and refined before its final casting in fiberglass. The body is sprayed, the face painted in oils, and the head is fitted with a wig that can be styled. These natural mannequins come complete with nipples, underarm hair, glass eyes, and teeth. It's said that the best mannequins, which designers always call by name and not by number, take nearly as long to make—from choosing a live model to presenting them to retail buyers—as it does to have a baby, but for all the pampering a mannequin gets, its life span in a top store is not likely to be more than two years. After that, fashion dated, most are relegated to interior displays, sold to other stores, or just destroyed.

Ads and window displays have always been used to attract customers to department stores, but other promotions have been just as effective over the years. In the early days the stores had airplanes land on their roofs, held exhibitions on paddle-wheel steamers, and arranged for appearances of every conceivable kind of celebrity. One of the most unusual goodwill promotions under-taken by a store—one which would go over big in New York City today—was conceived in 1913 by a Saint Paul emporium called The Golden Rule. Saint Paul was having trouble marketing city bonds, and the Golden Rule bought $123,000 worth, put them on sale with a store guarantee and sold them in less than five hours.

Through the years department stores have consistently served as educational centers in the process of attracting customers. Free lectures, educational displays, and classes are given on every imag-inable subject. At the time of one British coronation, Bloom-ingdale's transformed its auditorium into a reproduction of the Tower Room of the Tower of London, housing replicas of the English crown jewels. Stores have offered lessons in cooking, sew-ing, child care, typing, driving, music, painting, sculpture, interior decorating, doll's dressmaking, "space-saving"—just name it. Classes have been given in every sport, Jordan Marsh in Boston once constructing an elaborate setup to teach sailing, with a giant wind machine and a boat mounted on a revolving platform. Such institutional offerings attract customers, educate them to a desire for new merchandise, and create goodwill that will sooner or later be translated into dollars and cents.

Sale days draw more people into stores than any other promo-tion, and always have. Descriptions of some of these—such as the Strawbridge & Clothier's annual Clover Day sale—can be found in the store biographies elsewhere in this book, but others are held by almost all stores. The white sale, which originated in France and was first introduced here by John Wanamaker, is one of these. So is the $1 sale and the Washington Birthday sale. This last originated in Washington, D.C., during the 1930s and features many strategically placed low-cost items—such as dollar bills for ninety-four cents—to attract crowds to department stores. No longer with us are the mill-end sales of early times, these often consisting of merchandise odds-and-ends that the store bought cheaply at the end of a manufacturer's season. During the 1920s, stores frequently hired the flamboyant "C. H. Lockhart Mill End Sales" for such promotions. An extrovert of the first order, Lockhart toured stores throughout the United States and Canada promoting off-price events. Megaphone in hand, he'd act as a barker and was a crowd pleaser with a colorful humorous spiel who'd stroll down the aisles followed by throngs of customers as he touted his "sensational" and "irresistable" buys.

Next to sale days, the most common of department store promotions are probably fashion shows—which include everything from Hess's fashion caravans to the Fortnight formats of Neiman-Marcus that have their roots in the expositions and fairs held by Wanamaker's, Macy's, and all the pioneer stores at the turn of the century. The newest promotion idea among leading retail stores, suggested by *Clothes Magazine* at the 1977 National Retailers Convention, is to set up fashion shows to promote winter vacation clothes during June, July, and August—to create a "Fifth Season" and drum up business during the usual summer doldrums. Fashion shows were recently satirized by the mime Lavinia Plonka in her sketch, "The Inflation Collection," in which she wickedly but accurately portrayed a haughty, hollow-cheeked high-fashion model "chicly" using a sweater for a bib, a shopping bag for a hat and a bra for goggles. The best (or most expressive) fashions are usually "created" by someone; clothes that are "designed by" come a bit cheaper; and something that has merely "made" on the label can usually be afforded by most people.

The greatest of department store promotions come in the Christmas season. Where would department stores be without Christmas, and Santa Claus, who is the greatest salesman of all. The country's big department stores do up to 30 percent of their entire yearly sales volume during the Christmas season, normally amassing 20 percent of annual sales and 25 percent of annual profits in the holiday season, so they owe a lot to the jolly gentleman. Perhaps this is the logic behind the story that the abbreviation *Xmas* was the sacrilegious creation of a department store copywriter. *Xmas* however, is neither an abbreviation or "a vulgar commercial invention" of recent vintage. *X* has been used to symbolize the syllable "Christ" in English since at least 1100, when it was recorded in *Xtianity*, meaning "Christianity." The Old English word for Christmas recorded in the twelfth century *Anglo Saxon Chronicle* begins with an *X* and the word *Xmas* was used as early as 1551. Because the Greek word for Christ begins withthe letter *chi*, or *X*, some philologists believe that the *X* in *Xmas* symbolizes the cross.

The Christmas season traditionally begins on Thanksgiving for department stores, and it was a department store owner, Fred Lazarus, who got Thanksgiving stabilized as the last Thursday in November. Christmas promotions, however, seem to begin earlier and earlier every year and today most stores across the country start to don their holiday makeup at the beginning of November. Christmas displays, especially outdoor display windows, are always the most beautiful of the year, the designers outdoing themselves at this time of year. Macy's has been noted for its Christmas windows since the 1880s, while Richmond's Miller & Rhoad's religious windows are a traditional favorite. In Neiman-Marcus windows, and throughout the store, hundreds of Colorado aspen trees, stripped of foilage and sprayed white, are draped with thousands of tiny white lights. Traditional and modern displays grace the store windows of every city and suburban shopping center. Most are red and green and crystal, but there have been whimsical displays such as Santa Claus in a rocket ship, even one typically urban-paranoic window display showing Santa Claus coming out of a fireplace and everyone throwing their hands up in horror "because they're scared to death of that strange person." New York, a sentimental city under its diamondlike exterior, becomes a window wonderland in the Christmas season, its streets an outdoor museum of store displays. B. Altman, for example, has a large six window display called "The Day the Children Saved Christmas," which tells the tale, narrated from loudspeakers in each window, of Jim and Jill, who visit Santa at the North Pole, find him missing, and embark on a search to find him in time for Christmas.

Christmas shopping still isn't everybody's cup of tea. Last year a man in Bloomington, Illinois, dressed up as Santa and stationed himself in the Eastland Shopping Center, where he stayed until merchants had him arrested for handing out leaflets that deplored the greed and excessive commercialism of Christmas and urged shoppers not to shop, to "go home and celebrate Christmas." His sentiments are nothing new and have frequently been expressed by department store salespeople, Back in 1906 one saleswoman wondered in print "what the simple workman of Nazareth, if he looks down on things here below, thinks of the manner in which the most enlightened of nations celebrate His feast" every year. "The crowd of buyers this Christmas Eve assumed the aspect of a mob," she wrote, "and I should not have been greatly astonished if they had suddenly turned on one another and begun to tear and rend." Her Christmas stint in a department store filled her with a "sudden loathing and disgust for the whole Christmas idea . . . the restless, swaying, moving, perspiring mass of humanity," and "the heathen revel," made her vow that "I shall never give or receive another Christmas present as long as I live!" But then she was working weeklong fifteen-hour days for eight cents an hour.

Department stores often launch the Christmas shopping season with Thanksgiving Day Parades such as Macy's and Hudson's, both of which are over fifty years old. Hudson's Parade, the older of the two by a year, having been started in 1923, features 18 floats, 14 bands, and over two thousand participants. It is viewed by half a million people along its 2.5 mile route, and millions more see it on national television carried to 47 states. Because of a runaway horse team during one of the early Hudson parades, manpower was used for many years, with some 24 persons pulling a single float, but now all floats are mechanized. Ranging from depictions of the first Thanksgiving and Santa himself to the Little Old Woman Who Lives in a Shoe, the floats use nearly a mile of two-by-fours in their construction, plus about 4,800 cubic feet of Styrofoam, 75 reams of paper, and 200 gallons of paint.

Macy's parade, easily the most famous in department store history, was first held in 1924 with an audience of about ten thousand along the line of march. Today it is estimated that in good weather over a million men, women, and children crowd the parade route from Seventy-seventh Street and Central Park West to Herald Square. Macy's massive balloons, a parade trademark, first

came on the scene in 1927. Designed by artist Tony Sarg, Bill
Baird's mentor, who did so much to popularize puppetry in America, and sculptured out of air and rubber by the goodyear Tire and
Rubber Company, they have attracted national attention ever
since.

The job of inflating the balloons begins on Thanksgiving Eve. At
about 8:00 P.M. canvas ground cloths, similar to those used to keep
a baseball diamond dry, are taken to Seventy-Seventh Street (which
has been cleared of parked cars) and there laid out to cover most of
the street. The deflated balloons begin arriving in their shipping
cases at about 11:00 P.M. They are carefully unfolded on the ground
cloths, covered with nets and held down by sandbags. On Thanksgiving morning the countdown begins. The more than one thousand
Macy's employees who will march in the parade begin arriving at
the store for professional makeup and costuming. Goodyear "med-
ics," technicians sent by the company to repair any damaged
balloons, give the weather bureau a final check to determine
barometric pressure, which influences the amount of helium used to
inflate each balloon. Meanwhile, the handlers who will pull the
balloons down the parade route have arrived. The parade floats,
built and assembled in New Jersey, have been brought into Manhattan through the Lincoln Tunnel. Bands have arrived from all over
the country. At dawn they appear in their bright uniforms, and
each is given one final test performance at the staging area in front
of Macy's. Then each goes by bus to the parade's starting point and
the big show that lasts from 9:15 to noon.

Many celebrities appear in the parade, but the balloons are
always the favorites among the kids. Walt Disney and Norman Bel
Geddes, as well as Tony Sarg, have had a hand in creating these
behemoths, some of which require as many as 55 men to handle
them by their guide ropes. Though accidents have happened—
Mighty Mouse once struck a horizontal flagpole on the Hotel Astor
and was partially deflated—they are not usually serious because the
helium in each balloon is carefully balanced in separate compartments and if one balloon compartment is punctured, the gas in its
other compartments holds it aloft.

In a typical year, Macy's Parade will have 9 balloons, 45 floats,
14 bands, 400 clowns, and a bevy of celebrities. The Peanuts
character Snoopy is one of the kid's current favorites, as are the

cartoon characters Linus the Lionhearted, Kermit the Frog, Bull-winkle Moose, many fairytale characters, and, of course, Santa Claus. Another old charmer, Dino the Dinosaur, a four-story-high balloon that is 60 feet long and has a smile 2 feet wide, made a record 13 appearances in the parade. Dino was finally blown up and deflated for the last time in 1977 at a retirement party held at the American Museum of Natural History, down the hall from some of the most famous dinosaur fossils in the world. He had "lived" more than twice as long as any other character, the average life expectancy of each balloon being five years.

The 1947 film *Miracle on 34th Street,* starring Edmund Gwenn as Macy's Santa and Natalie Wood as the little girl who didn't believe in Santa Claus, was inspired by the Macy's Thanksgiving Day Parade, which is depicted in its opening scenes. *Miracle* and later television coverage of the parade, bringing it to some 100 million people, have made the parade almost the national symbol of Thanksgiving. The film itself is a perennial Christmas favorite shown every year on television, and it is safe to say that no other movie has so effectively publicized a commercial institution. Spin-offs of it include the Broadway musical *Here's Love* and a television special.

Interestingly, Kris Kringle, the Santa Claus in *Miracle* who has "latent maniacal tendencies," according to the store psychologist, Mr. Sawyer, but turns out to be a very real Santa, indeed, has a real-life counterpart. One of America's most active Santas, eighty-year-old Max Kramer of Brooklyn, began as a Macy's Santa about fifteen years ago. Kramer, who doesn't work for Macy's anymore but appears as Santa in numerous ads and at many public functions, considers himself synonymous with the legendary figure, just as Kris did. The name above his apartment bell in Ridgewood is S. *Claus,* a name he also signs to checks, and he at least occasionally answers the door with a "Ho, ho, ho!" When he isn't busy during the Christmas season, this S. *Claus* doesn't go back to the North Pole. He usually sits in a restaurant on Broadway during the warm months "watching the girls go by."

Marshall Field's sprite Uncle Mistletoe is very popular in Chi-cago, some children preferring to visit him instead of Santa Claus at Christmas time, but only one other department store creation has won the nationwide fame of Macy's Santa. In 1939 Robert May, a

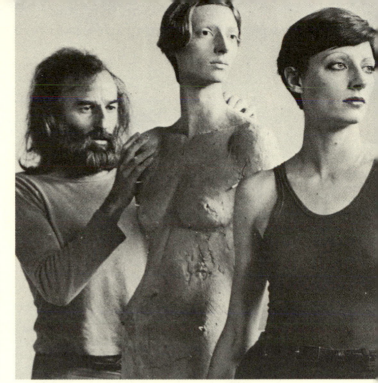

Right: Adel Rootstein sculptor, John Taylor, shapes a clay replica of top New York model Sara Kapp to be used to construct a mannequin.

Below: Some samples of completed Rootstein mannequins.

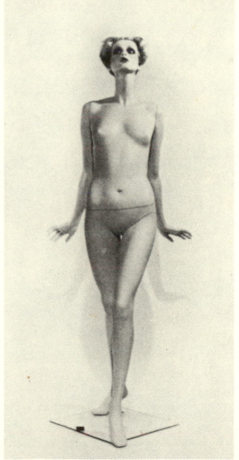

Bonwit Teller display windows on New York's Fifth Avenue are among the most visually striking in the city.

Window display at Gump's, San Francisco.

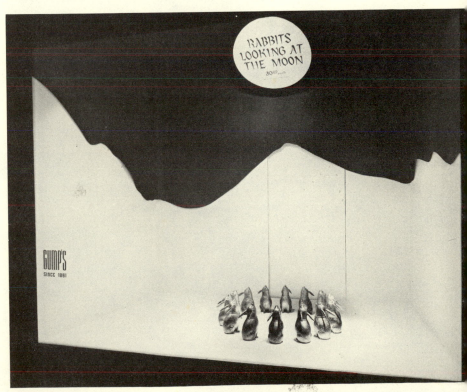

Window display from 1926 in the J. C. Penney Chanute, Kansas, store.

A Strawbridge & Clothier display window filled with "skimmers" in May 1916.

A "Flood Sale" at a J. C. Penney store in the 1920s.

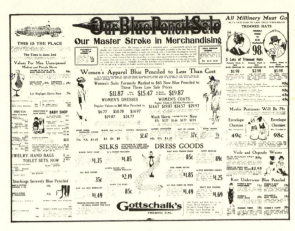

Above: In 1919 Gottschalk's of Fresno, California, held its first Blue Pencil Sale. Circulars like this were distributed and giant blue pencils hung in the windows as a symbol of cutting prices way down.

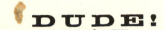

D U D E !

DO You Want Clothing? Give Us Your Shape.
DO You Require Boots or Shoes? Show Us Your Foot.
DO You Need Dry Goods? We Are They.
DO You Covet Jewelry Things? Them Are Us.
DO You Hanker for Musical Goods? Ring Our Bell.
DO You Ache for Crockery or Glassware? We Have One.
DO You Pine for Hardware or Tinware? Open Our Gate.
DO You Worry for Harness or Saddles? Enter Our Portal.
DO You Languish for Guns or Revolvers? Get in Our Range.
DO You Droop for Fishing Tackle? They Are Among Us.
DO You Mourn for Trunks? Climb Our Fence.
DO You Covet Groceries? That's We.
DO You Suffer from a Short Crop of Anything? You will find
it quoted in our Price List, which we will now send FREE to any
address upon receipt of the postage—7 cents. It is a book of 216
pages, 8½ by 11¼ inches (get out your rule), with over 3,000 illus-
trations (a whole picture gallery) of goods we carry. Stockmen
are particularly invited to visit us, with or without pikes and
lanterns. Look us over and buy wherever they please. We
never send a salesman outside of our door to solicit trade, and
have no branch stores. Look out for sharpers. We close at
6 p.m.

MONTGOMERY WARD & CO ,
227 and 229 Wabash Ave., near Exposition Building,
CHICAGO, ILL.

Left: Humorous ad placed in the *Drover's Journal* of Montgomery Ward & Co., 1883.

Below right: Evolution of a store's logo over a 75-year period as demonstrated by J. C. Penney's five changes since the original.

Part of an ad campaign to promote shopping at Boscov's in Reading, Pennsylvania.

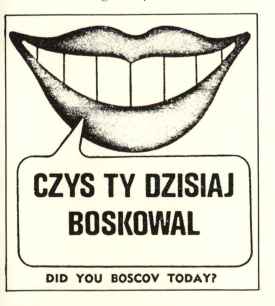

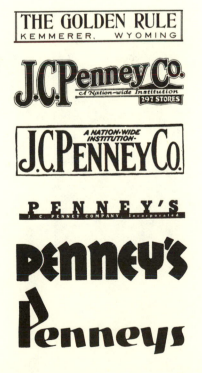

In 1922 Philadelphia's Strawbridge & Clothier's opened the first radio station in a department store with a musicale.

Left and below: Early in their careers Lauren Bacall and Susan Hayward posed for Ward ads.

To remind people that they needn't shop elsewhere, Hess's Allentown, Pa. store held fashion shows on trains bound for big cities.

A promotion featuring Robin of the Batman and Robin team at Hess's in Allentown, Pa.

OUR PALACE ADVERTISING CAR "SUCCESS."

Ward's used this Pullman car to carry a troupe of entertainers around the country and put on shows for potential customers.

Montgomery Ward used this early "electric horseless carriage" for promotion purposes in the 1890s.

Right: People come from a five-state area to see Dayton's annual spring flower show in its downtown Minneapolis store's huge auditorium. The theme of this show is "Scheherazade: Exotic Gardens of Morocco."

Below: The towering 45-foot Christmas tree at the old City of Paris, San Francisco, was an annual tradition for more than half a century. Liberty House continued the tradition when they purchased City of Paris in 1972 until moving into the new building in 1974.

The "Lighting of the Great Tree," an extravaganza that opens the Christmas season on Thanksgiving night every year at Rich's in Atlanta.

Above: Hess's of Allentown, Pa., parachutes Santa into the Allentown Fairgrounds.

Right: A booklet issued by Santa Claus Studios, a photography firm that takes photos of children posing with Santas, gives some rules for proper Santa Claus behavior.

SANTA'S MANNER WITH CHILDREN

Santa Claus, like any public figure, is always open to criticism. If anything is allowed to hurt the Santa illusion in the hearts of grown-ups, as well as children, considerable harm can be done. Santa must always remain a noble figure, kind, patient and understanding. The Santa of history and legend is also a jolly, robust sort of an individual with a ready smile, a hearty laugh and a cheerful disposition. And, needless to say, he never does anything to make a child unhappy (in spite of the piece of coal in the stocking legend) and never makes any kind of a promise that a parent may not fulfill.

1. **AS CHILDREN APPROACH** . . . or when traffic is slow, wave a cheery greeting to every child you see.

2. **GREET THEM CHEERFULLY** . . . A good hearty laugh is in order but it should not be too loud. Say, "Hello there! I've been expecting *you*."

3. **BE GENTLE** . . . Many children are nervous and easily frightened. A boisterous Santa with large, quick movements will make it difficult for such children.

4. **BE UNDERSTANDING AND PATIENT** . . . Remember the little ones are keyed up and excited in the presence of Santa and on occasion do strange things. Some are very shy and will not look at you, others may take a good tug at your beard.

5. **ASK THEIR NAME** . . . and then use it throughout the interview. Say, "That's a real nice name. I remember it from my good book."

6. **"WHAT DO YOU WANT FOR CHRISTMAS?"** . . . The age old question is always good. Listen carefully to their answers.

7. **WATCH PARENT FOR SIGNAL** . . . Do not promise anything unless the parent has indicated in some way that it is okay.

8. **ENCOURAGE GOOD HABITS** . . . Tell them you know they always put their toys away, help Mother, and eat all their dinner. Say, "Well maybe not absolutely always—but I know you try real hard, don't you?"

9. **NEVER SAY "I"** . . . Santa should always speak of himself as "Santa" or "Santa Claus." Say, "Well, Santa knows you want to be a real good boy."

10. **SAY GOODBYE** . . . "Well, goodbye Ann. Santa is so glad you came to see him. Santa will be sure to visit your house on Christmas."

Left: Dino the Dinosaur, long a favorite at the Macy's Thanksgiving Day Parade— probably the biggest promotion in department store history.

Below: The J. L. Hudson Department Store flag displayed here on its Detroit downtown store is the largest flag in the world.

Lawrence Welk, promoting a book at Rich's in Atlanta, poses with Chuck McGivern, and Faith Brunson, the store's book buyer.

Below: A home decorating class for Montgomery Ward customers.

Above: Fourth of July fireworks in New York Harbor sponsored by Macy's.

Left: A Montgomery Ward security guard spots a shoplifter on closed circuit TV and alerts his partner on the floor.

Below: Ads by S.T.E.M. Inc. (*Shoplifters Take Everybody's Money*) have proved very effective in reducing shoplifting in Philadelphia, Pa.

"**After I was caught, my 'friends' wouldn't have anything to do with me.**"

"Some initiation requirement," says Georgette, age 17, bitterly. "It was kind of a dare. If I could prove I'd shoplifted, I'd get into this club at school. Then I was caught. My parents were called. Everybody heard about it. Now the girls don't want me around—they say I'll give them a bad name."

copywriter in Montgomery Ward's advertising department, prepared a Christmas giveaway for Ward's featuring a character he called Rollo, then Reginald, and finally Rudolph—that famous reindeer with the glowing bulbous nose who has become part of American folklore. Over 6 million copies of *Rudolph the Red-Nosed Reindeer* were distributed, the company then generously assigning May all rights to the booklet. May had some trouble selling a commercial publisher a book that had already been given away 6 million times, but he finally did, and it has been doing well every year since then. His greatest break, however, came in 1949 when he sent the book to his friend composer Johnny Marks, who penned a song about Rudolph and persuaded Gene Autry to record it. "Rudolph" has since become the second biggest hit in the history of popular music, topped only by Irving Berlin's "White Christmas," and has sold more than 120 million records and made Marks a millionaire many times over. Its lyrics, according to one writer, are more familiar to most Americans than those of "Silent Night." You can safely bet at Christmas time that some Rome radio station is playing "Rudolph dal Naso Rosso" or that someone in Paris is listening to a recording of "Le P'tit Renne au Nez Rouge." As for May, he won't say what royalties he has received from his creation, only that "Rudolph is the first reindeer that ever kept the wolf from the door."

Right after the Thanksgiving Day Parade, Macy's Santa Claus is crowned on a throne of gold and makes his home at the Herald Square store for the Christmas season. Santas have been at home in American department stores since the early 1880s, a noted early one appearing in the elaborate Christmas pageants Mabley & Carew put on for children in Cincinnati during the Gay Nineties. Possibly the most famous was Miller & Rhoad's William C. Strother, who was also known as "the World's Champion Human Fly" for his work as a Hollywood stunt man and his exploits scaling tall buildings all over America. Strother's makeup, designed by Max Factor, took him over two hours to apply, and he was acclaimed as the most realistic Santa ever. Strother began his act by appearing out of a chimney, then took children on his lap and, by use of a concealed throat mike on an assistant, was able to address each child by name. He earned a thousand a week, the highest salary ever paid to a Santa Claus, and became a national celebrity before he died in 1958. Shortly after Strother's death, Miller & Rhoads inaugurated its Santa Claus trains in Richmond, Roanoke, and Lynchburg, which so many children came aboard that in one instance the Norfolk and Western Railroad had to run the largest passenger train in its history.

Legend has it that the wisest of Santas was the man who wouldn't parachute out of an airplane into one of the early open shopping malls. It seems that an elf who preceeded him got squished on the concrete when his chute didn't open and Santa refused to budge. But Santas arrive every year at centers in helicopters, fire trucks, and motorized sleighs.

Joske's in San Antonio has presented several notable Santas in recent times. One year its Santa, wearing a Stetson and packing a pistol, arrived in a covered wagon. Another Joske's Santa arrived by plane from the North Pole, was driven to the store in a bright red fire truck, climbed a fire ladder to the roof, and slid down the chimney to the photography studio. Joske's Texas-size mechanical Santa was a great crowd pleaser. Thirty feet tall while in a sitting position on a 20-foot chimney, he was wondrously contrived of iron, steel pipes, and fiberglass, and had to be dropped from a balloon each year onto the store's roof. For many years San Antonians enjoyed hearing his contagious "Ho-ho-ho" and seeing him move his arms in a 12-foot arc, but he finally fell victim to the ravages of time and weather.

By late November over twenty-thousand Santa Clauses are at their stations in department stores and shopping malls and on street corners across America—they start coming the day after Halloween, although only ten years ago it was thought grossly commercial to display Santas before the second week in December. Most Santas are from the ranks of retired or unemployed men—there are only eight women Santas in America—but many are drafted from salesmen, watchmen, and other store personnel. "A successful Santa has to combine the instincts, if not the expertise of both a psychiatrist and a mother," says one expert, yet most are paid the department store minimum wage.

There used to be a Santa Claus School in Albion, New York, run by Charles W. Howard, that turned out trained Clauses for department stores, teaching its students makeup, child psychology, and other relevant subjects and awarding B.S.C. (Bachelor of Santa

Claus) degrees to graduates. Today what was once the Santa Claus School is the Santa Claus Suit & Equipment Company, which sells complete Santa Claus costumes to stores for up to $325.

The nearest thing to a Santa School today is the American Photograph Corporation, which innovated the Santa and child photo promotions so popular in department stores and malls. American Photograph supplies stores with their brochures "The Successful Santa" and "How to Be a Real Santa," which give hundreds of tips on Santa Claus selection and etiquette. One rule, for example, states that Santas should "ask what a child wants, but never promise anything unless a parent has indicated in some way that it is okay." Most Santas like their work if they like children, says Jim Leidich, president of American Photograph. "And if they don't like children that much, watch out. Kids instinctively feel it when a Santa is reserved or withdrawn. They pull his beard."

Many Santas have more than their beards pulled, and last year one even reported having his wallet lifted by a little one he dandled on his knee, but usually Santa's problems are of a more diplomatic nature. A New York Santa, for instance, asked a little girl on his knee, "What would you like for Christmas?" and she advised him, "We don't have Christmas, we have Chanukkah." Said Santa, "So what would you like for Chanukkah?" and the little girl replied, "A Christmas tree."

Then there is the old story about the child taken to Macy's by his mother and plopped on Santa's lap. "What do you want for Christmas, lad?" Santa asked. "Better write it down," the child said, "or you'll forget it all," but Santa assured him that his memory never failed and the boy rattled off his demands. That afternoon, however, mother and child went shopping in Gimbels and the boy found himself on Santa's knee again. Gimbels Santa asked him the usual, "What do you want for Christmas?" and the boy leaped off his lap, kicked him in the shins, and yelled, "You numbskull, I *knew* you'd forget!"

❧ XI ❧

Rip-offs in Wonderland: Boosters, Snitches, Con Artists, Errant Easter Bunnies and Peeping Toms

Shoplifting is a business far more ancient, if not more honorable, than department store storekeeping—and a business that is nowadays threatening to become more profitable than the prey it feeds upon. Among the earliest accounts of a professional troupe of shoplifters is one written in 1592 by Shakespeare's detractor Robert Greene, who describes in unfamiliar argot an operation very familiar to store detectives today. Shoplifters caused English merchants such heavy losses in the early eighteenth century that they appealed to Parliament for help, and the government offered a reward and pardon to any shoplifter who informed on associates in crime. One stool pigeon turned in her two partners and their fence and all three were hanged at Tyburn for stealing a silver cup and about 25 pounds worth of silk, which the women had concealed and conveyed in a contrivance "not unlike two large hooks" under their petticoats. The execution of shoplifters didn't deter others, though, and by the nineteenth century there were kidsmen in London who actually trained child shoplifters in schools just as Fagin coached Bates and the Artful Dodger in *Oliver Twist*, the most documentry of Dickens' novels.

In 1857 an English police officer described a school where children were taught not only to shoplift but how to pick the pockets of shoppers. "From a line stretched across the room a coat was hanging," he testified, "along with a number of handkerchiefs tucked into its pockets. Each child in turn tried his skill in removing a handkerchief without moving the coat or shaking the line. . . . Other teachers used tailor's dummies and there was an exacting method in which the clothes used for practice were sewn all over with little bells that tinkled with the slightest vibration."

A book called *Criminals of America; or Tales of the Lives of Thieves Enabling Everyone to Be His Own Detective* tells how an American shoplifter in the 1870s filled a large bag under her loose dress with all she could carry. Another contemporary work, *Our Rival the Rascal,* describes the "hoisting kick," a "short overshirt covering an ordinary dress skirt so stitched that the lining and the skirt make a complete bag around the body from the waist to the heels." It was at about this time that the peerless Inspector Thomas Byrnes of the New York City Police Department referred to the amateur shoplifter in print. He was probably the first popular writer to label these women "kleptomaniacs," and there is still a tendency to call all amateur thieves by that name.

Merchants had to deal with extensive external and internal theft in early stores just as they do today. Shoppers who pay $1.98 for an item instead of $2.00 usually assume that this price shading is just a trick to make the purchase seem less expensive than it really is. But price shading may have originally been an antitheft device invented by R. H. Macy. This shrewd Yankee, it's said, reckoned that his sales force, in an era before cash registers and other checks on employees were common, would be more honest if prices weren't in round amounts. R.H. figured that customers almost always paid in even silver coin or bills. Salespeople giving back change from an odd-figured selling price would be compelled to make a full record of the transaction, and the temptation to pocket the entire amount of a purchase would be less inviting.

Internal theft was a big department store problem from the beginning. During one Easter promotion at Texas's Joske's the man-sized bunny rabbit hopping around the store was caught stuffing expensive men's suits into his bunny suit. A number of store Santa Clauses were caught stealing. But not only salespeople and other low-echelon employees accounted for the tens of thousands of dollars in cash and goods shortages every year. Buyers and other top management also lined their pockets. There is a record of one department head in an early Boston store who was discharged for buying $7,000 worth of furniture from a manufacturer for $40,000. A New York buyer purchased (for a kickback) over 250,000 red plush photograph albums of the same pattern, these so shabby that they had to be given away as souveniers after he was fired. For many years store owners were virtually paranoid about affairs between store managers and their female employees—especially bookkeepers—and often kept suspected "offenders" under surveilance long after working hours. In the days before sound auditing techniques such combinations could steal a store into bankruptcy, and thus love had no civil rights.

One well-known store of the time put its losses from shoplifting at over $15,000 a year in 1896. The store detectives who combated shoplifters never resembled the keen-eyed mysterious store Sherlock of fiction with his incredible disguises and strategems. As is still the case, they looked as inconspicuous and uninterested as possible. Most of the tricks used by shoplifters today were familiar to these detectives. Thieves dropped articles like lace handkerchiefs into unrolled parasols, used what was called a "kick," a long capacious pocket that ran the full length of a skirt, dropped items into loose blouse waists, even stashed stolen goods in the skirts of an infant in arms. Organized professionals were more accomplished, but the legions of so-called kleptomaniacs accounted for far more stolen merchandise. When apprehended these women—and amateur thieves were almost always women then—were escorted to a dressing booth where a woman searcher went through their clothes. Many came from prominent families, and the stores usually found it inadvisable to prosecute them for business reasons. Instead, a first offender was compelled to write out a confession, which was held as a warning. It's said that five or more New York stores held such confessions from a wealthy woman reputed to be one of society's Four Hundred.

An old story tells how Frank Woolworth checked security from time to time in his early five-and-dimes. Slipping into a store unnoticed on one occasion, he stole everything in sight, dropping three hundred picture postcards into his overcoat pocket, cramming other pockets with ribbon, cakes of soap, rubber balls, stick pins, bow ties, and even a claw hammer. It took him only three minutes to steal ten dollars' worth of goods, and he dumped these on the manager's desk acidly remarking, "I could have filled a delivery truck." Needless to say, forays like these resulted in tightened security.

Some oldtime thieves even had a preference for certain stores. Store detectives at Marshall Field once arrested a woman who had stuffed a fur coat, still on its hanger, into her "booster skirt." The old pro was asked why she kept bothering Marshall Field, why she didn't work the other stores occasionally. "Me work the other side of the street?" Millie cried indignantly. "I'm no jitney thief boosting cheap stuff. I work your store because you got all the best stuff in the city!"

Despite advances in technology, shoplifting is a far more serious problem today than it was in the past. Shoplifting is the fastest-growing crime in the nation, according to the latest statistics. Experts estimate that losses due to retail theft in 1977, and the constantly rising cost of trying to contain it (about half a cent on every sales dollar thus far), will total about $26 billion nationwide and that department store losses alone will account for perhaps $1.6 billion of this—or $8 million a day as another study claims. These "snowshovel estimates" include employee theft (studies by private security firms indicating that for every dollar's worth of merchandise a shoplifter grabs, a store employee will grab three dollars' worth). Furthermore, shoplifting and employee thefts—both are lumped together by the stores as "shrinkage"—have increased about 200 percent since 1960.

New York City's giant R. H. Macy, the world's largest store, was ripped off to the tune of $10 million in 1977. Theft losses among other stores around the country are running about 5 percent of their sales margins and cutting deeply into profit margins—which often are only 5 or 6 percent. "We're coming to the point of no return—literally zero profit," says the security manager of a Washington, D.C., department store, and some stores have already had to close because of high pilferage rates. *Security World* magazine, commenting on the sad situation, notes that far more than the retail value of an item is lost in a theft. For every $10 theft enough additional goods must be sold to pay the $10 out of profits—thus a store that has a 5 percent profit margin must sell $200 worth of goods to pay for the theft of a single $10 item before the normal profit cycle can be resumed.

Depending on whose figures are correct, 1 out of 10 or 1 out of 12 Americans is a shoplifter. The rule of thumb among store security officers is 1 out of 10, and the latter figure was established by a 1970 study made by Management Safeguards, Inc., a New York security company. For over six months, Management Safeguards staked out a midtown Manhattan department store and followed 500 shoppers—picked at random—from the time they entered the store until they left. Forty-two of the shoppers stole $300 worth of merchandise, about $7.15 each—which would mean that the store could expect to lose sixty cents for each shopper every day! A similar study made in Boston by Management Safeguards showed that 1 out of 20 shoppers were thieves, another made in Philadelphia revealed an horrendous 1 out of 10 figure, and finally the New York study was repeated again with the same 1 out of 12 result.

For the most part shoplifters steal small items—the five top choices are women's clothing, dress accessories, purses, women's coats, and jewelry. But thieves favoring the large brassy gesture have made some spectacular attempts. Dining room tables, couches, baby carriages, and demonstrator vacuum cleaners have all been carried out the front doors of stores. At New York's Lexington Avenue Alexander's a man was apprehended wheeling *two* bicycles out the door, and he had twenty stolen books in bags tied to the handlebars. But Macy's, in keeping with its image as the world's biggest store, has probably had the biggest thefts. Once, two men disguised as Macy porters calmly carried a canoe down the escalator from the sporting goods department and out into the street; they were later caught because they couldn't resist coming back for the paddles, legend says. In another incident a Macy's detective watched a man lift an aluminum kayak, balance it on his head and proceed on his way. According to one account, "He followed the man down six flights of stairs, past half a dozen store guards, out to a jammed Herald Square, and for several blocks down crowded streets to a parked car, where the man began to tie the kayak to its roof. At this point the detective flashed his badge." The shoplifter's reaction was more astonishment than dismay.

One Macy's shoplifter was found in the ladies' room, where she had fainted after opening a parcel she'd stolen from behind a counter—it contained a salesgirl's dead pet cat, which she had wrapped up that morning to take to the ASPCA for disposal. At a

Montgomery Ward store another woman was caught whose apartment yielded over $8,000 worth of stolen dresses that she had never worn. Many women are caught concealing stolen goods on their children, and one man nabbed in Macy's had trained his kids to jump up and down and make distracting noises while he grabbed things off the counters; he tried to escape, abandoning his children, when apprehended. Almost as reprehensible was the mother who sent her ten-year-old to a Chicago department store, where he was caught with a large shopping bag that he had been filling with items from a carefully prepared shopping list of merchandise she wanted him to steal.

Often a shopping bag, called "a bad bag," is the only equipment a shoplifter carries, but the tools of the trade range from belts studded with hooks worn inside a coat to skeleton keys for locked display cases. Some thieves dump merchandise into a dangling umbrella, others slip items like gloves into the folds of a newspaper, and still others have specially constructed pockets in which to slip small, expensive items like watches and jewelry. Women called "crotch workers" train themselves to hold merchandise under their dresses between their legs and walk quickly out of a store without dropping the merchandise. Booster skirts, pants, and coats—all garments especially designed to hold stolen merchandise—are common paraphernalia. Booster bloomers—old-fashioned bloomers with tight elastic at the knees—are worn under booster skirts, which have slits through which merchandise can be stuffed into the recesses of the bloomers. Booster boxes are frequently ingeniously designed to hold whatever the shoplifter intends to steal. A shoplifter stealing LP records, for example, might have a wrapped gift box under his arm with a concealed slit in the side or top through which he can insert a dozen or so records. The same can be done with briefcases, or even portable typewriters.

Shoplifters include people of all ages, from all walks of life, and several studies indicate that roughly the same percentages come from all racial and religious groups. Four major groups, however, constitute the worst offenders. The first two—shoplifting troupes and narcotic addicts—are the professionals who steal in order to sell to a fence for a profit and are called "boosters" by police. The last two—amateur adult and juvenile shoplifters—usually steal items for their own personal use and are termed "snitches."

Professional shoplifting troupes, which have been plaguing stores for centuries, amount to no more than 10 percent of department store shoplifters—they number far less than their amateur counterparts—but the value of the merchandise these boosters lift is far greater than the proportion of their numbers. These are the skilled artisans who use the most sophisticated schemes and equipment. One gang member actually uses a fake prosthetic limb for shoplifting and pickpocketing. He drapes a coat over his left arm and holds a briefcase at the end of his fake right arm, his real right arm hidden under his jacket. Since it appears that his both hands are immobilized, he can easily shoplift in crowds without being suspected.

South American nationals—mainly Chileans, Colombians, and Peruvians—are said to run shoplifting gangs around New York, Miami, Chicago, and Los Angeles that employ over a thousand people and steal about $150 million worth of goods a year. Those in the New York area meet early every morning in an uptown restaurant and decide which stores in the metropolitan area the dozen or so four-man gangs will cover. Then they drive or walk off to work. A member of one slick, well-dressed team recently described a typical operation to a *New York Times* reporter. "We'd go into a store like a group of friends and start browsing," he explained. "We'd decide the area we wanted to work and I would attract the salesman to another part of the store. I take a 36 regular suit but I'd ask for a 38. Of course the suit wouldn't fit and I'd make some excuse like 'I must have lost weight' to gain time and keep the salesman and any others not busy in the store, tied up with me." In the meantime, his accomplices would stuff their clothes with expensive merchandise. He'd take at least half an hour to be fitted properly and in that time they'd make three trips to the car while "waiting for him," filling it with stolen goods that they concealed in black plastic bags. Using this method each member of the gang netted a thousand dollars for a good day of work lasting only four hours. Some of the stolen goods, with just the price tags removed, were sold to fences operating store-front shops only a few blocks from the scene of the crimes.

Most gangs are small like the South American group, but another writer describes a native West Coast shoplifting troupe that consisted of 12 to 15 members. "They specialized in entering stores at about lunch hour," she writes. "Two 'stalls' would 'throw a hump' (create a distraction), which brought the store detectives to one spot and attracted the attention of the remaining salesclerks. While this disturbance progressed, about a dozen 'clouts' cleaned the rest of the store as thoroughly as their capacity to carry merchandise permitted. This troupe not only took display merchandise but stole 'understock' as well, *leaving whole shelves completely bare."*

Shoplifters aren't considered violent criminals by the police and will usually surrender without a fight when caught by security guards. The one exception is the narcotics addict, who steals to support his habit and occupies the borderline between professional and amateur shoplifters. Narcotic addicts, who constitute a minuscule number of store thieves, haven't the finesse of the true professional and are far more desperate than the neediest amateur. Often he or she "clouts and lams," that is, grabs an expensive piece of merchandise such as a fur coat and races down the aisles and out the front door. Since shoplifters get only a 10 percent return from fences on "hot goods," an addict must lift $1,000 of merchandise a day to support a $100-a-day habit. Woodward & Lothrup's department store in Washington, D.C., recently caught a shoplifter who confided that he had been an addict for twelve years. During six years of that time he had been making five or six visits a day to their store, walking out with $100 to $150 worth of merchandise, and had been hitting a store down the street between trips.

Amateur shoplifters used to be primarily adults, but in the last decade or so amateur juveniles have become the biggest single shoplifting group, accounting for over 50 percent of store thefts. In a random sampling of one thousand Delaware high school students, no less than 47.2 percent admitted to shoplifting at least once. The juveniles are often grammar school students, too. In Montgomery Ward's downtown Chicago State Street store ten-year-olds have been caught stealing from display cases that must be opened from the back. They crawl into the narrow space between the case and floor, hidden from sight, reach out with one hand, and open the cases with skeleton keys.

Adult amateur thieves usually steal items of more value than juveniles, and therefore cost the stores more money. They can range from panhandlers to the small merchant with a store across the street from the department store who sells what he steals from his competitor. More of them are women than men—a recent study has revealed that 1 out of 11 women shoplift while 1 out of 16 men steal from stores. Women may shoplift more than men because it "is the only thrill available for many women who received a traditional upbringing in the United States," as one psychiatrist puts it. Yet just as many women steal "to stretch the budget a little" or because they believe they're "just getting even" with the shop-keeper—an adversary who rips them off whenever he gets the chance. Kleptomaniacs—women who can afford to buy the things they shoplift but steal to satisfy their need for sex or love or their wish to get back at their mothers—are nowhere near as common as most people think. Many a wealthy businessman has an agreement with a store to have anything his wife or mother steals charged to his account, but no studies show that more than 2 to 3 percent of shoplifters are compulsive neurotic personalities, and a leading authority says that kleptomaniacs are only about 1 out of 500,000.

No more than 1 of 20 shoplifters is ever caught, according to a study made last year by the Criminal Service Systems of Van Nuys, California, but this figure is an improvement over the 24 out of 25 shoplifters who got away with their crimes a decade ago. Stores have developed some unique ways to combat shoplifters. Perhaps the oddest is the tarantula that one store displays prominently in its jewelry case to discourage wandering fingers—a decided deterrent even though the tarantula is harmless. Another interesting one is the rent-a-thief service provided to stores by the Rent A Thief And Sweet Revenge Corporation. Fear of public humiliation is the strongest shoplifting deterrent. Rent-A-Thief provides department stores with professional actors who are conspicuously "arrested" by store security guards in front of crowds several times a day, and this works so well that the stores are glad to pay $100 a performance.

Stores are buying more and more closed-circuit television cam-eras—Macy's Herald Square store has ten placed at strategic loca-tions—and are relying more on old standbys such as peepholes and two-way mirrors. Customers are completely deceived by these devices—men remove their false teeth for relief and women adjust their girdles in front of two-way mirrors without ever suspecting that they are being watched. Their use in dressing rooms and bathrooms has been discontinued by many stores because they are a blatant invasion of the honest customer's privacy, but nevertheless Big Brother still watches as we walk through most stores.

The newest wrinkle in antishoplifting devices is tiny sensitized tags that are put on merchandise; these miniature transmitters will trip an alarm as the culprit starts to leave the store if they haven't been removed or neutralized by a salesclerk. This service is available from firms like the Sensormatic Electronics Corporation of Akron, Ohio, which rents its system—ten thousand permanent sensitized tags and alarm—to hundreds of stores for about $4,000 a year. The only trouble is that salesclerks sometimes fail to remove the telltale tags, the alarm goes off when an innocent customer is leaving the store, and the store loses an old customer or is sued for false arrest.

A Philadelphia antishoplifting campaign called STEM ("Shoplifters Take Everybody's Money") has been notably effective in curbing shoplifting among teenagers, who as often as not steal for the thrill of it or to "rip off the Establishment" as for material gain. Financed mainly by Gimbels, Sears, John Wanamaker, and Strawbridge & Clothier, and created by the local Spiro & Associates advertising agency, STEM gets across two basic points, according to its chairman, Strawbridge & Clothier vice-president Frank Veale. "The first message," he says, "is that shoplifting is no joke, but a serious crime. Shoplifters over eighteen are given a provisional record and go to the police station. Our second point is that shoplifting costs everyone money because it raises prices." STEM television and print ads stress the fact that shoplifting can ruin a young person's life, driving the point home with poignant case histories that are based on actual arrests: "Ken swapped a college education for a $6.50 pair of jeans"; "Meg just traded her engagement ring for a $6 blouse"; "Karen exchanged a $2,500 scholarship for a $9.95 pullover"; "Carol just traded a $100-a-week job for a $3 belt." The decision to concentrate on teenagers—shoplifters who can be reached before the die is cast—has proved a good one, for Philadelphia retailers reported a 20 percent decrease in store shortages after STEM's first year, at a time when most cities were reporting increases.

Other stores feel that well-trained employees at point of sale and smarter merchandising are the answer to the shoplifting problem. Montgomery Ward, for example, takes special pains to screen and train its sales force and uses packaging that makes merchandise difficult to conceal in a coat lining, purse, or elsewhere. Still other stores don't make goods so available to impulse buying that they also provide an impulse for a thief—Macy's, for instance, no longer puts tie racks near the Seventh Avenue exit. Macy's also tried the procedure of asking all customers making cash purchases for their names and addresses and photographing all customers returning purchases for cash refunds. It was hoped that this rather illogical procedure (crooks could give false names, etc.) would scare off amateur shoplifters, but the policy had to be dropped due to public outcry about violations of privacy.

Many stores are getting tougher in prosecuting shoplifting offenders. Those that do usually have low shrinkage rates, like Montgomery Ward's amazing .3 percent—one-third of a cent on a dollar. Most experts say it is a shame that 75 percent of shoplifters are *not* arrested after being apprehended. For once arrested, prosecuted, and perhaps humiliated, pilferers apparently stop stealing. The recidivism rate is amazingly low, the rewards of shoplifting apparently not worth the cost to reputation and esteem.

No one knows why shoplifting has increased so tremendously in recent years—bigger stores with more accessible merchandise, inflation, youth rebellion against the Establishment, and a breakdown of the general moral fiber have all been blamed. But it's obviously going to be around for a long while and can only be curbed. "We're never going to eliminate shoplifting," says a Sears security superior, "any more than we can eliminate gambling or prostitution." The same can be said of the many other crimes department stores have to contend with, which range from armed robberies and con games to the bloody schemes of weirdos with or without a cause.

Department stores are occasionally the targets of armed robbers, though the crowded stores aren't a favorite of bandits. In 1965 two gunmen held up a Sears store in Troy, Michigan, and Sears employees chased them down the street and captured them. That same year Baltimore's Hutzler's made national news when three gunmen kidnapped the store's assistant manager and his family at their home, holding the man's family hostage while they forced him to open the store safe. Though the thieves got away with $23,000, they were eventually caught and their hostages escaped unharmed. This incident became the basis for several novels and a movie.

Thieves more often hide in a store after it closes, or break in late at night, and steal great quantities of merchandise, as they did in the 1977 burglary at Bergdorf Goodman in which $400,000 worth of jewelry was stolen. In 1964 Brooks Brothers lost over 1,200 suits worth some $200,000 to burglars. But Macy's and several other stores have made such thieves obsolete on their premises with the introduction of watchdogs that patrol the stores at night. These dogs are far more effective than the best alarm systems, which cost up to $15,000 in installation charges and $2,000 a month in maintenance charges for an average-sized 140,000-square-foot store. Probably the best novel ever written with a department store as its setting is James Gould Cozzens' *Castaway* (1934), the cryptic tale of a man lost at night in an empty department store crammed with material goods, a hapless twentieth-century Everyman trapped like Crusoe on his desert island. But Cozzens's Mr. Lecky wouldn't have survived Macy's superbly trained Doberman pinschers for an hour. Cash, Red Star, Mom (an acronym for Macy's Own Make), and Suzy (named after a Macy's perfume) were first put on patrol nights in 1952 (in the 1920s long-haired German shepherds had been tried, but they proved ineffective during the hot summer months), and today their descendants patrol the aisles. The dogs, worth up to $2,500 each, are released by their handlers after the store closes and commanded to search designated areas.

If a Macy's guard dog comes upon a prowler, he barks until his handler commands him to "Watch!"—the dog then holding the prowler motionless until the guard decides what to do. The Doberman will only attack when ordered to, or if the prowler moves as much as a half step. Then the 90-pound dog will be all over him in a flash, hanging on with a tenacity that has to be seen to be believed. The bite of a full-grown Doberman contains more than enough pressure to break human bone, and there are authenticated cases of the dogs hanging on to their prey even after they have been killed. It is impossible to bribe these watchdogs with food, for they are trained to eat only in their penthouse kennels. It's no wonder that they've caught only one or two prowlers since they went to work at Macy's. Most thieves are scared off just by hearing about them.

If Dobermans ever become extinct as after-hours store guards, they will probably be replaced by the 7-foot, 650-pound bulletproof guard that has been developed by Quasar Industries of Rutherford, New Jersey. This automated Century I robot, with a $75,000 price tag, is made of metal, plastic, and electronics, and is equipped with many "restraining systems" that make life impossible for burglars. Century I has one purpose: to search out and immobilize intruders. The prototype has sensors that can detect movement, body heat, or any noise, and when it detects an intruder, it stalks him at 20 miles an hour, orally instructing him to halt. If disobeyed, the robot gets tough. Its high-frequency sound transmitter can cause extreme pain in the inner ear; it can be equipped with a strobe light to temporarily blind an intruder, an electronic gun to deliver a powerful shock, and a mechanism that spurts laughing gas. The robot can also be programmed to kill, but Quasar says it will use only "nonlethal restraint."

Bad check artists and confidence men continue to plague department stores, as they have since the turn of the century. Bad checks have been passed by people as prominent as Queen Victoria's great-granddaughter, and con games have been played in the stores by the masters, including the late "Yellow Kid" Weil, on whose exploits the film *The Sting* may have been based in part. More than once con artists have tricked store detectives into arresting them as shoplifters and sued stores for false arrest. What a con man does here is to steal, say, a wallet while the guard is looking and then make his way to the door. Along the way, however, he will have "thrown" the wallet—dropped it through an open pocket leading to the floor and kicked it into an inconspicuous corner—so that when he is arrested, in front of reputable witnesses, he has no stolen merchandise on his person. Sometimes he will even provoke a guard to injure him and sue for the damage inflicted upon him.

Con artists occasionally purchase expensive items with stolen charge cards, but they must work fast in this case before the stolen card is reported. In another scam a con man buys something expensive and has it delivered COD to an apartment or hotel suite, where he takes the package—if the deliveryman is not alert—walks into an adjoining room on the pretext of going to get money, and skips out another door. But the cleverest confidence man in recent memory was a Texas "oil man" who paid a department store $5,000 cash for a beautiful pearl that he said was for his wife's birthday. A month later he returned and asked for a duplicate pearl—he wanted to have earrings made for his wife, he said, and when the store could find no duplicate, he insisted that he had to have one, he'd pay up to $25,000 for a perfect match! The store searched and finally found a matching pearl that a Chicago lady was willing to sell for $20,000 and bought it from her. But the "oil man" never showed up to buy the pearl from the store. The lady had been his accomplice and had sold back the original pearl at four times the price the con artist paid for it.

In another clever con game, the confidence man asks to see the best gems in a department store jewelry department. He or she steals an expensive stone while sitting examining the gems at a table, but sticks it under the table with a wad of chewing gum so that it isn't on his person when he is searched. A few days later he comes back to retrieve the gem and he sometimes sues the store as well. One con man pulled the gum trick, pretended to swallow the stone, was x-rayed and brought suit against the store.

In these troubled times department store security has to deal with slashers, who rip merchandise to pieces with razors for no sane reasons, "mad bombers" who threaten to plant bombs in stores (the original "Mad Bomber," George Metesky, threatened to blow up Macy's among other places), and unhinged political terrorists, who have planted bombs in crowded stores where their people shop to liberate their people. Recently, a child being held in the lost and found department of Boston's Jordan Marsh was claimed by a woman who heard his name announced on the public address system; luckily this "phony mother" was caught with the unharmed child a day later.

Everything considered, the stores have trouble enough, so it is hoped that the latest department store crime is "the first of a series of none," to quote the detective who investigated it. Police in Los Angeles recently arrested a man accused of molesting mannequins in a local department store. The man was seen fondling one dummy, peering up the dresses of two others, and then exposing himself to them.

⚘ **XII** ⚘

Workers in Paradise and the Great American Customer: Including Strikes, Unions, Credit Cards, and Many Unhappy Returns of the Day

Dandy frock-coated dudes with sideburns and "gentlemanly manners" did the selling in the earliest American department stores, and they were often hired for their looks, the owners figuring that this would appeal to women customers who liked to indulge in a little flirtation while shopping. But their lot was a hard one, marked by long hours, low wages, and working conditions that weren't much better than those of the sweatshops of a later time. Tuberculosis and other diseases caused by long hours in the cramped, poorly ventilated stores were a serious problem among the salesclerks, who had to abide by numerous rules that the store owners prescribed in little booklets issued to each employee. These rules often infringed on their private lives, as is shown by the following commandments handed down by a Chicago store in 1860:

> The store must be open 6 a.m. to 9 p.m. the year round. The store must be swept and showcases dusted; lamps dimmed, filled and chimneys cleaned; pens made; doors and windows opened; a pail of water, also a bucket of coal brought in before breakfast; and attend to customers who call. The store *must not* be opened on the Sabbath

unless necessary, and then only for a few minutes. The employee who is in the habit of smoking Spanish cigars, being shaved at the barbers, going to dances and other places of amusement, will surely give his employer reason to be suspicious of his integrity and honesty! Each employee *must* pay not less than $5. a year to the church, and *must* attend Sunday School regularly. Men employees are given one evening for courting and two if they go to prayer meeting. After 14 hours of work in the store, the leisure time should be spent in reading.

Scandalous working conditions continued to prevail when the Civil War made it necessary to employ women to take the place of the men who marched off to fight for the armies of the North or South. Women came behind the counters of the department stores in great numbers for the first time in this period, the first store to hire them being New Orleans' D. H. Holmes Company, and they had to work the same long hours for even lower pay. Women were scorned by some employees, but John Wanamaker and others championed them. "Men no longer monopolize the business places," Wanamaker wrote. "Women have been tried out, and have proven to have as great endurance as men. Women have more tact and accuracy than men. There is far more reciprocity in fine manners between women and women. Men have lessons to learn in speech and good manners toward each other. It is a fact that women are taking more pains to succeed in business than ever before and to make themselves independent as earners of their own support."

Because of the seasonal, transient nature of department store employment, unions had a hard time making any inroads during the early years. Working conditions depended entirely on the boss, and while there were always enlightened employers like Wanamaker's and Strawbridge & Clothier, who provided health, recreational, and incentive programs for workers, many couldn't have cared less for their employees' welfare in an age when "the mind of man was strained almost to the utmost tension in making money." Salesclerks had to put up with much worse than the stingy, irascible R. H. Macy, who once smashed to bits a glass shade a clerk had placed over one of his store's glaring gas jets, screaming: "I am paying for *all* the gaslight, and I intend to get *all* the gaslight!"

Some stores issued guidelines to clerks for dealing with customers, one specifying, among other things, that a sales clerk should:

- *Know yourself.*
- *Know your merchandise.*
- *Keep your mind on your work.*
- *Keep listening to your customers talking rather than yourself.*
- *Take firm hold of anything that displeases a customer and set it right before leaving it.*
- *Take no offense under any circumstances.*
- *Keep sweet.*

In 1898 Hess Brothers of Allentown, Pennsylvania, issued a card listing no fewer than 62 "Store Don'ts," including the following:

- *Don't dress dowdily, gaudily or dudishly, but cleanly, neatly and nicely.*
- *Don't wait upon customers with your hands dirty or your fingernails in mourning.*
- *Don't greet your customers with a tobacco or onion breath. It hastens them to move on to more fragrant surroundings. . . .*
- *Don't laugh loudly or use slang phrases. . . .*

The same store's chock-full rules and regulations booklet warned employees: "You would be very much surprised if you knew the trouble and expense we go to find out 'character and habits.' Detectives you don't know often are detailed to report all of your doings for a week." Above all a Hess employee was warned to ALWAYS SPEAK WELL OF THE HOUSE: "You should always uphold your house and its people. If you hear of anything wrong, repeat it. . . . If you see anything dishonest or against the interest of the house, report it; it is your duty. If you don't you are in a measure guilty, and if found to have concealed information which should have been reported you will lose your position. . . ."

Working conditions in New York grew so bad by the 1890s that the Consumers League of New York was organized with the object of compelling department stores to treat their employees equitably. The league fought for a minimum wage of six dollars a week, irrespective of sex; light, airy rooms; seats for the salespeople;

reforms in the system of fines for rule infractions; vacations with pay; and wages for overtime. How many employers complied with their demands and made the league "White Lists" isn't recorded, but those who didn't comply around the country were legion. In 1899, Annie Marion MacLean of the University of Chicago "adopted the disguise of a saleswoman" and found employment in a Chicago department store for two weeks, publishing an account of her experiences in the *American Journal of Sociology*. Her account brings to mind the sufferings of O. Henry's shop girls, even the conditions in Dickens's factories:

> The hours seemed days. "Can I possibly stand up all day?" was the thought uppermost in my mind, for I soon learned from my companions that abusive language was the share of one who was found sitting down. Later in the week I found this to be true. One of the girls who was well-nigh exhausted sat a moment on a little table that was for sale—there was not a seat of any kind in the room, and the only way one could get a moment's rest was to sit on the children's furniture that was for sale on one part of the floor. The manager came forth and found the poor girl resting. The only sympathy he manifested was to call out in rough tones: "Get up out of there, you lazy hussy! I don't pay you to sit around all day." Under such circumstances it is small wonder that the stolen rests were few. By night the men as well as the women were limping wearily across the floor, and any sales were made under positive physical agony.

Shop girls were sometimes used as demonstrators, too. The idea was to choose the youngest girl available to demonstrate a product. "Tell her to wear a short skirt and fix her hair like a high school girl," one manager in another store told his assistant who was selecting a girl to demonstrate a new coffee pot. "Choose the best looker you've got and the youngest-looking, because the theory is that even a child can work it."

Annie MacLean found that prices frequently changed during the day and that the penalty for selling under price was immediate discharge, while selling above price met with no disapproval. Workers often spied on each other, turning fellow employees in, but there was a certain camaraderie among salespeople as well. Another writer relates the following story:

Everyone of our furniture salespeople—and they were men by-the-way—in one store sold on commission. One of the best men died. His widow applied for his job and the men united in urging the buyer to take her on. And then developed the prettiest bit of chivalry. When her days were dull, when she would show goods to one "looker" after another without, of course, making sales, the men would call for her "book" and help her make a good day's showing. And the prettiest part of it all was that—not a man told. The grateful woman did.

Sanitary conditions for workers in the department stores were terrible, according to many observers. Annie MacLean reported:

The cloak, toilet and lunch rooms were the gloomiest and filthiest it was every my misfortune to enter. The cobwebs and dirt-smeared floors looked spooky under the flickering glare of insufficient gaslight. The only ventilation came through a foul basement and there the little girl attendants stayed all day and late into the night. And that was where the girls who brought lunches had to eat them. A few rough board tables and chairs in a more or less advanced state of ruin were provided and scores of hungry girls sat around and ate lunches from newspaper parcels and drank coffee from tin cans (supplied by the store at the rate of two cups for five cents). It was not a healthful atmosphere, either physically, or morally, and yet it was typical of the poorer class of stores.

Prostitution was a way of life for many of the shop girls; in fact, it was a common practice for retail stores to hire young women at almost no pay by pointing out that they would be in an ideal position to develop profitable liaisons with wealthy male customers. "The girls themselves," Annie MacLean reported, "said that more than a third of them were living lives of shame. . . . Lecherous men were always around ready to offer aid. They came, professedly, to buy, but it was not the wares of the store they wanted. The young and pretty girls yielded most easily. They would weep sometimes, and say: 'Good people look down on us. But they don't know—they don't know. *We have to earn our living!'* " Miss MacLean's solution to the problem was the "fostering of the trade union spirit" to bring the saleswoman's wages up "to a point where she can live without the wages of sin, without starvation or shame."

Annie MacLean had worked 175 hours over two weeks and received $11.88, a fraction more than six cents an hour. An accounting she made of her wages and expenses for the first week best illustrates the shop girl's plight at the time:

Wages	$2.00
Commission......................................	3.25
Less fines (10¢ for 3 latenesses)	.30
	$4.95

Expenses

Board for 1 week	$2.50
Carfare, 6 days @10¢	.60
Lunch, 5 days @15¢	.75
Lunch, 1 day @10¢	.10
Charity dinner	.13
Paper, 3 nights @ .02¢	.06
Postal cards.......................................	.05
Candy (treat)	.10
Stamps...	.10
Oranges (treat)	.09
Present for table girl	.05
Present for matron	.10
Laundry...	.16
Total expenses	$4.79

With a maximum savings of eleven cents a week there was little chance to "keep sweet," and Miss MacLean's earnings were no less than most of her coworkers, as the following chart she compiled shows:

American department stores never adopted the British "living-in system," but it was seriously considered by a number of early stores and tried on a very limited scale. Fortunately nothing came of these experiments, for "living-in" was usually the "slaving-in" that one critic called it. English stores and French department stores like Bon Marché, among others, often hired workers for the smallest salary they would work for and supplemented their meager wages

Name	Employment	Hours (A.M. P.M.)	Overtime	Weekly wage	For extra work	Cost of living per week	Conjugal condition	Health	Remarks
A......	saleswoman	8:00–6:00	none	$ 6.00		$2.50	single	fair	
B......	"	8:00–6:30	evenings till 10	3.00		2.50	"	"	same place 3 years
C......	"	8:00–6:00	none	5.00		3.00	"	"	
D......	inspector	8:00–6:30	till 10 or 11 P.M.	3.50		lived home	"	bad	
E......	wrapper	8:00–6:00	till 7 sometimes	4.00		" "	"	fair	
F......	buyer	8:00–6:00	none	10.00		" "	"	bad	
G......	enunciator	8:00–6:30	till 10 or 11	2.50	supper	$4.75	separated	good	
H......	saleswoman	8:00–6:30	"	3.50	supper	lived home	single	fair	
I......	cashier	8:00–6:30	"	6.50		$2.50	married	"	
J......	saleswoman	8:00–6:30	till 11	3.00	50c per week	3.00	single	"	husband and 4 children
K......	"	8:00–6:00	till 10	5.00	35c for supper	2.50	married	good	one child
L......	cash girl	9:30–4:30	none	3.25		lived home	widow	"	
M......	saleswoman	8:00–6:30	evenings	5% commission	supper	" "	single	fair	
N......	cash girl	8:00–6:30	"	$2.00	" "	" "	"	"	
O......	saleswoman	8:00–6:30	"	$2.00+5% com.		$2.50	"	good	
P......	"	8:00–6:30		$3.00	cup of coffee	2.50	"	"	
Q......	sewer	8:30–5:30	none	6.50		2.50	widow	"	one child
R......	saleswoman	8:00–6:00	evenings	5.00	30c for supper	lived home	single	fair	same place 7 years
S......	cash girl	8:00–6:00	none	2.00		" "	"	"	
T......	inspector	8:00–6:00	evenings	2.50	30c for supper	$1.50 at home	"	"	mother to help
U......	saleswoman	8:00–6:00	"	$4.50+1% com.	" "	$2.50	"	bad	
V......	"	8:00–6:00	"	4.00+1% com.	" "	$2.00 at home	"	fair	
W......	"	8:00–6:30	none	2.00+5% com.	supper	lived home	married	bad	husband had no work
X......	shirt-maker	8:00–6:00	"	40¾c per doz.		" "	"	fair	" ill; 2 children
Y......	wrapper-maker		"	12½c each			"	bad	
Z......	saleswoman	8:30–5:30		$7.00		$3.75	single	good	

* The "enunciator" cried out sales

with substandard food and lodging. The employer usually bought a block of houses, made alterations, and turned them into living quarters for his clerks, men in one house, women in another. After leaving these quarters in the morning, a worker couldn't reenter the premises for any reason until after work. As many as five workers slept in a room, frequently in the same bed; there were no keys for the rooms to allow any privacy at all; and no pictures or any other decorations were permitted. It was like living in a barracks, the workers responsible to a matron who even had the power to appropriate any garment not in its proper place. For whatever reason—a strong strain of individualism in the national character, a lack of paternal interest in most American employers—the living-in system never caught on in America. As unions gained power in England, the system disappeared or improved greatly, and the few remaining examples of living-in are model ones.

The first action resembling unionization among American retail store workers came as early as 1850, when New York dry goods clerks formed an association to encourage early store closings. Closing times meant even more than higher wages to the predominantly male clerks of the time. As one writer put it, "Men never saw their families by daylight except on Sunday, and in many cases then only half a day, being compelled to report for duty at the store on Sunday morning. What time did these men have to educate themselves?! How could they occupy their proper place in society under such conditions? They hardly had time to make the acquaintance of their family, let alone their neighbors, for when their day's work was done (generally at 9 p.m.), others were in bed." Thus, early closing movements flourished on both the East and West coasts. In 1853, for example, many merchants acceded to organized employee demands for an 8 P.M. closing during the winter months, and those who refused were boycotted.

Before the end of the nineteenth century early closing societies composed of retail clerks had formed several bona fide unions across the country, including one in Cleveland in 1865 and another in Providence, Rhode Island, four years later. Many of these local unions joined the Knights of Labor but looked to the American Federation of Labor (AFL) when they grew dissatisfied with the former national organization. It was 1890 when the AFL first chartered today's Retail Clerks International Association (then known as the Retail Clerks National Protection Association) as a national body with seven locals. There are several unions covering workers in the department store industry today, including the 118,000-member Retail, Wholesale and Department Store Union, but the Retail Clerks International Association with its 750,000 membership is the largest. Retail Clerks, whose members are now largely in the retail food and beverage industry, will probably merge with the RWDSU in the near future, giving workers greater strength in bargaining.

The RCIA has historically been a leader in improving department store working conditions. Its early efforts centered on shortening what was often a 112 hour workweek, in an age when it wasn't uncommon for an unmarried clerk to sleep on the counter in order to be ready to wait on whatever trade might chance to come by during the night. Equal pay for women, overtime pay, and a minimum wage were other important issues of the day. A Lynn, Massachusetts, local negotiated what was probably the first overtime contract for workers in 1906—insuring that clerks be paid thirty cents above the regular rate for all hours worked over 63 hours—but most stores resisted overtime for many years. The union tried to educate the public to early shopping, as did consumer leagues around the country, but this attempt largely failed, and seeking shorter hours became the official policy. By the 1920s the eight-hour day was a reality in some stores, but it wasn't until the coming of the Industrial Recovery Act (1938) and the Fair Labor Standards Act (1938) that the forty-hour week became the accepted workweek.

Wages for department store workers were as low as $1.50 a week up until World War I, and several stores required women to work a month free before they could get a job paying even that. In 1914 a study revealed that 70 percent of women in Philadelphia stores received "a wage insufficient to maintain them in health and efficiency." A study made in New York the same year found that over 63 percent of about 20,000 women working in department stores were paid less than $9 a week—the lowest reasonable living wage at the time—and that fully 2,500 of them made only $5 a week. Pay was worse, if anything, throughout the country, and working conditions were generally poor, when not downright dangerous. Stores were often fire traps, for example, mainly owing to the celebrated "open vistas" of American stores, which are not required by law—as are British and many foreign stores—to erect dividing walls at intervals on each floor in order to contain any fire that might break out. American stores never did give up the idea of the "open vista," but citizen campaigns in many cities citing famous stores as fire traps forced the industry as a whole to comply with all fire regulations. Overcrowded stores, blocked fire exits, inaccessible fire escapes, and other violations were dealt with severely, and the stores became safe despite their interior layout.

Most department stores exploited their employees in the early days, and this exploitation of workers by unscrupulous employers furnished the advertising that has frequently proved to be the incentive for a forceful reaction in labor history. Unions in retailing and many industries pressed for legislation regulating hours, wages, and working conditions, and their demands became New Deal laws in the thirties. As a result, many stores today that still haven't been organized by unions have been forced to adopt the forty-hour week and minimum hourly wage because they come under the jurisdiction of federal legislation.

The unions, of course, have as their ultimate goal the organization of all department stores, a difficult task for several reasons. Perhaps most important is the fact that retailing is still characterized by a high turnover in personnel; up to 30 percent a year of all workers leave their jobs. Another complicating factor is that unions must bargain separately with thousands of stores having different price, wage, and hour patterns within their own communities. Store workers are a heterogeneous collection, too, ranging from ribbon clerks in five-and-tens to high-commission salesmen in elegant specialty shops. Finally, white-collar workers as a group are difficult to organize, often regarding themselves as professionals or future executives rather than "retail clerks." This "white-collar psychology" isn't as prevalent as it was twenty-seven years ago— when Secretary of Labor Maurice Tobin said, "A white collar is not an honor, but a badge of slavery to a worker who thinks he is too good to join a union"—yet it still exists.

Opposition of the stores themselves has proved a formidable obstacle to unions over the years and has resulted in hundreds of strikes and boycotts. Generally, the unions consider a boycott more effective than a strike, for it amounts to a two-way squeeze:

utilizing only a small picket line, the union can keep its members working in a boycotted store—cutting down on the payment of strike benefits—and keep many customers out of it, while the store is losing business and having trouble meeting its payroll.

The unions claim that it is very difficult to organize department stores today because whenever there is a union election scheduled the stores can hire part-time people, who are eligible to vote under National Labor Relations Board (NLRB) rules, and influence them to vote against forming a union in the store. The union can protest violations of the law, but the NLRB has taken as long as five years to issue rulings and by that time—considering the high 30 percent annual turnover of department store workers—most of the employees have left and a new election must be held. "You have often heard the statement repeated that 'justice delayed is justice denied,'" the Retail Clerk's first-vice-president, Samuel J. Myers, wrote in a recent letter to the author. "The reason for most ... strikes and disputes lies in the fact that even where working people have utilized all the legal channels for the purpose of acquiring union representation ... management invariably uses litigation only for the purpose of delaying for years the employees' achievement of this goal.... It has been said by some ancient Roman statesman that if you are engaged in a war, unlimited sources of money is the best assurance of victory. This, of course, is more easily accessible to employers than to unorganized wage earners." While this is true, it should be remembered that over one million retail clerks *are* organized—not to mention store employees who are members of the Teamsters and other unions.

Department stores resist unionization simply because it puts them at a competitive disadvantage—for example, Retail Clerks admits that it would cost Sears about $64 million more to do business in California if it were unionized there. Many stores have gone to great lengths to avoid unionization, often to the point of flagrantly breaking the law. The best example is the case of Sears, Roebuck's Boston store, well-known in the history of labor relations, which shocked even the most cynical observers. In cooperation with union buster Nathan Shefferman, whose Labor Relations Associates (L.R.A.) had also worked for R. H. Macy, among many other companies, Sears had spawned a network of spies in 1953 and used them to destroy the unionization of its Boston employees.

There is no room to describe here the much-publicized machinations of Sears and the LRA—which included a cast of shadowy characters with aliases, as well as bribes, threats, setups, and plots and subplots worthy of a Grade B movie. Suffice it to say that Sears's vice-president for personnel later admitted to company wrongdoing and repudiated Shefferman before the Senate McClellan Committee in 1958. "The handling of the Boston situation," he said, "involved a series of mistakes highlighted by widespread use of pressure and coercion; discrimination against employees for union activities; favoritism, intrigue and unfair labor practices. I want to state, with the utmost candor and conviction, that many of the activities engaged in by Labor Relations Associates and certain company personnel acting with them were inexcusable, unnecessary, and disgraceful. A repetition of these mistakes will not be tolerated by this company."

Probably the most famous store labor dispute in history—and a dispute as memorable as any in all organized labor history—involved the other mail-order giant, Montgomery Ward & Company. The trouble at Ward's really began in 1942 when the National War Labor Board ordered the company to discharge union members of Local 20 of the United Mail Order, Warehouse and Retail Employees Union who failed to maintain their membership in good standing and to collect union dues in its plant. When Ward chairman Sewell Avery refused, President Roosevelt sent a letter directing Ward's to comply "without further delay . . . in the interest of the war effort." Avery eventually complied, but two years later, in 1944, he let Local 20's contract expire when the union refused to offer proof that it represented a majority of Chicago mail-order house and store employees. When the War Labor Board directed an extension of the contract pending an election, Avery contended that reinstatement of the union before balloting would violate nonunion employee rights and refused to do so. This led to a strike, which FDR ordered a halt to after twelve days, the president wiring Avery that the strike was delaying delivery of war-essential farm equipment and vowing "further action" if Ward's did not comply. Avery again refused, and Roosevelt directed the secretary of commerce to take possession of the company and run it for the government as an essential part of the war effort.

Avery refused to cooperate in any way with the government, and on April 27, 1944, an Army sergeant and private carried him out bodily from his office at Ward headquarters to the street, where a photographer snapped a picture of the seventy-year-old chairman and the soldiers that has become one of the most famous photographs in the history of photojournalism. Actually, Avery's refusal to move wasn't the act of a stubborn old man, as many still believe. Company president Stuart Bell had advised him that Ward's had no recourse to the government order and that it had to provoke an overt act to get its day in court, so Avery goaded the government into committing an overt act, actually winking at Ball and saying, "Is this what you want, Stu?" as he was being carried out. On the other hand, *Forbes* magazine has observed, "If a generation of Americans grew up thinking businessmen were Neanderthals, this picture of Sewell L. Avery convinced them." In any event, Ward's contested the government seizure in court, but the secretary of commerce ended control of the plant before the court made a decision, and the judge ruled that the need for a decision was no longer present.

Everyone thought the trouble was over, but the union persisted in its demands for a closed shop at Ward's, and Avery, for his part, refused to "coerce" employees. Late in December 1944, President Roosevelt ordered the secretary of war to take possession of all Ward's plants and the Army moved in again. The U.S. District Court in Chicago held the government seizure to be "illegal and unlawful" because War Labor Board orders were merely advisory and Ward's had no war-plant status, but the court added that the Army could remain at Ward's until the government appealed the case to the Supreme Court. The war ended before this came about—the justices declining to review the legality of the seizure— and by then the Army had been running Ward's for almost a year, the only time in American history that the federal government served as a private storekeeper. The seizure was condemned as "Communistic" and Avery was called "Neanderthal," but Avery had at least saved his company over a million dollars in retroactive pay increases ordered by the War Labor Board. The government's experience should have convinced it never to venture into retailing again, for besides its doubtless illegal seizure—regardless of the union demands—it paid out $300,000 more than it took in while minding the store.

THE WHITE HOUSE
WASHINGTON

November 18, 1942

Mr. Sewell Avery, President
Montgomery Ward and Company, Inc.
Chicago, Illinois

Dear Mr. Avery:

The National War Labor Board has notified me of your
rejection of the Board's Directive Order of November 5, 1942,
issued as its final determination of a labor dispute involving
your Company. The Board's Directive Order was rendered in
accordance with Executive Order 9017 and pursuant to the national
agreement between labor and management that there shall be no
strikes or lock-outs for the duration of the war, and that all
labor disputes shall be settled by peaceful means.

As Commander-in-Chief in time of war, I expect all
employers, including Montgomery Ward and Company, and all labor
groups to comply with the provisions of Executive Order 9017,
as supplemented by Executive Order 9250. I, therefore, direct
Montgomery Ward and Company to comply, without further delay,
with the National War Labor Board's Directive Order of November 5,
1942. I consider such a course of action essential in the interests
of our war effort.

Yours truly,

Franklin D Roosevelt

THE WHITE HOUSE
WASHINGTON

December 12, 1942

Dear Sir:

As Commander-in-Chief in time of war, I hereby

direct Montgomery Ward and Company to comply, without

further delay, with the National War Labor Board's directive

order of December eighth, 1942.

Yours truly,

Franklin D Roosevelt

Mr. Sewell Avery,
President,
Montgomery Ward & Company, Inc.,
Chicago, Illinois.

F.D.R. orders Sewell Avery to comply with an order of the National War
Labor Board in 1942.

Above: One of the most famous pictures in the history of photo journalism—Sewell Avery being ejected from his Montgomery Ward office in 1944.

Left: One of the most bitter department store strikes was directed against the May Company in 1946-47, when workers in Denver, Colorado, eventually won a union contract and an increase in clerks' starting salaries from $18.50 to $27.50 a week, among other benefits.

n Outline of Store Etiquette For Year 1918

is interesting to note, that while written in more up to date wording, every
e of these items are still included in our store policy today.

. Loud talking and calling distract customers. They also cheapen the individual and the tone of the store.

. Conversation in groups appears to the customer to be inattention to duty.

. Well-bred employees will refrain from the discussion of their personal affairs when any customer is near.

. Store and department problems are not to be discussed when a customer is present. These are all family matters, and discussing them *outside* the store is, distinctly, a breach of honor.

. A customer receiving attention from a salesperson must never feel that she is being stared at or even noticed by other employees. This is inexcusable.

. It is a wise policy, and also an evidence of good taste, never to discuss one customer with another.

. Comments on customers who have left the department are entirely unnecessary and exceedingly dangerous. Other customers overhearing, expect the same treatment. Laughing when a customer is leaving the department is also dangerous.

. Manicuring, powdering, and so on, in the department often appear to be a lack of proper training.

. The sight of gum chewing and candy eating gives an undesirable atmosphere to the store. It is also a great discourtesy to customers.

. Directing customers carefully, courteously and correctly is a service which means much to them. Personally conducting them to a department they are seeking is an added courtesy.

. An employee, if not busy, will wait until her customer leaves before picking up merchandise or entering into conversation with another employee.

. The use of a customer's name is pleasing to her, and the habit can be cultivated. The use of "lady" in addressing her is never permissable.

. The word "we" instead of "I" is recommended in speaking to customers of store matters, as "We have some fine material."

. The customer who is "just looking" is a welcome guest in our store. It is her privilege to look—our duty to make looking a pleasure.

. An employee will always allow customers to precede her in entering and in leaving cars.

. All conversation between employees is omitted in the elevator if a customer is present.

MILLER & RHOADS, INC.

Above: Telephone order board at Strawbridge & Clothier in Philadelphia, 1925.

Left: Virginia's Miller & Rhoads issued these guidelines to employees in 1918.

Below: Early storekeepers disliked extending credit and many of them hung this popular Currier and Ives print on their walls in the 1880s. Poor credit risks made up the letters in the words.

Woolworth pickets, shown here during the 1939 drive to organize the giant variety store chain, dramatized contrast between low-paid employees and Woolworth heiress Barbara Hutton. Though the RWDSU campaign that year failed, as had the sitdown strikes of 1936-37, steady progress has been made by the union since then in organizing units of giant five-and-dime corporations.

While department stores have traditionally opposed unionism, there were always stores that recognized the importance of their employees and looked out for their welfare. The paternalistic actions of some early stores toward their employees do seem ridiculous today. In the 1870s, for example, Hutzler's of Baltimore daily gave their women clerks a dime to buy an apple or two—this homely prophylactic was considered to be medical care, and was all the medical care their employees got. Los Angeles' Bullock's, and several other American stores, gave each employee a copy of Elbert Hubbard's "A Message to Garcia," that inspirational essay based on the exploits of a hero of the Spanish-American War that was supposed to inspire workers to greater efficiency with such sentiments as: "It is not book learning that young men need, nor instruction about this and that, but a stiffening of the vertebrae which will cause them to be loyal to a trust, to act promptly, concentrate their energies, do a thing—'carry a message to Garcia.' " Many workers, making $5 a week, better appreciated Hubbard's *Essay on Silence,* which contained nothing but blank pages.

On the other hand, there are records of early stores being willed to store employees by their employers. A number of stores had excellent relations with both employees and unions—Wanamaker's and the Philadelphia local of the Retail Clerks got along so well that union funds were used to advertise the store during the Great Depression. Filene's employee organization, the Filene Cooperative Association, formed in 1898, had more power than any union has ever had over a store. The F.C.A. had the power to arbitrate in any employee-store dispute—over wages, discharge, or store rules—with its decisions binding on management. Its rules were drawn by Filene's attorney Louis D. Brandeis, later a U.S. Supreme Court justice, and its originator, maverick Edward Filene (see Chapter 4), had hoped that it would prove a means for his employees' gaining ownership of the store. This never came about, but the association arbitrated disputes (settling them 55 to 45 percent in favor of employees over thirty years), formed one of the first store credit unions, a health clinic, and an insurance society, and ran its own restaurants. With the coming of the Wagner Act in 1935 it became an independent union and moved off the premises, conventional bargaining replacing its binding arbitration.

Filene's and other stores had minimum-wage policies, Saturday closings, pension plans, and staff discounts for employees early in this century, and decades before them Wanamaker's ran schools for its employees. The Quakers' Strawbridge and Clothier declared that one of the reasons they were in business was "to elevate the conditions of employees." Today most stores with any savvy at all realize that their employees are as important as their merchandise and prices—one study shows that shoppers patronize department stores primarily because of the quality of their sales help—and they try to treat their people accordingly. At Penney's the words *clerk* and *employee* aren't even used—the 162,000 people who work at Penney's are all called *associates.* Penney's, Sears, and Lazarus, among many stores, have generous profit-sharing plans (pioneered by the founders of Bon Marché, the world's first department store), and corporate training programs like Ward's and Penney's, using the latest teaching machines, are common. Wages, which constitute about two-thirds of department store operating expenses, are still low compared to many industries, but have risen steadily over the years, and working conditions, which have improved immensely since World War I, are now exemplary for the most part. The stores give employees discounts ranging from 10–25 percent on all purchases. Women, who constitute the majority of store employees, receive equal pay for equal work today and hold 46 percent of all retail executive jobs. The old canard that women work in department stores for pin money (when according to government studies at least half "work out of compelling economic necessity" and most others work to maintain a higher standard of living) is voiced by few employers today.

Prodded by the Equal Employment Opportunity Commission since the late 1960s, department stores have also made great strides in hiring and advancing members of all minority groups. Minorities are still a rarity at the very top in most stores, but that too will change within the next decade unless a period of reaction sets in. Sears, for example, is justly proud of its affirmative action program, which it calls M.A.G., Mandatory Achievement of Goals. The company, which completely discloses minority representation in its annual reports, has more than doubled the number of blacks working for Sears since 1969, blacks now constituting 13.4 percent of its work force, a figure greater than blacks' proportion in the population. In 1977 the Equal Employment Opportunity Commission did find that Sears had violated Federal law by discriminating against blacks, women, and Spanish-surnamed Americans, but the company appealed that the decision (its exact contents still secret under the law) be reversed because the Commission came under the improper influence of NOW, the National Organization of Women. Sears also ran into trouble recently when the United States Court of Appeals ruled that the company had appropriated a socket wrench invented by one of its employees, Peter Roberts, by fraudulent means. In 1965, the decision said, Sears told Roberts, then a teenager, that his wrench would cost much more to manufacture than it actually did and he accepted $10,000 for an invention that sold over 19 million wrenches. Mr. Roberts was awarded $1 million damages and the right to go to a lower court to get back his patent.

The style for salespeople is different in each department store, depending on the customers, but the most amusing or exasperating salespeople—depending on one's outlook—would have to be the haute help in the specialty stores, those haughty aristocrats who pointedly direct people to *fragrances* or *hosiery* when asked for the perfume or stocking departments. Mostly it's all a façade to match the store's. A clerk at a fancy Fifth Avenue emporium, for example, once corrected an unpretentious lady who had asked for a box of chocolates. "Ah, madame means our bonbons, no doubt," he told her. "Yeah, I'd also like five pounds of those cookies," said the lady. "Yes, our petits fours," the clerk replied. "Shall we deliver your purchase, madame?" "Nah," the lady said, "I'll carry it home myself." Finally the clerk reverted to true form. "What's the matter with you?" he burst out. "Why schlepp a big package like that around the street!"

This Christmas an overworked clerk was heard to remark after a particularly hard day that he wished there were such a thing as reincarnation and that his customers would come back as salespeople. But the Great American Customer isn't that bad. She and he are hard to generalize about. In the early days shoppers were mainly women, and they still are today, though women no longer constitute 90 percent of the customers in most stores as they did sixty years ago. Customers range from reliable credit risks to deadbeats, from bargain hunters to hunters on the track of girls behind the counters. There are as many discriminating shoppers as there are people who want to order van Gogh's "Sunflowers" in a different color, to match their wallpaper. Clerks, however, *are* taught to classify customers in some stores, and in case you've ever wondered if salespeople are sizing you up when you approach a counter, Macy's once issued a sales pamphlet to its people giving an appraisal of customer types and telling how to handle each one. Not to mention the "downright nasty," we are either:

1. Impetuous, nervous, tense
2. Slow, difficult, hard to satisfy
3. Decisive, confident, aggressive
4. Indecisive, changeable
5. Friendly, sociable, reasonable
6. Intelligent, analytical, critical
7. Quiet, timid, indifferent

Famous department store customers have ranged from Kokomo the chimp to Queen Elizabeth, from Teddy Roosevelt, who shopped in person at Field's, to the voluptuaries of a Saudi Arabian harem, who were outfitted by mail at Macy's. They have been remarkably loyal to their favorite stores. Stylish heiresses will go on shopping sprees and load their limousines with $50,000 worth of dresses from one store; a shabby old woman will peel fifty bills off a roll of hundreds to buy a $5,000 etching she likes.

Several stores—including G. Fox and The Emporium—were saved from financial ruin after they were destroyed by fire when customers paid all their bills, despite the fact that all records were destroyed. Customers are remarkably loyal to favorite salespeople, too. A seventy-year-old saleswoman at I. Magnin's in Los Angeles has been selling to generations of Pasadena and Hancock Park women for forty-five years. Though she comes in at ten, leaves at four and takes a two-month vacation every year, she writes up at least $200,000 in telephone orders every year.

In early times the stores were proud to have clergymen and teachers among their customers, and many stores, including Hess's gave them a 6 percent discount. Dry goods clerks, dressmakers, and milliners were also entitled to discount cards. From the beginning, bargain hunters had to be contended with, according to a *Harper's Magazine* correspondent describing them at an 1857 sale held at A. T. Stewart's Marble Palace, which may have been the first American department store. "I had to storm *cheveaux de frise* of hoops to reach the counter," he wrote. "Observe your wife at dry goods if you know her. She may be sweet in the parlor, but she is like a ghoul at the counter, as if she might steal a dress or tear the eyes out of a clerk who refused to abate the price. . . . The shopping mania is a disease peculiar to women. It is a species of insanity."

There were always, however, "sensuous shoppers" like the fellow who described D. H. Holmes's New Orlean's store in 1849. "The paneling alone is a relief to the weary eye," he effused, "and picturesque flower groups which ornament its surface, give the whole a pleasant appearance. . . . You might loiter away half an hour there amid dreams of embroidery as agreeably as in a gallery of pictures. Like Tennyson, while you gaze on the gossamer thread, which sits like the reflection of an artist's thought on the rose-misted marble of a lady's neck, you, too, will have dreams of fair women. And then the silks, the rich gorgeous silks, which appear to clasp the whole brilliancy of Samercand in their lustrous tissues, and the satins which look as if they were designed to loll in many folds about the glowing limbs of Venus, or to rise and fall, in luxuriant fullness, on the queenly bust of Juno, when her proud thoughts flutter like frightened birds beneath—and the magnificent brocades, whereon Oriental flowers have been sown to glow and bloom into a parterre of gold and vermeil-tinted beauties—all charm the observer and suggest feelings which are sensuous without sensuality."

Department stores have long known that "the customer is always right," or almost always right. "If your customer thinks the moon is made of green cheese, let it go at that, just so you can make your sale," instructs an early salesman's manual. Try and help him even if he wants "a blue-covered book by an author whose name begins with 'C' or maybe 'G'." But the stores just haven't figured out how or why customers buy. Some blame it on the weather. Back in 1946 a now defunct mail-order house made an attempt to measure sales by "customer temperature," using weather bureau reports. A state's average temperature for a week was multiplied by the number of customers in that state, then an average or "normal" index or temperature figure for the country was developed. Upon adding the totals for all states and dividing by the number of customers the company actually had during that week, it found what was called its "customer temperature." In extreme hot spring and summer weather, sales were as adversely affected as during a warm fall and mild winter. The higher the customer temperature index went, the lower the chances for normal sales.

No store has worked out a system involving the phases of the moon yet, but one retailer who prefers anonymity has been daring enough to list ten reasons why women buy:

1. Her husband says she can't have it.
2. It will make her look thin.
3. It's on sale.
4. It comes from Paris.
5. Her neighbors can't afford it.
6. She can't afford it.
7. Nobody has one.
8. Everybody has one.
9. It's different.
10. Just because.

During the Great Depression, Macy's, Kresge's (now K mart), and other stores conducted "elections" among their customers to determine their preferences in material, style, weight, type, and price range of merchandise ranging from dresses to furniture. As for customer credit, department stores at first followed the advice of the Persian poet Omar Khayyam, who wrote, "Ah, take the cash and let the credit go." Early department store tycoons would have been outraged at even the old ultraconservative plan of 30 days to pay at no interest. Field's co-founder Levi Leiter, for example, was notorious for chasing delinquent debtors out of the store even after they had paid their bills, brandishing his cane and refusing to sell to them again for cash or credit. But the stores were granting credit liberally by the 1920s, when Americans, who had always preferred to pay cash, were already learning to extend their credit (once defined as "suspicion asleep") and were making 15 percent of all retail purchases on the installment plan. Charge accounts were made simpler by the Charge-plate system originated by the Farrington Manufacturing Company in 1927 and which Filene's was the first department store to use. Each approved customer received a small metal plate with his name, address, and account number embossed on it and bearing his signature for identification. An imprinting machine in each department made a printed impression of the charge plate or any itemized sales check that was to be charged, a copy of the check going to the customer, and another to the store.

Over 30 million people had charge plates in various stores across the country before most stores switched to their own credit cards in the 1960s. Today, in an era when there are ten thousand different credit cards available in the United States alone and many people believe "charge" is the opposite of "buy," department stores often accept not only their own store credit card, but bank credit cards as well. Fees for bank credit card service to stores range from 3 percent to as high as 6 percent, the average being about 2.5 percent; but department stores, unlike small shops, will not bargain and offer a discount to customers paying in cash. Under one new bank card plan, offered by New York's Greenwich Savings Bank, a bank depositor can obtain a 2 percent rebate on purchases at Alexander's department store by using a special card that immediately transfers funds from his savings account to the store—the loss of interest to the saver's account is far less than the rebate. Such a plan might answer the prayers of many department stores, whose credit collection problems are so bad that they don't even want to talk about them (not with me, at least). The National Retail Merchants Association says that the stores all lose money servicing revolving credit accounts. It claims that the 18 percent annual rate (1.5 percent on every monthly balance) that a customer is charged for credit is not sufficient to cover the cost of the service itself—citing one recent study where the cost of providing revolving credit was found to be $1.29 for every dollar of finance charge revenue paid in by the customers.

Compulsive shoppers, who "frantically require things to satisfy unfulfilled needs, such as sexual needs," in the words of one psychiatrist, pose especially difficult collection problems. Those people, whose lives amount to "perpetual buying binges," buy things whether they want them or not and run up bills they often can't pay. But then stores have always had trouble collecting from customers, even healthy customers who are well intentioned. "I got your letter about what I owe," wrote an early customer of the Hudson Bay Company. "Now be pachant. I ain't forget you. Please wait. When I have the money I will pay you. If this was the Judgement Day, and you was no more prepared to meet your maker than I am to meet your account you sure would go to hell. Trusting you will do this."

Perhaps it's best to end with the complaining customer, who for over a century has made salesclerks wince at the expression, "Many happy returns." Liberal return privileges have been a hallmark of department stores from their beginnings, and the policy isn't likely to change in the near future. Doubtless there will be some ingenious complainers who will surpass even these customers:

• The farmer who wrote, "Dear Monkey Ward, What the hell is wrong with the zippers in your overalls? They keep coming open at the damnest times, and a few times I was downright embarrassed when it happened in public!"

• The lady who complained to Sears that she wasn't able to cook the "decoy ducks" the company had sent her.

• The man who complained that his false teeth, found in a Korvette's *Ladies Room,* had been damaged by Lost and Found.

• The old woman who in 1957 returned nine cents' worth of pins and needles that she had bought in 1927, explaining to Macy's that there was nothing wrong with the pins but that her eyesight had failed and she didn't do much sewing anymore.

• The Macy's shopper who complained; "As far as exchanges go, you are not as courteous as some other department stores. I returned a pantie (silk) that split at the seams. One of your Section Managers, (a lady?) asked me to try them on and bend over, as she doubted my word about the size. Do you think this is a proper way to treat an honest customer?"

• Or finally, the lady who wrote in verse to Macy's:

> *I think that I shall never see*
> *A bra that's fashioned just for me;*
> *I thought that I should order "C",*
> *Surveyed again, and ordered "B";*

"B" is too large, to my dismay,
And yet I am too big for "A".
Poems are made by fools like me;
I guess my bras will have to be.
The gist of this is just to say,
Please come and take the bra away.

To whom Macy's replied:

We received your poem and do agree
You have a problem twixt A & B.
Our heads went together, our minds were knit;
The solution to your enigma is "custom fit."
So to our shop on the second floor
We suggest you come at least once more;
You'll see our clerks and then the fitter,
And after that, you can't be bitter.

PART THREE

A GALAXY OF
GRAND EMPORIUMS

More Great American Stores—
Past, Present, and Future

Some fourscore and seven days ago what its owners called "a gay department store catering to homosexuals" opened its doors on Amsterdam Avenue on New York City's Upper West Side. Terry McNulty, the proprietor, announced that his Leather Loft had expanded to triple its size and now included a gay travel agency, hair cutting salon, bookshop, and greeting card shop, as well as traditional departments offering clothing, boots, jewelry, and other merchandise.

In the future the Leather Loft may or may not become a full-line department store, one of America's grand emporiums—certainly stranger things have happened in the history of American retailing, as the following stories of over one hundred stores conclusively show. The gay department store, while it isn't exactly earth-shaking news, is the latest of an infinite variety of stores that have included everything from giant chains that started as ships and Indian trading posts to stores founded by churches, ethnic groups, baseball players, snake-oil salesmen, a few latter-day saints, and more than a few present-day sinners. This chapter will examine important stores among them that haven't yet been covered, try to briefly account for the successes or failures of department stores in general, and take a quick glance at their future as well.

Unfortunately, there is no room to include the many foreign stores that have been mentioned in passing throughout these pages. Much more could be said about grand emporiums like London's fabulous Harrod's, where the Queen shops, a huge palace with silver and china departments that go on forever and even a meat department featuring all kinds of exotic game; the Orosi-Back department store in fabulous Baghdad overlooking an ancient marketplace; La Samaritaine, the biggest of many Parisian stores;

Moscow's giant state department store, GUM; Tokyo's Mitukoshi store, where salespeople come to the front of their counters to bow to customers at the beginning of every day and where weddings are often performed for customers; Sweden's ancient Nordeska Kompaniet; the Hudson Bay Company and Eaton's in Canada. . . . But that is another book; the stores here are no farther away than Hawaii.

It is hard to generalize about so complex a subject, but the earliest founders of American department stores from Hawaii to Alaska generally fall within three broad groups: British immigrants escaping poverty in that country; descendants of Quaker families who had settled in New England in early colonial times; and Jewish refugees from oppression in Germany and eastern Europe. There are, of course, many exceptions to the rule, Felix Vernier, the founder of San Francisco's City of Paris, and one of the few Frenchmen to found an American store, being but one of them. Germans, Scandinavians, Italians, Poles, Chinese, Japanese, and members of practically every nationality group have founded department stores here. So have representatives of every race, the small Plaza Exchange department store recently opened in Brooklyn being the newest example of a black-operated store.

As far as religion is concerned, a theory advanced by Professor N.S.B. Gras of the Harvard Graduate School of Business half a century ago held that Calvinism (Presbyterianism) and Judaism produced the greatest department store merchants. "According to a theory worked out by Werner Sombart, now of the University of Berlin," Gras wrote, "there is a real connection between the development of the modern spirit of capitalistic enterprise and the progress of Calvinism. While Catholicism, Anglicanism and Lutheranism were staid, dignified religions, Calvinism was a religion of enthusiasm, fervor and hustling. . . . Calvinism seems to assume or perhaps even assert that work is next to godliness and that man should keep books when dealing with the Deity. It might be expected that there would arise out of this form of Protestantism, therefore, a great capacity for work and for saving. . . . According to the theory of Sombart, Calvinism is most like Judaism— Calvinists and Jews have the religious fervor necessary for capitalistic enterprise." An interesting theory—although one automatically suspects any theory on religion emanating from 1930s Germany—

but just a theory. Many Presbyterians and Jews founded American department stores, but so did Anglicans, Catholics, Buddhists, and Mormons—as these biographies show. It can be said, though, that Presbyterians and Jews produced department store founders far out of proportion to their numbers in the population.

Judging by the reports of its legion of detractors through the years, the American department store has died about a hundred times over the past century. These reports were highly exaggerated. Despite the predictions of doomsayers, who even this year are tugging at the church bells, the department store is still alive and thriving on these streets, and all signs indicate that it will be around to celebrate America's tricentennial. Whatever problems have arisen over the years have been solved by innovative thinking, and there's no reason to think that new problems won't continue to be solved.

Those department stores that have survived many years have passed through roughly five stages: (1) birth, (2) growth, (3) maturity, (4) decline, and (5) comeback. Those that didn't make it past stage four of this life cycle—stores like Emery-Bird-Thayer, the White House, Scruggs-Vandervoort-Barney, Lit's, and others noted in these pages—died from a Pandora's box of diseases. Some succeeded because they were dominated by creative charismatic leaders; others failed precisely because of this. There are stores that do well because they are safely grouped together in a concentrated area of department stores; still others found no such safety in numbers.

According to *Here, There & Everywhere,* a newsletter for retail executives, most department store failures suffered from Weknowitall, "a virulent form of marketing sleeping sickness" whose symptoms are cockiness, resistance to change, and "taking customers, competition and resources for granted." Yet nepotism killed almost as many, as did disorganization—a division of a store going its own way, "as if run by a feudal baron and giving only lip service to overall store policies." Egomaniacal empire building probably took as many down as panics, depressions, and recessions over the years. A recent example of this is W. T. Grant, which in trying to duplicate the wondrous growth of rival S. S. Kresge (now K mart) succeeded only in bankrupting a huge, profitable company. In its haste to become another K mart, Grant's granted credit indiscriminately to hype sales and opened over 400 new stores in five years, once opening 15 new stores in a single day!

What the future holds for the department store is anybody's guess. Certainly there are a lot of new inventions on the horizon:

• Quasar Industries of Rutherford, New Jersey, the same firm that invented the security guard Century I has built five-foot robots designed to walk back and forth outside department stores and entice customers to come inside—something like the human "puller-ins" of last century.

• Complex electronic cash registers like Singer's Modular Data Transaction System (MDTS), which do everything that a standard cash register can do and can transmit sales and inventory data to a central office as well, are now commonly used in many stores. Electronic funds transfer systems (E.F.T.) from banks to stores are also becoming more common.

• Sears-Simpson in Canada is already experimenting with an IBM system allowing day and night telephone ordering into a computer, which checks a customer's credit by the credit card number he punches out on a push-button telephone.

• An experimental shopping service employing the Bell System's Picturephone has been offered by numerous firms, including Bonwit Teller, and a closed-circuit device on which pictured merchandise can be ordered by shoppers who push appropriate buttons has been proposed several times.

• No doubt the day isn't too far in the future when stay-at-home shoppers will buy goods pictured on cable television. "Two-way cable television, with its multitude of channels, makes in-home electronic selling feasible," says Montgomery Ward President Edward S. Donnell. "A miniature, up-to-date, flexible and economically practical electronic catalog already is foreseeable."

But despite the many technical innovations that are inevitably in store for the stores, most experts predict that the department store won't change basically within the next century. Some say there will be more specialty stores, while others—probably nearer the mark—insist that discounters will lead the way. But it is a better guess that the line between traditional department stores, specialty stores, and discount stores will become more blurred every year and that a new hybrid will eventually be born. In the immediate future, look for the stores to go all out in promoting sales, increased productivity the only answer to the great expenses they have incurred in

expansion over the last decade or so. Marginally profitable departments such as furniture operations and barely profitable nonretail-
ing sidelines, like the hotel interest Marshall Field recently sold off,
will be given up by more and more stores. In general, there seems
to be a period of slow growth in the offing, with smaller stores,
smaller shopping centers, and so forth being built in select fast-
growing areas—especially in the Sunbelt.

One does wonder if humorist Frank Sullivan's prediction about
tomorrow will come true. "Shopping will not be the bedlam it is
today," Sullivan wrote in his essay "The Christmas of the Future"
(1933). "It will be controlled. The energies of American women will
be harnessed. There will be national leagues of shoppers. Teams
from stores like Macy's, Lord & Taylor, Marshall Field, Filene's and
Wanamaker's will compete with each other in shopping bouts
under the rules now governing wrestling. It will be no time at all
before controlled Christmas shopping has developed a hardy,
buxom race of American women shoppers which might well serve
as a first line of national defense in case of emergency. Perhaps it
may eventually be said of the United States that our victories were
won on the notion counters of Gimbels."

There are now anywhere from four thousand to seven thousand
department stores in America, depending on whose definition of a
department store one accepts. The U.S. Bureau of the Census
considers "stores organized by department handling a wide variety
of merchandise, including ready-to-wear, dry goods and home
furnishings, and having sales of over $100,000 annually," as bona
fide department stores. Other authorities further stipulate that such
stores must have at least 25 employees to qualify, and still others set
additional requirements. The buying public, however, usually looks
upon several thousand of what most authorities would call "smaller
general merchandise stores," and large specialty stores as department stores, for all practical purposes, giving us the higher figure. It
would obviously be impossible to describe even briefly all seven
thousand American department stores in this small space, but no
account of the development of the department store in America
would be complete without bringing up to date the histories of a
good selection of some of the more famous stores not already
mentioned. These capsule biographies, only a paragraph in some
cases, are arranged by the dates when the stores were founded, to
form a chronological history of sorts. But these dates do *not* indicate

when a store became a full-fledged department store; sometimes it took a century or more for what were established as dry goods stores, trading posts, *tiendas,* or country stores to evolve into grand emporiums.

Two further apologies should be made. Profit margins are not mentioned here. Department stores are notoriously closemouthed about the money they make—it was tough enough getting approximate sales figures from some—and too much guessing would have been involved. Most analysts say that 6 to 7 percent of sales is a typical department store profit margin and that any store that does 10 to 13 percent pretax profits—like Bloomingdale's and a few others—is in a rarefied area. Neither will many names of present-day store executives be found in these biographies. As one joke has it, "Ten, fifteen years ago, things were so good, you could open a new store, put a gorilla in charge and be successful. Nowadays, the gorilla wouldn't have a chance." But it's *not* that store executives mean little to a store's success—just that top retail executives have been playing a game of "musical stores" in recent years, going from one company to another so often that it's impossible to keep up with them. Some stores follow the policy of losing the battle and killing the commander. Other executives move out on their own. In most cases the heads of stores here are confined to historical figures—for the leader of Macy's today might tomorrow be telling Gimbels.

1766

GLADDING'S—*Providence, Rhode Island*

(See Chapter 5)

1821

America's Oldest Department Store

HAGER AND BROTHER, INC.—*Lancaster, Pennsylvania*

Hager and Brother had the distinction of being the full-line department store with the earliest history in America, although several foreign stores made it seem young in comparison. Hager's began life as a general store founded by Christopher Hager in Lancaster, Pennsylvania, well over half a century before Frank Woolworth founded his first successful five-and-ten in that city. It became a true full-line department store toward the end of the nineteenth century and until it closed in 1977 was still operated by Hager's descendants on the original site where the family patriarch built his general store. Watt & Shan, another early Lancaster store, dating back to 1878, took over Hager's after it failed but finally abandoned the operation, which competed with their own beautiful old store in town.

1823

A. T. STEWART'S—*New York, New York*

(See Chapter 2)

1825

ARNOLD CONSTABLE & COMPANY—*New York, New York*

(See Chapter 5)

1826

LORD & TAYLOR—*New York, New York*

(See Chapter 5)

1827

Macy's First Rival

JAMES A. HEARN & Son—*New York, New York*

Few shoppers know that Hearn's, not Gimbels, was Macy's great rival in the early days, and a far more bitter rivalry it was. In a 1902 price war, for example, Macy's offered Japanese silk at forty-one cents a yard and Hearn's quickly reduced its price to thirty-nine cents. Throughout the day a battle was waged that one observer described as "the wildest excitement ever witnessed in a retail store," women in both stores tearing and pulling at the ribbon, which at the end of the day was practically given away at eleven yards for one cent!

Hearn's had been founded by James Hearn's father, George A. Hearn, Jr., who had emigrated to America from England's Isle of Wight just as Aaron and James Constable had emigrated from the little island before him. Marrying into the Arnold family, he became a partner of Aaron Arnold, then founded his own store at 425 Broadway near Canal Street in 1842. His son James eventually moved the store to its location near the old Macy's on Fourteenth Street in 1886. There it remained until it closed down in 1955. Only a ghost of the venerable, once-powerful institution remains today—the Hearn branch in the Bronx, which is owned by the giant City Stores Company. (See also Arnold Constable, Chapters 5 and 11.)

1830

The Emporium in Porkopolis

JOHN SHILLITO COMPANY—Cincinnati, Ohio

"The oldest store west of the Alleghenies" was founded almost 150 years ago when John Shillito opened his modest dry goods store on Main Street in "Porkopolis," as Cincinnati was nicknamed for its hog-slaughtering industry. Nearly a half century later, in 1877, Shillito had prospered enough to build an imposing six-floor emporium at what is now Shillito Place. This building, called Shillito's Mammoth Dry Goods Store, had a great rotunda 60 feet in diameter rising 120 feet to a large glass dome that let air and sunlight into the store.

With its one thousand employees, and the giant palomino horses that pulled its delivery wagons, Shillito's was the largest and best-known department store in the city for many years; but by 1925 it had fallen behind the times and was no longer number one in Cincinnati. Purchased in that year by F. & R. Lazarus & Company, which later formed the vast Federated Department Stores, Inc., the store was revitalized and modernized, even adding a 300-car garage building, the first to be built by any department store in the city. Sales increased by nearly a million dollars the year Lazarus took over, and Shillito's went on to achieve a sales volume greater than the combined sales of Cincinnati's next three leading department stores.

Shillito's has a long, interesting record of community service. During the 1937 flood of the Ohio, the store turned all of its well water over to the city, pumping 72,000 gallons for hours into the city's mains and even mounting spigots on the store's outer walls to provide drinking water for thirsty citizens. Today, Shillito's sponsors a junior Town Hall for debates by high school students on important questions and gives free space to a Craft shop of the Handicapped. When you telephone for the time in Cincinnati, a Shillito recording provides it, along with a suggestion that you support some civic enterprise.

1838

BON MARCHE—*Paris, France*

(See Chapter 2)

1840

Working on the Levee

GODCHAUX'S—*New Orleans, Louisiana*

Of all the stories of American peddlers who became department store multimillionaires—and there are a score such tales—none is more Algeresque than the saga of Leon Godchaux. For while most of the others had brothers or relatives here in America to help them, even when they were immigrants, Godchaux had no one. Born of a poor Jewish family in Herbeville, France, in the province of Alsace, Leon left home alone at the age of twelve with just enough money to pay his passage to America aboard the *Indies*, which took a full year to reach New Orleans in 1837. The boy, who spoke only French, introduced himself to the wealthiest merchant in town, Leopold Jonas, and convinced the old man to lease him a backpack filled with pins, needles, ribbons, and other sundries—to lease it to a twelve-year-old on credit. Leon then set out to call on the plantations along the Mississippi River. Within several days he had sold all his merchandise and made enough money to pay off Jonas, buying additional supplies with his profit and making his path along the river once more. The youngster soon established himself as a reliable, friendly hawker, and ladies on the great plantations grew to depend on him for his merchandise and for news of the big city as well. Leon soon retired his pack for a wagon, increasing his stock tenfold, and within three years had the means to acquire his own country store.

The fifteen-year-old store owner chose a site near Convent, Louisiana, conveniently situated between a convent and a plantation and when this store prospered he took the opportunity to open up a men's store on Levee Street (now Decatur) in New Orleans. His new store, up on the levee and within easy access of sailors landing at port, did so well that by the end of the Civil War, Leon found himself in the ironic position of lending money to the plantation owners he had once peddled notions to along his route in sugar cane country. When slavery was abolished after the Civil War, sugar production suffered a tremendous loss for lack of labor, and many plantation owners were forced to liquidate their holdings. Leon bought his first plantation from the Boudesques family, and because he had long before promised to return their kindness for nursing him through an illness when he was a boy, permitted them to stay on, rent free, for the rest of their lives. But the Reserve Plantation was only the first of 14 that the young man would ultimately own. Leon had hit upon a new idea that revolutionized the sugar industry—instead of letting each plantation grind its own cane, he devised a way of producing sugar cheaper by setting up central factories. By the time he died in 1899 he was the most prominent sugar merchant in the South and his store in New Orleans was six stories high.

After Leon's death his son Paul took over the store, added departments for women, and relocated it to the building on Canal Street where it still stands. He in turn passed on the business to his son Leon, who is today chairman of the board of what has become one of the most exclusive specialty stores in the South. The fourth and fifth generations of the Godchaux family now operate the beautiful Canal Street store and five others, four in Louisiana and one in Biloxi, Mississippi—a multimillion dollar empire in stores and sugar that grew from the small pack on the back of a twelve-year-old boy.

1841

The Oldest and Biggest Store in Boston

JORDAN MARSH COMPANY—*Boston, Massachussetts*

Up to the time he left his home in Maine at age fourteen with only $1.25 in his pocket, Eben Jordan was so poor that he could truthfully say "he had never in his life spent a nickel in currency." Only five years later, however, he had been set up in a little dry goods store in Boston by a local merchant who had recognized his merchandising ability when Eben worked for him as a dry goods errand boy and ribbon clerk. Some ten years later Eben went into partnership with Benjamin L. Marsh and a great Boston store was born, a store older than all the many Boston stores that have celebrated their centennials.

Jordan Marsh's early business prospered, due mainly to Eben Jordan's tireless travels across the Atlantic to buy quality merchandise, and the original wholesale house added a retail store as an adjunct, the tail soon wagging the dog. By the time Eben Jordan died in 1895 there was a complex of buildings within the bounds of Washington, Summer, Chauncey and Bedford streets that formed Boston's largest department store. Eben Jordan had pioneered in enlightened personnel policies for his day and adopted many "new-fangled contraptions," including the first telephone to be used in a department store (1876), a passenger elevator operated with ropes, electric lighting, a pneumatic tube system, and glass showcases that were the talk of Boston. A farsighted merchant, he instituted liberal return privileges and either coined or was one of the first to use the slogan, "The customer is always right." His son Eben Jr. was no less enlightened and, in addition to contributing much to the store as president, built the Boston Opera House for the city, maintaining it for many years at his own expense. He also built Jordan Hall, an auditorium for the Boston Conservatory of Music.

After Eben Jr.'s death, Jordan Marsh was guided by George W. Mitton, the son of Edward H. Mitton, a former errand boy who had risen to the store's vice-presidency, and later, by his son Edward R., who represented the third generation of Mittons to be associated with the store. In 1947 work was begun on the present downtown store occupying the old Jordan Marsh site, five units done in colonial style with such modern conveniences as radiant-heated sidewalks for snow removal and indoor lighting to simulate daylight. "New England's Greatest Store," as it bills itself, now has divisions in Boston and Miami and is a principal unit of the Allied Stores Corporation chain with annual sales of about $335 million.

1842

R. H. MACY & COMPANY—New York, New York

(See Chapter 4)

1842

GIMBEL BROTHERS, INC—*New York, New York*

(See Chapter 4)

1842

"Free Showers for the Ladies"

THALHIMER BROTHERS, INC.—*Richmond, Virginia*

Thalhimer's is doubtless the only department store in history to have provided free showers for its women customers to make their shopping more pleasant summers, and is probably the only store ever to be founded by a university professor—one from a renowned university at that. William Thalhimer had been a professor of history at the University of Heidelberg before emigrating to Richmond and opening a one-room dry goods store in 1842, when John Tyler was president of the United States. Fourth-generation Thalhimers run the store today, which makes Thalhimer's one of the oldest department stores in the country still managed by the founder's family, but the store is nonetheless a public company with 48 percent of its stock publicly held. Thalhimer's anchor store in downtown Richmond was the first aluminum-clad store in America. The company, which had sales of over $140 million and profits of $5.3 million in 1977, operates 26 stores in 11 Virginia and North Carolina cities. This is an amazing record, considering that though the department store is over 135 years old, it didn't begin branching out from its downtown store until 1960. Long-range expansion goals include Thalhimer stores in South Carolina, Tennessee, and West Virginia. In June 1978 it was reported that the Carter Hawley Hale department store chain would acquire Thalhimer's for $70 million, giving the chain a stronger presence in the East.

1842

America's First Delivery Service

D. H. HOLMES—*New Orleans, Louisiana*

Daniel Holmes, the founder of this noted Louisiana store, left the family farm near Point Pleasant, Ohio, the town where Ulysses S. Grant was born, when only sixteen and worked at a number of retailing establishments, including New York's Lord & Taylor, before he opened his New Orleans emporium. Something of a scholar—self-taught in French, Spanish, Italian, Hebrew, and Sanksrit—he traveled widely overseas to stock his little shop, and by 1849 business had grown so that he had to open a larger dry goods concern on Canal Street, where the present D. H. Holmes store is located.

Holmes's retailing practices, contrary to the attitudes of the time, sent customers scurrying to his store. There was a "no questions asked" return or refund policy and the store stayed open 12 months a year, including at night after the opera. Daniel Holmes's selling maxims were the following: "Sell to others as you would buy yourself," "Good merchants make small profits and many sales," "Goods must come up to claims" and "Deal fairly and be patient, and in time you will crowd your store with customers." These are

ABCs of modern retailing, and combined with other innovations, made the store a great favorite of New Orleanians.

Daniel Holmes instituted a number of nationwide retailing firsts. When wives of army officers stationed at Jackson Barracks in 1845 told him that robberies along the river road made them afraid to carry packages home, he obliged them by sending their purchases to the barracks in his personal carriage. This service was so successful that soon several high-stepping horses drawing wagons with the Holmes name on the side became a familiar sight in New Orleans and the first department store delivery service was born. Holmes was also the first to employ women clerks—during the Civil War when many families were destitute and women had to earn the livelihood their husbands or fathers at the front couldn't provide.

D. H. Holmes, with sales of about $125 million a year, now operates eight stores in greater New Orleans, Baton Rouge, and Houma, most of them modern in design. Its most noted store stands on the original Canal Street location, a Gothic building with arched double windows, shutters, cast-iron balcony, and full-length pilasters. At street level, under a wide marquee, is the famous Holmes clock, which inspired the saying "Meet you under the clock at Holmes," a slogan familiar to generations of New Orleans shoppers.

1845

"More Merchandise for Less Money"

BACONS—*Louisville, Kentucky*

Bacons, the oldest retailing name in the Bluegrass State, is another store founded on an early bit of market research. Jeremiah Bacon made a careful personal survey of all the turnpikes and roads leading to Louisville before opening J. Bacon & Sons in the spot that attracted the most traffic. His little business prospered, several stories were added to the old store, and finally a spacious emporium was built on Market Street near Fourth in 1901, a store that displayed its slogan, "More Merchandise for Less Money," on a placard in the center of the first floor. Jeremiah Bacon's three sons however, wanted no part of the new big business and sold the store, retiring from retailing in 1903. Bacon's became part of the H.B.

Claflin Company chain, which owned many stores and had important interests in Lord & Taylor and James McCreery & Co., and came into the hands of Mercantile Stores, Inc. when Claflin went into receivership in 1914, shaking the foundations of the department store business. The store has prospered under Mercantile's direction and now has branches in Saint Matthews, at Bacon's Shopping Center in Shively, and across the state line in Jeffersonville, Indiana. Bacon's historic old downtown store was closed in 1972, and an ultramodern store, one of the shopping showplaces of Louisville, was opened to replace it in Bashford Manor.

1847

The Store That Shoppers Built

G. FOX & COMPANY—*Hartford, Connecticut*

When in 1917 fire completely destroyed the G. Fox store in Hartford, and all records were lost, faithful customers came forth to pay their bills "from their memory and hearts" and it was estimated that practically every dollar owed was paid. G. Fox was already a Connecticut institution at the time, having been founded by dry goods merchants Isaac and Gershon Fox seventy years before on Centinel Hill overlooking the Connecticut River, the same site on which the G. Fox store stands today. This one-room fancy goods shop heralded "LATE AND IMPORTANT NEWS FOR THE LADIES" in its first advertisement, offering items like "silk fringes, fabrics of all description, kid gloves and stockings of all numbers," and closing with the assurance that "particular attention is given to calls from the Ladies." The last was fitting for a store that later sold the first pair of nylon stockings in America and still counts women as constituting about 80 percent of its customers. The shop was a tiny one, little more than 7 feet x 9 feet, whose counters "left scant room for two people to pass," according to a newspaper account of the day, which adds that Gershon Fox's "mischievous" lady customers "invariably irreverently called him 'old man Fox'." As business grew, a new four-story store had to be built on the same site and more wheelbarrows had to be bought—for Fox had been one of the first stores to make home deliveries and made them by wheelbarrow until late nineteenth century, when horse-and-wagon deliveries were started.

After the G. Fox store burned to the ground in 1907, an 11 floor department store was built in its place, a structure that was at first know locally as "Fox's Folly." The new store, which eventually contained a fully equipped hospital, a theater for community events, and an invisible glass display window with full lighting, among other novel features, is an interesting building containing many examples of the rediscovered art deco period, especially in its marquee design and in Centinel Hill Hall on the eleventh floor. Next door to it is another Fox store, the 1876 Cheney or "Brown Thompson" building, which is considered the triumph of Henry Hobson Richardson, the best-known architect of the Romanesque revival in America, and which was recently placed on the National Register of Historic Buildings. In 1937 this building, weighing 8,000 tons, was moved to its present site—a move considered one of the great engineering feats of the day.

Beatrice Fox Auerbach, Gershon's granddaughter, succeeded her father Moses as president of G. Fox in 1938—becoming the first woman president of an American department store—and continued in this capacity until her retirement in 1967. Two years before that the company had affiliated with the giant May Department Store Company, but still maintains autonomous management. The store, with sales of about $120 million, is now the leading and largest store in southern New England and has six branches, only one of them, the new store in Warwick, Rhode Island, outside of Connecticut's borders.

1849

Dynasty in the Pacific

LIBERTY HOUSE-HAWAII AND LIBERTY HOUSE-MAINLAND—*Honolulu, Hawaii*

Captain Henry Hackfeld sailed from Germany to Honolulu in 1849 with a cargo of fashion merchandise, household articles, and ship fittings for the missionaries and settlers of the Hawaiian

Islands. His profits were handsome, and in the same year he established a small store on what is now Fifth Street with the blessings of the Polynesian monarch Kamehameha III. H. Hackfeld & Company prospered. Hawaii's ports were a stopover for fur traders on their way to Far Eastern markets, and were the major provision stops for thousands of whalers plying the Pacific. Then gold was discovered at Sutter's Mill in California, and hordes of miners who descended on the state not only cleaned out all supplies in the area, but bought from the Hawaiian Islands whatever could be shipped—clothing, food, shovels, boots, fabrics, animals, flour. With a northeaster behind him, a Hilo sea captain could reach the Golden Gate with cargo in two weeks. Hackfeld's capitalized on this, and California's gold rush turned the little Honolulu store into a giant of commerce.

During World War I, H. Hackfeld & Company was seized by the Alien Property Custodian as a German-owned business and in 1918 a group of American businesses purchased it, Hackfeld's becoming part of the conglomerate American Factors, Ltd. The firm continued to expand and prosper, eventually changing its name to the Amfac Merchandising Corporation, and formed a merchandising division called Liberty House to handle its 29 stores in Hawaii. Today its beautiful flagship store in that state, anchoring one end of Ala Moana Center, located between Waikiki and downtown Honolulu, is the leading department store in Hawaii.

Liberty House began to expand to the mainland in 1969 when they purchased the seventeen Rhodes Western department stores in Washington, Oregon and California. Rhodes had been a leader in spearheading the march of department stores to shopping centers throughout the West after World War II. Another important acquisition was the Joseph Magnin stores (see Chapter 5), which retain their original name—unlike the Rhodes stores under the Liberty House banner. All and all, Amfac has 88 stores, 51 Joseph Magnin and the rest Liberty House, producing revenues of $335 million. These include the world-famous Liberty House at City of Paris and the first Liberty House on the mainland in San Jose's Eastridge Shopping Center. One arresting novelty in this store is the "satellites," handsome display cages containing Liberty House fashions that move vertically through the central atrium court of the store from ground level to top. Five Liberty House stores in

Washington and Portland were purchased by Marshall Field & Co. in 1978 for $14 million in cash.

1849

The Store Without a Back Door

FAMOUS-BARR COMPANY—*St. Louis, Missouri*

"All the farmers out yonder are talkin' 'bout this place and it's gittin' to be quite famous," a rural customer purportedly said to the Messrs. Motte and Specht in complimenting their men's clothing store on Franklin Avenue in Saint Louis, and the proprietors immediately adopted the Famous Company as the name of their little shop, which they had founded several weeks before in 1870. The store prospered until 1892, when a fire all but destroyed it, and David May of the thriving May Company (see Chapter 4) bought its name and salvaged stock at a fire sale for $150,000 in cash.

The rapid growth of the Famous Company continued under May, who rebuilt it, adding many more lines, and became even greater with the purchase in 1911 of the nearby William Barr Company, a dry goods store that had been founded in 1849 as H.D. Cunningham and Company. The 21-story building erected to house the merged stores two years later occupied the entire block surrounded by Olive, Locust, Sixth, and Seventh streets and was one of the largest retail buildings in the world at the time, the Famous-Barr Company at first occupying only its basement and first seven floors, with the rest of the space rented as offices for local business concerns. This building, incidentally, was proudly described as "the only store without a back door," it being considered quite prestigious that no delivery horses and carts were ever seen leaving Famous-Barr, all deliveries handled at the service annex nearby.

The new store boasted a cafeteria that could be converted into a gymnasium and a theater where actor-employees gained national recognition because of the success of the store's "Famous Follies" in the pre–World War I era. Within a few years after the merger, Famous-Barr was handling the greatest volume of business of any department store west of Mississippi. Sales growth continued, but it wasn't until 1948 that the store opened its first branch in Clayton, Missouri. Since then Famous-Barr has encircled the outskirts of the metropolitan area with stores, many of them topped with the distinctive F-B dome, its ten branches making it Saint Louis's largest department store. Now the second largest unit of the May Department Store chain, the store's $240 million in annual sales places it twenty-first among American department stores. Plans are being formulated for new branches in the near future, in keeping with the store's slogan, "Partners in Progress—Greater St. Louis and Famous-Barr."

1849

Delivery by Wheelbarrow

JOSEPH HORNE COMPANY—*Pittsburgh, Pennsylvania*

Today this great store is part of the vast Associated Dry Goods Corporation department store chain, but it was founded as a tiny trimmings and fancy goods shop at 63 Market Street in Pittsburgh. The original store belonged to Lorenzo Eaton, but in 1849 the aging merchant made his young clerk Joseph Horne a partner in the enterprise and Horne eventually became its sole owner, although he later took on partners himself. The little store prospered, making its first free deliveries in a wheelbarrow "driven" by a former slave. By 1893 Horne's had moved into a new building on what is now Stanwix Street, the first of three buildings that constitute the store today. Horne's was one of the original 18 members of the Retail Research Association formed by Lincoln Filene in 1916 (see Chapter Nine). The company presently has ten branches in Pennsylvania and three in Ohio. It also operates Associated Dry Goods' three Boston stores in Erie, Pennsylvania.

1850

Gone, But Still Remembered

JAMES McCREERY & COMPANY—*New York, New York*

Many New Yorkers still remember James McCreery & Company, and the store will always have its place in history because it was immortalized in Lindsay and Crouse's play *Life with Father*. Mc-

Creery's began as a dry goods store in lower Manhattan, and like most New York stores, moved uptown as the city expanded northward. After a period near A.T. Stewart's historic Cast Iron Palace on Eleventh Street, the store moved to Twenty-third Street and then to Thirty-fourth Street, where it became as famous in its day as the nearby Macy's. The conservative old store finally went out of business in 1954 after more than a century in retailing, unable to change with the times. Today its 11-story building, completely remodeled, houses Orbach's.

1850

"A Business That Knows No Completion"

LEH & COMPANY—*Allentown, Pennsylvania*

Five generations of the Leh family have operated H. Leh & Company since its founding almost 130 years ago, making it one of the oldest family-owned stores still doing business at the same location. The company is possibly the only American department store that is a partnership, but has never been incorporated.

Henry Leh, a local Heidelberg Township Farmboy who had worked as a canal boatman and apprenticed as a tailor, was only twenty when he opened the H. Leh & Company Temple of Fashions in Allentown, which wasn't yet a city. Though his store was housed in a building only 20 feet wide and 110 feet deep, Leh quickly took on other lines besides clothing and, before the end of his first year in business, even began making shoes and boots. Emphasis was initially on the manufacture and selling of quality footwear—which Leh supplied to the Army, among other customers—but the department store business prospered as well. Over the years Leh acquired additional space for the store, and in 1884 he took former schoolteacher Horatio Koch as a partner, bringing his two sons, George and John Leh, into the firm five years later.

A year after the founder died in 1910, the company shoe factory, which occupied the store's two upper floors, was discontinued to make room for department store expansion. Today, after numerous expansions and renovations, the original little 2,100-square-foot shop is a modern department store with nearly 250,000 square feet for sales and service. H. Leh & Company opened a Quakertown branch store in 1972. Managed by a fifth generation of Lehs and descendants of Horatio Koch (who married the founder's sister) the completely family-owned store now serves a market area with over half a million population, in contrast to the 3,778 inhabitants of Allentown it served in its first years of business. "We're proud of our past and our tradition," says partner John Leh II, "but we don't want to live on our laurels. We'd rather build a business that never knows completion."

1850

Customers in Rowboats

LIBERTY HOUSE AT THE CITY OF PARIS—
San Francisco, California

This unique emporium is probably the only department store in America named after a ship—and is no doubt the only store that made its first sales to customers in rowboats. It all began in May 1850, when French silk-stocking manufacturer Felix Verdier, acting on the advice of his perspicacious young wife, sold his business in Nimes, chartered a brig named the *Ville de Paris* and sailed to San Francisco with a splendid cargo of silks, laces, and fine wines to sell to the luxury-starved forty-niners of gold rush days. Verdier, disgusted with the French politics of his times, found in America a political climate more to his liking and riches he hardly believed possible. Before he could even unload his splendid cargo at Yerba Buena Cove, hundreds of miners in small rowboats surrounded the brig, waving bags of gold dust and clamoring for his goods, especially the fine wines, champagnes, and cognacs. Within a few hours all was sold, the miners and their women rowing back to shore attired in finery and drinking toasts from bottles ripped from the cases of burgundy and bordeaux, chablis and champagne they had bought.

Verdier returned to Paris, had the name *City of Paris* painted on his brig, and bought an even greater quantity of French finery, sturdy boots, woolen coats, heavy underwear—and of course fine wines—with which to return to America. Landing at San Francisco again in 1851, he opened a little waterfront store, called the City of Paris after his ship, at 152 Kearny Street that catered to the miners and their women, giving it the motto of the French capital—*"Fluctuat nec mergitur*—It floats and never sinks." Before it moved to its famous site on Union Square, the store changed locations three times, and when it was destroyed by fire in 1906, Felix's grandson, Paul, and granddaughter, the Comtesse Suzanne de Tessan, rebuilt it, several generations of the Verdier family guiding its destiny as it grew into a great and distinctive department store.

The City of Paris became famous for its elegant goods and the French vintages stored in the noted Verdier Cellars, certainly the most worthy wine cellar in an American department store. After Prohibition, the Verdiers converted the lower level of the store into a miniature French village named after the luxurious French liner, the S.S. *Normandie*, but a sign painter changed this to "Normandy" Lane and so it remained. The store and its numerous branches became a San Francisco landmark, establishing many city traditions, such as the enormous Christmas tree that, beginning in 1909, rose under it dome every Thanksgiving Eve to become the official Tree of the City.

The fine old City of Paris closed its doors in 1974, two years after it had been purchased by the Liberty House chain, part of the merchandising division of Hawaii-based Amfac, Inc. (see the Liberty House entry). Liberty House shut down and eventually sold the Union Square store to Carter Hawley Hale, which wants to demolish it for a new building, much to the dismay of preservationists. In any event, Liberty House built a new Liberty House at the City of Paris on Stockton and O'Farrell streets. What the new six-floor store lacks in Old World charm, it makes up for with its bold modern architecture, which is reminiscent of Amfac's Hawaiian heritage. The store has retained the Verdier wine cellar, including the old wine racks and furnishings and the Chilled Room where the wines are stored under controlled temperature and humidity. In Normandy Lane there is now a restaurant called The Plum featuring excellent country French cuisine, and a beautiful Lagoon Garden shares the seventh floor with the Amfac mainland executive offices. The placid lagoon is surrounded by a lush garden with some 20 varieties of vegetation, ranging from 11-foot sculptured trees to sugar cane and ground cover, and a unique "white noise" sound generating system is used to eliminate any loud noises in this haven, 55 speakers continuously emitting "a soft rushing of air sound."

1851

F. & R. LAZARUS & COMPANY—*Columbus, Ohio*

(See Chapter 4)

1852

Elegance in the Queen City

McALPIN'S—*Cincinnati, Ohio*

George Washington McAlpin didn't become sole owner of McAlpin's—which he had founded, with partners, as Ellis, McAlpin & Company, Wholesale Dry Goods—until about 1880, when the store moved to its present downtown location at West Fourth Street in the Queen City. The firm remained wholesale, with trade extending throughout Ohio, Indiana, Illinois, West Virginia, and Alabama, until the founder died in 1890 and his brother William reorganized it into a wholesale-retail operation, building an elegant new department store at the same location. A newspaper clipping of the day described the new store in glowing terms: "There is no such beautiful interior to be found in the country as is presented in this model establishment. So greatly has the fame of the interior finish of McAlpin's traveled over the county, that merchants come hundreds of miles to see the designs for themselves." William also gave Cincinnati one of its present-day landmarks. In 1901 he purchased a famous English clock to decorate McAlpin's first entrance, and the clock is still there for all to see and hear as it strikes the hours.

McAlpin's eventually became part of the early H.B. Claflin group and was purchased by the Mercantile Stores chain when Claflin failed in 1914. The store's initial branch opened in 1954, when its Western Hills store became Cincinnati's first suburban department store. The Kenwood Plaza branch, opened two years later, was for a time the largest single-floor suburban store in the entire Midwest.

McAlpin's with sales of $85 million, now has eight stores in all, including two across the Ohio River in Lexington, Kentucky, right in the heart of blue grass country.

1853

A Pioneer Merchandiser

RIKE's—Dayton, Ohio

This old Dayton store, formerly the Rike-Kumler Company, was another charter member of the Retail Research Association. In 1959 Rike's was purchased by the Federated Department Stores chain. Today it has sales of about $125 million annually from its main store and four nearby branches, all of which have been built since Federated took over.

1854

One of the Earliest Chain Stores

CARSON, PIRIE SCOTT & COMPANY—Chicago, Illinois

A mere shipwreck didn't prevent Samuel Carson and John T. Pirie from continuing their journey from northern Ireland to America, nor did it disturb their dream of founding a store here. Salvaging what they could when *The Philadelphia* went aground off Newfoundland, the two young men sailed on another ship to New York, working their way west, They opened their first store in the railroad town of Amboy, Illinois, this small dry goods shop housed in a remodeled saloon—an ironic beginning for a firm destined to make its home in one of America's most distinctive buildings. Within four years members of the Scott family had migrated from Belfast to Amboy to work in the already expanding store, and the youngest of them, John E. Scott, became the firm's first errand boy at the age of fifteen. His son Robert was to become the third partner of Carson, Pirie Scott & Company in 1890.

By 1858 Carson & Pirie had opened branch stores in four nearby

Illinois towns, becoming one of the first (if not, in fact, the very first) chain store in the United States. Six years later the store had its first Chicago operation, a shop at 20 Lake Street where the firm's wholesale business was located. The time when retailers would deal directly with manufacturers was a long way off, and wholesale operations were immensely profitable, especially when they also supplied retail outlets of their own as Carson & Pirie's did. Business flourished, and after the Civil War the company built new quarters on the west side of State Street; but in 1871 the great Chicago fire claimed the store as it did most of the city. The firm's losses would have been much greater if another partner, Andrew MacLeish, hadn't acted quickly. As flames licked against the walls he flagged down passing teamsters. "Fifty silver dollars for every wagonload of merchandise you save out of this building," he cried over and over, and about 40 percent of the goods inside were saved.

Carson, Pirie Scott & Company rebuilt after the great fire and by 1904 leased and moved into a building designed by the American architect Louis Sullivan at the center of State and Madison in Chicago. The 12-story building, purchased by the firm in 1955, and named a Chicago Historical Landmark in 1959, was exciting in itself as an outstanding example of the Chicago School of Architecture. With its distinctive entrance of fine iron grillwork, it is still the store of which Carson's is most proud. It was one of the first buildings to prove the skyscraper principle of steel and masonry construction, and it became a model for countless other department stores built in America and Europe.

In 1953 Carson's became the first department store anywhere to sell insurance policies to its customers, issuing a personal effects floater. An original member of the Associated Merchandising Corporation, a cooperative buying venture financed by 31 leading U.S. department stores, Carson's today operates 15 Chicago stores and 11 stores outside the Chicago area. These include stores in the shopping center at Edens built by the firm and in the enclosed Randhurst Shopping Center owned by Carson's, Wieboldt Stores, and Montgomery Ward. Other divisions of the company, which has sales of over $300 million, are its wholesale floor covering division, and Carson International, a restaurant and hotel management operation. In 1968, almost a century after the first devastating

Carson blaze, the firm's main store on State Street caught fire again. All customers and workers were evacuated safely, and the store was back in business on a limited basis within five days.

1854

From Company Store to Department Store
PENN TRAFFIC—*Johnstown, Pennsylvania*

Stiles, Allen & Company, the forerunner of Penn Traffic, began as a little general store on the bank of the old Portage Canal in Johnstown. That same year it was sold, becoming the King, Buchanan & Company store, and not long after, King, Buchanan merged with the company store of the Cambria Iron Works, being named Wood, Morrell & Company after Cambria's owners.

For almost forty years Wood, Morrell operated as the company store of Cambria Iron, which issued script that workers could exchange for goods that they needed. In this period it was the great store of Johnstown, a three-story brick-and-iron building unmatched for miles around. Finally, in 1891, Wood, Morrell built an even larger store, changed its name to Penn Traffic, and for the first time established itself as a full-line department store. No one seems to know where the unusual name Penn Traffic came from, though. One theory is that Penn is meant for Pennsylvania and that Traffic means trade or business, while another holds that Traffic was chosen because the store was located on the main traffic routes of canal and railroad between Pittsburgh and Philadelphia.

In its long history, Penn Traffic has survived two disastrous Johnstown floods and a 1906 fire that burned the store to the ground. In 1908 it opened its $500,000 "mercantile palace" with a three-day reception that included the exhibition of Henry Hammond Ahl's noted painting, *In the Shadow of the Cross*, famous at the time for its "miraculously changing luminosity." Today the former company store is a six-store complex with two branches in Johnstown and one each in Somerset, State College, Du Bois, and Indiana, Pennsylvania.

1854

From Tienda *to Department Store*

STEINFELD'S—*Tucson, Arizona*

Aaron Zeckendorf arrived in Santa Fe in 1854, the same year that the Gadsden Purchase from Mexico opened up a vast new southwest territory, to establish a general store or *tienda* as it was called in the area. Almost twenty years later his nephew Albert Steinfeld, who had immigrated to America from Germany as a child, went to work for him in Tucson, where he had moved his little store. At the time the whole territory had less than ten thousand inhabitants, about a thousand of them in Tucson, where the Apaches were a constant source of danger, often raiding the town to drive off cattle and horses. The Zeckendorf store, located in an old adobe at the corner of Maine and Pennington was a shambles, merchandise scattered all over the floor, and the new fifty-dollar-a-month clerk put some order in the place. Within seven years the eager Steinfeld was manager of the firm, by the 1890s he had become a full partner, and in 1904 he bought the Zeckendorf family out and became sole owner of the store, changing its name to A. Steinfeld & Company.

Albert Steinfeld was a great Arizona merchant who played pioneering roles in many state industries, including mining, agriculture, livestock, real estate, banking, construction, hotel keeping, and manufacturing. But his major interest was the store that is his monument. Steinfeld's, always the heart and nerve center of all Steinfeld enterprises, has had a colorful history, One famous customer was Doc Holiday, who often rode up from Tombstone to buy firearms from the store's noted gun department. One time, word came that Pancho Villa was planning to raid Tucson, and fearing that he would make Steinfeld's firearms collection his first stop, store employees barricaded its doors, put mattresses up against windows, and waited with guns loaded for an attack that never came. The store never offered "white shotguns" for fathers of the brides at shotgun weddings—although this suggestion was made to the firearms department—but has presented a number of unusual promotions. Steinfeld's centennial year was ushered in with "the fastest moving man of 1954 in the fastest moving conveyance of 1854"—prominent New York builder William Zeckendorf, grandson of the founder, aloft in a covered wagon, touring Tucson behind a team of white oxen. Still owned and operated by the Steinfeld family (his nephews Lee and Jim Davis inherited it on the death of Harold Steinfeld, Albert's son), the modern Tucson store, a far cry from the adobe shack it evolved from, is one of the oldest family-owned department stores in America.

1854

San Francisco's Finest

THE WHITE HOUSE—San Francisco, California

So many Frenchmen lived in San Francisco in the mid-nineteenth century that the founders of the White House hired Raphael Weil, an eighteen-year-old boy who spoke French, as a salesclerk and hung a sign in their window reading "Ici on parle francais" to attract business. Raphael Weil eventually became sole owner of the White House and built it into a renowned department store, earning a reputation as a great connoisseur, citizen, and philanthropist, as well as a great merchant over the years. Weil always claimed to have placed the first full-page newspaper ad ever run by a store. When he was nearly seventy, the White House was totally destroyed in the 1906 San Francisco earthquake, but he started rebuilding the store "while the ashes were still hot." The great merchant so admired Abraham Lincoln that he closed his store every February 12 after Lincoln's death. Weil saw to it that this was store policy until his own death in 1919, at age eighty-four, and the White House carried on the tradition for many years. The store went under in the 1960s, a difficult era in retailing when many stores either merged or failed, and no one since has seen fit to revive its honorable name.

1855

Another Rags-to-Riches Story

MANDEL BROTHERS—*Chicago, Illinois*

So poor that they had little more than the clothes on their backs when they emigrated to America from Bavaria in 1848, the four Mandel brothers opened a tiny store in Philadelphia where they tried to replenish their pockets and learn the language and the dry goods business at the same time. Leon, Emanuel, Simon, and Solomon soon went west to Chicago, where a kindly uncle who owned a dry goods store on Clark Street had offered to take them into the business. By 1855 the brothers had earned the right to add their name to the store, and Klein & Mandel did so well in the next five years that they moved into a new building at Clark and Van Buren. Here the business prospered, becoming Mandel Brothers on Klein's retirement, but the great fire of 1871 that has traditionally been blamed on Patrick O'Leary's cow kicking over a lighted lamp and setting its barn ablaze seemed to have ruined the brothers as it did many Chicago merchants.

What the fire didn't claim those October days, looters did. Drunken men smashed store windows and threw out bolts of fabrics to the crowds, women staggered along weighed down with stolen dresses, grimy street urchins sported suits several sizes too big for them and expensive white kid gloves, people even draped their animals in expensive silks. All in all, the fire claimed three hundred lives and led to the destruction of about $200 million of property. The Mandel Brothers lost everything they had. Undaunted, they were one of the first stores to set up shop in temporary quarters, but Marshall Field, determined that the new "market street" in Chicago be on State Street, where he had rebuilt his grand store, persuaded them to relocate there in 1877.

The Mandels were big enough by the new century to be considered one of the "department store octopuses" by small retailers and in 1906 began looking for larger quarters elsewhere, but Marshall Field again intervened, promising them a ninety-nine-year lease if they remained. The store stayed on State Street, rebuilt in 1912 as a large department store and completely modernized in 1948 in a renovation that saw the addition of all the amenities modern stores boast. Though it went out of business ten years later, the historic store was managed by descendents of its founders till the last.

1856

Abe Lincoln Shopped Here

ROOT'S—*Terre Haute, Indiana*

Root's, the largest department store in the Wabash Valley, has had a reputation as a fashion leader since its earliest days. Its founder Andrew Jackson Edsall was among the first retailers to eliminate bargaining by setting established prices on every item he sold. His Edsall & Company, first located on Sixth and Main, became Edsall, Root & Company when Boston merchant L.B. Root joined him in 1863, by which time the store had been relocated to Fourth and Main. Here Edsall offered his rich midwestern clientele such luxurious novelties as imported paisley shawls, laces, linens, and French toilet soap. He even sold linen handkerchiefs to Abraham Lincoln. After Edsall died, his partner Root eventually took over total management of the firm, and moved it to its present location at 617 Wabash, continuing its policy of supplying its customers with the latest trends in fashions. Root sold his store to the H. B. Claflin chain in the early 1900s, and when that group failed, it passed into the hands of its present owner, Mercantile stores. There are branches now in Honey Creek, Sullivan, and Robinson, Illinois. The multimillion dollar Root Store in Honey Creek Square is the largest department store between Indianapolis and Saint Louis, or between Chicago and New Orleans.

1856

Iowa's Biggest Store

YOUNKER BROTHERS—*Des Moines, Iowa*

The first Younker Brothers store is listed in the first Keokuk, Iowa, city directory, a notable one because it was set in type by

Samuel L. Clemens, the same printer who became better known as Mark Twain. But then great names keep turning up in Younker's history—a long family genealogy shows that one descendant of the store's founders, Donna Lindsay, married Dr. Jonas Salk. "The biggest store in Iowa" was started by Lytton, Samuel, and Marcus Younker, who emigrated to America from Poland in 1856. Choosing Keokuk, Iowa, as a site because it was a prosperous town owing to its strategic position on the Mississippi River, they opened a retail dry goods store business and, using the store as a base, traveled the countryside as itinerant peddlers. The brothers explored the Des Moines River valley and found much business there, staying with farmers along their route, paying for their keep with merchandise from their packs and planting the first seeds of goodwill for the store. Meanwhile, the store in town prospered, even though the merchants, religious Jews, early placed an ad in the *Daily Gate City* (Keokuk was called Gate City because of its situation at the foot of the Mississippi rapids) advising that it would "be closed on every Saturday" to observe their sabbath.

Business began to sour for the Younkers by 1874, when riverfront towns started to decline, and they invested in a Des Moines branch store. From its rude beginnings at Fifth and Main streets, across the street from the Estes House—then "the only hotel west of the Mississippi with a heating stove in every room"—this store moved several times over the years in becoming the Younkers that thousands of Iowans know today. The Des Moines store opened with an ad reading: "We have come to live here and mean to do right. If you want honest goods at bottom prices, call at Younker Brothers." It was the first store in town to hire women, and a description of that saleswoman's lot shows how ways have changed since then: "For the first few days, Mrs. McCann was anything but happy. She kept herself discreetly in the rear of the store, feeling strange and out of place in this business world dominated by men. In a short time, however, the women customers were seeking her out, because they liked the idea of being waited on by a woman. Mrs. McCann's success was so decided that much jealousy was felt among the men."

Younkers moved to its present location in 1899 and by store purchases, expansions, and mergers came to occupy the whole block on Seventh and Walnut. The acquisition of Wilkens department store (1923), the merger of Younkers' and Harris-Emery's, and the purchase of J. Mandlebaum & Sons (1928) made the store Iowa's largest and foremost. It now has 23 branches throughout Iowa and Nebraska, with combined sales of over $110 million a year and twenty-five thousand employees.

1857

"Meet Me by the Lions"

THE LION STORE—*Toledo, Ohio*

The descendant of an old New England family whose great-grandfather had fought at Bunker Mill, Frederick Eaton learned retailing as a fifty-dollar-a-year clerk in a country store near his Sutton, New Hampshire, farmhome. Agreeing with Horace Greeley that a young man's future was in the West, he journeyed to Toledo, Ohio, where he opened a dry goods store, Frederick Eaton & Company, at 115 Summit Street in the same year that the dirt streets of young Toledo were first paved with 2-inch thick pine planks. Despite the failure of the Ohio Trust Company and the great panic in Toledo that year, the Eaton Company made $15,000, no doubt owing in great part to the frugal Frederick, who "slept upon the counter at night as a substitute for insurance policies and burglar-proof safes." The store soon moved to larger quarters at 79 Summit, and it was at this location, sometime between 1859 and 1865 (no one is sure of the date), that the famous Eaton lions made their appearance. Eaton purchased the two life-size cast-iron beasts, installing them outside the entrance to his store, and within a few years people were referring to it as the Lion Store. When in 1866 he moved to the store's present Summit Street site, the lions went with him, and they have remained guarding the front doors for over a century, surviving a fire that burned the store down in 1870 and many enlargements and modernizing since. They have become a Toledo landmark, an object of affection, legend, and stability for Toledoans as the Wanamaker eagle is to Philadelphians and the Rich's clock is to Atlantans.

The Lion Store was primarily a wholesale dry goods store in its early years, Eaton's now-defunct Bee Hive branch serving as its retail outlet. The Lion became part of the H.B. Claflin Company on

Frederick Eaton's death in 1890 and was subsequently acquired by the Mercantile Store group when the earlier chain folded twenty-four years later. The two cubs in the Lion pride are the first branch store, opened in the Westgage Village Shopping Center in 1957, and the Lion store opened in Southwest Toledo's Southwyck Shopping Center in 1972. The downtown store was completely remodeled in 1962 and features a popular restaurant called the Copper Kettle. One of Lion's firsts in the "Glass Capital of the World" was its highly mechanized warehouse, opened in 1970, which has one of the 30 or so storage and retrieval systems in the country.

1857

Working by the Railroad

SANGER-HARRIS—*Dallas, Texas*

After he opened the first Sanger store in McKinney, Texas, Isaac Sanger was joined by his brothers Lehman, Samuel, Alexander, and Philip, who journeyed one by one from Germany to join him in America. The Sangers were sensitive to the rapidly changing Texas marketing scene during this early period and frequently relocated at any place they felt was becoming a new center of trading activity. One of the country's earliest chain stores, they owned little 400-square-foot dry goods shops throughout Texas, boasting about 11 branches by 1871.

Wherever the railroads went, the Sangers followed, and when the railroads expanded to Dallas in 1872, the first Sanger store opened there a few weeks later. This store grew into the largest retail store in the Texas of its day. Among retailing "firsts," Sanger Brothers was the first Dallas store to sell ready-made clothes for women, the first to offer customers credit, a telephone shopping service, a mail-order service, and home delivery, and the first Dallas advertiser to use fashion sketches in its ads. Sanger's was also the first store in Dallas to use passenger elevators, escalators, gas lights, and electric lights. The store pioneered in employee relations, too, establishing the first night school for employees and the first employees' savings and loan association. But it was not generous with wages—when young Herbert Marcus demanded a raise at Sanger Brothers, the store granted their buyer of boy's clothing only $1.875 more, and he quit, going on to found Neiman-Marcus, Texas's most famous store today.

For many years Sanger Brothers dominated the Texas retail field, but after the death of the dynamic Philip Sanger in 1902, it began to decline and was an ailing business by the time the Sanger family sold the company to Stifel, Nicholaus & Company of Saint Louis in 1925. Under the leadership of E.P. Simmons the store prospered, but following his death in 1951, it was purchased by the Federated Department Store group. Ten years later Sanger Brothers, operating under its own name within the group, purchased A. Harris & Company and became Sanger-Harris. Anticipating the rapid development of the suburbs, Sanger-Harris was the first Dallas store to build suburban stores in growing areas of the city. Today it has 10 branches, including the giant in Fort Worth's climate-controlled Hulen Mall Shopping Center, which opened in 1977. Sanger-Harris has sales of about $125 million yearly. Its six-floor, block-size downtown Dallas store, built in 1965, is one of the few new downtown Dallas stores to be built in America in the last twenty-five years, its striking modern architecture offering a startling contrast to the tiny shanty of a store that began it all.

1857

Oregon's Biggest Store

MEIER & FRANK COMPANY—*Portland, Oregon*

Meier & Frank is probably the only store whose owner became governor of a state, Julius L. Meier having served as Oregon's governor, in which position he organized the state police force. Today the store is part of the huge May Company chain and has one of the highest per capita sales records of any store in America, with $100 million in sales. Headed by Aaron M. Frank, a grandson of the founder, it is now the largest department store in Oregon. Meier & Frank has a branch in Lloyd Center, a mile from the center of Portland and America's largest downtown shopping center.

1858

One Price, One Place, One Family

HUTZLER'S-*Baltimore, Maryland*

Hutzler's, a Baltimore institution, has occupied the same site under the same family ownership for over a century. Moses Hutzler, father of the three founders, operated a dry goods store in Baltimore before setting his sons up in business at the Howard Street location where Hutzler's still stands. Abram, Charles, and David Hutzler ran the store jointly and even in the early days had a reputation for fair trading and dependable quality goods. Much early merchandise was imported from Europe, and a guarantee of quality went with everything sold, especially the laces that "Mr. David" Hutzler made his specialty. By 1868, when bargaining was still the rule in retail shops, the store was advertising its "one-price" policy, and in 1874, when Hutzler's moved into a new three-story building a couple of doors south, it proudly displayed the slogan "One Price House" in large letters under its name. To customers attempting to bargain over an item the invariable reply began with "Sorry . . ."

The delivery service by horse and wagon that Hutzler's began in 1874 was the first in Baltimore, and horses delivered many a package to customers until 1899, when the store introduced the first power-driven truck used by a store in the city—an electric model that broke down frequently and was derided by onlookers gleefully shouting, "Get a horse!" Hutzler's also pioneered in novel, eye-catching newspaper ads to attract customers. By 1888 the modest buildings housing the store proved entirely inadequate, and they were razed to make room for a much larger store. Called the Palace, as were many grand emporiums of the day, this five-floor stone building with a handsome carved façade was typical of the eclectic style that was the architectural favorite of the era. Today it constitutes the south building of the present Hutzler's, a great part of the original façade remaining, and were Baltimorians of that day to return, they would have little trouble recognizing it, so little has the intricate exterior been altered. David Hutzler was so enamored of the Palace that he had a handsome china cabinet built as a model of it, presenting this to his wife on their golden wedding anniversary.

After the death of David Hutzler, the last of the founders, in 1915, Hutzler's continued to grow. The following year another five-story annex was erected on the south side of Saratoga Street, and in 1924 this building was raised from five to ten stories. Finally the modern "Greater Hutzler's" on Howard Street was built in 1932. In addition to this complex of downtown stores, Hutzler's has circled Baltimore with four suburban stores. The little shop on Howard Street has become a department store giant employing 3,500 in help and doing a yearly business of over $50 million in sales. In 1965 Hutzler's made national news when three gunmen kidnapped the company's assistant manager and his family at their home, holding the man's family hostage while they forced him to open the store's safe (see Chapter 11).

1860

Arizona's Best-Known Store

GOLDWATERS, INC.—*Phoenix, Arizona*

Goldwaters is well known nationally because it bears the name of Arizona's Senator Barry Goldwater, unsuccessful Republican candidate for President in 1964. Senator Goldwater has no connection with the firm, which was founded by his grandfather Joseph, a former peddler. (Interestingly, the father of Arizona U.S. Senator Carl T. Hayden was also an early merchant.) Today Goldwaters is a star in the crown of the giant Associated Dry Goods department store chain.

1860

"Grass Roots Service"

THE HECHT COMPANY—*Baltimore, Maryland, and Washington, D.C.*

The original Hecht store was founded in Baltimore, Maryland, by Samuel Hecht, whose three remarkable sons would go out on their own in years to come and make the family name one of the most respected in American retailing. The first to do so was eldest son Moses, who at the tender age of fourteen, with a little experience under his belt from working in the patriarch's store, opened a small dry goods store in the early 1890s, following this up with a store in Washington, D.C. By this time Moses had been joined by his brothers Alexander and Emmanuel. Together they opened the Hub, on Baltimore and Light streets in 1897, replacing this with another store on Baltimore and Charles when it burned to the ground in the great Baltimore fire of 1904.

Both the Baltimore and Washington D.C., stores were successes from the start, thanks to what the Hechts called "grass roots service." Alexander Hecht, for example, placed his office on the balcony overlooking the main floor of the Washington store. Like his brother he strongly believed in personal involvement with his customers and showed his concern for their welfare by coming down frequently to give personal service and attention to their shopping needs—and to help solve any problem in question.

Over the years Hecht's pioneered in many areas and claims a number of Washington department store firsts—first with escalators, charge plates, and a company-paid pension plan, to name just a few. The company built its present downtown Washington store on F Street at Seventh in 1924, a modern building that was expanded seventeen years later. By the time the Hecht Company became part of the prosperous May Department Stores Company chain in 1959, it had, besides its Washington and Baltimore locations, a modern New York Avenue Service Building in Washington and five branches in Virginia and Maryland. Under the May Company the branch expansion that began in 1947 at Silver Spring, Maryland continued, and today the Hecht Company consists of 19 stores in all, plus several service facilities. Last year the Baltimore/Washington Hecht's ranked thirteenth among the nation's leading volume department stores, with $275 million in sales.

1861

JOHN WANAMAKER—*Philadelphia, Pennsylvania*

(See Chapter 4)

1861

GUMPS—*San Francisco, California*

(See Chapter 5)

1862

"The Biggest, Best, and Busiest"

O. T. JOHNSON COMPANY—*Galesburg, Illinois*

O. T. Johnson's is possibly the only store in America that isn't called by its name. Not long after O. T. Johnson hung up the sign on his dry goods store over a century ago, people began calling the store O. T.'s and today it is known almost exclusively by these initials. O. T.'s has changed hands and locations in Galesburg several times over the years. It first became a bona fide department store at the turn of the century when it proudly advertised itself as "The Big Store—Galesburg's Biggest, Best & Busiest Store." Eventually O. T.'s was purchased by the Alden's mail-order firm (see Chapter 7), coming under the control of Gamble-Skogmo in 1963 when that merchandising chain purchased Alden's, but it is still operated autonomously.

1862

A Store Founded by Huguenots
STEKETEE'S—*Grand Rapids, Michigan*

The Steketees offer still another example of an immigrant family fleeing persecution in Europe and eventually founding a department store dynasty in America. This time the immigrants were Protestants, French Huguenots who were driven from France to the Netherlands, where the father was a government overseer of the dikes holding back the North Sea. The family finally fled to America when they could not find religious freedom even among the tolerant Dutch.

The Steketees settled in Michigan, where Paulus, the youngest son, in 1862 joined local merchant John Doornink in opening a store called "Doornink and Steketee, Merchants, Tailors and Clothiers" at the corner of Monroe and Division avenues in Grand Rapids. The little store prospered until it burned to the ground in 1871, at which time John Doornink decided to sell his interest in the firm to his partner. Paulus took over, and in another seven years the store became P. Steketee and Sons, doing business at 100 Monroe Street, the site it occupies today. Here the Steketee system of apprenticeship began, each member of the family who wants to be associated with the firm working at all basic retailing jobs from the bargain basement up until he or she learns the business.

Steketee no longer has the wholesale business it had at the turn of the century, and the store has been enlarged and renovated extensively over the years. The large clock on the main floor is a city landmark, "Meet me at the clock at Stek's," long a familiar phrase to Grand Rapids shoppers. One complete wing of the seventh floor houses a computer center that handles not only the store's records, but also provides computer programming service for many other businesses in West Michigan. The family-owned firm, one of the state's largest chains, has a second store in Grand Rapids and branches in Grand Haven, Holland, Kalamazoo, and Muskegon.

1863

"Lest Customers Be Tempted to Frivolous Thoughts"

THE H. & S. POGUE COMPANY—*Cincinnati, Ohio*

Isabella Pogue, a matriarch of formidable influence, sailed to America from famine-stricken Ireland with her seven children in 1849. Most of her sons took retailing jobs of one kind or another in Cincinnati, and two of them—Henry and Samuel—in 1863 bought a dry goods business from their uncle John Crawford, for whom they had worked several years, and renamed it the H. & S. Pogue Dry Goods Company. Three other brothers joined the firm shortly after, and all were responsible to the remarkably shrewd Mrs. Pogue, who demanded that one or another of her sons report to her every day at lunchtime with news of the store's progress and problems. The Pogue boys were wily enough themselves, though. When they expanded in 1878, for example, they hadn't enough merchandise to fill the numerous shelves in their new quarters. They had anticipated this, however, and for months before their move to Fourth Street had begun hoarding all the empty boxes they could lay their hands on. When the store opened, these cartons simulated acres of goods, and old customers were under the impression that the Pogue inventory had quadrupled. The ruse worked, although the clerks sometimes had trouble remembering which boxes contained merchandise and which were empty.

The brothers were generally above such tricks, however; in fact, they were rather stern Presbyterian teetotalers who never cursed, permitted themselves no extravagances, and even kept their store windows curtained on Sunday "lest customers be led to frivolous thoughts." Decent men, who were fair to their employees and gave generously to charities out of religious convictions, they made their store one of the most famous in Cincinnati and turned it into a full-fledged department store by the late 1880s, when the store's corporate name was changed to the H. & S. Pogue Company, "Dry Goods" no longer part of the title.

Members of the Pogue family were still running the store in 1916, the year that Pogue erected a building with six acres of floor space on Fourth Street, this store being the basis for the present downtown Pogue's. It wasn't until 1961, three years after James Petty, the first president of the store from outside the Pogue family, came into office that Pogue's was sold to the Associated Dry Goods chain. The company now has five branches with sales of over $65 million annually.

1863

A Step on the Way West

EMERY-BIRD-THAYER—*Kansas City, Missouri*

In the midst of the Civil War, Emery-Bird-Thayer opened their store on Second and Main streets in Kansas City, which was considered almost a part of the frontier at the time. It would be two years before the first train connected the town with Saint Louis, making the run in over twenty hours, and the only practical way west from Kansas City was along the Santa Fe Trail until the famous Atchison, Topeka and Santa Fe Railroad was completed in 1880. In 1850 a monthly stage line had been established between Kansas City and Santa Fe, and Emery-Bird-Thayer took advantage of the former city's position as the chief outfitting point for travelers heading West. Their little store supplied provisions and dry goods to stages setting out from Kansas City. The artfully painted stages of the day, which had water-tight bodies to ford streams, stopped for fresh teams every 20 miles, and furnished their 15 passengers with rifles to defend themselves against Indians, charged $175 in gold for the journey. Emery-Bird-Thayer profited from their steady, weekly business. Thousands of pioneer wagons took the trail every year, too, and the store sold them bacon, groceries, coal-oil, hardware, fabrics, blankets, and notions, selling its share of the $5 million in merchandise said to go West along the trail every year. Over a period of almost two decades Emery-Bird-Thayer profited from the trade and gradually evolved into a department store—one of the handful of American general stores to do so. The pioneer store prospered up until the 1950s when, like Scruggs-Vandervoort-Barney, another century-old Missouri store, it closed its doors in the face of retailing's discount revolution.

1864

Another Western Pioneer

DANIELS & FISHER STORES, COMPANY—
Denver, Colorado

In 1957 the May Department Stores chain took over this early western store, which had long been its competitor. It is now known as May-D & F and still operates in Denver, with yearly sales of $80 million. (See Chapter 4.)

1865

MARSHALL FIELD & COMPANY—*Chicago, Illinois*

(See Chapter 4)

1865

B. ALTMAN & COMPANY—*New York, New York*

(See Chapter 5)

1865

A Store Grows in Brooklyn

ABRAHAM & STRAUS—*Brooklyn, New York*

Duh Dodgers is long gone and Brooklynese is a dying dialect, but Abraham & Straus, or A & S's, as it is usually called by denizens, remains a Brooklyn institution. It has been for over a century, thanks to the sagacity of its founder. Abraham Abraham, the founder of Abraham & Straus, clerked in Newark's Bettlebeck &

Company dry goods store—along with future department store founders Benjamin Altman and Lyman Bloomingdale—for three years before he decided to run away from home and enlist in the Union Army when he turned eighteen. Though he had all the makings of a great general, his parents had other ideas for his future and tracked him down in Chicago before he could enlist, dragging him home to New York much against his will. Time, or the end of the Civil War, seems to have ended his romantic dream, for within three years he had opened a small dry goods store on Fulton Street in Brooklyn in partnership with Joseph Wechsler.

Wechsler & Abraham's tiny three-employee shop survived the post–Civil War depression and grew to occupy three floors of its original location by 1883. That engineering marvel called simply the Brooklyn Bridge opened the same year and so did Abraham's new store farther up on Fulton Street, which was housed in the five-story Wheeler building. Locals referred to the building as Wheeler's Folly because it was so far removed from the contemporary commercial center, but Abraham sensed that the new bridge would change the business topography of Brooklyn and his decision to move is one of the two most important turning points in the store's history. The other was Abraham's lobbying to bring the New York City subways into Brooklyn, a dream that became reality in 1908 when the first of subway shoppers from New York paid their nickels to journey over to A & S's and fight for bargains in its basement.

Wechsler & Abraham became Abraham & Straus in 1893 when Joseph Wechsler sold his interest in the business to the three Macy's partners, Isidor and Nathan Straus and Charles B. Webster. The store did not become a part of Macy's, though it had a close association with the New York store and shared overseas offices, but Isidor Straus kept a stern eye on the business. One of his courteous but scolding notes to poor Abraham made no fewer than five complaints about various department operations ("It is utterly impossible for you to make money in that department under such conditions!") and closed with line, "I guess I have done enough scolding for one letter."

To cushion the shock of Straus, Abraham took as many of his family as possible into the business. When he died in 1911, an obituary described him as "an ideal American merchant," one who had built a little dry goods shop into a department store with annual sales of $13 million and had proved himself a public-spirited progressive employer as well. It was under his grandson, Walter N. Rothschild, general manager of A & S at the time, that the store became a member of the Federated Department Store coordinating group—in fact, Federated itself was born on Rothschild's yacht in Long Island Sound, where he met to discuss the plan with two other stores A & S had long been associated with in the Retail Research Association and the Associated Merchandising Company (see Chapter 8). Today the store is an assortment of old and new buildings at the Fulton Street location and remains Brooklyn's busiest department store. Of A & S's branches, the store in Hempstead, Long Island, was long the largest suburban store in the eastern United States, but the company's Brooklyn flagship is among the few downtown stores left in the country that still consistently does better than its suburban counterparts. Bargains and promotions ranging from sports seminars to modern poetry readings still draw many New Yorkers from across the river to the store, and sales of close to half a billion dollars yearly make A & S's one of the top three nonchain department stores in America.

1866

THOMPSON'S PREMIUM HOUSE—*Bridgewater, Connecticut*

(See Chapter 7)

1867

ZIONS—*Salt Lake City, Utah*

(See Chapter 4)

1867

From City to Suburbs
STERN BROTHERS—*Paramus, New Jersey*

Toward the beginning of 1867, when Andrew Johnson was hanging on in the White House by the skin of his teeth, when the United States would purchase Seward's Folly from Russia, and "Weston the Pedestrian" would collect ten thousand dollars for walking 1,238 miles from Portland, Maine, to Chicago, the Stern Brothers quietly opened a one-room dry goods store at No. 367 Sixth Avenue in New York, a location skirting the edge of old Chelsea Village, where so many of the first families of New York had built palatial residences. Isaac, Louis, Bernard, and Benjamin Stern, sons of a German immigrant watchmaker, were all partners in the store at one time or another, but it was started by the two older brothers, Isaac being the early visionary and driving force of the business. From earliest days the little store earned the reputation of being "the best in dress goods, laces and silks" and within a decade had to add larger quarters at No. 110 West Twenty-third Street. Here Stern's became famous for imported merchandise at popular prices and a large stock that included even "Mrs. Moody's special corset for those ladies inclined to an excess of avoirdupois," as the brothers, always quick with a euphemism, put it in their ads.

Business proved so lively on Twenty-third Street, an area that most merchants had considered too far uptown for commerce, that in 1878 a new building had to be built to accomodate Stern's customers. This was to be one of the grandest of the old grand emporiums, a building that still stands today, and is one of the best preserved cast-iron façades in the city. It was hard for a retailer to go wrong in a neighborhood where shoppers like Lily Langtry, Commodore Cornelius Vanderbilt, Edwin Booth, S. J. Tilden, and Russell Sage strolled along the street.

In his book *Forty Years on Twenty-third Street*, Henry Irving Dodge reminisced:

When Isaac Stern let it be known that he was going to pull up stakes from Sixth Avenue and establish himself on Twenty-third Street, opposite the Fifth Avenue Hotel, he was called a lunatic by the wiseacres. But Stern was a man of courage. Also, Stern had dreamed dreams of long lines of the carriages of the fashionable drawn up before his store, so he planted his banner right in the heart of the most aristocratic section of the city. Nor did the blue-noses turn him down. In fact, the long line of carriages—Stern's realized dream—was the talk of the day. And Stern Brothers stayed right there and prospered for thirty-five years. The eyes of New York were on the Isaac Stern venture. The ice being broken, Best & Company followed Stern Brothers in 1880. Then came Bonwit Teller. Twenty-third Street was regarded as the highest-toned retail street in New York. None but the fashionable concerns obtained there.

According to Valentine's *Manual of Old New York*, there were "exciting arrangements of the departments" in Stern's Twenty-third Street store. "Goods were displayed to great advantage and altogether the store presented an inviting appearance to the public. For many years, Stern Brothers in Twenty-third Street was the Mecca for thousands of the most opulent buyers in New York."

Stern's next pioneering venture was its store built on Fifth Avenue and Forty-second Street near the New York Public Library, which had opened its doors two years before in 1911. This site is practically the geographical center of the city, and the "Great Department Store Opposite Bryant Park" prospered here for fifty-six years. It continued to cater to the "carriage trade" until about 1917, when World War I brought an end to the importation of luxuries upon which so much of its business depended and it changed its merchandise policy to become a medium- to better-priced store.

Stern Brothers passed from Stern family hands in 1925 when Benjamin, the one surviving brother, retired and a banking syndicate obtained control of the firm, shares of common stock publicly offered for the first time. Over the next decade Stern's became noted for its promotions and earned the title of "the show business store" because of the close to a hundred celebrities that appeared annually at its fashion shows and other special events. Stern's became a member of the Allied Department Store chain in 1951 and under the aegis of Allied began opening suburban shopping center stores in New Jersey. During the 1960s, the Stern's Forty-second Street store experienced problems similar to many urban area department stores throughout the country. This led to a bold decision to close the New York store early in 1969 and concentrate Stern's growth in the New Jersey market, where the store now has four branches.

1867

"The Greatest Store in the Greatest State"

JOSKE'S—*San Antonio, Texas*

German merchant Julius Joske came to San Antonio on his first visit to America and opened a small store on Main Plaza, later returning to Berlin for his family. The J. Joske & Sons store prospered and made several moves to larger quarters before settling at the site of the present downtown store in 1888. Expanded and renovated many times over the years, this grand emporium has traditionally been called Joske's Big Store—and billed as "the biggest store in the biggest state" until Alaska was admitted to the union and it became "the greatest store in the greatest state." It is probably the only department store built directly next to a church—St. Joseph's—which it still surrounds today.

Julius Joske and his son Alexander after him were great innovators, promotors, and public relations geniuses. Joske's, for example, was the first store in the Southwest to eliminate the five-cent nickel as the lowest standard of value, substituting copper pennies that Texans had traditionally scorned. But the store pointed out that customers had been taken advantage of under the old Texas rule of trade—where two items for 12¢ each sold for 25¢—and convinced them that they were saving money at Joske's.

Oddly enough, big sales at Joske's in the early days were often called "slaughter sales," a term apparently peculiar to this one store. The Big Store was once advertised with a three-thousand-candle power searchlight on its roof. It also had what has been described as "the world's greatest electric sign," a thoroughly Texan 50-foot × 50-foot, six-ton contraption dismantled in 1938.

Incandescent lights operated by a 7-foot flasher showed a cowboy on horseback galloping after a running steer. The cowboy twirled his lariat over his head and lassoed the steer's horns. The steer reared on his haunches and was jerked over on his back. Then everything was dark and quiet for a moment until the action began again. All the while the words "Joske's the Big Store" flashed across the top of the sign and an 8-foot Texas star radiated blue and green lights, the border of the picture all flashing and whirling circles changing colors at each reversal.

A few years after Alexander Joske died in 1925, his store was purchased by Hahn Department Stores and it is now a member of the Allied Stores Corporation department store chain that evolved from Hahn. Today Joske's has 11 stores in Texas with a total selling area of almost 2.2 million square feet and combined annual sales of over $150 million.

1868

STRAWBRIDGE & CLOTHIER—*Philadelphia, Pennsylvania*

(See Chapter 4)

1869

E. C. ALLEN COMPANY—*Augusta, Maine*

(See Chapter 7)

1870

For Love and Money

HERP'S—*Grand Rapids, Michigan*

Herpolsheimer's, or Herp's as it is called today, was founded in Grand Rapids because one of the store's founders was courting his future wife in that city. Before the Civil War, Hoosiers William G.

Herpolsheimer and Carl G.A. Voight had planned to open a dry goods store in Indiana, but had to cancel their plans when Herpolsheimer was drafted into the Union Army. After the war, the two men resumed their planning, but had to choose another location because Voight's fiancée lived in Grand Rapids. Herpolsheimer, a former clerk, managed the Voight-Herpolsheimer Dry Goods Company, while Voight managed a milling company the two men had also founded in Grand Rapids, but after a fire that burned the store to the ground in 1902, the two partners went their separate ways, Herpolsheimer taking the store and Voight the milling company.

William Herpolsheimer and his son Henry built the dry goods shop into a true department store well before World War I, and Henry's son Arthur expanded it more during the prosperous 1920s. But in 1928 the Herpolsheimer family sold out to Hahn Department Stores, Inc., a chain that became the powerful Allied Stores Corporation seven years later. Herp's has continued to grow and prosper in Grand Rapids, a city of over half a million. Its modern four-story store has the distinctive street address "Number One Division." and a unique feature of the store is the "Hot Lines" on each floor that connect customers directly with the president's office.

1871

The Grand Depot

KAUFMANN'S—*Pittsburgh, Pennsylvania*

Hawking sundries from door to door in Pittsburgh, Jacob and Isaac Kaufmann, immigrant brothers from Germany, managed to save $1,500, enough to open a 17-foot × 34-foot merchant tailor shop at 1916 Carson Street on Pittsburgh's South Side. Kaufmann's still prides itself on being the greatest "Store for Men," even though it is a department store, and it is interesting to note that this first shop was intended primarily to serve the industrialists of the nearby Jones & Laughlin Steel Corporation, supplying these affluent businessmen with their morning coats and stiff shirt collars. Astounding first year sales of $21,585 enabled the owners to begin a series of moves to larger quarters that culminated in the big store they opened fifteen years later in an ornate building at the corner of Fifth Avenue and Smithfield. This store came to be known as the Grand Depot when between 1891 and 1913 Kaufmann's acquired the remainder of the block on both streets. The fashionable emporium, the first to use electric lights in the city, had a tower topped by a statue of the Goddess of Liberty holding aloft a flaming torch lighted by natural gas, and a huge four-faced clock, still adorning Kaufmann's, that bears the legend, "Meet me under the clock."

The Grand Depot was the first Kaufmann's store that offered women's ready-to-wear—the store had dealt exclusively in men's clothing before this—and to promote the "Ladies Day" in 1886 on which it added this line the store unrolled a red velvet carpet to welcome new customers. By this time two more Kaufmann brothers, Morris and Henry, had emigrated from Germany to become partners in the family concern. It was Morris's son Edgar who began a new era for the store when he became president in the 1920s. Pittsburgh's "Merchant Prince" came to the store with worldwide retailing experience, having worked in stores ranging from Marshall Field in Chicago to Paris's Galleries La Fayette and Hamburg's Karlstadt Department Stores. E.J., as he was known, established buying offices in 27 foreign cities, and under him Kaufmann's was completely renovated in 1930. At this time Boardman Robinson was commissioned to do his distinguished murals depicting the history of commerce and these, on the main floor, along with the angled counters and black marble pillars throughout the store, became the talk of the industry. E.J. himself presided over Kaufmann's in an office that was a monastery taproom brought intact from Europe. Another noted store feature was the beautiful Vendome Shops on the top floor, which sold paintings and other *objets d'art.*

In 1946 Pittsburgh's largest store became a member of the May Company department store chain. Kaufmann's first branch store opened in Monroeville, Pennsylvania, in 1961 and since then six more branches have been established throughout the state. Another important building program was launched in 1952, resulting in an addition to the main store downtown that substantially increased the frontage on Fifth Avenue. This expansion was made possible by the purchase of the Carnegie-Illinois Building, which was razed to erect the new modern building now attached to the old store. Kaufmann's downtown and its branches now occupy over 1.8 million square feet of space, employing six thousand people, and do an annual business exceeding $200 million—quite a difference from the little 17-foot × 34-foot shop that had sales of $21,585 its first year.

1872

MONTGOMERY WARD & COMPANY—*Chicago, Illinois*

(See Chapter 7)

1872

BLOOMINGDALE'S—*New York, New York*

(See Chapter 4)

1872

"An Elegant Mart of Fashion"

L. S. AYRES—*Indianapolis, Indiana*

N. R. Smith & Company's Trade Palace on Washington Street was in the days of bustles and bombazine, surreys and broughams, called "the most imposing structure in Indianapolis," an "elegant mart of fashion." Lyman S. Ayres, a successful German New York merchant who had begun as a wagon peddler, must have jumped at the chance when Mr. Smith offered to let him buy a controlling interest in the store and come to the Midwest to run it. In any event, Ayres immersed himself in the new business, and within two years he took over complete management of the Trade Palace and moved it across the street to an even bigger building; it became L. S. Ayres and Company. Today the Ayres's flagship store at this location covers half a city block and leads 13 up-to-date Ayres branch department stores, which generate more than $250 million in sales every year and make Ayres fifteenth in a list of America's one hundred top-volume stores. Among Ayres branches is the John Bressmer Company, a 120-year-old Springfield, Illinois, department store that it acquired in 1958.

In the early days L. S. Ayres pioneered in many areas. It claims to have been the first department store to install electric lighting in 1876, and was one of the first stores to use the telephone in its business. The store's delivery fleet was motorized in 1906 and by 1912 consisted of seven electric automobiles with a maximum speed of 20 miles an hour. Ayres was one of the founders of the innovative Retail Research Association in 1916 and a charter member of the Associated Merchandising Corporation buying group that grew from it two years later (see Chapter 8).

Once affectionately called "the old dowager of Washington Street," L. S. Ayres is now a modern store in every respect, though an Indiana institution with strong ties to the past. Members of the Ayres family remained in operational control of the firm until it was acquired by the Associated Dry Goods Corporation in 1972. Perhaps the store's most distinctive feature is the great bronze Ayres Clock, an Indianapolis landmark that hangs on the corner of its building at Meridian and Washington streets. The 10,000-pound clock, with illuminated dials 8 feet in diameter, facing in every direction, is seen by over half a million people every week.

Ayres, which has sales of about $90 million a year, has always been famous for its promotions and good works. Back in 1939 it initiated "Ayres' Audichron," an automatic time-of-day telephone service that is now used by Indianapolis people over a million times a month. Just this year the firm opened Christmas Angel Shops in all its stores. The shops sell Christmas cards, seals, and tree ornaments made by mentally retarded adults and designed by sheltered children, all profits going to the Indiana Association for Retarded Children.

1873

"The Busiest Store on the Busiest Corner of the Busiest Street in the West"

JOSLINS—*Denver, Colorado*

In the Gay Nineties, J. C. Penney clerked at Joslins before moving on to found his own retailing empire, and the elegant store's rich clientele included such celebrities as Molly Brown, the colorful mining heiress, and Baby Doe Tabor, who must have been fond of the "filmy French creations" Joslins was famous for. The store was founded by John Jay Joslin, a prosperous thirty-three-year-old merchant from Vermont, who decided to move West while visiting his brother in Denver and purchased the New York Dry Goods Store, a two-story building on the corner of Larimer and Fifteenth street, renaming it the Joslin Dry Goods Company. This was three years before Colorado statehood came, a time when Denver was a free-wheeling gambling and dance-hall oasis for miners who emerged from the silver-rich Colorado mountains with fortunes in their saddle packs. The shrewd Joslin, as did David May, sold the big-spending miners the luxurious things they wanted, and his store soon outgrew its original site. By 1887 Joslin had erected what is the nucleus of the present store, a grand emporium with plate-glass display windows fronting the entire building, which was the most elegant Denver had ever seen.

J. J. Joslin remained as head of the store when he sold it to the H. B. Claflin chain in 1910, and he continued as its president under Mercantile Stores, which bought Joslins when Claflin failed four years later. The famed Denver climate must have helped him as much as it did J. C. Penney, for he too was one of the grand old men of retailing, dying a year after he retired in 1925, aged ninety-six.

Joslins's first branch opened at Denver's Merchant's Park Shopping Plaza in 1944. In 1965 all its stores became officially known as Joslins, without an apostrophe. Today, with stores in downtown Denver, Pueblo (the old Crew Beggs store, dating back to 1885), Englewood, Boulder, Aurora, and Lakewood, Joslins now boasts that it serves all the residents of the Colorado front range. Old J. J.

Joslin called his store "the busiest store on the busiest corner of the busiest street of the busiest city in the West!" and his vision may yet be realized.

1874

A Dream Come True

J. B. WHITE—*Augusta, Georgia*

At the age of sixteen James Bryce White ran away from his home in Ireland to seek his fortune in New York City, where for sure, he knew, the Yankee streets were paved with gold. After working a short time as a cash boy in a dry goods store, he headed for Augusta, Georgia, then a winter resort for rich New Yorkers, and worked in a small department store for six years, saving enough money to go into business for himself with two partners in 1874. After another year he bought out his partners and concentrated on establishing both a wholesale and retail business. A creative merchandiser who ran an elite store staffed with formally attired floorwalkers, White prospered beyond even his boyhood dreams. After his store burned to the ground in 1899, he erected a larger building at 732 Broad Street, which remained in use until 1924, when the present flagship store was erected at 932 Broad.

James White became a multimillionaire in 1904 when he sold out to the Claflin company chain. The rags-to-riches process had taken thirty years, but proved that at least the streets of Augusta were paved with gold. When Claflin's failed in 1914 the Mercantile Stores chain purchased J. B. White. Under Mercantile the store's first branch was opened in 1930 at Aiken, South Carolina. Additionally, there are now branches in Augusta's National Hills Shopping Center, and in Richland Mall and Dutch Square Mall in Columbia, South Carolina.

Right: Hutzler's Palace Building, built in 1888, stands almost unchanged next to today's Hutzler's ninety years later.

Below: The first Carson Pirie Scott store opened in this building in Amboy, Illinois in 1854.

The way a well-groomed store used to look—Younker's De Moines' store back in the early 1900s.

Construction of the downtown Washington Hecht Company.

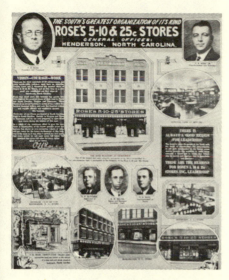

Left: Rose's Stores were a growing variety store chain in the 1930s.

Below: Crowley, Milner's massive downtown Detroit store, scheduled to crumble under the wrecker's ball in June 1978.

Left: Buffums' first store on Pine Avenue in Long Beach, built in 1925.

Dayton's flagship store in downtown Minneapolis.

Broadway's first downtown store, the biggest store west of the Mississippi when built in 1913, closed sixty years later in 1973.

The Sanger Brothers store as it looked on Elm Street in downtown Dallas in 1895.

The second Liberty House to be built on the mainland in 1972 in Hayward, California. This three-level store has 180,000 square feet of floor space.

The interior of G. Fox's downtown Hartford, Connecticut, store.

1875

"The Largest Small-Town Store in the State"
WYCKOFF'S—*Stroudsburg, Pennsylvania*

The New York Store—one of many at the time named after great cities like New York or Boston—was founded by Amzi Wyckoff, the son of a peddler, and local merchants James Cooke and William Bell. Actually no more than an 18 foot × 25 foot room located in his father's house, the little store on Main Street prospered under Wyckoff's "Small Profit and Quick Sale" policy, which he advertised widely. Wyckoff took over the store completely in 1892, after Bell died and Cooke retired. By the time he himself died twenty years later, the store occupied the whole family house and included another building as well, Amzi's son succeeding him and erecting most of the buildings on the site of the present store.

Wyckoff's has always had a great sense of showmanship. Store-sponsored excursions have attracted thousands of people over the years—eleven thousand, in fact, visited the 1939 World's Fair on Wyckoff excursions. The store has brought Santa Claus to town by train, plane, and "autogyro," and holds promotions like doll parties, art exhibits, and an annual childrens' Halloween parade. In 1933 the firm became an authorized selling agent for Sears, Roebuck and Company, a mutually profitable partnership. Today Wyckoff's is proud to call itself "the largest small-town store in the state."

1875

Chicago's First Department Store
THE FAIR—*Chicago, Illinois*

"Everything for Everybody under One Roof," E. J. Lehmann advertised, when he opened his first store on State Street and Adams, words that could have been the credo for department stores in general. Lehmann was one of those merchants with great flair and panache who contributed significantly to the development of the American department store, in contrast to more sedate types like John Wanamaker, who did just as much in their own, quieter way.

Lehmann came to America from Germany as a youngster and worked as a bellboy and peddler, among other jobs, before he founded The Fair, which concentrated on cheap notions and houseware a full four years before Frank Woolworth's first store. His store overflowed out into the street, with penny, nickel, and dime goods heaped on stands by the sidewalk, but Lehmann sold dry goods and apparel almost from the start, too, and was thus probably the first Chicago store that resembled a full-line department store. The seemingly tireless merchant bought up neighboring stores, and rebuilt his own so that within four years The Fair was four times its original size. A staunch believer in advertising, he placed the first full-page ad in a Chicago newspaper. Unable to delegate authority, Lehmann was involved in the smallest details of store operations, from greeting customers at the door to supervising wrapping of purchases, and the stress finally proved too much for him. A nervous breakdown in 1890 forced him to retire, and he died ten years later when only fifty-one years old; his son E. J. Lehmann, Jr. assumed control of the business.

The Fair, incidentally, is one of the few department stores in America that has belonged to two great chains. First, S. S. Kresge (now K mart) acquired a controlling interest in the store and made it a part of its great five-and-ten empire. It was under Kresge that The Fair, by then an 11-story store a block long on its original site, opened its first branch in suburban Oak Park in 1929. In 1957 Montgomery Ward bought The Fair Company and its three branches, and it remains under Ward's control today.

1875

An Old Family Business

HIMELHOCH BROTHERS & COMPANY—
Detroit, Michigan

After emigrating to America from Latvia as a young man, Wolf Himelhoch pack-peddled merchandise throughout the East until he reached Caro, Michigan, in what is called the Thumb district of the state. There the locals treated him so kindly that he decided to settle down with his wife and eight children and build a small clothing store. The first shop was little more than "a hole in the wall," according to one contemporary, and when the Himelhochs spotted prospective customers in the street they had to hurry outside, marshal all their charm, and try to lure them inside. They must have been convincing, because the "hole in the wall" soon became a sizable shop at the site of the present Gamble's store in Caro. This store was doing a booming business in 1907 when Wolf sold it and moved to Detroit, where he opened another store with some financial backing from Chicago's Marshall Field.

Wolf Himelhoch's first Detroit store stood on what is now the site of the J. L. Hudson store in Woodward Avenue. His sons Zella, Herman, and Moses were partners, but it was the patriarch who made all important decisions and like so many merchants of the day personally greeted his customers each morning dressed to the nines in frock coat and stiff collar. The next great presence in the family business was to be Wolf's youngest son, Israel, who earned his degree at Harvard Law School and practiced law for a time before coming to Himelhoch's. Israel worked with the great William Travers Jerome on the famous Harry K. Thaw murder case, and when Thaw escaped from prison, he and Jerome brought in their client before he crossed the Canadian border. Unfortunately, the legal life wasn't always so exciting; in fact, one story has it that Israel decided to return to the fold one day when his boss, looking around at all his legal help, commented: "I feel like I am only a floorwalker in a great legal department store." More likely, Israel returned because his brother needed him, but, in any event, he remained the real force in the family business from the early 1920s until his death in 1973.

One of the first downtown Detroit stores to venture out into the suburbs, Himelhoch's (pronounced Himelhoke's, with the hard German sound at the end) now has eight branches. Though it is strictly speaking a woman's specialty chain that carries a line of men's wear as well, it is certainly one of the grand old family-operated stores in the country. Headed by a third-generation Himelhoch, Israel's youngest son, Charles, it is still completely family owned and Charles's son and daughter have already worked in the store, indicating possible fourth-generation leadership. Charles Himelhoch is guardedly optimistic about the downtown operation. The shopping area, which was built up in the 1920s to rival New York's Fifth Avenue, has greatly deteriorated in recent years, as have so many urban shopping areas across the country. "I don't see any sudden miracles taking place downtown," Himelhoch says. "It took many years for Detroit to deteriorate and it will take many years to improve ... but just as blight can spread, improvements also can spread." The downtown store, like all the others, carries merchandise in the medium- to upper-price range, but is the best Himelhoch's for bargain hunters, as it is a central clearing point for marked-down items from all the stores. Himelhoch's new Fairlane store in Dearborn, Michigan, is in keeping with a newer trend in retailing. Featuring a greenhouse-type glass front, simulated skylights, and lots of greenery, it was designed to be completely flexible, making it possible to expand or contract any department at any time, even the fitting rooms being portable.

1876

I. MAGNIN—*San Francisco, California*

(See Chapter 5)

1876

Old-Fashioned Bargains

BRAGER-GUTMAN'S—*Baltimore, Maryland*

Brager-Gutman's is an old-fashioned department store in the sense that it hasn't forsaken bargains; it still has a bargain basement, in fact, and even offers a modern version of its old "four-cent table" of notions—an inflationary "bargain table" offering items for ten cents or three for twenty-nine cents. Brager-Gutman's has always featured value-priced "more-for-your-money" merchandise, and the firm was the first store in Baltimore to run $1 Day Sales. During such sales, back in the early 1900s, cash sped through the pneumatic tube system to the counting room so fast that it had to be stuffed in wastebaskets. The store also introduced Baltimore to the traditional George Washington Birthday Sale.

Brager-Gutman's was founded over a century ago by Julius Gutman, a German immigrant, who formed a partnership with Aaron Brylawski to open a "silk, laces and fancy goods business" in a leased house at 122 West Lexington Avenue. This cash-only business—credit installment selling wasn't instituted until 1955—did well, and Gutman eventually bought out his partner, enlarging the store all the while. On his death in 1921, his son took over the reins and seven years later built the present-day store at Lexington Mall. Things were tough for a while during the depression, when the store could only buy merchandise COD, but the real crisis came in the late 1950s, after middle-class flight to the suburbs brought on the deterioration of the downtown retail district, a familiar story all over America. Gutman's made a mistake in not expanding to the suburbs, but recouped its position to a large extent by merging in 1959 with Brager-Eisenberg, Brager having been a rival since its founding in 1883 (in 1929 it had merged with Eisenberg). Brager closed its store at Eutaw and Saratoga and moved its merchandise to Gutman's, the new store called Brager-Gutman.

The Brager family gained control of the new company by acquiring the capital stock of Brager-Gutman, but sold it to the Scranton Corporation in 1968 for $1.24 million when it became apparent that young members of the family had no interest in continuing in the business. In 1974 the company was sold to H.R.T. Limited, an Hawaiian-based corporation, but it still remains the bargain department store it has always been. "The day we stop going bargains," says one executive, "that's the day people won't come in any more."

1876

"Above All No Bargaining"

POMEROY'S—*Reading, Pennsylvania*

The 20-foot × 100-foot Globe, which was the original Pomeroy's, wasn't much of a store, but it was all the three ambitious young clerks from Connecticut who opened it could afford. George Pomeroy, Josiah Dives, and James Stewart had only invested a thousand dollars, all the money they had between them, but they believed their three-point program of "same price to all; guarantees always honored; and above all no bargaining" would attract many customers in a day when haggling was the rule and cheating too often wasn't the exception in stores.

The policy worked, and within two years the Globe had moved to larger quarters and opened a branch store in Harrisburg. Business continued to grow rapidly, two more branches were established, and by 1888 Pomeroy and Dives (Stewart had since retired) took over the entire five floors of their main store building in Reading. During the next fifteen years, a six-story annex was added, adjacent property was purchased and a "seven-story skyscraper," Reading's first, was erected on the city's main downtown corner. Pomeroy and Dives were innovative when it came to employee benefits, establishing one of the first low-cost employee group insurance plans in 1903. After a partnership of forty-four years, Josiah Dives died in 1922 and George Pomeroy became the sole owner of the store, its name changed to Pomeroy's at the time. In 1932 Pomeroy's was purchased by the giant Allied Stores chain, and today the firm has 10 branches in eastern Pennsylvania and western New Jersey doing over $125 million in sales.

1877

MAY DEPARTMENT STORES—*St. Louis, Missouri*

(See Chapter 4)

1877

BUTLER BROTHERS—*Boston, Massachusetts*

(See Chapter 7)

1877

A Pioneer Promoter

MABLEY & CAREW—*Cincinnati, Ohio*

He sponsored pie-eating contests and foot-races, stabled horses in his store show windows and raffled them off, gave free gifts for every four purchases, painted his store's name on the sides of barns, fences, and hillsides. One of the most colorful promoters in merchandising history, Christopher R. Mabley began as a pioneer in the men's ready-made clothes field, which became big business only after manufacturers proved that mass production of clothing was practical by producing uniforms for Union soldiers during the Civil War. Mabley usually went into partnership with promising young merchants wherever the prospects seemed good, and he often had several clothing stores flourishing at once—at one time, in fact, he was a partner of Joseph Lowthian Hudson, who went on to found the great J. L. Hudson department store in Detroit.

Once a store was on its feet, Mabley generally went off to Europe on vacation, for he liked the good life better than business life. Probably his empire would have been greater if he hadn't been such a *bon vivant*—at one time he had stores in 10 cities—but he was one of the wealthiest and best-known merchants of his day. Born in Cornwall, England, Mabley had moved to Canada with his family when he was a boy of thirteen and worked in his father's clothing store there for five years. After opening his first store in London, Ontario, he moved on to the United States, where he started stores in Milwaukee and several Michigan towns. By 1870 he was in Detroit operating a store under what he called the "one price rule." There he became "the pioneer clothier of the West" with his slogan "Our Rule of Three: One Price—One Principle—One Profit." Mabley used the most modern business methods of his day, especially excelling in advertising, and by 1885, the year of his death, he had stores in Detroit, Baltimore, Louisville, Cleveland, Cincinnati, Pontiac, and Jackson, Michigan, and several other cities. Several of these, including the Detroit store, were full-line department stores by this time, as his ads clearly show.

Mabley and Company failed in 1896, "went to the wall," as a Detroit newspaper put it, with a total indebtedness of about $400,000. But the Cincinnati store, which passed entirely into the hands of partner Joseph Carew on Mabley's death, was not affected. Mabley and Carew, according to an old story in the *Cincinnati Times Star*, was founded wholly by accident. As tradition has it:

It was only through the fact that Mr. Carew and his old partner C. R. Mabley, passing through Cincinnati from Detroit to the South, missed their train connections here that the business of the Mabley & Carew

Company was established in Cincinnati. Mr. Mabley and his brilliant young business lieutenant, Mr. Carew, started from Detroit on a business trip to Memphis, Tennessee, in 1877. Missing their train connection at Cincinnati they walked around town and reached Fountain Square. At No. 66 Fifth Street, the corner of the alley between Vine and Walnut Streets, Mr. Carew saw a "For Rent" sign. Immediately he grasped the idea that here was a splendid business opportunity.

From the beginning Carew had charge of the Cincinnati store— in fact, Mabley never visited the city again. Joseph Carew was a Canadian of Irish descent who had emigrated to the United States in 1869 shortly after his twenty-first birthday to work in Mabley's Detroit store, where he quickly became the merchant's right-hand man. Using all of Mabley's advertising and promotional techniques, plus many of his own, he made the Cincinnati store one of the leaders in the city. Carew established a Mabley & Carew Arbor Day custom that lasted for fifty years until the 1940s, in which time over 5 million trees were donated to Cincinnati school children to be planted. In the early 1890s he became the first merchant to give elaborate Christmas pantomime performances for children, building a balcony on the store for showings of Bluebeard, Little Red Riding Hood, and other favorite stories. Speaking of these holiday pantomimes, one venerable Cincinnatian recalled, "I doubt very much if the children of the present day have such a Christmas treat as the Mabley Pantomimes on Fountain Square. How we would stand for hours laughing away the time and then going home to dream of the Sleeping Beauty!"

The old store—on West Fifth Street was bulging at the seams when Carew built a grand emporium on the site in 1887. Several sources described this new building, which was illuminated every night with ten thousand electric lights on its façade, as having "the greatest electrical illumination on any mercantile building in the world." It served as Mabley & Carew's home long past Mr. Carew's death in 1914—until 1930, when another store was built nearby. After the Allied Stores Corporation chain purchased the Mabley & Carew Company in 1962, the store moved to another location on the corner of Fifth and Vine, where it stands today still overlooking Fountain Square. (See also J. L. Hudson, Chapter 4.)

1878

From Full-Line to Specialty Store

LEOPOLD ADLER COMPANY—*Savannah, Georgia*

"Savannah born, Savannah owned, Savannah operated," has been Adler's slogan for almost a century now. Founded by Leopold Adler and operated today by his son and grandson, Sam Adler and Sam Adler, Jr., this family firm illustrates the trend toward specialization that is becoming increasingly popular among stores today. Adler's grew into a full-line department store that eventually operated in a massive building on the corner of Bull and Broughton streets, Savannah's main downtown shopping district. After the entire store burned to the ground in a tragic 1958 fire, business was conducted in a variety of temporary locations for about a year and a half. Adler's then reopened their business in the suburban Victory Drive Shopping Plaza, where it eliminated several departments previously carried—including men's wear, piece goods, hoseware, glassware, and china. Ten years later the store moved again, to the enclosed Oglethorpe Mall in the southern section of the city, where it built a modern store of over 25,000 square feet. Adler's dropped children's wear, toys, and linens at that time and became strictly a ladies' specialty shop.

1879

From Lilliputian to Giant

BEST & COMPANY—*New York, New York*

The Lilliputian Bazaar, later a department for infants in Best's, was the store's original name when it was founded on Sixth Avenue and Twelfth Street by Albert Best and James A. Smith a century ago. The store's trademark was a hand of Gulliver on which children were playing, but over the years the little shop moved northward with the wisest of New York merchants and expanded its line to include clothes for children of all ages. After James Smith retired, selling his interest in the business to Thomas Ball, and Albert Best died, the store was incorporated under the name Best & Company, which seemed infinitely better to its principals than Smith & Company or Ball & Company. By 1924 the last of the Ball family put his shares on the market and Best & Company went public.

Colorful Philip LeBoutillier, president of Best's for many years, developed the store to its fullest potential. Not long after he came on the scene in 1917 LeBoutillier decided that his department buyers should have a free hand in selecting styles from manufacturers instead of being responsible to a merchandise manager, as was the case in most stores. He followed up by establishing a bonus system for buyers as an impetus to sales. In 1928 LeBoutillier enlarged Best's main store on Fifth Avenue and Thirty-fifth Street, and the following year he established the first of Best's branches in Garden City, New York. He was also responsible for Best's move to its location on Fifth Avenue at Fifty-first Street, where it remained one of the city's finest stores, specializing in women's clothes from cradle to adulthood, until it went out of business in the 1960s.

1879

F. W. WOOLWORTH COMPANY—*Lancaster, Pennsylvania*

(See Chapter 4)

1879

The Matriarch of Fargo Stores

DE LENDREICIE'S—*Fargo, North Dakota*

Onisime de Lendreicie may be the only French-Canadian ever to found an American department store. He and his partner Charles Chiniquy originally named their store The Chicago Dry Goods House, locating it in a fine two-story brick building on Front Street. The 554 pioneer women of a town then part of the Dakota Territory were dazzled by what the local newspaper called "an elegant store with everything a lady could want . . . the finest store in North Dakota," and its proprietors were amazed when these women from sod and log cabins bought elegant silks and satins, imported velvets from Scotland and England—an array of luxurious merchandise from all over the world that they had never seen before. When Chiniquy left the firm, Eugene de Lendreicie joined his brother, and the two began an enterprising delivery service, shipping goods by stage to Grand Forks, by railroad to Bismarck, and by steamboat as far as Winnipeg in Manitoba. By 1893 business was so good that a new store called de Lendreicie's Mammoth Department Store was built downtown, this store becoming even larger a few years later when three more stories were added to the original two floors.

After the de Lendreicie brothers retired in 1920, members of the family ran the O. J. de Lendreicie Department Store until the Mercantile Stores chain purchased it in 1955. In 1972 the historic downtown store was closed and a new luxurious de Lendreicie's was opened in the West Acres Shopping Center. The store still serves the 21 prosperous farming counties in North Dakota and Minnesota that have historically used Fargo as their shopping city. On the opening of the new store, the *Fargo Moorhead Forum* commented: "In its sprightly young garb at West Acres, the matriarch of local department stores has changed her face, her style, and her way of life—with the same respected service left as a reminder of the fresh upstart's breeding."

1880

A Chain of Family Stores

L. S. GOOD & COMPANY—*Wheeling, West Virginia*

L. S. Good, a peddler who had emigrated to America from a town on the German-Swiss border, founded this Wheeling store in 1880. It remained a single family-owned store, operated by the founder, his sons, and finally his grandsons for eighty-two years, until 1962 when the company began to expand. Still controlled by the Good family, which owns 74 percent of the firm's stock, and operated by the founder's grandsons Lawrence and Sidney Good, the store has in a little over a decade grown from one store with sales of about $1.5 million to a national department store chain with sales in the $100 million range. Good's expansion began when the Good brothers noticed that an extensive renovation of their Wheeling store in 1962 increased business tremendously. They decided to embark upon an expansion plan where they would purchase and renovate family-owned department stores with sales of from $5 to $25 million, stores that the large department store chains considered too small to acquire. Often these were stores where there were no young family members moving up to perpetuate the name, and they were usually stores whose growth was limited because they were unable to finance expansion. In any case, the plan worked, and Good's is now a prosperous "family store chain," or "federation" as the brothers like to call it, that includes well-known local stores such as Fowler's of Binghamton, New York; Gable's, Altoona, Pennsylvania; The Hub, Steubenville, Ohio; Smith-Bridgman, Flint, Michigan; Christians, Owosso, Michigan; Robinson's, Battle Creek, Michigan; Knapp's, Lansing, Michigan; and Kann's, Washington, D.C.

1880

"The Finest Small City Department Store in America"

PECK'S—*Lewiston, Maine*

The first day's receipts were only thirty-seven cents for one pair of stockings, but Peck's founder Bradford Peck, a former cash boy at Boston's Jordan Marsh, believed better times would come. Peck had started retailing when a boy of twelve and attended night school while working himself up to a traveling salesman for an importing company. Not a man to be easily discouraged, he worked tirelessly to improve his store and within a few years was making enough from it to be able to buy out his partner, Edward Plummer. The store soon outgrew its location on Music Box Street and moved across the street to larger quarters, but even these premises didn't suffice, and in 1898 the present building on Main Street was constructed. Though this site was away from the main business district at the time and people predicted no store could last there— one local wag suggested that "the building could easily be converted to a barn"—Peck's succeeded in attracting shoppers and formed the nucleus for a new shopping center in town. Peck's was well known outside its trading area and *Collier's Magazine* once called it "the finest small city department store in America." In 1947 Boston's great Filene's purchased the store, Peck's being the only complete department store ever bought by Filene's and their only store allowed to retain its original name. Filene's sold Peck's to Alden's in 1963, and it became the property of Gamble-Skogmo a year later when that large chain bought Alden's.

1881

WILLIAM FILENE'S SONS COMPANY—*Boston, Massachusetts*

(See Chapter 4)

1881

THE J.L. HUDSON COMPANY—*Detroit, Michigan*

(See Chapter 4)

1882

SPIEGEL, INC.—*Chicago, Illinois*

(See Chapter 7)

1883

"Honest Goods from Top to Bottom"

WIEBOLDT STORES, INC.—*Chicago, Illinois*

Married just one week when they opened their little 10-foot × 25-foot store on Grand Avenue in Chicago, William Wieboldt and his wife lived in the back of the store building, which they rented for sixty-five dollars a month. Working by themselves because their budget allowed no help, the venturesome young couple managed to make a profit the first year, but they had to move twice before finding a really profitable location in 1887 at the corner of Paulina Street and Milwaukee Avenue. Eventually, they added a fourth floor to the three-story building housing their store, which had a 50-foot sign reading, "Honest Goods from Top to Bottom," and the figure of a gilded Lion about 3 feet high that stood facing the street on a platform above the entrance. The Wieboldts, like many merchants of the day, displayed merchandise on the sidewalks adjoining the store, not only to sell the goods but as a means of directing traffic inside. They also had a watchman whose main duty was to check baby carriages for customers while they were shopping, some customers checking their babies as well as the carriages.

When his wife retired from the business near the turn of the century, Wieboldt formed a partnership with local merchant Carl Hanson. A fire completely destroyed the Lion store soon after and the partners designed a four-story and basement building almost four times bigger than the one that had burned down. Various additions were made to the new building after its erection until it finally became the largest department store in the area. The business grew rapidly, and by 1912 there was a branch in the Lakeview area; this store expanded five years later to twice its size. During the 1920s and 1930s Wieboldt and his sons ran the stores and consistently plowed back their profits into the business. As a result, Wieboldt came out of the depression with seven stores serving Chicago's middle-income shoppers. The company, which has since gone public and is no longer controlled by the Wieboldt family, now has 13 stores located throughout Chicago and in four adjoining counties that had sales of over $160 million last year. Its largest store is on the corner of State and Madison, where along with the other grand emporiums it helps State Street retain its reputation as the "Great Street" of Chicago retailing.

1883

"Boston Service" in Los Angeles

J. W. ROBINSON COMPANY—*Los Angeles, California*

As hard as it is to imagine, Los Angeles had a population of only thirteen thousand when Joseph Winchester Robinson, arrived there from Massachusetts in 1882 to launch a new career as an orange grower. Robinson quickly decided, however, that the City of the Angels was a better place to start a dry goods store such as the one he had operated back home and, after returning East to buy stock, opened the Boston Dry Goods Store at Spring and Temple streets, where he rented a small shop for $125 a month.

The little store, featuring the "Boston service" that the rest of the country thought was the ultimate at the time, prospered beyond Robinson's expectations, and he soon had two clerks in help. After adding a wholesale operation on Temple Street, he moved his retail operation into larger quarters opposite the old City Hall in 1891 and five years later acquired a four-story building on South Broadway serviced by over one hundred employees. At this time the store's name was changed to the J. W. Robinson Company.

The spread of the railroads West, the discovery of oil in Bakersville, and the rise of the motion picture industry had made Los Angeles a wealthy community by the time J. W. Robinson opened its new store on Seventh Street between Grand and Hope in 1915. Robinson's continued to grow with the city and by 1934 had added another unit to the store, doubling its size, and completely modernized it. The store remained in family hands, under the son and then the grandson of the founder, until 1955, when it was purchased by the Associated Dry Goods Corporation chain. Robinson's was operated autonomously like the other stores in the group, and continued its branch development, which had begun in 1947 with a shop at Palm Springs. Today the store ranks thirty-second among American department stores, with $175 million in sales, topped in California only by Broadway-Hale, May, Macy's, Bullock's, and the Emporium.

1885

MILLER & RHOADS—*Richmond, Virginia*

(See Chapter 4)

1885

From $8.33 a Month to an Empire

J. B. IVEY & COMPANY—*Charlotte, North Carolina*

Joseph Benjamin Ivey, the founder of Ivey's, was the son of a circuit-riding Methodist preacher, who apprenticed him to the mercantile business after deciding that his weak eyesight, caused by a childhood attack of measles, wouldn't allow the reading and close work college demanded. Finding employment in a one-room country store at the age of seventeen, Joseph worked hard for the then common wage of $8.33 a month (employers generously made this a round $100 a year) and so impressed his boss that when, after some four years, he left the store for pastures promising more greenbacks, Captain Hoyle hired him back and made him a partner, changing the name of the store to Hoyle and Ivey. This 1885 general store in Belwood, North Carolina, was thus Ivey's first, and he increased business by such promotions as hiring a brass band, floating hot-air balloons over the store, and setting up a huge purple tent to accommodate the biggest crowd ever to attend a retail sale in town. But old Captain Hoyle was too conservative for him, rejecting most of his ideas, and in 1893 Joseph left Belwood and joined the Henrietta Mills store in Rutherford County, remaining there until 1900, when he opened his own store in Charlotte.

His new store, founded with capital of $3,000, half from his savings and half borrowed from his brother George, was in a poor location on North Tryon Street, too far from the central town square, and Ivey's sales the first day totaled only $33.18. Business didn't get better and not being a man to live with a mistake, J.B. moved within the first year to a prime location on West Trade Street. Over the next five years he worked fourteen hours a day, doing the store's buying, training the salespeople, keeping the books, and writing all the advertising. Assisted by manager David Ovens, a remarkable man who established the credit system at Ivey's in 1912 and in later years dictated his interesting autobiography to his secretary in five weeks, he made his store a great success. By 1924, when the present downtown store was built, Ivey's was a large urban department store in every modern sense of the term.

J. B. Ivey wasn't afraid of new ideas, or much of anything for that matter. Once he attended Daredevil Little Joe Weisenfeld's Riding School in Baltimore to learn how to ride a bicycle and upon "graduation" went home to open an agency for Columbia bicycles in a store he managed. When news of the great stock market crash came in 1929, he shut down his Charlotte store at twelve and took all the employees out for a picnic and an afternoon of golf.

Men like that don't jump out of windows and usually live to a ripe old age, so it is no surprise that when J. B. Ivey died in 1958 he was almost ninety-five, still another of the grand old men in the department store world. The founder's only son, George M. Ivey, who had joined the store in 1920 and was responsible for converting it to a corporation two years later, then headed the company until his death in 1968, aged seventy-two. His son, George M. Ivey, Jr., is now chairman of the board of one of the handful of large department stores in America still actively controlled by the founding family. At present there are 23 Ivey stores in North and South Carolina and Florida, with revenues of $90 million a year, the store ranking sixtieth in sales among the thousands of American department stores. That, counting Sunday closings, comes to average sales of over $290,000 a day, almost ten thousand times more than J. B. Ivey's opening day receipts of $33.18.

1886

SEARS, ROEBUCK AND COMPANY—*Chicago, Illinois*

(See Chapter 7)

1886

"The Store That Quality Built"

MYERS BROTHERS—*Springfield, Illinois*

Sam Rosenwald, a former peddler and father of the great Julius Rosenwald of Sears, sold his store for men and boys in Springfield to the Myers brothers in 1886. By 1900 Lewis and Albert had taken their younger brother Julius into the firm and had built a new store on the site where the downtown store stands today. This five-floor emporium served as Myers Brothers until it was destroyed by fire in 1924 and the present-day 10-story flagship store was built on the same site. The company is now owned and operated by second- and third-generation members of the Myers family and has eight quality stores in central Illinois, including one in Springfield's White Oaks Shopping Center. Albert Myers, the firm's president, was in the first group of American merchants to visit mainland China recently when it reopened trade agreements with the United States.

1886

"The Biggest, Best and Busiest Store in Montana"

HENNESSY'S—*Butte, Montana*

Three years before Montana entered the union, Canadian Daniel J. Hennessy, who had clerked in Butte's E. J. Bonner & Company dry goods store, opened a store of his own on Main Street. Hennessy catered to the pioneers in the rough frontier town, his "grand opening" advertised in the *Butte Daily Miner* featuring:

$50,000 worth of clothing, hats, boots, shoes, shirts, and underwear. Men's and boys' clothing. The best nailed boots and brogans. All goods warranted as sold. We have the best stock and will give the best prices in the city.

Three years later a fire completely destroyed the prospering D. J. Hennessy Mercantile Company, but, fortunately, insurance covered most of the $125,000 stock loss, and Hennessy's was soon back in business on a grander scale. By 1889 Daniel Hennessy had established a second department store called Copper City in Anaconda and was being called "the Merchant Prince of Montana and the Northwest," his influence so great in the community that he was elected to the first state senate of Montana when the territory became a state that same year. Two more branches were to be added and a new six-story store constructed in downtown Butte before the H. B. Claflin Company chain bought Hennessy's stock in the early 1900s.

When Mercantile Stores purchased Hennessy's after Claflin went bankrupt in 1914, it bought four of the company's stores, but by the 1920s Mercantile had sold all but the Butte flagship. Under Mercantile's direction this Hennessy's remains "the biggest, best, and busiest store in Montana," with modern branches in Helena, Montana's capital, and Billings, the largest city in the state.

1887

Duluth's Biggest Store

GLASS BLOCK—*Duluth, Minnesota*

The oldest and largest department store in Duluth, Minnesota, Glass Block, was founded by John Panton, a young Scotsman, and Joseph Watson, a Belfast Irishman, under the name Panton & Watson. This small store on the corner of First Avenue West and Superior Street outgrew its original space within eight months and the partners had to move lock, stock, and good will to a larger two-story building down the street. Finally, in 1893, the new "merchandising marvel" still in use today was erected at 128 West Superior Street. Consisting of two floors above street level and two floors below, the store was truly a marvel for its day, with its own electric power plant, an electrically driven cash carrier cable system to transport sales slips and money from various departments to a central cashier, twelve big arc lights on every floor, and stock valued at over $300,000.

William White joined Panton after Joseph Watson retired in 1896, the new partnership prospering like the original one and three new floors added to the store. In 1911 the partners sold out to the F. A. Patrick Company of Duluth, which changed the store's name to the Glass Block Store Company. The Mercantile Store Company acquired Glass Block in 1944. Mercantile has extensively remodelled the downtown store since then and opened a modern branch in Duluth's Miller Hill Shopping Center just a few miles away.

1887

From Wigwam to Millionaire

THE JONES STORE COMPANY—*Kansas City, Missouri*

A pioneer from birth—he was born in an Ottawa Indian wigwam in the Kansas Territory—J. Logan Jones was by temperament a wanderer who didn't linger long in one place when opportunities seemed better elsewhere. He only lasted three years in Stafford, Kansas, where he and his wife opened a little general store called the Cyclone in 1887. Taking his profits, Jones moved his family and store to Kansas City, Kansas, where he stayed in business five years before deciding that the other side of the river looked greener and making his final move to Kansas City, Missouri. There the Jones Dry Goods Company opened for business in a seven-story building complete with fancy elevators. Jones proved an enterprising merchant who made his store a local institution, vigorously participating in civic affairs and introducing such innovations as a baby nursery where customers could leave their children. Not a man to be intimidated by bad luck, he had a new store erected little more than a year after the old one burned to the ground during a city carnival in 1899.

The Jones Store Company, which made its founder a millionaire, had a large mail-order business and was big enough to be represented by buying offices in New York, London, Paris, and Berlin before the stock market crash of 1907. The store then had to be sold to the H. B. Claflin chain, which failed itself seven years later, the Jones Store Company passing into the hands of Mercantile Stores. Since then the seven buildings constituting the downtown store have been extensively remodeled and expanded, all but two being completely rebuilt, and branches have been established in Blue Ridge, Missouri; Overland Park, Kansas; and Prairie Village, Kansas. Jones, which does over $70 million in sales a year, is recognized as the fashion leader in the vast area it serves. Future stores are being planned for the greater Kansas City area, "the Gateway to the Southwest," which has the largest livestock exchange and the second largest grain milling industry in America.

1888

A *Pioneer Department Store*

PEOPLES—*Tacoma, Washington*

Tacoma's streets were still unpaved and there were only a few hitching posts in front of the store in 1888, when the parent company of Garretson, Woodruff and Pratt opened The Peoples Store on Pacific Avenue. But, according to a local newspaper, "The crowd came in and bought so heavily that the shelves were pretty near cleaned." The store grew along with Tacoma and in 1896 moved to larger quarters on the corner of Eleventh and Pacific Avenue, where it still does business today. It offered a wide and sophisticated selection of goods, ranging from silks and satins to silverware, perfumes, and art works, not to mention a complete line of dry goods and home furnishings, and was a true department store—the largest one in the state of Washington at the time.

In 1912 the Peoples Store joined the H. B. Claflin chain, but only two years later was purchased by Mercantile Stores when Claflin failed during an inflationary period. Under Mercantile the old downtown store has been extensively remodeled and Peoples, as it is now called, has opened branches in Lakewood, Olympia, Port Angeles, Sea-Tac, Wenatchee, and Yakima.

1889

"Quality Tells—Price Sells"

ROOBINS—*Cordele, Georgia*

Here's still another peddler-to-palace story—one that began on the back of a Polish immigrant named Abraham Roobin. "Old Abe," as people called him, peddled the sawmill roads of south Georgia, and within a few years saved enough money to send back to the old country for his younger brother Louis, the two of them peddling together until they put enough aside to open a small dry goods establishment called the Daylight Store in Cordele. Business prospered, but Abe decided to relocate to a larger city and sold the store to his brother, its name changed to L. J. Roobin at that time.

Roobin's has remained in family hands since Louis Roobin died in 1925, his son Jake Roobin heading the store today and Jake's sons Joe and Sam active in management. In 1948 the store opened a unique Store for Homes branch, taking their former family residence on the corner of Thirteenth Avenue and Seventh Street and converting it into a homelike store building where shoppers could see just how a sofa, lamp, or picture would look inside a real house. Recently, however, this operation was moved to the main store, allowing the complete Roobin operation to be under one roof. Though Cordele has a population of only twelve thousand, the store considers its trading sphere to be a seven-county area. Roobin's has remained strong in the face of major chain branches and shopping centers in its trade area mainly because the owners and employees of the small department store know its customers personally, can in fact call most of them by name. The store has no major plans for expansion or change of any kind and intends to keep serving families it has served for generations under the slogan "Quality Tells—Price Sells."

1889

A Store Growing in the City

SAGE-ALLEN—*Hartford, Connecticut*

With net sales of over $38 million a year Sage-Allen is one of Connecticut's leading independent specialty department store organizations, selling no furniture, floor coverings, appliances, toys, or sporting goods. Known to three generations of Connecticut and western Massachusetts families, it features medium- and higher-priced wearing apparel and accessories for men, women, and children, in addition to a broad range of nationally known domestic merchandise and giftwares. The firm has 12 stores across the state and operates Sage-Allen Budget outlets as sources of well-known but lower-priced clothing. Leased departments such as photography and beauty salons account for about 12 percent of sales. The company, which went public in 1972, employs two thousand people at peak seasons and has more than doubled its stores since 1962. Its flagship store in downtown Hartford, built in 1898 and last renovated in 1968, is one of the few urban stores in the country showing signs of an upturn, in great part because of increased traffic resulting from a revitalization of the downtown area by the city. To attract mothers and young children to the downtown Hartford store, the company provides special shows and entertainment and maintains a supervised fun room for children called Our Backyard. A fleet of 28 trucks is maintained for home delivery.

1889

"A Family Fashion Center"

LAZARUS—*Wilkes-Barre, Pennsylvania*

Henry and Asher Lazarus (no relation to Simon Lazarus, the founder of the great Ohio department store dynasty, who had emigrated to America from Prussia a half century before them) came from Russia to booming Wilkes-Barre on the banks of the Susquehanna at a time when the one-price idea was sweeping the country. So the two brothers took as their motto for their new enterprise at 11 South Main Street: "The One Price Dry Goods House." In an early ad they set forth their policy: "With the newest and best, we buy low, but we boast also that we sell the best. . . . Money savers will be able to make a little money go a great ways here." From miles around "money savers" responded to the Lazarus idea and their store prospered. Yet when Asher Lazarus died in 1911, his brother didn't want to continue in business without him, and Henry sold the store to the H. B. Claflin chain, which failed in 1914, the Lazarus Store was purchased by the Mercantile Store group at that time. Under Mercantile the store moved to West Northampton and South Main streets, where in 1928 a handsome new Lazarus Store with 55,000 square feet of selling space was opened. Over the years this three-story emporium has been expanded several times and is now double its original size. Throughout the years it has been regarded as the "family fashion center" of the northeastern region and works hard to maintain this image. Lazarus suffered severe damage in the floods caused by

Hurricane Agnes in 1972 but was quickly restored to its original state.

1890

ALDENS, INC.—*Chicago, Illinois*

(See Chapter 7)

1890

HENRI BENDEL, INC.—*New York, New York*

(See Chapter 5)

1890

JOSEPH MAGNIN—*San Francisco, California*

(See Chapter 5)

1890

The American Bon Marché

BON MARCHE—*Seattle, Washington*

This great Seattle store, named after the famous French prototype of all department stores, is now owned by the giant Allied Stores Corporation chain. Besides its large 878,000-square-foot flagship store in Seattle, Bon Marché has 10 branches in Washington, 5 in Idaho, 2 in Oregon, and 1 in Lowell, Massachusetts. In all, these 20 Bon Marché stores have a total selling space of over 3 million square feet and sales of about $200 million annually. Two wholly owned subsidiaries of Allied Stores—Allied Marketing Corporation and Allied International—provide merchandising research and information and act as merchandising consultants to the stores, which are as renowned for quality in their trading areas as is their namesake in France.

1891

From Fur Factory to Department Store

HALLE'S—*Cleveland, Ohio*

Halle's of Cleveland has always been noted for its personal touch; in fact, the late Walter Halle, the founder's son, used to write personal letters to all customers who charged one thousand dollars or more a year at Halle's. This department store began as a small Public Square fur factory and retail shop operated by Solomon and Samuel Halle, brothers who had bought the even older fur business of Captain T. S. Paddock. The store soon began selling men's, women's, and children's clothing as well as furs. In 1896, the year ready-to-wear clothing for women first made its appearance, Mrs. William McKinley, wife of the future president who was then governor of Ohio, wore a blue serge dress and a sealskin coat from the Halle establishment. The store didn't become a full-line department store until 1914, when it had already moved to the site of its present downtown store on Euclid Avenue and added such departments as furniture, toys, and sporting goods. Halle's opened its first branch in 1929 in Erie, Pennsylvania, the first of many to be opened over the years. In 1970 Halle's was purchased by Marshall Field by an exchange of stock agreement. The company, which operates under its original name, has 10 stores in all, with net sales of about $75 million a year.

1891

Another Dead Giant

LIT BROTHERS—*Philadelphia, Pennsylvania*

Samuel and Jacob Lit, whose parents emigrated to America from Holland in the 1830s, were born right on Market Street in Philadelphia, not far from where they later founded their department store. Actually, the store was started by their sister Rachael Wedell as a dress shop, but they joined her two years later, adding dry goods to the line, and helped build it into a great department store. The first little shop, famous in the city because Rachael trimmed hats free if the materials were bought in the store, was located at 45 North Eighth Street, but in the panic year of 1893 the Lit brothers and their sister moved to the northeast corner of Market and Eighth streets, where they soon built an imposing five-story store with a cast-iron façade. The three partners added more merchandise to their stock every year, and by the turn of the century Lit's was a full-fledged department store.

Lit Brothers—the name was a misnomer, as Rachael was always an active partner in the family operation—began to purchase adjacent stores, until by 1918 it occupied the whole city block, with a continuous five-story facade for its store. Purchased from the family in 1928 by the City Stores Company chain, which came under the control of the Bankers Securities Corporation during the depression, Lit's remained a Philadelphia institution until the store finally closed its doors for the last time one night in late 1976, a victim of urban decay, even though it was among the top 50 or so American stores with over $100 million in annual sales. In its day, Lit's had formed part of one of the greatest concentrations of department store business in America—the intersection of Market and Eighth streets boasting Lit's, Gimbels, and Strawbridge & Clothier on three of its corners. In fact, it was in 1927 one of six department stores on Market Street—along with Gimbels, Strawbridge & Clothier, Frank & Seder, N. Snellenburg's (now also deceased) and Wanamaker's—that did a full one-quarter of the city's retail business, a record that isn't likely to be surpassed anywhere in the near future.

1895

A Favorite Capital Store

WOODWARD & LOTHROP—Washington, D.C.

Fondly called "Woodies" by its patrons, Woodward & Lothrop is one of Washington, D.C.'s two biggest department stores. Along with Hecht's, the capital's other big store, it pretty much had the market to itself until department store chains began opening branches in the area over the past decade or so. Exclusive stores, such as Neiman-Marcus, Saks Fifth Avenue, Lord & Taylor, Bloomingdale's, and I. Magnin, now have stores in the District of Columbia suburbs or city, which has the largest median family income of America's 10 major metropolitan areas. Woodward & Lothrop's reaction has been to eliminate their budget stores, upgrade their merchandise, and increase prices to match the opulent allure of their competitors—still another example of a traditional department store putting on specialty store airs. Woodward & Lothrop ranks as America's twenty-fifth leading store, with its 13 units doing over $240 million in sales.

1895

BONWIT TELLER—*New York, New York*

(See Chapter 5)

1896

THE EMPORIUM—*San Francisco, California*

(See Chapter 5)

1896

COINER'S—*Berryville, Virginia*

(See Chapter 4)

1896

From Bankruptcy to Billions

THE BROADWAY—*Los Angeles, California*

Arthur Letts, a young Englishman who had been apprenticed to a dry goods merchant as a boy, clerked for a time in Toronto, in what is now the Walker Stores, but he opened his first store in

Seattle—a men's clothing store that he operated under a huge tent. Unfortunately, four years of hard work came to nothing when the panic of 1893 bankrupted him and after paying his creditors thirty-five cents on the dollar, he journeyed south to Los Angeles. There Letts eventually purchased a bankrupt store called The Broadway Department Store on Broadway and Fourth Street for $8,167. Adhering to the relatively new policies of fixed price and liberal refunds, he made the store a great success. Interestingly, its slogan was "All cars transfer to Fourth and Broadway," referring to the electric trolley cars that converged near the store and almost identical to Bloomingdale's slogan in New York.

Lett's was also responsible for founding Bullock's department store (q.v.), and after he made his fortune he settled accounts in full with his creditors of Seattle days. The Broadway, with 35 stores, is today one of the most important divisions in the billion-dollar Carter Hawley Hale chain (see Chapter 9), which owns The Emporium, Bullock's, Neiman-Marcus, Capewell, Bergdorf Goodman, Waldenbooks, and other stores mentioned in these pages.

1897

K MART, INC. (S. S. KRESGE)—*Troy, Michigan*

(See Chapter 6)

1897

HESS'S—*Allentown, Pennsylvania*

(See Chapter 4)

1898

A Nashville Landmark

CASTNER KNOTT COMPANY—*Nashville, Tennessee*

Nashville's oldest department store was founded by merchants Charles Castner and William Knott on Summer Street (now 5th

Avenue) and quickly became one of the city's favorite shopping places. By 1906 the store outgrew its original quarters and moved to a much larger building on Seventh Avenue and Church Street, a location Castner Knott still occupies today. This site was the former home of the De Moville family, who represented southern culture at its best, which makes the store doubly an historical landmark.

A few years after their only move, Castner Knott's founders sold their store to the H. B. Claflin Company, and when this chain failed in 1914, Mercantile Stores bought the landmark department store. The original store has been renovated several times since then, but branch expansion for Castner Knott had to wait until the end of World War II, when the store's first branch was opened in Shelbyville. Since then new stores have been built in Donelson, Green Hills, Harding Mall, Harfuth Square, Rivergate, and Bowling Green, Kentucky.

1900

Business under the Big Top

BROCKS—*Bakersfield, California*

In 1952 the Tehachapi-Bakersfield earthquake damaged Brocks so badly that the firm was forced to evacuate the building until extensive repairs could be made. Brocks became possibly the only department store in modern times to operate under circus tents, setting up a temporary branch called Brocks Big Top in the nearby Westchester area. For over a year the company did business under the Big Top, only moving back to its present location downtown after the building was reinforced, enlarged, and remodeled.

This hadn't been the first misfortune to befall Brocks, fire having destroyed another building in 1919. Brocks has its roots in an old Bakersfield store called Hochheimer's, which dated back to 1900 and was founded by Moses and Amiel Hochheimer, merchants in the area since 1876. Malcolm Brock, a nephew of the Hochheimers who had worked for them off and on for thirty years, purchased their store from them in 1924 and formed the Malcolm Brock Company. Brocks, which now has branches in Westchester and Valley Plaza, is today operated by descendants of both the Brock and Hochheimer families, the Hochheimers having changed their family name to Homer during World War I, at a time when superpatriotism reached such extremes that Americans were re-naming everything German—making sauerkraut "liberty cabbage," a hamburger a "liberty sandwich," and even changing German measles to "liberty measles."

1900

The Biggest Sales in Texas
FOLEY BROTHERS—*Houston, Texas*

Pat and James Foley had to borrow two thousand dollars from an Irish immigrant uncle to found their Houston store, which has since become the largest volume department store in Texas. The store long ago passed out of the hands of the Foley brothers, first sold to the George S. Cohen family in 1917 and then acquired by the Federated Department Stores chain in 1945. Federated paid $3,250,000 for the store and property that Foley's owned, made a profit of over $2 million selling off some of the extra property, and in 1947 built a modern $13 million store designed by Kenneth Franzheim and Raymond Loewy. Within three years sales had more than quadrupled from the $6.5 million gross Foley's had been doing when the chain purchased the store. Today sales are about $265 million annually, sixteenth highest in the nation, a figure that includes the receipts of the seven Foley branches in or around Houston that have been built since 1961.

1901

BERGDORF GOODMAN—*New York, New York*

(See Chapter 5)

1902

A *Fine Fashion Store*
FRANKLIN SIMON—*New York, New York*

Franklin Simon was only thirteen when he left school to take a job at Stern Brothers department store in 1878. The New York store hired him as a stock boy at $2.50 a week, giving him two nights off a week to complete his education at night school, and he worked there nearly twenty-five years before opening his first specialty and fashion store for women on Fifth Avenue and Thirty-eight Street.

Simon's choice of location was astute—there was no other women's fashion store in the area at the time—and by the late 1920s the former $2.50 a week stock boy was grossing $25 million a year at his store. Simon never forgot his past, however, and before he died in 1934 he had instituted classes at Franklin Simon's for young employees who hadn't finished school and established two scholarships for employees at New York University's School of Retailing.

After the founder died, his widow sold the store to the Atlas Corporation, and in 1947 it was acquired by City Specialty Stores, Inc., now the City Stores Company chain, which operates 65 Franklin Simon specialty stores across the country.

1902

J. C. PENNEY COMPANY—*Kemmerer, Wyoming*
(See Chapter 4)

1902

SAKS FIFTH AVENUE—*New York, New York*
(See Chapter 5)

1902

One of America's Biggest Retailers

DAYTON'S—*Minneapolis, Minnesota*

Perhaps one of your ancestors caught a glimpse of George Draper Dayton at the turn of the century as he traveled through the Midwest. Dayton must have seemed a bit odd to people in many towns as he stood on street corners and counted with pad and pencil the passersby. But it was this crude application of the statistical method that enabled him to choose Nicollet Avenue in Minneapolis as one of the busiest and most promising streets in the Midwest region on which to open a dry goods store. Dayton, a Minnesota banker, helped finance a store named Goodfellow's at Third and Nicollet, expecting to remain a silent partner, but bought out his partners the next year, moved the store to Seventh and Nicollet, and renamed it Dayton's Daylight Store.

In time Dayton's Daylight Store changed its name to the Dayton Dry Goods Company, which eventually became known as Dayton's. The principles of liberal credit, no-questions-asked returns, and good service established by the systematic founder were responsible for the store's growth into a full-line 12-story department store in the heart of Minneapolis. Dayton's was a founder of Associated Merchandising Corporation, formed by a group of department stores in 1912 for the cooperative mass buying of merchandise (see Chapter 8). The store's first expansion outside downtown Minneapolis did not come until 1954, when a full-line Dayton's was established in Rochester, Minnesota, home of the Mayo Clinic. This was followed by eight more Minneapolis stores over the years and one Dayton's in Fargo, North Dakota. These stores, run by third-generation members of the Dayton family, occupy about 3 million square feet of space, employ over thirteen thousand people, and serve over 10 million customers each year. Included among them is Dayton's million square foot Southdale center, built in 1956, which was the first fully enclosed, air-conditioned shopping center in the world.

In 1969 the Dayton regional stores merged with the J. L. Hudson

Company to form the Dayton Hudson Corporation, America's ninth largest nonfood retail chain (see Chapter 8), with Bruce Dayton becoming chairman of the board. Previous to the merger the store had acquired Diamond's of Phoenix, John G. Brown in Tulsa, and Lipman Wolfe in Portland, Oregon. It had to rebuild its watered-down executive buying force following these acquisitions, but now boasts revenues of over a quarter of a billion dollars from all the Dayton stores.

Dayton's strength is most apparent in its great appeal to the more affluent and more sophisticated, fashion-conscious consumer, the store a cut above any of its competition in both quality and price. But the full-line department store doesn't specialize in fashions, and the store prides itself on the Customer Service Memo advertisements that it has published as buying guides to customers on everything from clothing to refrigerators and air conditioners. Its 12,000 square foot main store auditorium is well known in Minneapolis for the free public service events held there. These have included fashion shows, art shows, discussions on women's lib, a senior prom for oldsters, and an orphan animal sale. The store's animated Christmas display is visited by a quarter of a million people from mid-November until Christmas, and each spring the auditorium is transformed into a fantastic garden, with hundreds of thousands of blooms, shrubs, and trees. This flower show has become an upper-Midwest tradition, people coming from a five-state area to get a "preview of spring" at Dayton's.

1902

An Old-Fashioned Store

J. E. MANN—*Brattleboro, Vermont*

J. E. Mann was founded by John E. Mann in 1902 and has been handed down through three generations of the family. Now one of Vermont's largest women's and specialty department stores, it is operated by the founder's son John, Sr., its president, and grandson Kim Mann, the store's general manager. A typical small department store, employing about 28 salespeople—most of whom do their own buying and stocking—Mann's reflects "the traditional Vermonter's taste," according to Kim Mann, "in which high fashion plays a very small part." The store has a familylike relationship with its customers—one saleslady has been with the company since 1919. Most customers are permanent residents from a 40-mile radius around the store, but like many stores along Vermont's southern border, Mann's also depends on the flood of tourists to the area in the winter and summer seasons.

1902

A Store Inspired by Filene's

B. FORMAN COMPANY—*Rochester, New York*

Forman's, which prides itself on being "the largest fine specialty store between New York City and Chicago," owes its life to one of the most notable talents in retailing, the brilliant Louis Kirstein, general manager of Filene's in Boston. It was Kirstein who encouraged and aided Benjamin Forman, a young tailor who operated the Vienna Tailor Shop in Rochester, to open a ready-to-wear store on his North Clinton Street premises. Soon the store was doing so well that it moved to its present location on Clinton Avenue South in the heart of Rochester's business district, occupying a building that was expanded to six floors in 1923.

Benjamin Forman established a legacy of fine merchandise and customer satisfaction in Rochester. Following Kirstein's advice again, he became a charter member of the Associated Merchandising Corporation when it was formed in 1918, enabling his store to join in the cooperative mass buying of merchandise that Lincoln Filene had originated (see Chapter 8). The prosperous business that he left behind when he died in 1951 was inherited by his three sons, under whom the company expanded.

After the death of Edward Forman in 1958, his brothers, Maurice and Fred, along with Gilbert and Gordan McCurdy, formed the Midtown Holding Company with the purpose of building an urban shopping center. Four years later the Midtown Mall, with an entrance leading to the Forman store, was completed, becoming an integral part of the Rochester community and a showplace for visitors from around the world. Besides its main store in the mall, B.

Forman has branches in Pittsford, the Culver Ridge Shopping Center, Irondequoit, and Greece, New York. The company was sold to McCurdy & Company, Inc., in 1968 but operates as an autonomous division of the corporation.

1903

Growing with the West

LEVY'S—*Tucson, Arizona*

From its modest beginnings as the little Red Star Store, founded in Douglas by Jacob Levy and his wife when the state was a territory, Levy's has become one of the biggest retailers in Arizona. The story of the store's growth is to a great extent the story of the growth of the American Southwest. As did many pioneer merchants in the area, Jacob Levy started small, expanded as population grew, and made his fortune.

Along with his brother Ben, Jacob Levy incorporated the thriving Red Star Store as Levy Brothers Dry Goods Company in 1912, and seven years later the brothers opened a second store in Douglas called the El Paso Store, which was located on the border and catered almost entirely to a Mexican trade. Levy Brothers next bought out the Fair Store of Bisbee in 1925 and did well enough in the midst of the depression to take over the Myers and Bloom Men's Store in Tucson. By 1933, two years after its purchase, the Tucson store had proved so prosperous that additional space was added on the corner of Pennington and Scott, and women's apparel, shoes, and housewares were added to the men's line.

Jacob Levy and his brother Ben parted company in 1935, with Ben and his two sons taking the Douglas and Bisbee stores, while Jacob and his two sons kept the Tucson operation, which was incorporated under the name Levy's. The store continued to grow and after World War II ended was over three times the size of the original, one of the most modern stores between Dallas and Los Angeles.

Early in 1960 Levy's became part of Federated Department Stores, Inc., the largest chain of conventional department stores in the country. At that time, a decision was made to close the downtown Tucson store, which was experiencing difficulties, as were many urban stores across America, and a complete department store was opened in the El Con Shopping Center, where a Levy's branch store was located. In 1969 the new two-story store of Indian Pueblo design opened and proved so successful that another floor had to be added to accommodate customers.

1904

California's Largest Independent

E. GOTTSCHALK & COMPANY—*Fresno, California*

Gottschalk's is now California's largest independently owned department store, with 1,400 employees and sales of about $50 million. The store, which operates 6 major department stores and 12 specialty stores in the central part of the state, was founded by Emil Gottschalk, a German immigrant who came to America with his family as a boy, worked his way through Columbia University in New York City, and then moved West, where he gained retailing experience working in several department stores. Leaving Kutner-Goldstein, a store in which his wife's father was a partner, he capitalized on his outstanding reputation in the community by raising enough money to open a spacious full-fledged department store on the main floor of a new building being erected on Fulton Street.

On opening day the National Guard band was on hand to entertain the crowd. But the four thousand boxes of fine French candies given away to customers weren't nearly enough to supply the people who made Fresno's downtown streets impassable gaping at the huge Gottschalk show windows and the "beautiful wax figures ... draped in artistic style ... which certainly would not have been any truer to life and taste had they been arranged by the deft fingers of a French modiste." Kutner-Goldstein, angered that Gottschalk had left their employ—taking 14 other workers with him—vowed that his operation wouldn't last six months and set aside a large promotional budget to insure this prediction, but as it turned out Gottschalk's was quite successful and Kutner-Goldstein closed forever before the end of the year.

Emil Gottschalk was an extraordinary mathematician; he delighted in adding up three-column figures of the day's receipts simultaneously and arriving at the correct result before the columns could be tallied by someone on a Comptometer. He was seldom wrong, and the figures were seldom disappointing. Gottschalk made "service" his byword—the store's horse and carriage delivery teams often made special runs with a few yards of material or a five-cent spool of thread. His clientele increased year by year, and in 1914 he built a much larger air-conditioned store to accommodate them on the corner of Fulton and Kern, which is still the site of the Gottschalk flagship store. The business prospered, featuring free delivery, "one price for all," a money-back guarantee, a "Bright-light Basement," and even coupons that were used like trading stamps.

Gottschalk's was famous into the 1930s for its annual Blue Pencil Sales, instituted in 1904, when huge blue pencils hung in the windows and customers fought over the marked-down goods. The store was the first in the area to employ Armenians, often discriminated against in Fresno, as salesclerks. When Emil Gottschalk retired, his nephews Abe Blum and Irving Levy, who had joined the firm earlier, took charge of the store, and it has been in their hands and the hands of their descendants ever since.

1904

LANE BRYANT—*New York, New York*

(See Chapter 5)

1904

"Fashion right ... Quality right ... Service right"

BUFFUMS—*Long Beach, California*

Harry Buffum, the second of only four presidents to head Buffums over its seventy-four-year history, once described the company's first store on Pine Avenue, as it looked in the year his father C. A. Buffum and his uncle E.E. ("Double E") Buffum purchased it from the Schelling Brothers Company. "It was a typical store of the times," he recalled. "There was a potbellied stove in the middle, yardage and notions on one side, men's wear on the other, and in the rear and up three steps, women's ready-to-wear."

Buffum, who began his retailing career as a sweep-out boy in the store at nine years old, might have mentioned the wooden gallery and iron hitching rod out front, the flickering gaslight inside, the rustle of silks, the smell of men's high button shoes highly greased with wax, and the pail of water standing next to the telephone, a precaution all early stores took against fire. Long Beach was only a lazy town of 4,500 in those days, southern California itself far from being the largest retailing area in the country next to New York, as it is today, but from the beginning the two-story brick store took as its motto the three-fold creed "Fashion right . . . Quality right . . . Service right . . . ."

Buffums prospered, and in 1925 a handsome six-story department store was erected alongside the original building. Harry Buffum was president when the store's first branch opened in Santa Ana during the prosperous post–World War II years, but expansion really accelerated under Vaile G. Young, who succeeded him eleven years later. Buffums, which now has 13 modern branches and is led by William Hansen, the firm's president since 1970, doesn't even try to outbuy giants like Carter Hawley Hale, the May Company, or Bullock's. A specialty department store that sells no appliances, floor coverings, or other hard goods, it specializes in high-fashion ready-to-wear, offering "the finest selection and service possible." The policy seems to work, for Buffums is doing $65 million a year in sales today. Recently, the store passed out of the hands of the Buffum family when it was purchased by David Jones, Ltd., the fourth largest department store chain in Australia, because, as Hansen says candidly, "We couldn't refuse the price. . . . There was no urgency . . . we had ready cash for expansion and we were well capitalized. The offer was simply too good to refuse."

1905

The Only Store with an Ombudsman

HARRIS DEPARTMENT STORES—*San Bernardino, California*

Undoubtedly, no other department store in America has an official ombudsman as Harris does. This family-operated store's motto is "Servimus—We Serve," and it obviously takes these words seriously. James K. Guthrie, its ombudsman (which, loosely translated from the Swedish, means a "mediator or go-between") has, in the store's words, "complete authority to investigate all complaints and to override any middle or top management decision which is not to the liking of the customer."

Harris has believed "the customer is always right" since its founding in 1905, when the brothers Harris—Arthur, Herman, and Philip—opened a small dry goods store with only a 25-foot frontage in the old San Bernardino Armory Building. These German immigrants stated in an opening-day newspaper ad, "If courteous treatment, low prices, good goods and honest methods are appreciated here, we will certainly have no difficulty in gaining trade." Their virtues were appreciated, for the store did very well indeed, moving to larger quarters and opening its first branch operation at Redlands within three years.

In 1927 a big new Harris store was built on the corner of Third and E streets in San Bernardino, the site of the present downtown store. Harris—where fourth-generation family members work today—serves a market area (Riverside–San Bernardino) that ranks a surprising thirtieth in the nation. Besides its recently remodeled six-floor downtown store, part of an urban regional mall, it has modern branches in Riverside, Indio, and Redlands.

1906

From Storeroom to Department Store

GLOSSER BROTHERS, INC.—*Johnstown, Pennsylvania*

When founded 72 years ago, Glosser Brothers occupied only a small storeroom in the large four-story building that is its anchor store today. The firm, still managed by members of the Glosser family, now has sales of more than $116 million a year and runs twelve self-service Gee Bee discount department stores as well as its 32-department flagship store in downtown Johnstown. There is also a Glosser supermarket operation consisting of 10 stores, and a Glosser home improvement center store. The department stores, which account for about 65 percent of company sales, feature a number of special events annually, especially the main Johnstown store, which holds fashion shows, Halloween window-painting contests, and Christmas promotions. Glosser's has won several awards for innovative television commercials.

1907

NEIMAN-MARCUS—*Dallas, Texas*

(See Chapter 5)

1907

A Giant California Store

BULLOCK'S—*Los Angeles, California*

Many local stores went out of business during the financial panic of 1907, the year Bullock's opened its doors, but the new department store managed to hang on, though at times, "You could shoot a cannon through the aisles without hitting anyone." To keep up appearances, the store sent out its horse-drawn delivery wagons every day, even when there was nothing to deliver, and stocked some shelves with empty cartons rather than betray the fact that there wasn't enough money to buy ample stock. Such tactics succeeded; the store survived the depression, and the following year reaped a profit on over $2 million in sales.

Bullock's was founded by John Bullock, a young Canadian who had left a job as a delivery boy in Paris, Ontario, to try his luck in California, the El Dorado of the day to Americans and foreigners alike. Starting as a salesman in Arthur Lett's Broadway Department Store, Bullock worked his way up to store superintendent, and when Letts decided to complete a new store on the corner of Broadway and Seventh Street, where another merchant had begun construction and died before the seven-story building was finished, he asked Bullock to run it for him. John Bullock was appointed president of the store, the store was named after him, and another young Canadian, Percy Winnett, who had started as a cash boy in Broadway, was made his assistant. Bullock's opened after a nonselling preview of the store to the public, which included a band concert on the lower floors and a pony show in the roof garden. On opening day customers were treated to an exhaltation of canaries singing throughout the beautiful store, and violets were given away to all shoppers, a custom that Bullock's continued over the years.

Bullock's was noted from the start for its unitization of goods, the now common practice of arranging merchandise departments into separate units according to type—establishing separate sections, for example, in its underwear department for women's and children's underwear. The store's early ads were conservative and honest for the era, one of them astounding and amusing the public by offering "$15 suits for $15" when other stores were advertising "$25 suits for $15." Service was unparalleled in Los Angeles—once when a Bullock's driver delivered Christmas presents too early and the children in the house opened the packages, ruining their widowed mother's Christmas surprise, the store sent them free toys from Santa Claus. It was no wonder that Bullock's grew in prestige and sales. In 1912 a new 10-story building was erected adjacent to the original building, this the first of many new store buildings. By 1927, when Bullock's, Inc., was formed by Bullock and Winnett to purchase the store from the estate of Arthur Letts, who died that year, Bullock's had a sales volume exceeding $22 million.

Before John Bullock died in 1933, Bullock's had opened its

showplace store on Wilshire Boulevard in Beverly Hills (1929), its Bullock's Palm Springs branch (1930), and Bullock's Westwood (1932). Inside the downtown store is a bronze bust honoring the founder, who had built his store into a giant, made it a charter member of the Associated Merchandising Corporation (see Chapter 8), and was a leader in Los Angeles civic affairs, playing a major role, for instance, in arranging the construction of the Colorado River Aqueduct that supplies vital irrigation water to southern California. Percy Winnett took over as president of the firm, which he led through the depression without an unprofitable year, and he arranged the 1941 merger of Bullock's with the famous I. Magnin's (see Chapter 5).

Under Winnett, Bullock's opened its widely acclaimed $6 million Pasedena branch in 1947, one of the most beautiful stores in America with its unique architecture and the lovely view of the mountains from the Coral Room. Among other developments was the Fashion Square Shopping Center, built in Santa Ana in 1958. Six years later all the Bullock's and I. Magnin units were purchased by the Federated Department Store chain, which operates the stores separately, Bullock's now America's sixteenth leading department store with over $265 million in sales.

1908

From City to Suburbs

CROWLEY, MILNER & COMPANY—*Detroit, Michigan*

Joseph Crowley wasn't a gambler by nature—in 1905 he declined the opportunity to invest five thousand dollars in Henry Ford's new venture. But he thought he knew a lot about retailing, and when a Detroit bank offered him a chance to reorganize the failing Pardridge and Blackwell Department Store, he didn't think this was a gamble at all. Leaving his Crowley Brothers Wholesale Dry Goods Company, he asked William Milner of Toledo's W. L. Milner Department Store, a firm in which Crowley Brothers had an interest, to join him, and the two merchants took over the almost bankrupt old store. This was at a time when Crowley, Milner's retailing neighbors included J. L. Hudson, Taylor Wolfenden, Ernst Kern, and Newcomb Endicott, which served the "carriage trade." Crowley and Milner rejuvenated the store, and it grew slowly at first, then suddenly boomed thanks in great measure to Henry Ford's five-dollar day and high employment in Motor City. By 1917 Crowley, Milner had expanded to the point where it was Michigan's largest store, an honor it held until J. L. Hudson assumed the title a few years later.

Milner was killed in an auto accident while trying to better his commuting time between the store and his home in Toledo one night, and Crowley died two years later of a heart attack. Control of the firm eventually passed into the hands of the Crowley family after some bitter fighting. The store prospered until the depression, when sales plummeted from $40 million in 1928 to under $10 million five years later. With few customers, and shelves and racks meagerly stocked, prices were below any hope of profit. Sales featuring ruinous markdowns were staged fruitlessly, and the scrip paid to Detroit city workers was accepted instead of cash—policies that led retailing expert Amos Parish to comment quite seriously that Crowley, Milner would profit by paying every customer five dollars not to buy. With the help of a bond issue, however, the firm did come through the depression intact and recouped its losses during the prosperous World War II years. This was an era of great promotions. During the Christmas season, for example, the toy department had not only its enthroned Santa greeting long lines of children but a minicarnival on the floor below complete with a merry-go-round and other mechanical rides.

Crowley, Milner started losing money again at its downtown store when the urban deterioration began affecting Detroit in the 1960s; sales for 1976 were only $9 million, below even the lowest point of the depression era. Most of the buildings that occupied the original Pardridge and Blackwell site were torn down in accordance with lease termination requirements in June, 1978, and only one building remains of the old Detroit landmark, this serving as administration headquarters for the company's prospering eight suburban stores. The company sees no hope for a new downtown unit presently and there are no plans to build in Detroit in the near future.

1910

"An Old-Fashioned General Store Grown Up"
MARLOW'S, INC.—*Manchester, New Hampshire*

Nathan Marlow, still another grand old merchant who lived nearly a century, worked in his Manchester department store at least eight hours a day, six days a week from the time he founded it until he died in 1975, age ninety-seven and a half. Even in his last year, "Papa," as his employees and customers called him, knew the location of the store's more than sixty-eight thousand items and could locate each within seconds for a customer. The patriarch, who smoked three packs of cigarettes a day until the end, never even let the weather phase him, sleeping on the premises whenever a snowstorm threatened so that he could open his store the next day.

Nathan, a shipping clerk in his native Russia, had clerked for three years in Japan, learning to speak the language fluently, before he emigrated to America. Working as a suit cutter for several years, and then operating a grocery store in Jamaica, New York, he finally journeyed to Manchester, where he and his brother Sam opened a five-and-ten on Main Street that came to be known as The Quaker Store. The store stocked a wide variety of goods and by 1926 had overflowed its boundaries, moving to its current location beneath the Orford Hotel. "We're just an old-fashioned general store that grew up," says Nathan's son George, sixty, who runs Marlow's today. The small department store, which was renovated in 1949 and employs 40 people now, is still known as "the store that has everything" to Manchester residents; even obscure, no-longer-manufactured merchandise can often be found at Marlow's. Marlow's remains a timeless haven on a street that has seen many changes, a refreshing rarity in an industry that has increasingly become depersonalized. There is no indication that this tradition will end. "People said we'd go out of business every time a chain opened on Main Street," George Marlow says. "But they've all closed up and we're still here."

1911

A Long Island Favorite
GERTZ—Jamaica, New York

Gertz is probably the only major department store in America that began as a corner stationery store. Benjamin Gertz's unpretentious little shop was started at an original investment of ten thousand dollars. Wisely, he sold excellent goods at attractive prices and the business grew, until by the time all his four sons had joined him in 1941 the family concern had evolved into a $10 million a year full-line department store occupying the entire block between 168th and 169th streets on Jamaica Avenue. In that year the Allied Stores Corporation chain assumed ownership of the firm and accelerated expansion. In 1946 an extensive addition was made to the store, and Long Island branches were eventually opened in Flushing (1951), Hicksville (1956), Great Neck (1961), Bay Shore (1962), East Hampton (1969), and Sunrise Mall in Massapequa (1973).

In 1977 Gertz ranked forty-fourth among American department stores, with $125 million in sales. But rumors persist that the five-story Jamaica emporium, a favorite of Long Islanders for over half a century, will close when the store's lease expires in 1980. Macy's has already announced that it will close its Jamaica branch, despite the fact that the area is being extensively renovated in an attempt to make it once again New York City's second busiest shopping section outside of Manhattan. If Gertz picks up the business that Macy's has abandoned, the flagship store may remain at its old stand.

1911

"More for Less or Your Money Back"
OHRBACH'S INC—New York, New York

A few venerable retailers still remember the 1923 grand opening of Ohrbach's Union Square store in the building where film pioneer

Adolph Zukor had operated the world's first nickelodeon. After converting the fire-damaged building into a store, Nathan Ohrbach and his partner Max Wiesen, a dress designer, held an opening day bargain sale that drew such large crowds that windows were broken, 20 people were injured, and the police has to be called in to restore order. Similar scenes were to be repeated several times in Ohrbach's history, as would be expected of a specialty store whose slogan is, "A business in millions, a profit in pennies." Twenty-five years later, in fact, so many bargain hunters invaded its new downtown Los Angeles store that Ohrbach's had to take spot radio advertisements to warn customers to stay away from the store for a week—a nightmare for police, perhaps, but a retailer's dream that is seldom realized.

Nathan Ohrbach had migrated to America from Austria with his parents when he was two years old and worked as a store sweeper, lifeguard, and Macy's delivery boy, among other jobs, before beginning his storekeeping career with a small specialty shop on Brooklyn's Fulton Street. The twenty-year-old called his store Bon Marché, Inc., a name that not only brought to mind the great French department store, but which he knew meant "cheap bargain." Soon afterward, he opened his first store in Manhattan on Fourteenth Street, where he continued to sell ready-to-wear clothing at a low markup, making his profit from many sales.

Ohrbach and his financial backer Wiesen never got along, and five years after the grand opening on Union Square, Nathan bought his partner out for $650,000, over ten times the amount Wiesen had originally invested. Sales were approaching $3 million that year, and Ohrbach decided to trade up, or upgrade the quality of the merchandise he sold, but the specialty store was to grow into the giant it is by sticking to its original policy of low markup. Another Orhbach's slogan was, "More for Less of Your Money Back" and any customer who could prove that she had purchased an item that cost less at another store was returned not only the difference but ten percent of the other store's price as well.

All early Ohrbach sales were for cash, there was no fancy wrapping or delivery, no alterations, semi-self-service, and no discounts for employees, and the store spent less than half of what its rivals did on its remarkably effective institutional advertising, which never cited prices—as if low prices were to be taken for granted at Ohrbach's. These economies enabled the store to sell fashionable garments to shoppers who otherwise could not afford them. Style was what Ohrbach's stressed in its distinctive ads, such as those famous cartoons of the voluptuous Melisse, "the girl in the Ohrbach dress" who always got her man. Stylish bargains appealed to rich and poor alike, and there are true stories of women filling chauffeur-driven limousines with Ohrbach garments, of Vanderbilts and Astors, princesses and movie stars shopping in the store.

When the founder's son Jerome Kane Ohrbach succeeded his father as president in 1946, Ohrbach's sales were well over $30 million a year. Jerome Ohrbach expanded the organization, opening its store on Wilshire Boulevard's Miracle Mile in 1948 and arranging for the purchase of Millirons, a downtown Los Angeles store dating to 1905 that Ohrbach's modernized and occupied under its own name in 1953. Ohrbach's finally moved from its New York Union Square location the following year, when it leased the 11-story store formerly occupied by the James McCreery Department Store (q.v.) on West Thirty-fourth Street across from the Empire State Building. Noted industrial designer Raymond Loewry remodeled the interior at a cost of $2 million, and on the first day of business some 100,000 people stormed the store looking for bargains.

Ohrbach's is now entirely owned by the Netherlands-based Brenninkmeyer Company, which also owns over two hundred stores in Europe. Brenninkmeyer bought into the firm in 1962 and increased its holdings until by Nathan Ohrbach's retirement in 1965 it had complete control. The store's founder, one of the most respected merchants of his generation died in 1972 at the age of eighty-seven.

Not long after Ohrbach's opened at the Zukor nickelodeon building in 1923, his competitor Sam Klein, a Russian immigrant who with pushcart methods had made "S. Klein, On the Square" a New York institution, predicted that the new store would last only seven months. As it happened, Ohrbach's, with sales approaching $200 million today, would not only wrest sales leadership from Klein's in "the toughest retail market in the world," but would outlive the older store, which went out of business in recent years. Today the faded signs of both stores on Union Square are about the only reminder of the great price wars waged between Ohrbach's and what was once the largest women's wear shop in the world.

1912

Sincerity, Honesty, and Loyalty

OPPENHEIM'S—(SCRANTON DRY GOODS COMPANY)—*Scranton, Pennsylvania*

It took over sixty years for this store to be named after its founder. I. E. Oppenheim had called his little establishment the Scranton Dry Goods Company when he opened it at 111–113 North Washington Avenue in 1912, promising his customers "sincerity of purpose, honesty in dealings and loyalty to truth." A tireless worker, Oppenheim rapidly built up his business and by 1917, after six expansions, was operating a full-line department store in a modern building. This store, too, was added to over the years and in 1968 underwent a $500,000 renovation. The Oppenheim family continues to own and operate the firm, which now includes a specialty store branch in Clarks Summit and a complete department store in Mount Pocono's Pocono Village Mall. Since "dry goods" is no longer a familiar term in the lexicon of most Americans, the firm's name was changed to Oppenheim's in 1972, a name many customers had been using for years prior to this because of the widely advertised Oppenheim Sale Days instituted in 1925. Oppenheim's has traditionally helped the city's poor, even outfitting needy families without cost in the past, and today completely finances a charitable fund called the Oppenheim Foundation.

1913

L. L. BEAN—*Freeport, Maine*

(See Chapter 7)

1913

"The South's Greatest Organization of Its Kind"

ROSE'S STORES, INCORPORATED—*Henderson, North Carolina*

P.H. Rose began his business career in 1898 as the owner of a small, makeshift soda pop and soft drink stand outside a one-room post office in Seaboard, North Carolina. Fifteen years later dreams that the boy had while selling his penny lemonade came true when Rose took his savings from many another retailing job and opened the first "Rose's 5-10-25¢ Store" in Henderson. This was to be only one of a family-owned chain of variety stores that he visualized throughout the South selling good merchandise at "the lowest possible prices." Rose's long billed itself as "The South's Greatest Organization of Its Kind," and this remains true today. The firm has widened its line considerably, and its stores, called simply "Roses," are now considered discount department store or variety chains. As are K mart stores, they are one-level, self-contained buildings provided with large parking lots. Shoppers wheel carts throughout the store and pay at checkout counters. Though not nearly as prosperous as K mart, Rose's Stores now has 266 units with total sales of well over $400 million, making the chain twenty-fifth among America's nonfood retail chains.

1914

FISHER'S BIG WHEEL—*New Castle, Pennsylvania*

(See Chapter 6)

1920

The Fashion Store Built by a Baseball Player

LOEHMANN'S INC.—*Brooklyn, New York*

Frieda Mueller Loehmann, a former coat buyer for Stewart & Company, launched her first store on Nostrand Avenue in Brooklyn, a small shop in which customers could purchase designer dresses at discount prices. It was such a success that Mrs. Loehmann moved it to larger quarters on Bedford Avenue several years later. Loehmann's expansion began when Frieda's son Charles C. Loehmann joined the company in 1925. Charles, a pro-baseball player for a short time on the Cincinnati Red's farm team following his graduation from the University of Cincinnati, opened a Loehmann's store on Bainbridge Avenue in the Bronx with his wife Anita. Business boomed, and with George J. Greenberg, now head of the store, he expanded the business into a discount high-fashion chain with 38 stores in 16 states grossing over $100 million in sales annually. Loehmann, an energetic, athletic person all his life, remained active in the business until his death this year at the age of eighty-three.

1921

From Peddler to Department Store

BOSCOV'S—*Reading, Pennsylvania*

Young Solomon Boscov, a Russian immigrant who landed here in 1911 with $1.37 in his pocket, came to Reading because he had trouble speaking English and had heard that everyone in town spoke Yiddish. The Pennsylvania Dutch spoken there was hardly that, but it was close enough for him to understand and be understood. Solomon obtained credit from a friendly supplier for thread, suspenders, salt and pepper—everything that farm wives might need—and forthwith he became a peddler. At first, he often had to exchange merchandise for meals, but business grew better and he soon bought—of all things—a motorcycle and side car to carry him over his route through Bucks and Lancaster counties. After a few nasty spills, this unlikely conveyance was traded in for a horse and wagon, and Solomon resumed selling his wares.

At the end of World War I, Boscov quit peddling and in 1921 opened the Economy Shoe and Dry Goods general store on Ninth and Pike streets in Reading, he and his family living in the back of the store. Solomon also branched out into home building, and business went well until the Great Depression, when he had all he could do to keep his employees on the payroll and was forced to house his family in the unsold homes that he had built.

Expansion of the Boscov retail store didn't really come until 1959, when Solomon's son Albert injected new ideas into the business and sales volume more than quadrupled to $1.5 million within five years. In late 1963 the company began its first full-line department store operation with a new store in Sinking Spring called Boscov's West. Since then the concern has grown to six stores with sales of about $50 million, up from $6 million in 1965 despite the fact that two stores burned to the ground and were rebuilt in that time.

Boscov's is noted in its trading area for its promotions—the latest store opening featured a ribbon cutting ceremony where the ribbon was made of $10 bills. The family-owned store follows the unusual practice of moving its entire management staff into each new store as it is opened, converting the executive offices left behind into additional selling space. Albert R. Boscov, the store's president, a man with a sense of humor, recently announced the first "transatlantic Boscov's" in the store's newspaper—"Scheduled for opening aboard the *Queen Elizabeth 2* as soon as we can float a loan!"

1924

A Growing Discounter

THE WILMINGTON DRY GOODS COMPANY— *Wilmington, Delaware*

"The Dry," as it is called locally, was founded on Market Street by merchant F. M. Lazarus and operated by him until 1924, when he sold it to SCOA Industries, formerly the Shoe Corporation of America. That first store, the anchor for the chain that SCOA started, has been expanded nine times since it was built sixty-four years ago. The Dry is a highly promotional department store whose philosophy is simple: "Give the best possible value at the lowest possible price, and back up each purchase with a cash refund guarantee." Its Wilmington flagship has been described as "a cross between Disneyland and the World Series" during one of its sales of label-less brand-name men's shirts and designer dresses, and often sells as many as a thousand men's suits a day. The chain at present has five stores besides its flagship: in surburban Wilmington; Huntington, West Virginia; Claymont, Delaware; Vineland, New Jersey; and Lancaster, Pennsylvania. These 100,000 square feet discount stores often average sales of over $100 per square foot per year. To help cut costs, all sales are cash, there is no gift wrapping, boxing, or alterations, merchandise isn't price-ticketed (prices are posted on counter signs), and advertising is styleless and scrupulously straight forward.

1925

The Forty-Three-Year-Old Centennial Store

GAMBLE-SKOGMO—*Minneapolis, Minnesota*

After selling cars for several years, Bertin C. Gamble and Philip W. Skogmo opened a retail automotive accessory store in Saint Cloud, Minnesota. From this small beginning the company has become the twenty-fourth largest merchandising company in America, with annual sales of about $1.6 billion. It is also one of the few giant chains in America with a founder still living and actively associated with his company.

Gamble's has branched out into many fields since its founding. Besides its 1,200 auto accessory stores, the company is involved in banking, insurance, importing, automobile leasing, home improvement and hardware stores, real estate, and shopping center construction. Its retailing softwear operation includes supermarkets and drugstores as well as department and discount stores.

Bertin Gamble and Philip Skogmo first entered into the softlines field during World War II, when automotive accessories became unavailable and they sold men's and women's clothing in their auto stores. This proved so successful that new franchised units under the name Skogmo were opened, and today 137 Skogmo dealer stores continue to satisfy the needs of small-town and rural families in the midwest. After Philip Skogmo died in 1949, the company continued to expand. In 1962 Gamble's entered the mass-merchandise market with its Tempo and Buckeye stores, which now number over 70, and the following year brought the purchase of the Stedman Brothers variety store chain in Canada. A year later saw the acquisition of Alden's, Inc., one of the nation's oldest mail-order catalog companies, both Alden's and its department store chain having a rich history that far outdates that of the parent company (see Chapter 8). Acquisitions that followed included Founders, Inc., with its almost one thousand Mode O'Day ladies' ready-to-wear outlets; Cussins & Fearn variety stores; Rasco variety stores; the J.M. McDonald Company department store chain with 85 retail outlets (which had been founded in 1929 by a J.C. Penney merchandising executive); and the 29 Women's World stores located mainly in the western and southern states. All and all, Gamble's giant merchandising operation consists of over 3,500 stores in the United States and Canada.

Bertin C. Gamble hasn't wielded real power at Gamble's since being deposed by a palace coup several years ago. But back in 1960 the firm conceived the novel idea of celebrating its centennial anniversary sixty years ahead of time—"because neither the present management nor the employees would be around to celebrate the actual 100th anniversary in the year 2025." The company celebrated by producing a one-hour television spectacular called "Way Back in 1960" with an all-star cast—including Herb Shriner, Tom Poston, J.P. Morgan, Phyllis Newman, and Dennis Day—that was viewed in 20 states throughout the midwest.

1928

A Leading New York Store

ALEXANDER'S—*New York, New York*

Alexander's was founded as a small clothing shop on Third Avenue in Manhattan. Today, along with Macy's, Gimbels, Korvettes, and Bloomingdale's, it is one of New York's five leading department stores. Its nine branches in the city and suburbs had sales of $365 million in 1976, eighth in the nation for individual department stores. Alexander's is noted for its attention to style and quality as well as price, although it is generally regarded as a discount department store whose chief competitors are Korvettes and Mays. Its suburban stores are typified by the modern structure decorated with murals housing the branch in the Green Acres Shopping Center in Valley Stream, New York.

1934

The Department Store in "Middletown"
BALL STORES—*Muncie, Indiana*

The Ball Brothers Company, which still makes home canning jars used for putting up fruit, vegetables, and other foods, opened its department store in an old building at what is now "Munseetown Square" on Charles and Walnut streets. After four years, Fred J. Petty, director of Ball Stores and the Ball Brothers Company, and his wife Margaret Ball Petty, purchased the store from Ball Brothers, making it the independent operation it is today. The store was completely remodeled and prospered over the years under the leadership of Fred Petty, who died in 1949, his wife assuming the presidency.

Ball's furniture unit was added to the store in 1963, making it a full-line department store. Munseetown Square (Muncie was originally called Munseetown) is, in effect, an urban shopping center, featuring these two Ball Stores and the firm's Rose Court shops, located in the heart of the small city, which was, incidentally, the original of the famous "Middletown" in the book of that name by sociologists Robert and Helen Lynd. Ball Stores first expanded in 1957, establishing a branch store in Marion, Indiana. In 1968 the company acquired the Collegienne Shops located near Ball State Teachers College, these shops featuring women's fashions and giftware. Mrs. Petty is now the store's chairman of the board, and her son Edmund is president.

1937

MASTERS—*New York, New York*

(See Chapter 6)

1938

"There Grows Dillard's"

DILLARD DEPARTMENT STORES—*Little Rock, Arkansas*

The experts warned that anyone opening a department store during the Great Depression, when stores were failing every day, was foolhardy at best, but William F. Dillard's investment of eight thousand, all the money he could scrape up, proved to be a good gamble indeed. Since that first store opened in Nashville, Arkansas, Dillard's has averaged almost a new store every year and has been described as the "fastest growing department store in the west" by a leading retail publication. To date there are 40 Dillard Department Stores in Arkansas, Texas, Oklahoma, Louisiana, Kansas, and New Mexico, and the chain has its eye on other states. Its stores include the 113-year-old Pfeifer's of Arkansas, purchased in 1963 (Pfeifer's has the catchy motto, "There grows Pfeifer's . . . the store that will never be completed"), the 10-story Brown-Dunkin store in Tulsa, and the ninety-year-old Mayer and Schmidt store in Tyler, Texas—all of which operate under their original names. William Dillard, a native Arkansan who learned retailing from floor sweeping on up in his father's Mineral Springs general store, is today assisted by two sons in his $100 million operation. "As I have acquired stores," he says, "my primary thoughts have not been on how to make them grow, but rather how they can better serve the community; how they can create new jobs and . . . earn profits for the people who have invested in my enterprises."

1943

Success in the City

HARVEY'S—*Nashville, Tennessee*

Nashville's leading store was a dying urban deparment store with sales of little over half a million dollars in 1943 when the late Fred Harvey purchased it. Harvey, a former Marshall Field department manager, renovated the store, changed its name, and advertised it with ads carried by blimps. Night openings also attracted shoppers, who were made good customers by the store's exceptional values and friendly atmosphere, and within a decade sales were more than 20 times what they were when Harvey took over. Fred Harvey's son Fred Harvey, Jr., is president of the store today.

1947

TWO GUYS—*Garfield, New Jersey*

(See Chapter 6)

1948

KORVETTES—*New York, New York*

(See Chapter 3)

1953

ANN & HOPE—*Cumberland, Rhode Island*

(See Chapter 6)

1970

JGE STORES—*Bayside, New York*

(See Chapter 6)

1977

THE PLAZA EXCHANGE—*Brooklyn, New York*

(See Chapter 7)

1977

THE CITY DUMP—*New York, New York*

(See Chapter 7)

The Great American Department Store Pages of Superlatives

THE DEPARTMENT STORE HALL OF FAME: AMERICA'S 25 GREATEST RETAILERS *

1. Alexander Turney Stewart—(A. T. Stewart & Co.)
2. John Wanamaker
3. Rowland Hussey Macy
4. Aaron Montgomery Ward
5. Richard Sears
6. Marshall Field
7. Edward Filene
8. Abraham Lincoln Filene
9. Frank Woolworth
10. James Cash Penney
11. David May
12. Joseph L. Hudson
13. Sebastian S. Kresge (K mart)
14. Fred Lazarus, Jr.
15. Adam Gimbel
16. Eugene Ferkauf (Korvettes)
17. Dorothy Shaver (Lord & Taylor)
18. Isidor Straus (Macy's)
19. Louis Kirstein (Filene's)
20. Julius Rosenwald (Sears)
21. Morris Rich

* The merchants are not ranked here in any particular order, and those not bearing a present-day store's name are so indicated. More about all of them can be found on the preceding pages.

22. Robert E. Wood (Sears)
23. Walter Hoving (Tiffany's)
24. Stanley Marcus
25. Harry B. Cunningham (K mart)

A LIST OF PEDDLERS WHO FOUNDED
GREAT DEPARTMENT STORES °

1. Adam Gimbel
2. Morris Rich
3. Leon Godchaux
4. Andrew Saks
5. Joseph Goldwater
6. L. S. Ayres
7. Nathan Snellenberg
8. Jacob and Isaac Kaufmann
9. The Younker brothers (Lytton, Samuel, and Marcus)
10. L. S. Good
11. Abraham Roobin
12. Solomon Boscov
13. Wolf Himelhoch
14. Marcus Spiegel

THE WORLD'S SEVEN OLDEST DEPARTMENT STORES °°

1. Bon Marché—Paris, France
2. A. T. Stewart & Company—New York, New York
3. R. H. Macy—New York, New York
4. John Wanamaker—Philadelphia., Pennsylvania
5. Zions—Salt Lake City, Utah
6. Marshall Field—Chicago, Illinois
7. Arnold Constable—New York, New York

° Two others who founded stores not bearing their names are E. J. Lehman (The Fair) and Henry Siegel (store now out of business).
°° See Chapters 2-4 for more details.

THE TEN BIGGEST VOLUME
DEPARTMENT STORES °

1. Macy's—New York
2. Hudson's—Detroit
3. Abraham & Straus—Brooklyn
4. Broadway—Los Angeles
5. Marshall Field—Chicago
6. Korvettes—New York
7. Bamberger's—New Jersey
8. Alexander's—New York
9. May Company—California
10. Bloomingdale's—New York

THE WORLD'S SIX BIGGEST STORES °°

1. Macy's—New York, New York
2. Hudson's—Detroit, Michigan
3. Marshall Field—Chicago, Illinois
4. GUM—Moscow, U.S.S.R.
5. Harrod's—London, England
6. La Samaritaine—Paris, France

THE TWELVE MOST RENOWNED FOREIGN
DEPARTMENT STORES

Bon Marché—Paris
GUM—Moscow [1]
Harrod's—London
Mitsukoshi—Tokyo

° As of July 1977
°° In order of size; see Chapter 4 for more details. Some writers have Field's tied with Macy's for first place with 2,200,000 square feet of selling space, but the consensus is that Macy's is the winner.
[1] State owned.

Galeries Lafayette—Paris [2]
La Samaritaine—Paris [3]
La Ville de Paris—Paris
Takashimaya—Tokyo [4]
Maison Blanche—Paris
Orosi-Back—Baghdad
The Hudson's Bay Company—Winnipeg [5]
Nordeska Kompaniet—Stockholm [6]

THE TWENTY-TWO BILLION DOLLAR CHAINS (in sales) [*]

Sears Roebuck	$22,024,000,000	(7)
K mart	10,064,000,000	(18)
J. C. Penney	9,369,000,000	(21)
F. W. Woolworth	5,543,000,000	(45)
Montgomery Ward	5,000,000,000	(50)
Federated Dept. Stores	4,923,000,000	(54)
Winn-Dixie Stores	3,997,000,000	(66)
Lucky Stores	3,914,000,000	(72)
American Stores	3,465,000,000	(88)
May Dept. Stores	2,370,000,000	(143)
Dayton-Hudson	2,191,000,000	(159)
Rapid-American	2,046,000,000	(175)
Allied Stores	1,927,000,000	(191)
R. H. Macy	1,661,000,000	(223)
Gamble-Skogmo	1,634,000,000	(228)
Carter Hawley Hale	1,505,000,000	(256)
Associated Dry Goods	1,468,000,000	(266)
McCrory Corp.	1,350,000,000	(343)
Zayre Corp.	1,261,000,000	(348)
Genesco	1,015,000,000	(369)
Gimbels	1,000,000,000	(371)
Vornado	1,000,000,000	(375)

[2] Today's Parisian style-setter.
[3] Paris's biggest store.
[4] Has a New York branch.
[5] The world's oldest retailer.
[6] Perhaps the firm with the most ancient lineage, though not as a department store.
[*] For 1977; figures in parentheses indicate rank among all U.S. businesses, which General Motors led with $55 billion in sales. Chains' income includes mail-order operations, discount department stores and variety stores. See Chapter 8 for more details, and an extended list of chains.

THE THIRTEEN MOST PROFITABLE
DEPARTMENT STORE CHAINS °

Sears, Roebuck	$836,000,000	(11)
K mart	302,900,000	(43)
J. C. Penney	295,000,000	(44)
Federated Dept. Stores	196,600,000	(71)
F. W. Woolworth	91,900,000	(228)
May Dept. Stores	84,000,000	(250)
Dayton-Hudson	80,900,000	(260)
Allied Stores	74,200,000	(282)
Winn-Dixie Stores	70,000,000	(295)
Lucky Stores	61,300,000	(339)
R. H. Macy	52,800,000	(395)
Carter Hawley Hale	50,100,000	(409)
Associated Dry Goods	42,100,000	(459)

THE ELEVEN RICHEST
DEPARTMENT STORE CHAINS °°

Sears, Roebuck	$23,086,000,000	(18)
Mobil Oil (Montgomery Ward)	20,575,967,000	(17)
J. C. Penney	4,106,000,000	(116)
K mart	3,428,000,000	(142)
Federated Dept. Stores	2,520,000,000	(207)
F. W. Woolworth	2,214,000,000	(249)
May Dept. Stores	1,651,000,000	(350)
Arlen Realty (Korvettes)	1,563,000,000	(373)
Rapid-American	1,485,000,000	(390)
Allied Stores	1,295,000,000	(448)
Dayton-Hudson	1,219,000,000	(470)

° Profits for 1977; figures in brackets show ranking among all U.S. businesses, which American Tel & Tel led with about $4.544 billion in profits.
°° Assets as of 1978; numbers in parentheses indicate rank among all U.S. businesses, which are led by American Tel & Tel with $93,972,000,000 in assets. Includes the full assets of corporations controlling department store chains, not assets of the retailing chains alone.

THE SEVEN TOP INDEPENDENT
DEPARTMENT STORES (in sales) °

Marshall Field (31)	$611,000,000
Carson Pirie Scott (26)	360,000,000
Woodward & Lothrup (13)	241,000,000
Strawbridge & Clothier (17)	240,000,000
John Wanamaker (14) [1]	238,000,000
Higbee (10)	187,000,000
B. Altman (6)	180,000,000

THE CHAINS WITH MOST EMPLOYEES °°

Sears, Roebuck	430,200	(4)
K mart	206,000	(9)
F. W. Woolworth	199,700	(12)
J. C. Penney	193,000	(13)
Federated Dept. Stores	109,000	(27)
Montgomery Ward	103,000	(32)
May Dept. Stores	63,500	(61)
Allied Stores	55,000	(75)
Lucky Stores	47,000	(102)
R. H. Macy	41,000	(128)
Carter Hawley Hale	35,700	(156)
Dayton-Hudson	35,000	(162)
Zayre Corporation	25,000	(240)
G. C. Murphy	21,000	(282)
Gamble-Skogmo	17,500	(329)
Marshall Field	14,900	(381)
Scoa Industries	14,000	(401)

° As of 1977; figures in parentheses are the number of units the store has. These so-called independent stores don't like to call themselves chains, but in reality they are; what they *aren't* is ownership group chains like Federated Department Stores. See Chapter 8 for more details.

°° As of 1978; figures in parentheses show rank among all American businesses; American Tel & Tel leads with over 946,000 employees.

[1] Wanamaker was acquired by Field's in 1978.

Rose's Stores	13,000	(434)
Goldblatt Bros.	11,000	(497)

THE FIVE LEADING MAIL-ORDER HOUSES °

1. Sears, Roebuck
2. Montgomery Ward
3. J. C. Penney
4. Spiegel's
5. Alden's

THE WORLD'S SEVEN BIGGEST SHOPPING CENTERS °°

1. Lakewood Center—Lakewood, California
2. Woodfield Mall—Schaumberg, Illinois
3. Randall Park—Cleveland, Ohio
4. Roosevelt Field—Garden City, New York
5. Cinderella City—Engelwood, California
6. Metrocenter—Phoenix, Arizona
7. Yorktown Shopping Center—Lombard, Illinois

THE SEVEN STATES WITH THE MOST SHOPPING CENTERS

1. California—2,044
2. Texas—1,470
3. Florida—988
4. New York—868
5. Ohio—737
6. Pennsylvania—730
7. Illinois—628

° See Chapter 7.
°° In order of largest selling area; see Chapter 9 for particulars.

AMERICA'S ELEVEN MOST BEAUTIFUL
DEPARTMENT AND SPECIALTY STORES °

1. John Wanamaker's—Philadelphia, Pennsylvania
2. Marshall Field—Chicago, Illinois
3. I. Magnin—San Francisco, California
4. I. Magnin—Los Angeles, California
5. The Emporium—San Francisco, California
6. Lord & Taylor—New York, New York
7. Bullock's—Pasadena, California
8. Neiman-Marcus—Dallas, Texas
9. Gump's—San Francisco, California
10. Carson, Pirie Scott—Chicago, Illinois
11. Sanger Harris-Dallas, Texas

ELEVEN REMARKABLE WOMEN IN RETAILING °°

1. Marguerite Boucicaut—Bon Marché
2. Margaret Getschell—Macy's
3. Mary Magnin—I. Magnin
4. Lena Bryant
5. Dorothy Shaver— Lord & Taylor
6. Hortense Odlum—Bonwit Teller
7. Geraldine Stutz—Henri Bendel
8. Beatrice Fox Auerbach—G. Fox
9. Bernice Fitz-Gibbon—Macy's
10. Margaret Fishback—Macy's
11. Lucina Wyman Prince [1]

° A purely subjective listing that doesn't include office buildings like the magnificent Woolworth Building and the immense Sears Tower, the world's tallest building. Brief biographies of these stores can be found in the text. See also Chapter 2 for a tour of elegant old New York emporiums no longer used as stores but still standing.
°° See the preceding pages for brief biographies.
[1] Founder of Boston's noted Prince School, which trained many women as department store personnel directors.

ELEVEN GRAND OLD PEOPLE OF RETAILING °

1. Sebastian Kresge—99
2. Nathan Marlow—97
3. J. J. Joslin—96
4. J. C. Penney—95
5. Mary Magnin—95
6. Morton May—95
7. J. B. Ivey—95
8. James E. Casey (United Parcel Service)—95
9. L. L. Bean—94
10. Lincoln Filene—92
11. Robert E. Wood (Sears)—90

THE THIRTEEN HIGHEST-PAID RETAILERS ° °

Name	Age	Company	Remuneration
Arthur M. Wood	65	Sears, Roebuck	$573,000 †
Donald V. Seibert	54	J. C. Penney	$520,000
Thomas M. Macioce	59	Allied Stores	$512,000
Ralph Lazarus	64	Federated Dept. Stores	$478,000
William A. Andres	51	Dayton-Hudson	$390,000
Robert E. Dewar	55	K mart	$380,000
Leon F. Winbigler	52	Mercantile Stores	$335,000
David E. Babcock	63	May Dept. Stores	$327,000
Donald B. Smiley	63	R. H. Macy	$310,000
Angelo Arena	54	Marshall Field	$300,000

° Brief biographies of these "longest-lived" retailers can be found in the preceding pages. Morton May is still living and active in May's, and James Casey is living and active in U.P.S.

° ° For the year 1977. Includes salary, bonuses, and director's fees but excludes stock options and long-term contingency payments. This list does not include heads of conglomerates who own department stores, such as Mobil Oil's (Montgomery Ward) Rawleigh Warner, Jr., who made $745,000 in 1977.

† Succeeded by Edward R. Telling on February 1, 1978. By way of comparison, Mr. Wood ranked fifty-first among all highest paid U.S. executives. Hawley, number twelve on this list, ranks number 414 overall. The highest-paid American executive is fifty-six-year-old J. Robert Fluor, head of The Fluor Corporation. He made $1,121,000 in 1977.

Edward F. Gibbons	58	F. W. Woolworth	$299,000
Richard R. Pivirotto	47	Associated Dry Goods	$260,000
Philip M. Hawley	52	Carter Hawley Hale	$256,000

A LIST OF MORE WORDS AND PHRASES
BORN OF RETAILING °

Acid test—Frontier peddlers determined the gold content of an object traded to them by scratching it and applying nitric acid—which came to be called *the acid test,* the term quickly coming to mean a severe test of reliability.

Blow your own horn—medieval peddlers frequently used horns to attract a crowd of customers, and having no servants to herald their arrival, as nobles did, they had to blow their own horns. Since their merchandise often seemed hardly worth all the fanfare, *to blow your own horn* came to stand for any display of boasting. (That is one explanation of the phrase, anyway.)

Buck—bucks, our slang for dollars, were first simply deerskins, which were commonly used as a medium of exchange in backwoods' country stores.

Chap—the old English word *chop* meant "to barter" and gave us the words *cheap* and *chapman,* a wandering peddler. *Chapman* lives in the language long after the last chapmen have passed from the scene. For the English term *chap,* fellow or man, is simply an abbreviation of *chapman*—a good *chapman* or *chap* became in time a good fellow.

Dicker—a *dicker* was originally a bundle of ten animal skins, deriving from the Latin *decuria* for any set of ten articles. Since fur trappers and other customers often bartered these skins at trading posts and country stores for merchandise and there was quite a lot of haggling over the worth of the ten skins, *dicker* came to mean "to haggle."

Lagniappe—probably comes from the Peruvian Quechuan Indian *yappa,* a present made to a customer. The Spanish called this *la napa* and French Creoles who operated stores in Louisiana con-

---

° See index for many other examples

verted the Spanish word into the *lagniappes*, or free gifts, still given customers today.

Micah Rood's apple—any apple variety or "sport" with streaks of red running through its white flesh. Folklore has it that on a fine spring day in 1693 a jewelry peddler visited old Micah Rood's farm at Franklin, Pa. Shortly afterward the peddler was found murdered under an apple tree in Rood's orchard, but his jewelry wasn't recovered and the farmer was never convicted of the crime. However, all the apples harvested from Rood's tree that autumn had streaks of red inside and Rood died of fright when he bit into one and saw this "blood," the red streaks called "Micah Rood's curse" from that day on.

Mosey—to stroll or saunter about leisurely. Possibly derives from "the slouching manner of wandering Jewish peddlers in the West," many of whom were named or called Moses, Mose, or Mosey, and who walked slowly or slouched over because of the heavy packs weighing them down.

P.M.S.—a term of unknown origin that means "a reward paid to a salesperson for selling a particular piece of merchandise, usually a slow-moving item."

Shoddy—During the Civil War suppliers cheated the Union Army with cheap uniform cloth called "shoddy" that literally unravelled on the wearer's back—which gave the name *shoddy* to a whole new class of fortunes and a new adjective to the language.

Ye Olde Gifte Shoppe—As a matter of fact, such shops never existed, despite their host of imitators today. *Ye* did yeoman service in the past as both the plural of "you" and as a mark of respect when talking to a single person, but it has never meant "your" in English. The Ye's on those signs adorning half-timbered Tudor-style establishments, the ones that read Ye Olde Gifte Shoppe, Ye Olde Hot Dogge Haven, etc., should actually be pronounced "the," not "ye," for that was what they meant in Ye Olde English terms. The letter Y in Ye is really not a "Y," but a "thorn," the Anglo-Saxon symbol for "th." This Anglo-Saxon dipthong was originally written something like a *p*, but careless writers and sign painters in later years left it partially open at the side so that it came to resemble a *y*, early printers presenting it as such. Neither was the Ye in old manuscripts and signs ever pronounced as anything but "the" up until modern times.

A LIST OF TRADITIONAL DEPARTMENT STORE
SALES BY MONTH °

Air conditioners: Aug., Sept., March
Appliances: Feb., Oct.
Bedding: Jan., May, Aug.
Bicycles: Jan., Feb., Sept., Oct., Nov.
Blankets: Jan., May, Nov., Dec.
Boats: Oct.
Books: Jan.
Car accessories: Sept., Feb., Aug. (tires)
Carriages: Jan. Aug.
China, glassware: Jan., Feb., Mar., Sept.
Cleaning supplies: April
Clothing (boys'): Jan., Mar., Apr., June, Dec.
Clothing (men's): Jan., Mar., Apr., Aug., Dec.
Clothing (women's): Jan., Feb., Apr., Aug., Dec.
Coats (men's and boys'): Mar.
Coats (women's): Feb., Nov.
Cooking utensils: Jan., Feb., Sept.
Cosmetics: Jan., Feb., July
Curtains, drapes: Jan., Feb., May, July., Aug., Nov.
Dishes: Jan., Feb., Sept.
Dresses: Feb., Nov.
Drug items: Jan., Feb., July, Dec.
Fabrics: Sept., Jan.
Floor coverings: Jan., Feb., July, Aug.
Furniture (indoor): Jan., Feb., July, Aug.
Furs: Jan., Feb., Mar.
Garden supplies: July, Aug., Sept., Oct.
Hats (children's): July

° In addition, look for sales in traditional bargain centers such as Filene's Automatic Bargain Basement and the "clearance corners" of posh stores like Saks, B. Altman, and even Tiffany's; Christmas items sales in January; February Washington and Lincoln's birthday sales; Memorial Day and Labor Day specials; Fall sales on Columbus Day; and July summer clearance sales.

Hats (men's): Jan., July
Hats (women's): Feb., May, July,
Hosiery: Mar., Oct.
Housecoats: Apr., May, June, Oct., Nov.
Housewares: Jan., Feb., March, Sept.
Jewelry: Feb., July
Lamps: Feb., Aug.
Linens: Jan., May
Lingerie: Jan., Feb., Apr., May, Oct.
Mattresses: Feb.
Notions: Feb.
Radios, stereos: Jan., Feb., July.
Refrigerators, freezers: July
School supplies: Aug.
Shirts (boy's): Jan., Mar., Apr., June, Dec.
Shirts (men's): Jan., July
Shoes (boys' and girls') Jan., Mar., July
Shoes (men's and women's): Jan., July
Silverware: Feb.
Sports equipment: Jan., Feb., July, Aug.
Stationery: Feb.
Storm windows: June
Stoves: Feb.
Suits (men's): Jan., Mar., Apr., July, Dec.
Suits (women's): Jan., Feb., April, May, Aug.
Toys: Jan., Feb.
Televisions: Jan., Feb., May, June, July
Washers and dryers: Mar.
Washing machines: Jan., Feb., July
Watches: Feb.
White goods: Jan., May, Aug.

Addendum
An Honor Roll
of Other Notable
Department Stores

Perhaps in a future edition there will be room for the fascinating stories of the following 500 or so department stores, which can merely be listed here by city and state. Many of these stores have long histories and deserve full treatment as much as the stores preceding them, but there just wasn't enough space for their stories or pictures. So we'll have to hold off on provocative names like The Original Twelfth Street Store and Mr. Wigg's Department Store until next time.

ALABAMA
Alabama Novelty House, Inc.—Birmingham
Burger-Philips—Birmingham
V. J. Elmore—Birmingham
Gayfer's Montgomery Fair—Montgomery
Loveman's—Birmingham
Pizitz—Birmingham
Rogers, Inc.—Florence
Super Stores—Prichard
Top Dollar Store—Jasper

ARIZONA
Babbitt Bros.—Flagstaff
Jacome's Department Stores—Tucson
Malcolm's Dept. Store—Phoenix
Meyerson Stores—Tucson

ARKANSAS
Pollock Stores—Fort Smith
M. M. Cohen—Little Rock
Sterling Stores—Little Rock
Wal-Mart Stores—Bentonville

CALIFORNIA
Boston Stores—Carson
Comet Stores—Pasadena
Dearden's—Los Angeles
Dick Bruhn Inc.—Salinas
Fed-Mart Stores—San Diego
Charles Ford Co.—Watsonville
Fedco, Inc.—Los Angeles
Harris'—San Bernardino
L. Hart & Son Inc.—San Jose
H. C. Henshey—Santa Monica
J. F. Hink & Son—Berkeley
Hinshaw's Department Stores—Whittier
Holman's Department Store—Pacific Grove
Komoto's Dept. Store—Fresno
Livingston Bros—San Francisco
Lucky Stores, Inc.—Dublin
Marshall's Dept. Store of California—Granada Hills
W. W. Mertz—Torrington
Mervyns—Hayward
Moore's Dept. Store—Lompoc
F. C. Nash & Co.—Pasadena
Pic N' Save—Carson
Ransohoffs—San Francisco
Rasco Stores—Burbank
Sherwood Swan & Co.—Oakland
Walker-Scott—San Diego
Weinstock's—Sacramento

COLORADO
Denver Dry Goods—Denver
Neusteters—Denver

The Denver—Denver
Valco Inc.—Rocky Ford

CONNECTICUT
Ames Dept. Stores—Hartford
James H. Bunce Co.—Middletown
Caldor, Inc.—Norwalk
D. & L Stores, Inc.—New Britain
Davidson & Leventhal—New Britain
First Hartford Corp.—Manchester
Griswold's Dept. Store—Guilford
Howland Hughes Co.—Waterbury
The Edward Malley Co.—New Haven
Raphael's Dept. Store—New Britain
D. M. Read Inc.—Bridgeport
D. W. Rogers Co.—Greenwich

DELAWARE
Kennard-Pyle Co.—Wilmington

FLORIDA
Beall's Dept. Stores—Bradenton
F. C. Daffin Co.—Marianna
Eagle Family Discount Stores—Opa-Locka
Eckerd Corp.—Clearwater
Furchgott's Inc.—Jacksonville
Jefferson Stores—Miami
Maas Brothers Inc.—Tampa
B. E. Purcell Co.—Orlando
Richard's—Miami
Rutland-King, Inc.—St. Petersburg
Sav-A-Stop—Jacksonville
Southwest Florida Enterprises—Fort Myers
Sunshine Dept. Store—Tampa
Webb's City Inc.—St. Petersburg
Winn-Dixie Stores—Jacksonville

GEORGIA
Alford Bros.—Lawrenceville

Burden, Smith & Co.—Macon
Churchwell's—Waycross
Cullum's, Inc.—Augusta
Davison-Paxon Co.—Atlanta
C. Goldstein & Sons—Millegeville
H. Kessler & Co.—Atlanta
J. A. Kirven Co.—Columbus
Levy's of Savannah—Savannah
Mansour's—La Grange
I. Perlis & Son—Cordele
Rosenberg Bros.—Albany
Standard Stores—Macon
Witt Dept. Store—Columbus

HAWAII
Alexander & Baldwin—Honolulu
Carol & Mary—Honolulu
Hana Ranch Inc.—Maui
Hawaii Corporation—Honolulu
N. Kamuri Ltd.—Honolulu
Maui Stores—Honolulu
Paia Mercantile Co.—Paia
Servco Pacific Inc.—Honolulu
Shirokeyo Inc.—Honolulu

IDAHO
C. C. Anderson Stores—Boise
Bazaar, Inc.—Boise

ILLINOIS
Belscot Retailers—Chicago
A. Bergner & Co.—Peoria
The John Brommer Co.—Springfield
John Bessemer Co.—Springfield
City Products—Des Plaines
Community Discount Stores—Chicago
Crawford Dept. Stores—Chicago
Fellner's, Inc.—Belleville
Frank's Dept. Stores—Chicago

Gilmore Associates—Oak Park
Globe Outlet—Waukegan
Goldblatt Brothers—Chicago
Hoffing's Dept. Store—Chicago
The Home Store—Chicago
George Ingraham—Chicago
Jewel Companies, Inc.—Chicago
Klaus Stores, Inc.—Chicago
Linn & Scruggs Co.—Decatur
Madigan Bros.—River Forest
Myers Brothers—Springfield
Original Twelfth Street Store—Chicago
Peoples Store of Roseland—Chicago
Robeson's Inc.—Champaign
Roland's—Bloomington
Schultz Bros.—Lake Zurich
Joseph Spiess Co.—Elgin
Spurgeon Mercantile Co.—Chicago
Charles Stevens—Chicago
D. J. Stewart & Co.—Rockford
Street Leader Dept. Store—Chicago
TSC Industries—Chicago

INDIANA
Danners, Inc.—Indianapolis
William H. Block—Indianapolis
The Evansville Store—Evansville
Index Notion Co.—Sullivan
Loeb's Inc.—Lafayette
Edward C. Minas Co.—Hammond
Robertson Bros. Dept. Stores—South Bend
Schultz & Co.—Terre Haute
M. B. Thrasher Co.—Frankfort
George Wyman Co.—South Bend
Zielsel Bros.—Elkhart

IOWA
Armstrongs, Inc.—Cedar Rapids
James Black—Waterloo
Boston Store—Ft. Dodge

Graham Dept. Stores—Ottumwa
Killian's—Cedar Rapids
Martin Dry Goods—Cedar Rapids
M. L. Parker Co.—Davenport
Petersen-Harned-Von Maur—Davenport
J. S. Schram Co.—Burlington
Tuerke Mercantile Stores—Fort Dodge

KANSAS
Chaffin Inc.—Dodge City
Duckwall Stores—Abilene
Eckles Dept. Store—Dodge City
Pegues Inc.—Hutchinson
Pelletier Stores—Topeka
MFY Industries—Wicheta
Topeka-Crosby Corp.—Topeka

KENTUCKY
S. W. Anderson Co.—Owensboro
Behr Stores—Louisville
Byck Bros.—Louisville
Consolidated Sales Co.—Louisville
Dollar General Corp.—Scottville
Lerman Bros.—Louisville
Maloney Enterprises—Mt. Sterling
National Industries—Louisville
Shapira Corp.—Louisville
Stewart Dry Goods Co.—Louisville
Ben Snyder Inc.—Louisville

LOUISIANA
W. F. Beall Corp.—Shreveport
Howard Bros. Discount Stores—Monroe
Krauss Co. Ltd.—New Orleans
Labiche's Inc.—New Orleans
Muller Co., Ltd.—Lake Charles
West & Co.—Minden
H. J. Wilson Co.—Baton Rouge

MAINE
Porteous Mitchell & Brawn Co.—Portland
Rines Bros.—Portland

MARYLAND
L. Epstein & Sons—Baltimore
Forbes, Inc.—Baltimore
Feldman's, Inc.—Baltimore
Charles Fish & Sons—Baltimore
Four Besche Bros.—Baltimore
Al Franklin Co.—Baltimore
Hochschild, Kohn & Co.—Baltimore
Kirson's, Inc.—Annapolis
Levenson & Klein, Inc.—Baltimore
Rosenbaum Bros.—Cumberland
Routzahn's—Hagerstown
Sandler's Dept. Store—Baltimore
Stewart & Co.—Baltimore

MASSACHUSETTS
Almy Stores—Boston
Arlan's Dept, Stores—New Bedford
Barnard, Summer & Putnam Co.—Worcester
Corcoran's—Cambridge
Grover Cronin—Waltham
England Brothers—Pittsfield
Forbes & Wallace—Springfield
Gilchrist's—Boston
Harvard Cooperative Society—Cambridge
Andrew T. Johnson Co.—Boston
Kings Dept. Stores Inc.—Newton
Mammoth Mart—Bridgewater
Mars Bargainland—New Bedford
Marshall's, Inc.—Wobum
R. A. McWhirr—Fall River
Mitchell & Co.—Haverhill
Parke Snow, Inc.—Fitchburg
H. W. Pray Co.—Newburyport
T. W. Rogers Co.—Lynn
R. H. Stearns Co.—Boston

Albert Steiger, Inc.—Springfield
System Co.—Lynn
United Overton—Newton Highlands
Zayre Corp.—Framingham

MICHIGAN
Boyer-Campbell—Detroit
Borman's, Inc.—Detroit
Cowan's Dept. Stores—Sault Ste. Marie
Federals, Inc.—Detroit
Gilmore Bros. Inc.—Kalamazoo
J. W. Knapp—Lansing
W. R. Knepp & Co.—Bay City
Meijer, Inc.—Grand Rapids
O'Donnell-Seamans Co.—Ivonwood
John Priehs Mercantile Co.—Mt. Clemens
Wm. C. Wiechmann Co.—Saginaw
The Wurzburg Co.—Grand Rapids

MINNESOTA
H. Choate & Co.—Winona
Donaldson's—Minneapolis
Dueber's Inc.—Waconia
G. R. Herberger's—St. Charles
C. F. Massey Co.—Rochester
Powers Dry Goods—Minneapolis
Salkin & Linoff—Minneapolis

MISSISSIPPI
Egger's Dept. Store—Columbia
The Lampton Co.—Columbia
McRae's Inc.—Jackson
W. E. Walker Stores—Jackson

MISSOURI
Edison Bros. Stores, Inc.—St. Louis
Flanders Dept. Store—Excelsior Springs
Gideon Anderson—Gideon
Heer's—Springfield
Interco Inc.—St. Louis

Lammert Co.—St. Louis
Mattingly Stores—Lexington
Missouri Farmers—Columbia
National Bellas Hess Inc.—North Kansas City
Newman Mercantile Co.—Joplin
Parkview-Gem, Inc.—Kansas City
P. M. Place Stores—Bethany

NEBRASKA
J. L. Brandeis & Sons—Omaha
Harold Mangelsur & Sons—Omaha
J. M. McDonald Co.—Hastings
Miller & Paine Inc.—Lincoln
Richman Gordman Stores—Omaha
Skagway Discount Department Stores—Grand Island
Wheeler Stores—Grand Island

NEW JERSEY
Bamberger's—Newark
S. P. Dunham & Co.—Trenton
Hahne & Co.—Newark
Jamesway Corp.—Secaucus
Miller-Wohl Co.—Secaucus
Meyer Brothers—Paterson
Reynolds Brothers—Lakewood
Unishops Inc.—Jersey City
Valley Fair Corp.—Little Ferry

NEW HAMPSHIRE
The Lynch Corp.—Manchester
Speare Dry Goods—Nashua
Ward's Dept. Store—Hanover

NEW YORK
Abrahamson-Bigelow Co.—Jamestown
Abrahams Bros.—New York City
Acme Markets—Tazewell
Adam Meldrum & Anderson Co.—Buffalo
Almart Stores—New York City
Atlantic Dept. Stores—New York City

Barbara Lynn Stores—New York City
Boardman Ltd.—Albany
Bond Industries—New York City
Bradner's Inc.—Olean
Bressec's Oneonta Dept, Store—Oneonta
Buy-Rite Discount Centers—Brooklyn
C. E. Chappell & Sons—North Syracuse
City Stores—New York City
Conran's—New York City
Cornwall Equities—New York City
J. M. Field's Inc.—New York City
E. W. Edwards & Son—Syracuse
Genung's Inc.—White Plains
Hampton Sales—Garden City
Hartfield-Zody's—New York City
Hens and Kelly—Buffalo
Honig's Parkway, Inc.—Bronx
Interstate Boston Corp.—New York City
S. F. Iszard Co.—Elmira
Kline Brothers—New York City
Kleins—New York City
M. H. Lamston—New York City
Luckey, Platt & Co.—Poughkeepsie
J. W. Mays—Brooklyn
McCurdy & Co.—Rochester
McLean's Department Stores—Binghamton
Mid Island Department Stores—Seaford
J. J. Newberry Co.—New York City
Neisner Brothers—Rochester
S. E. Nichols, Inc.—New York City
Oneonta Department Store—Oneonta
Raylass Department Stores—New York City
Rosenthal & Rubin—Binghamton
Rothschild Bros.—Ithaca
Sattler's, Inc.—Buffalo
Sibley, Kindsay & Curr—Rochester
Sullivan's of Liberty—Liberty
Swezy & Nevins—Patchogue
Takashimaya—New York City
Times Square Stores—New York City

Tompkins Dry Goods—Middletown
Twin Fair—Buffalo
Volume Merchandise—New York City
Weston's Shoppers City—New York City
Whitney Stores—New York City

NORTH CAROLINA
K. M. Biggs Inc.—Lumberton
Bon Marché Inc.—Asheville
Boylan-Pierce—Raleigh
Brown's Dept. Store—Yadkinville
Capitol of Fayetteville—Fayetteville
W. S. Clark & Sons—Tarboro
Davis, Inc.—Winston-Salem
Dupree's Dept. Store—Farmville
R. W. Goodman—Rockingham
Hudson Belk Co.—Raleigh
Ideal Dry Goods—Winston-Salem
Mack's Stores—Sanford
John F. McNair—Laurinburg
B. C. Moore & Co.—Wadesboro
Myers Department Store—Greensboro
Z. V. Pate—Laurel Hill
B. A. Sellars & Sons—Burlington
Sky City Stores—Asheville
Spainhour Co.—Hickory
Super Dollar Stores—Raleigh
The Washington Group—Winston-Salem
H. Weil & Bros.—Goldsboro

OHIO
Big Bear Stores—Columbus
Carlisle-Allen Co.—Ashtabula
J. A. Conley Co.—Canton
Cook United, Inc.—Cleveland
Elder-Burman Stores Corp.—Dayton
Fries & Schuele Co.—Cleveland
Giant Tiger Stores—Euclid
Halle Brothers—Cleveland

Hub of Steubenville—Steubenville
La Salle & Koch—Toledo
Marting Brothers—Portsmouth
McAlpin's Plaza Store—Middletown
G. M. McKelvey—Youngstown
Mr. Wiggs Dept. Stores—Cleveland
D. M. Ogilvie & Co.—East Liverpool
M. O'Neil Co.—Akron
A. Polsky—Akron
M. Schachne & Sons—Chillicothe
Schottenstein Stores—Columbus
Swallens—Cincinnati
Edward Wren Store—Springfield

OKLAHOMA
C. R. Anthony Co.—Oklahoma City
John A. Brown Co.—Oklahoma City
Daube Co.—Ardmore
Froug Co., Inc.—Tulsa
Gosselin Stores—Oklahoma City
Katz Department Store—Stillwater
Kelso Department Store—El Reno
Scrivner, Inc.—Oklahoma City
Vandever Co.—Tulsa
T G & Y Stores—Oklahoma City

OREGON
Bazaar, Inc.—Portland
Hub, Inc.—Coos Bay
Sprouse-Reitz—Portland
G. F. Wacker Stores—Pauls Valley

PENNSYLVANIA
George Allen, Inc.—Philadelphia
J. M. Balter Co.—Braddock
Bankers Security—Philadelphia
Charles H. Bear—York
Bergman's Dept. Store—Kingston
Bloomgarden's Dept. Store—Milford

Bouman's Dept. Stores—Harrisburg
Bright Stores—Lansford
Celento's Dept. Store—Canonsburg
Chatlin's Dept. Store—Norristown
Cleland-Simpson—Scranton
Eureka Stores—Windber
Fellers Inc.—Harrisburg
Fowler, Dick & Walker—Wilkes-Barre
William F. Gable Co.—Altoona
M. T. Garvin—Lancaster
R. Guinan & Co.—Mt. Carmel
Heinsmans Dept. Store—Columbia
Hershey Dept. Store—Hershey
O.W. Houts & Son—State College
Katz Bros. Inc.—Honesdale
Kraus Dept. Stores—Erie
Laneco, Inc.—Easton
Le Fevre Bros—Boyertown
Leitzinger Bros.—Clearfield
Levenson Bros.—Warren
G. Mankin Dept. Store—Prospect Park
S.W. Metzler Stores—Uniontown
Mosteller's Inc.—West Chester
G. C. Murphy—McKeesport
New York Store—Pottstown
Silo Inc—Philadelphia
Slatter's Dept. Store—Chester
Stan-Mail Inc.—York
L. L. Stearns & Sons—Williamsport
Stern & Co.—Philadelphia
A. E. Troutman Co.—Greensburg
Schoenfeld's Dept. Store—Portage
Watt & Shand—Lancaster
Welker & Maxwell—Oil City
C. K. Whitner—Reading
P. Wiest's Sons—York
Zollinger-Harned—Allentown

RHODE ISLAND
William Ley's Dry Goods—Newport

Outlet Co.—Providence
The Shephard Co.—Providence
McCarthy Dry Goods—Woonsocket

SOUTH CAROLINA
Myers Arnold Co.—Greenville
Bailes Dept. Store—Charleston
J. L. Coker & Co.—Hartsville
Jas. F. Condon & Sons, Inc.—Charleston
Edwards—Charleston Heights
Kerreson's Dept. Store—Charleston
Mutual Home Stores—Greenville
Novit Siegel Co.—Walterboro
The Aug. W. Smith Co.—Spartanburg
Sam Solomon Co.—Charleston
James L. Tapp Co.—Columbia

TENNESSEE
Cain-Sloan Co.—Nashville
Draper & Darwin—Lebanon
Emery Stores—Knoxville
John Gerber Co.—Memphis
J. Goldsmith & Sons—Memphis
H. P. King Co.—Bristol
Kuhn's Big K Stores—Nashville
Lay & Co.—Cleveland
Loveman, Berger & Teitlebaum—Nashville
Proffitts Inc.—Alcoa
Miller Bros. Co.—Chatanooga
Miller's Inc.—Knoxville
National Stores—Nashville
Ira A. Watson Co.—Knoxville

TEXAS
Drydens—Groves
Duke & Ayres—Dallas
Dunlap Co.—Lubbock
J. M. Dyer Co.—Corsicana
The Fair, Inc.—Beaumont
Goldstein-Migel Co.—Waco

Hemphill-Wells—Lubbock
Howard Discount Centers—Texarkana
Kallison's—San Antonio
Lack's Inc.—Houston
E. S. Levy & Co.—Galveston
McClurkan's Inc.—Wichita Falls
Meyer Bros, Inc.—Houston
Monning's—Ft. Worth
Moore Brothers—Abilene
M. E. Moses Co.—Dallas
Perry Bros.—Lufkin
The Popular—El Paso
Sage International—Houston
Sakowitz-Gulfgate—Houston
Solo Serve Co.—San Antonio
Stripling's—Fort Worth
Titche-Goettinger—Dallas
Three Beall Brothers 3—Jacksonville
Winn's Stores—San Antonio
Zale Corp.—Dallas

VERMONT
Abernathy-Clarkson-Wright—Burlington
Economy Dept. Store—Rutland
F. C. Luce Co.—Waterbury
David Shapiro Dept. Store—Brandon

VIRGINIA
Altschul's Dept. Store—Norfolk
Ames & Brounley—Norfolk
H. B. Carter & Co.—Warrentown
Gammon's—Rural Retreat
Globeman Stores—Martinsville
S. H. Heironimus Co.—Roanoke
Morton's—Arlington
Smith & Welton—Norfolk
Southern Department Stores—Petersburg
Rices Nachmans Inc.—Norfolk
Paul H. Rose Corp.—Norfolk
Tilman's—Charlottesville

C. H. Williams—Charlottesville
Williams Dept. Store—Pembroke

UTAH
Grand Central—Salt Lake City
The Richer Department Store Corp.—Salt Lake City

WASHINGTON
Nordstrom, Inc.—Seattle
Pay 'N Save—Seattle
Roundup Co.—Spokane
Spokane Dry Goods—Spokane

WASHINGTON, D.C.
The Kann Corp
Lansburgh's
Long's Dept. Stores

WEST VIRGINIA
Anderson-Newcomb Co.—Huntington
A.W. Cox Dept. Store Co.—Charleston
Dils Bros. & Co.—Parkersburg
L. S. Good & Co.— Wheeling
J. M. Hartley & Son—Fairmont
Heck's Inc.—Charleston
McCormick's Inc.—Logan
Parsons-Souders, Stone & Thomas—Clarksburg

WISCONSIN
T. A. Chapman Co.—Milwaukee
Farmers Store Co.—Cau Claire
John Hill's Inc.—Wisconsin Rapids
Kohl Corp.—Milwaukee
Lauerman Bros. Co.—Marinette
Harry S. Manchester Inc.—Madison
Milwaukee Boston Store—Milwaukee
H. C. Prange Co.—Sheboygan
Roth Bros. Co.—Superior
Schuette Bros.—Manitowac

Index